POWER AND LANDSCAPE IN ATLANTIC WEST AFRICA

This volume examines the archaeology of precolonial West African societies in the era of the transatlantic slave trade. Using historical and archaeological perspectives on landscape, this collection of essays sheds light on how involvement in the commercial revolutions of the early modern period dramatically reshaped the regional contours of political organization across West Africa. The essays examine how social and political transformations occurred at the regional level by exploring regional economic networks, population shifts, cultural values, and ideologies. The book demonstrates the importance of anthropological insights not only to the broad political history of West Africa, but also to an understanding of political culture as a form of meaningful social practice.

J. Cameron Monroe is Assistant Professor of Anthropology at the University of California, Santa Cruz, and Director of the Abomey Plateau Archaeological Project in the Republic of Bénin, West Africa. He serves on the editorial board of *Azania: Archaeological Research in Africa* and has published in various journals, among them *Historical Archaeology*, *Journal of African History*, *Journal of Social Archaeology*, and *Current Anthropology*.

Akinwumi Ogundiran is Professor of Africana Studies, Anthropology, and History at the University of North Carolina, Charlotte, and Director of the Upper Osun Archaeological and Historical Project. He is the author or editor of several publications, including *Archaeology and History in Ilare District, Central Yorubaland*; *Precolonial Nigeria*; and *Archaeology of Atlantic Africa and the African Diaspora*.

Power and Landscape in Atlantic West Africa

ARCHAEOLOGICAL PERSPECTIVES

Edited by

J. Cameron Monroe
University of California, Santa Cruz

Akinwumi Ogundiran
University of North Carolina, Charlotte

CAMBRIDGE
UNIVERSITY PRESS

University Printing House, Cambridge CB2 8BS, United Kingdom

One Liberty Plaza, 20th Floor, New York, NY 10006, USA

477 Williamstown Road, Port Melbourne, VIC 3207, Australia

314-321, 3rd Floor, Plot 3, Splendor Forum, Jasola District Centre, New Delhi - 110025, India

79 Anson Road, #06-04/06, Singapore 079906

Cambridge University Press is part of the University of Cambridge.

It furthers the University's mission by disseminating knowledge in the pursuit of education, learning and research at the highest international levels of excellence.

www.cambridge.org
Information on this title: www.cambridge.org/9781108978309

© Cambridge University Press 2012

This publication is in copyright. Subject to statutory exception and to the provisions of relevant collective licensing agreements, no reproduction of any part may take place without the written permission of Cambridge University Press.

First published 2012
First paperback edition 2020

A catalogue record for this publication is available from the British Library

Library of Congress Cataloging in Publication data
Power and landscape in Atlantic West Africa : archaeological perspectives / [edited by] J. Cameron Monroe, Akinwumi Ogundiran.
   p. cm.
Includes bibliographical references and index.
ISBN 978-1-107-00939-4 (hardback)
1. Africa, West – History – To 1864.   2. Social structure – Africa, West – History.
3. Political culture – Africa, West – History.   4. Africa, West – Commerce – Social aspects – History.   5. Africa, West – Commerce – Political aspects – History.
6. Landscape archaeology – Africa, West.   I. Monroe, J. Cameron.   II. Ogundiran, Akinwumi.
DT476.P68   2011
966´02–dc23   2011019257

ISBN 978-1-107-00939-4 Hardback
ISBN 978-1-108-97830-9 Paperback

Cambridge University Press has no responsibility for the persistence or accuracy of URLs for external or third-party internet websites referred to in this publication, and does not guarantee that any content on such websites is, or will remain, accurate or appropriate.

For Merrick Posnansky

Contents

Foreword by Merrick Posnansky		*page* ix
Preface		xv
Contributors		xix
1	Power and Landscape in Atlantic West Africa *J. Cameron Monroe and Akinwumi Ogundiran*	1

PART I. FRAGMENTED LANDSCAPES

2	Atlantic Impacts on Inland Senegambia: French Penetration and African Initiatives in Eighteenth- and Nineteenth-Century Gajaaga and Bundu (Upper Senegal River) *Ibrahima Thiaw*	49
3	Political Transformations and Cultural Landscapes in Senegambia during the Atlantic Era: An Alternative View from the Siin (Senegal)? *François Richard*	78
4	The Eguafo Polity: Between the Traders and Raiders *Sam Spiers*	115
5	From the Shadow of an Atlantic Citadel: An Archaeology of the Huedan Countryside *Neil L. Norman*	142

PART II. STATE-GENERATED LANDSCAPES

6	Segou, Slavery, and Sifinso *Kevin C. MacDonald and Seydou Camara*	169

7 Building the State in Dahomey: Power and Landscape on the Bight of Benin 191
J. Cameron Monroe

8 The Formation of an Oyo Imperial Colony during the Atlantic Age 222
Akinwumi Ogundiran

PART III. INTERNAL FRONTIER LANDSCAPES

9 The Rise of the Bassar Chiefdom in the Context of Africa's Internal Frontier 255
Philip de Barros

10 Fortified Towns of the Koinadugu Plateau: Northern Sierra Leone in the Pre-Atlantic and Atlantic Worlds 278
Christopher R. DeCorse

11 Rethinking the Mandara Political Landscape: Cultural Developments, Climate, and an Entry into History in the Second Millennium A.D. 309
Scott MacEachern

PART IV. CONCLUSION

12 The Local and the Global: Historiographical Reflections on West Africa in the Atlantic Age 339
Ray A. Kea

Index 377

Foreword

Merrick Posnansky

The development of West African archaeology has been much more rapid than most Africanist researchers once thought possible. *West Africa before the Europeans: Archaeology and Prehistory*, written by Oliver Davies (1967), was the first synthesis of archaeological scholarship on West Africa. Preceding it had been Raymond Mauny's *Tableau géographique de L'Ouest Africain au Moyen Âge d'apres les sources écrites, la tradition et l'archéologie* (1961), which combined both archaeological and historical sources to cover the more geographically restricted Sudanic and Sahelian belts from Senegal to Tchad. Although national archaeologies of Nigeria (Shaw 1978) and Ghana (Anquandah 1982) were subsequently published, regional syntheses were not attempted, and the next book-length work with a claim to some comprehensiveness was Christopher DeCorse, ed., *West Africa during the Atlantic Slave Trade: Archaeological Perspectives* (2001). Separated by thirty-four years, Davies and DeCorse clearly defined their chronological parameters.

Archaeology forty years ago was still divided between Stone Age studies and the Iron Age and historical archaeology, although the latter term was not employed for West African studies. Seventy-two percent of Davies' study dealt with environmental change and Stone Age studies. The emphasis was on the nature of sites and the classification and association of artifacts. The study of West Africa before the impact of the Europeans was considered purely as prehistoric archaeology. European terminologies were employed, and there were huge gaps on the map, for which there was no evidence, and research was largely restricted to fieldwork conducted from the principal centers where Europeans were based, such as Dakar, Conakry, Abidjan,

Bamako, Accra, Lagos, and Freetown, or where research institutes such as the Institut Fondamental d'Afrique Noire (IFAN) had been established. There were only five full universities and a little more than a dozen West African-based archaeologists by 1967. In contrast, there are now more than fifteen universities where some archaeology is or has recently been taught, and more than a hundred trained archaeologists working in museums, antiquities services, monument boards, and universities.

By the time of the publication of DeCorse's *West Africa during the Atlantic Slave Trade*, the picture had changed considerably in terms of the increased number of archaeological personnel and institutions and the volume of archaeological research, but the time periods and geographical areas involved were limited. The focus was on the Atlantic seaboards of West Africa. Although there was effective regional coverage, as that for the Cameroons, there were still huge areas omitted because of the lack of solid field research. Themes other than the slave trade were minimized. During this period from the sixteenth to the nineteenth centuries, major changes were happening – many the result of European contact. However, changes in the trans-Saharan trade, many aspects of state formation in the Sudanic zone, and increasing competition for resources also had their origins in regional developments that were considered in less detail. The volume by DeCorse, a model for new archaeology at all levels, set the stage for much more vigorous work in historical archaeology in previously less studied areas, such as Bénin.

Research in the past half century posts definite red flags about the dangers of approaches that are too discrete to West African history and archaeology. In the first generation of African historical scholarship in the 1960s, many African historians, proud of their own local histories, returned from Europe to write about the states from which they came. There was a flurry of doctorates that dealt with the politics and trade of their home areas. These had the result of emphasizing differences over relatively small distances. Access to European archives resulted in greater significance being given to Dutch, Danish, French, and British company histories, and less reliance was placed on West African state histories. Although the present study contains chapters by seven of the writers contained in DeCorse's volume, this emphasis has been avoided. Scholarship has matured and archaeology has more than kept up with research on documentary sources. The present volume provides a corrective balance by including several penetrating studies of states that grew up away from the coast and discusses developments that took place in nonstate situations. This new volume represents a clear break with past research because it covers all of West Africa and brings the study of West Africa's past into the present in a continuous discussion of some of the dominant themes of human settlement.

Instead of dealing with distinct time periods as evidenced from changes in tool technology, from stone to copper and its alloys, from stone to iron, from locally smelted iron to imported iron bars, the authors emphasize the landscape. The authors thereby deal with West Africa in a seamless, fluid capacity. Recent research (Posnansky 2004) has demonstrated that hunting and gathering persisted through agricultural times, and many present-day communities still collect snails and oil palm grubs, trap small rodents like grasscutters, or *agouti*, and birds, and make use of an extensive natural pharmacopoeia. Humans are part of the landscape, and the landscape was a dynamically changing backdrop to cultural, humanly determined, developments that had pronounced impacts on the landscape. Such developments included the reduction of tree cover for agriculture and fuels, the creation of settlement sites by building mounds above water levels, and changes to the botanical and animal biospheres. But in this volume landscape goes beyond the purely environmental to embrace the spatial relations of the societies under discussion. The authors are dealing with a competitive and fluid world. One of the principal achievements of archaeology has been to deal in space in a much more dynamic way.

Geographic Positioning Systems (GPS) and spatial imaging accessible from virtually continuous global monitoring are enabling archaeologists to see the vicinity of their sites within completely new perspectives. Different categories of sites are seen, past waterways are revealed, and dynamic maps are produced combining traditional forms of archaeology, such as shovel sampling and questioning of local elders, with the results of the new satellite imagery. This is facilitating the coverage of areas away from excavations on the more obvious archaeological sites. A totality of cover is thus feasible. What is still lacking is the archaeologist's ability to walk the landscape in a total fashion. Even this restriction is becoming lessened as the number of archaeological surveys increases and the number of observers expands. In 2009 alone, more than a dozen foreign teams went to West

Africa to work with local institutions that also sponsored departmental groups, including archaeology students fulfilling the "long essay/dissertation" requirements for their degrees. The use of similar equipment by different international teams is leading to greater regional compatibility. Some of the dreams of the dedicated scholars who produced the *Atlas of African Prehistory* (Clark 1967) are at last beginning to be realized. Sites are parts of landscapes; individual finds help interpret those landscapes; and fitting the parts into a whole is leading to new conclusions based on the observed relationships. A very definite contribution of the editors is to stress that in West Africa we are dealing with a fragmented landscape that cautions us to beware of simplistic generalizations.

Although the new technologies facilitate the comprehension of larger geographical areas, allowing skilled regional interpretations from which aspects of the landscape can be quantified, the realization has to be accepted that the landscape is both eternal and ephemeral. The changing relationships between humans and the landscape have been appreciated for a long period, particularly after the brilliant synthesis of scholars such as Bovill (1958) working on the Sahara. Whereas the past scholarship on West African landscape has been focused on ecology, this collection of essays is about social transformations and how differing spatial relationships have produced different historical experiences at regional levels. For example, the location of the Hueda and Dahomey states – similar in ethnic origins and traditions of leadership – had very different histories, because one was located nearer to the coast where major changes were occurring. Both had to react, and their locations were affected differentially. Dahomey ultimately grew when faced by Oyo aggression, whereas Hueda was unable to adapt or expand when menaced by aggressive powers on both the land and sea frontiers.

The most dramatic conclusion of this volume is how meaningless old time ascriptions now appear. Except on the coast where new towns were created, there is no sharp distinction between the prehistoric and historic periods. What was significant were the changes that took place at a societal level. States formed, chieftaincies arose, and populations agglomerated. In writing about time, periods have been typecast. There is a tendency to speak of the "age of maritime expansion," of the era of the "slave trade," or of the "industrial age." All of these are accurate for some areas but not for all – West Africa was changing; there was a vigorous trade from the north, and religious movements had social, political, technological, and cultural ramifications. Much of West Africa at different times was affected neither by the Atlantic trade nor by revolutionary movements in the Sudanic belt and Sahel. Dealing with discrete geographical areas that shared a universal timescale in this volume enables the editors to avoid overall generalizations. One of the major scholarly achievements of the past half century has been to secure a more acceptable chronological framework. Besides the obvious scientific methods, such as radiocarbon and thermoluminescence dating, oral history combined with more precise dating of imported ceramics, glassware, and pipe bowls and stems has provided a more precise chronology than was once thought possible. With better dating of mixed imported and local assemblages, we are closer to erecting more secure sequences of local and regional ceramic wares that will ultimately provide a stronger framework for our historical reconstructions.

Regardless of time, trade was an important variable. In the past, scholars fixated on long-distance trade as a major factor of change, but all the studies included in this volume emphasize the importance of both local and long-distance networks. Trade ultimately rests on the exchange of resources that are reflective of landscape variations. In this way, datable objects are transmitted outside of their areas of manufacture, and trade facilitates the transmission of knowledge, including technologies. Foreign objects became ritualized, as in the case of brass bowls of North African manufacture located in obscure West African contexts, such as Nsawkaw in Ghana (Wilks 1961). In such situations, the presence of new imports was far more important than the lack of contemporary written accounts.

Local accounts of interactions elaborated and embroidered over the years have also become valuable. In such situations, it is meaningless to attach the ascription of "historic" to one and not to the other. In West Africa, many different sources of information inform us about past behavior, technology, creativity, economy, and social organization. Some sources are less subjective than written observations; others, especially oral histories, are richer in personal detail; but all must be combined to provide a fabric of past experiences. In this sense, archaeological, oral, and documentary sources are relevant and of equal value in taking us further back into periods for which we have less information but for which we can anticipate new interpretations. They are complementary methodologies in cooperation rather than being in opposition. It is time for the horizontal lines that once separated prehistoric from historic periods to be dispensed with when dealing with the past 1,000 years or so of West African history. Only by accepting this continuum can we truly appreciate the dynamic forces, both ecological and cultural, that have affected the various political landscapes examined in this volume.

Monroe and Ogundiran have provided remarkable coverage, not only in terms of geography but also in terms of field methodologies. The editors and their collaborators represent some of the up-and-coming scholars who will make their marks as surely as Shaw, Davies, and Mauny did in the past. The political landscape takes center stage, and in this sense this is a volume that points the way to the future for West African archaeology, providing a history of the region from multiple sources.

BIBLIOGRAPHY

Anquandah, J. (1982). *Rediscovering Ghana's Past*. Longman, London.

Bovill, E. W. (1958). *The Golden Trade of the Moors*. Oxford University Press, London.

Clark, J. D., ed. (1967). *Atlas of African Prehistory*. University of Chicago Press, Chicago.

Davies, O. (1967). *West Africa before the Europeans: Archaeology and Prehistory*. Methuen, London.

DeCorse, C. R., ed. (2001). *West Africa during the Atlantic Slave Trade: Archaeological Perspectives*. Leicester University Press, New York.

Mauny, R. (1961). *Tableau géographique de l'Ouest Africain au Moyen Âge d'apres les sources écrites, la tradition et l'archéologie*. IFAN, Dakar.

Posnansky, M. (2004). Processes of Change – A Longitudinal Ethno-Archaeological Study of a Ghanaian Village: Hani 1970–98. *African Archaeological Review* 21 (1): 31–47.

Shaw, T. (1978). *Nigeria: Its Archaeology and Early History*. Thames and Hudson, London.

Wilks, I. (1961). The Northern Factor in Ashanti History: Begho and the Mande. *Journal of African History* 2 (1): 25–34.

Preface

Intellectual projects that tap into a diversity of perspectives to address a common theme generally emerge out of a sense of both frustration with, and the possibility to transcend, the prevailing status quo. For one of us (Monroe), such frustration emerged at the Society for American Archaeology (SAA) meetings held in Salt Lake City, Utah, in 2005. Having submitted an individual paper on Dahomean architecture, Monroe was charged with the responsibility of chairing a general session given the imaginative title "African Archaeology," to which it was assigned. As many readers of this volume are well aware, such sessions are compiled by the SAA Program Committee out of individual paper submissions. Although the papers were of high quality, they spanned historical periods and regions and drew from a host of unrelated themes and theoretical perspectives. Despite the fact that general sessions are a necessary component of large professional meetings, Monroe was immediately concerned that such a session provided the *primary* platform for the presentation of Africanist research at the SAAs that year. To the degree that it lacked any semblance of thematic coherence, Monroe took to heart a passing comment he heard a notable Mesoamericanist make upon exiting the session: "Is that all that African archaeology has to offer?"

Reflecting on that experience, Monroe approached Akinwumi Ogundiran about the idea of organizing a session on a coherent theme in African archaeology for the 2006 SAA meetings in San Juan, Puerto Rico. Noting a recent growth in the archaeological analysis of materiality and political process in Africa in the recent past, we saw the opportunity to focus on the theme of social complexity in the second millennium A.D., exploring the relationship between political processes and the sorts of transcontinental cultural and economic entanglements that gripped the subcontinent in that period. Hence, initial frustration transformed into an opportunity to collaborate with colleagues who were just returning from the field with fresh data and insights into the issues of power and political processes in the recent past. The result was a well-attended session titled "African Complex Societies in Transition: Transformation, Continuity, and Process in the Second Millennium AD," which was composed of participants working principally in Eastern and Western Africa, and for which Adria LaViolette and Norman Yoffee graciously agreed to serve as discussants.[1] The majority of the papers, however, focused on West Africa, undoubtedly the product of the professional networks of the session organizers.

Participants were asked to think broadly about how their research spoke to issues of relevance to scholars working on social complexity around the world, and the result was a series of exciting and very high-quality papers. Rather unexpectedly, however, two unifying themes emerged in the West Africa papers during the session. On the one hand, these papers were all engaging long-standing historical debates regarding the nature of social and political transformation in West Africa during the Atlantic Era. These papers were not only engaging historical debates, however. Rather they also represented clear methodological advances in how archaeologists might productively integrate documentary, oral, and archaeological source material. The historical richness of these case studies yielded a particular interpretive strength, resulting in textured perspectives on the dynamics of political process in the past. On the other hand, West Africanist presenters were unified in engaging broader theoretical issues centering on the theme of "landscape." Whereas, and with notable exceptions, archaeological research in West Africa has been dominated by questions of technological change and long-distance trade for decades (see Posnansky, Foreword to this volume), each of these papers drew from various "landscape" perspectives to explore the nature of power and political economy across the region.

We decided this emerging thematic unity among West Africanist scholars was worth exploring further, and despite the high quality of the papers on East Africa, we resolved to focus on West African case studies from the Atlantic Era alone. Seeking broad geographic coverage, we solicited additional contributors who are creatively deploying a variety of landscape perspectives to explore the Atlantic Era in contexts across West Africa (Christopher DeCorse, Scott MacEachern, Sam Spiers, and Ibrahima Thiaw). Although Adria LaViolette and Norman Yoffee were unable to continue with the project because of other commitments, we were fortunate that Ray Kea was willing to play ball with this group of historically attuned archaeologists.

Our goal in this volume is to build on the rapid pace of research over the last decade on the nature of social complexity in sub-Saharan Africa broadly, and in the Atlantic Era particularly. Edited volumes by Susan McIntosh (1999), Christopher DeCorse (2001), Andrew Reid and Paul Lane (2003), and, most recently, Akin Ogundiran and Toyin Falola (2007) have called for new ways of conceptualizing the political processes through which societies in the region responded to the emergence of the Atlantic economic system. We believe the following chapters have answered that call, revealing the wide spectrum of political landscapes through which West African expressions of political authority were materialized in response to both the opportunities and constraints presented by Atlantic commercial entanglement. The result is a series of theoretically robust and historically nuanced contributions to our understanding of political dynamics. We expect these studies will be of interest to both West Africanist historians and archaeologists concerned with the dynamics of social complexity more broadly.

The volume that has resulted from this productive dialogue would not have been possible without the valuable contributions of many people. First and foremost, we would like to express our sincere thanks to each of the volume's contributors, who demonstrated unparalleled patience and flexibility as this project has come to fruition since 2006. We are also indebted to Beatrice Rehl and the editorial staff of Cambridge University Press for their support and professionalism during the review and editing stages. Two anonymous reviewers provided invaluable comments on each chapter and on our introduction, and we thank both of them for their willingness to contribute their perspective on the volume. The chapters in this book have been unquestionably improved as a result. Our wives, Stephanie Monroe and Lea Koonce Ogundiran, provided the emotional and editorial support that have kept us coming back to the project since 2006, and we cannot thank them enough for their support, patience, and encouragement.

Last, this volume would not have been possible without the professional contributions of Merrick Posnansky, who was gracious enough to write its foreword. Directly or indirectly, each contributor to this volume has been influenced heavily by his work. Indeed, it was Merrick who began to wrestle with the complex relationship between long-distance trade and political complexity in West Africa during his Begho research in the 1970s, and it was Merrick who led the charge for an archaeology of the transatlantic slave trade in West Africa. In one way or another, we have all had the good fortune to have him as our guide and mentor at some point in our careers, and we are better scholars for it. It is in light of his undeniable influence on each of us that we dedicate this book to him.

J. Cameron Monroe and Akinwumi Ogundiran
March 11, 2011

NOTE

1. Participants in this session included Philip de Barros, Jeffrey Fleisher, Chapurukha M. Kusimba, Sibel B. Kusimba, Kevin MacDonald, J. Cameron Monroe, Neil Norman, Akinwumi Ogundiran, Francois Richard, and Melanie A. Zacher.

BIBLIOGRAPHY

DeCorse, C. (2001). *West Africa During the Atlantic Slave Trade: Archaeological Perspectives.* Leicester University Press, New York.

McIntosh, S. K. (1999). *Beyond Chiefdoms: Pathways to Complexity in Africa.* Cambridge University Press, Cambridge.

Ogundiran, A. and T. Falola (2007). *Archaeology of Atlantic Africa and the African Diaspora.* Indiana University Press, Bloomington.

Reid, A. and P. Lane (2004). *African Historical Archaeologies.* Kluwer Academic/Plenum Publishers, New York.

Contributors

Philip de Barros
Department of Anthropology, Palomar College

Seydou Camara
Institut des Sciences Humaines, Bamako, Mali

Christopher R. DeCorse
Department of Anthropology, Syracuse University

Ray A. Kea
Department of History, University of California, Riverside

Kevin C. MacDonald
The Institute of Archaeology, University College London

Scott MacEachern
Department of Sociology and Anthropology, Bowdoin College

J. Cameron Monroe
Department of Anthropology, University of California, Santa Cruz

Neil L. Norman
Department of Anthropology, College of William and Mary

Akinwumi Ogundiran
Department of Africana Studies, University of North Carolina at Charlotte

Merrick Posnanksy
Departments of History and Anthropology, University of California, Los Angeles

CONTRIBUTORS

François G. Richard
Department of Anthropology, University of Chicago

Sam Spiers
Archaeology Program, La Trobe University

Ibrahima Thiaw
Institut Fondamental d'Afrique Noire (IFAN), Université Cheikh Anta Diop

1

Power and Landscape in Atlantic West Africa

J. Cameron Monroe and Akinwumi Ogundiran

INTRODUCTION

The Atlantic Era, which spanned the seventeenth through the nineteenth centuries, was a period of intense commercial integration linking key economic players in Western Europe, the Americas, the Indian Ocean littorals, and much of West and Central Africa. The period was marked by dramatic increases in the volume of commerce at both the regional and global levels (Curtin 1998), and both the nature and the structure of political organization in all of these core areas was transformed radically. In fact, it is arguable that few communities on earth escaped the wide-reaching effects of commercial expansion and integration in this period (Wolf 1982). In North Atlantic Europe, the rising tides of commerce led to the emergence of a mercantile class, destabilizing feudal power structures and leading to the modern capitalist nation-states of the West. The Americas were transformed into an economic extension of Europe through colonization. Colonial polities thrived in North and South America by exploiting the mineral and agricultural resources that fueled commercial transformations across the entire Atlantic Basin. West Africa was not excluded from these political and economic transformations, the regional manifestations of which are the subject of this volume.

Beginning in the second half of the seventeenth century, as long-distance commerce came to be dominated by the export of human captives in the trans-Atlantic slave trade, West African political economies were transformed dramatically, resulting in a complex network of polities linking coast and interior in new ways

2

POWER AND
LANDSCAPE IN
ATLANTIC WEST
AFRICA

(Eltis, et al. 1999) (Figure 1.1). Within a few decades, between the late seventeenth and early eighteenth centuries, polities and elites whose economic survival rested on specializing in slave raiding and slave trading developed across West Africa. As a result, peer-polity rivalry and bitter conflict intensified, and old regional hierarchies began to give way to new cleavages and political configurations that were characterized by militarism and the intensification of centralized political landscapes in some areas and by decentralized political formations in others.

The impact of Atlantic trade on sociopolitical form in West Africa has been a subject of intense historiographical debate for decades. At the core of this debate is the degree to which the Atlantic slave trade affected political formations, political economies, and ideologies of power that characterized Atlantic West African societies during the seventeenth through the early nineteenth centuries (Barry 1998; Curtin 1975; Fage 1969; Rodney 1970). Until very recently, our understanding of social and political change in the Atlantic Era depended almost exclusively on documentary and oral evidence. In contrast, archaeological research tended to focus on topics relevant to the more distant or ancient African past, an intellectual division of labor that resulted in what Jan Vansina referred to as 'sibling rivalry' between the disciplines of history and archaeology (Vansina 1995). Vansina's comment has resulted in important dialogues of great value amongst archaeologists, and to a lesser degree between historians and historical anthropologists. These dialogues have emphasized how the integration of historical and archaeological data can contribute substantially to our understanding of social, economic, and political processes in West Africa during the Atlantic Era (DeCorse 1996, 2001b; DeCorse and Chouin 2004; Denbow 2003; Falola and Jennings 2003; S. K. McIntosh 2005; Robertshaw 2000; Stahl 2001, 2009; Stahl and LaViolette 2009).[1]

At a primary level, this volume represents an archaeological contribution to our understanding of political culture and sociopolitical relations in the era of Atlantic commercial revolutions. Using both historical and archaeological tools, this collection of essays sheds light on how entanglement in the Atlantic economic sphere shaped West African political processes. The central argument of the book is that the commercial revolutions of the seventeenth and eighteenth centuries dramatically reshaped the regional contours of political organization across West Africa. The book serves, therefore, to fill some

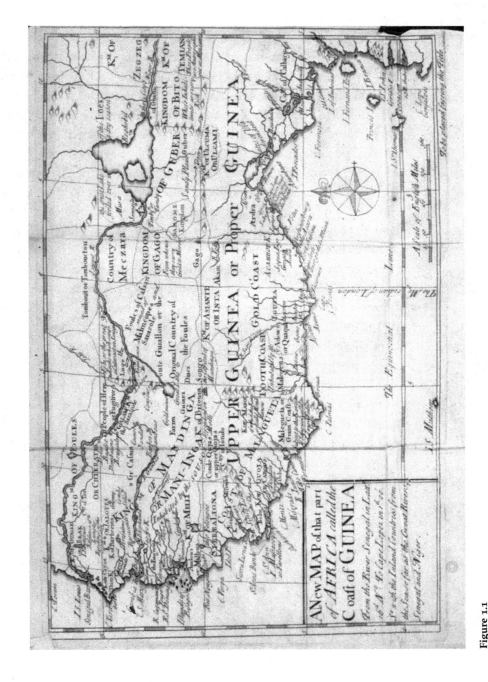

Figure 1.1
Eighteenth-century political map of West Africa, from "A New Map of that Part of Africa called the Coast of Guinea" (Snelgrave 1754).

of the critical gaps in the historiography of Atlantic West Africa's political formations, while at the same time applying an anthropological perspective on the forms of political culture that evolved in this region during the early modern period.

Additionally, however, these insights are important not only to our understanding of the broad political history of West Africa, but also to archaeological perspectives on political culture as a form of meaningful social practice. Atlantic West Africa, as a distinctive historical and regional unit, has been almost entirely absent in the empirical and theoretical understanding of political processes that have characterized the study of complex societies worldwide (S. K. McIntosh 1999b). The study of West African societies, begun long ago by scholars interested in non-Western political systems, identified a range of political forms from centralized states through decentralized lineages (Brown 1951; Fallers 1964; Forde and Kaberry 1967; Fortes and Evans-Pritchard 1940; Goody 1971; Lloyd 1960, 1971; Southall 1956). Until the last few decades, however, scholars commonly argued that the former were the product of either Islamic or European intervention in the second millennium A.D. The precolonial state in Africa was thus viewed as "a superstructure erected over village communities of peasant cultivators rather than a society which has grown naturally out of them" (Oliver and Fage 1962:36), and it was examined in terms of markers of civilisation introduced from elsewhere (see Connah 2001 and Mitchell 2005 for discussion). In contrast, African decentralized societies were seen as the product of a deep and unchanging past untouched by outside influences, providing ideal staging grounds for building anthropological models of the primitive (Stahl 2001; Wolf 1982).

These assumptions have had deep and long-lasting consequences for anthropological and archaeological conceptualizations of Africa's past. On the one hand, as cultural evolutionists of the 1960s increasingly turned towards archaeology to identify the processes of cultural evolution uncontaminated by outside influences, West African cases were deemed of little comparative value. Indeed, as Elmen Service, author of the extremely influential volume *Origins of the State and Civilization*, once wrote, "the various instances of state-making in West Africa . . . have no direct or focal bearing on the problem of the origin of primary states" (Service 1975:137). Similarly, African case studies were almost entirely absent from the chiefdom debate of the 1980s and early 1990s (S. K. McIntosh 1999b). Viewed within the framework of cultural evolution, furthermore, nonstate societies were judged 'people without history' (Wolf 1982), rendering the archaeological study of such communities of little value to a discipline devoted to the explanation of processual change. The aforementioned assumptions about West Africa's past thereby lent credence to the marginalization of case studies from the region within anthropological archaeology more broadly.

However, as archaeologists have shifted their objectives from outlining universal evolutionary trajectories to illuminating variable pathways towards social complexity (S. K. McIntosh 1999a, 1999b), West Africa in the era of the expanding modern world system emerges as valuable context in which to explore the dynamics of political organization from a comparative perspective (DeCorse 2001c). Indeed, we believe that the often microhistorical precision with which archaeological research can be conducted in West Africa, reflected in the following essays, makes the region *ideal* for exploring the dynamics of power, social complexity, and political economy unencumbered by threadbare evolutionary typologies (Stahl 1999a).

This volume adopts a *landscape* perspective, outlined in detail here, to contribute to our understanding of the particular nature of social and political change in West Africa in the Atlantic Era, and the relationship between political organization and cultural entanglement more broadly. Rather than promote one particular vision of landscape in this volume, however, each chapter reflects a diverse approach to the archaeology of landscape, examining a plethora of ways in which social and political transformations in West Africa are observable in reference to regionally defined archaeological remains. What were the regional manifestations of power and authority in this period? How were West African communities able to establish or resist dominance in their respective regions? How were the peripheries, frontiers, and boundary zones of states constituted? What forms of political and economic articulation took place between centralized and decentralized polities? What roles did trading entrepôts and trade routes play in contests for authority, power, hegemony, conquest, and resistance? Incorporating perspectives on regional economic networks, population and settlement shifts, and the regional manifestation of cultural values, memory, and ideology, the chapters in this volume seek to answer these and other questions. In all, they cast significant light on how a landscape approach to the material manifestations of power can advance our understanding of the nature of political authority in Atlantic West Africa.

In this chapter we introduce the problems and prospects in accounting for the nature of West African responses to entanglement within Atlantic commercial spheres. First, we outline the nature of the historiographical and archaeological discussion to date, highlighting the role material culture has played in constructing historical narratives of Atlantic commercial entanglement. Second, we introduce the potential for a landscape perspective to address some of the questions left unanswerable by this approach, illuminating broader issues of social, cultural, and indeed political change in this period. Last, we draw on the case studies presented in this volume to introduce three broadly inclusive landscape forms that resulted from the complex nature of political maneuvering in Atlantic West Africa: *fragmented landscapes*; *state-generated landscapes*; and *internal frontier landscapes*.

WEST AFRICA AND THE ATLANTIC WORLD: MATERIAL NARRATIVES OF CULTURAL ENTANGLEMENT

The impact of Atlantic-Era commercial revolutions on West Africa's domestic economy (particularly in regard to the organization of production, consumption, and exchange of goods and services and their relationships to political organization across the region) has been the focus of a long-standing academic debate (Alpern 1995; Eltis 2000; Inikori 2001; Inikori, et al. 1992; Lovejoy 1989; Rodney 1966; Thornton 1998). Historical and archaeological research on West Africa in the Atlantic Era has brought to the foreground the study of material practices from a variety of perspectives (documentary, archaeological, and art historical), making specific claims about the close relationship between Atlantic commercial processes and both cultural and political transformations across the region. This has resulted in contrasting narratives of West African entanglement within Atlantic commercial spheres (e.g., Stahl 2001). In this section, we explore the sorts of narratives of entanglement that have emerged from this dialogue, suggesting that they represent only one way of understanding the range of responses to Atlantic commercial expansion across West Africa's littoral and hinterland. These observations encourage the inclusion of a broader landscape approach that examines how transformations in material life were positioned within political economies, cultural ideologies, and regional power relationships.

The historiography of the trans-Atlantic economy, viewed through the prism of available documentary sources (merchant records, ships' logs, company account books, and so forth) has primarily offered metahistories of imports and exports, focusing on human and material capital flows within the African littorals of the Atlantic Basin (e.g., Inikori 2002). Some have argued that the volume of both was so great that local industry was diminished, that Africa was drained of necessary labor supplies, that indigenous slavery intensified dramatically, and that the influx of guns and gunpowder triggered the emergence of centralized militaristic states (Austen 1987; Goody 1971; Inikori 1977; Klein 1992; Lovejoy 1983; Rodney 1966). According to this view, the rising demands for human cargo as the dominant African export "retarded the development of market economies in western Africa and kept the region's economies largely out of the integrated commodity production processes of the Atlantic economy until the abolition of that trade in the mid-nineteenth century" (Inikori 2007:86). This resulted in political entities fully dependent on expanding European commercial forces for both their structure and their survival (Rodney 1981; Wallerstein 1974).

In contrast, others have argued that the Atlantic economy, and the commerce that supported it, was of minimal consequence in West Africa because the share of African exports and European imports was insignificant relative to the value of other economic circuits. In this view, European imports were never in significant demand, and were able neither to penetrate African markets nor to threaten domestic industry until the third quarter of the nineteenth century (Eltis and Jennings 1988). The import of exotic trade goods, rather, fulfilled a demand for prestige goods alone, and had minimal impacts on the broader West African economy. Based on his assessment of mercantile patterns on the Gold Coast and in Senegambia, for example, John Thornton has suggested that "Africa's trade with Europe was largely moved by prestige, fancy, changing taste, and a desire for variety – and such whimsical motivations were backed up by a relatively well developed productive economy and substantial purchasing power" (Thornton 1998:45). According to this view, Atlantic exchange was epiphenomenal to local political trajectories.

As a measure of economic impact, this historiographical debate has largely depended on the use of quantitative measures of the *volume* and the *value* of goods and captives traded in the Atlantic Era, measured in terms of European monetary standards and market logic. As such, this debate reflects a decidedly *formalist* approach

8

POWER AND
LANDSCAPE IN
ATLANTIC WEST
AFRICA

to understanding the impact of the slave trade on local community dynamics, depending as it does upon gross assessments of capital flows into and out of the West African littoral, far removed from the immediate social context in which such goods were circulated, used, and discarded. As a result, social and cultural change has been assessed in relatively one-dimensional terms, focusing on whether or not indigenous political economies expanded as a result of contact, at the expense of a more nuanced understanding of the variable responses to local entanglement within Atlantic commercial systems (DeCorse 2001a:11–12).

Scholars are cognizant, however, of the need to explore the social context in which global commerce was operating at the local level in West Africa during the early modern period (DeCorse 2001a; Stahl 2001; Wolf 1982). Long has it been argued, for example, that internal socioeconomic factors were the primary force in determining the paths taken by many African societies in response to the opening of early international trade (Austen 1978; Polanyi 1966). The key question is not how much trade took place, or whether economies were stimulated or retarded along a sliding scale of 'development,' but rather precisely how local economic and political systems were shaped by and also shaped the evolving capitalist world economy. That is, we should be seeking to understand how West African political economies were increasingly articulated into an expanding capitalist commercial system, what Eric Wolf defined long ago as the primary work of historical anthropology (Wolf 1982).

Archaeological research is increasingly central to this debate, drawing from anthropological perspectives on the role of exotic material culture in preindustrial societies. In non-capitalist economies, luxury or wealth goods may serve as the primary social currency for underwriting political legitimacy, expansion, and long-distance trade over broad areas (Earle 1997). For Timothy Champion, 'prestige-goods' economies "seem particularly common on the fringe of early states and empires, and are a regular means of articulating societies with very different structures of economic and social organization" (Champion 1989:12). Rather than economic epiphenomena, therefore, the flow of new exotica into West Africa would have impacted local polities in very powerful ways (Appadurai 1986; Ekholm and Friedman 1979; Kohl 1987; Larsen 1987; Renfrew 1986; Rowlands 1987; Schneider 1977). *Volumetric–valumetric* approaches to Atlantic commerce are ill equipped to address this issue because of the basic nature of the source material, which is extremely limited in its ability to achieve an understanding of the social context in which such goods were exchanged, consumed, and discarded.

In the past three decades, archaeologists have taken up the daunting challenge of understanding the implications of Atlantic commercial entanglement for both coastal and interior societies in Atlantic Africa. Whereas historians have focused largely on quantitative measures of trade and value, archaeologists, largely working at the household level, have examined patterns in the production, exchange, consumption, and discard of exotic and local material culture (DeCorse 2001a; Goucher 1981; Kelly 1997a; Ogundiran 2002, 2007; Stahl 1999b, 2001). This research has placed high analytical value on understanding the social roles of, and cultural values attributed to, imported trade goods in West African contexts, transforming our understanding of the nature of material practices in West Africa in this period.

For example, excavations within the Fante community surrounding the slave-trading fort of Elmina in Ghana (DeCorse 1992, 1998, 2001a), and within the Huedan palace community of Savi in the Republic of Bénin (Kelly 1995, 1997a, 1997b, 2001), have examined the social and cultural values attached to imported goods in these contexts. Framed in reference to cultural continuity versus change, Christopher DeCorse and Kenneth Kelly examined how European trade goods were used, and indeed displayed, in terms of local cultural and political values, allowing a new appreciation of how European imports were integrated into deeply rooted material practices in West African communities. Ongoing research in the West African interior, furthermore, has shed light on the wide-reaching impacts of global trade in West Africa beyond the reach of coastal enclaves. Ann Stahl, for example, has documented how the Atlantic economy resulted in broad transformations in production, consumption, and taste in smaller-scale hinterland communities in the Banda regions of Ghana, an area on the margins of multiple commercial spheres in the past (Stahl 2001, 2007; Stahl, et al. 2008). This agenda has been carried forward by Akin Ogundiran in the Yoruba hinterlands of the Bight of Benin, with an emphasis on gauging the social value of Atlantic imports at the local level and the transformations in material culture that accompanied the commercial revolutions of the Atlantic Age (Ogundiran 2002, 2003, 2007, 2009).

Importantly, however, these studies are not limited solely to imported goods. Rather, they interrogate the entire corpus of material life – local and exotic – towards a broader understanding of how local commodity production chains were impacted by Atlantic commercial encroachment (Cruz 2003; Ogundiran 2001; Stahl, et al. 2008; Usman 2000). As a result, archaeological research conducted at the household level has provided valuable insights into the dynamic nature of material practices in this period. Such research has had the added benefit of highlighting clear linkages between contact-period communities and their precontact antecedents, lending credence to long-standing attempts by scholars to situate the archaeology of West Africa in the Atlantic Era squarely within a *longue durée* perspective (Stahl 1999a, 2001). Household-level research has thus reframed our understanding of the political economy of West Africa in the Atlantic Era in reference to indigenous social and cultural value systems, enhancing our understanding of the social dynamics of a wide range of communities implicated by Atlantic commercial pressures.

Drawing from their unique methodological strengths, historical and archaeological research on the nature of material life in Atlantic West Africa has gone far in illuminating the relative impact of global trading networks on West African communities in the Atlantic Era. For a number of reasons, however, these approaches can go only so far in addressing the broad impacts of the Atlantic economy on political organization and political process in West Africa.

Throughout the seventeenth and eighteenth centuries, a bewildering variety of polities developed in Atlantic Africa, whose economic survival rested on complex commercial relationships with the coast. Likewise, the political institutions of several pre-Atlantic polities witnessed significant transformations, from expansive territorial states such as Oyo (Law 1977), Dahomey (Bay 1998; Law 1991), Benin (Ben-Amos 1999; Ryder 1969), Asante (McCaskie 1995; Wilks 1975) and Segu (Roberts 1987), to small-scale polities like the Efik city-states of Old Calabar (Lovejoy and Richardson 1999), the Akwamu, Akyem, Kwaku, and Krepi of the Gold Coast (Daaku 1970), to trading confederacies such as the Aro of the Bight of Biafra (Northrup 1978; Okpoko and Obi-Ani 2005). Some of these polities specialized in slave raiding and slave trading; some served as social networks for slave-trading merchants and as refuge from expansionist slave-raiding polities (Inikori 2003; Klein 2001; Lovejoy 1983). Still others flourished because of their participation in the broad commercial revolutions that accompanied the integration of the region into the Atlantic economic orbits. Importantly, each of these polities adapted to this new world order in its own contingent ways. Alone, neither the formalist histories nor substantivist archaeological counternarratives have been able to account for the degree to which the variable nature of West African political structures was connected to broader Atlantic economic processes.[2]

Additionally, as archaeologists devote greater attention to exploring communities that thrived in the West African interior in this period, durable trade goods – those same goods deemed central for lubricating the wheels of social transformation – are identified with much-lower frequency (DeCorse 1980; Ogundiran 2007; Stahl 1999b). Indeed, the same may be said of communities in the near hinterlands of major coastal centers as well (DeCorse 2001a). This pattern suggests that such resources were concentrated within political centers across West Africa, serving as important material resources for elites attempting to inculcate a sense of status distinction (Stahl 2008). At the same time, however, the overall impact of integration into Atlantic commercial spheres was no less dramatic for communities that lack clear material evidence of contact (DeCorse and Spiers 2009; Ogundiran 2009). Eighteenth and early-nineteenth-century European observers, as well as the historical traditions of both the littorals and the hinterlands, indicate that the Atlantic commercial revolutions translated into an economic boom across West Africa (Adams 1966; Barbot, et al. 1992; Bosman 1967; Clapperton, et al. 2005; Curtin 1997; Lander, et al. 1832; Manning 1982; Snelgrave 1754). Likewise, whether directly or indirectly, Atlantic encounters clearly had transformative impacts on the cleavages and distribution of power and authority at the local and regional levels in West Africa. The kinds of material narratives of Atlantic commercial processes outlined above cannot alone account for the broad transformations that took place across West Africa during this period.

Mounting historical and archaeological research does suggest, however, that this gap may be bridged by the adoption of a *landscape* perspective, broadly defined. Whereas the direct material implications of Atlantic commerce may be masked beyond centers of trade, historical research has demonstrated that Atlantic commercial processes had wide-reaching and universal impact on the way diverse sets of communities were organized spatially across West Africa's coast and hinterlands (Kea 1982; Klein 2001). Royal capitals of those kingdoms that actively engaged in the Atlantic slave trade expanded rapidly, providing a safe haven for those fleeing slave-raiding neighbors as well as for those profiting from the new economic opportunities introduced by Atlantic commerce. New towns rapidly emerged in the interior to control important nodes in emerging regional exchange systems. Populations flocked to the European-controlled coastal communities, resulting in towns with populations in the tens of thousands (DeCorse 2001a). Others were depopulated, reflecting a pattern of de-urbanization (Kea 1982). Still others fled conflict to mountainous regions, building complex defensive systems to avoid capture (Klein 2001). The result of these processes was a series of distinct yet interconnected political landscapes structured to maintain order and foster trade with the Atlantic world, as well as to resist the onslaught of expansionist polities. Overall, therefore, the period can be considered one of major demographic upheaval characterized by new manifestations of power and cultural memory that had profound effects on the way people lived in and thought about the world around them.

Scholars have wrestled with how regional landscapes were transformed in the Atlantic Era. Historians and historical anthropologists have made important contributions to our understanding of urbanism (Anderson and Rathbone 2000; Coquery-Vidrovich 1991, 2005; Hull 1976; Law 2004), trade and economic networks (Barry 1998), regional settlement dynamics (Kea 1982), and the relationship between settlements and historical memory (Greene 1996, 2002; Shaw 2002). Despite invaluable contributions on these and other topics with a 'regional' bent, we remain unable to overcome the near lack of even coverage (over time *and* space) regarding historical references to the nature of regional social, cultural, and political dynamics.[3] Our understanding of the contours of power and authority is therefore based largely on limited source material from a handful of documentary 'hot-spots' that stand out historically in high relief (DeCorse 2001b). Thus, research drawing from documentary and oral archives alone has produced only partial histories of the West African response to the slave trade – histories that focus on charting social, economic, and political change in a restricted set of settlements across what undoubtedly was a dynamic and heterogeneous political landscape.

Increasingly, historical–archaeological research drawing from a variety of landscape approaches is filling these gaps in the documentary record. Indeed, as Christopher DeCorse has noted, "More important than the presence or absence of trade items, it is the changes in settlement patterns, defensive features, and settlement organization that testify more eloquently to the transformations that occurred in African societies" in the Atlantic Era (DeCorse 2001b:10; see also Stahl 1999a). In the last decade, archaeological research across West Africa has demonstrated the power of a landscape perspective to address broad-scale political and economic processes in the Atlantic Era, reflecting a veritable revolution in the methods and goals of historical–archaeological research in the region (Chouin 2008, 2009; de Barros 2001; DeCorse 2005; DeCorse and Chouin 2010; DeCorse, et al. 2000, 2009; DeCorse and Spiers 2009; Gronenborn 2001; Holl 2001; Kelly and Norman 2007; MacEachern 1993, 2001b; McIntosh and Thiaw 2001; Monroe 2003, 2007a, 2007b; Norman 2009; Norman and Kelly 2006; Richard 2007; Smith 2008; Swanpoel 2004; Thiaw 1999). These research projects have adopted a variety of methodological and theoretical viewponts that may be conceptualized in terms of a landscape perspective, broadly defined. Building upon this recent trend in the region, we propose that a landscape approach can contribute significantly to our understanding of transformations in political processes, power relations, and authority that fundamentally defined how West African communities experienced and reacted to global economic pressures. In the following section, we outline an archaeological approach to landscape, emerging out of a productive dialogue with research in other world regions and its potential application to the Atlantic West African context.

ARCHAEOLOGIES OF POWER AND LANDSCAPE

Ask ten archaeologists to define 'landscape' and one will undoubtedly receive at least as many answers. In North America, landscape archaeology has its roots in the regional settlement archaeology of the post–World War II era, wherein patterns in the distribution of human settlement were used to make broad conclusions about the causative relationship between environmental forces and social organization (Ammerman 1981; Johnson 1977; Parsons 1972; Smith 1976). Although regionally focused archaeology continues to have a deep-rooted bias towards the study of settlement patterns, archaeologists also appreciate what lower-density, nonsettlement remains can tell

14

POWER AND LANDSCAPE IN ATLANTIC WEST AFRICA

us about human social and cultural behavior in the past (Bintliff and Snodgrass 1988; Cherry, et al. 1991; Ebert 1992; Foley 1981; Gosden and Head 1994; Knapp 1997; Rossignol and Wandsnider 1992; Yamin and Methany 1996). Building on a parallel tradition of the archaeology of field systems and mortuary monuments in the British Isles (Bender 1993; Bradley 1978; Hoskins 1955; Tilley 1994), the term *landscape archaeology* is commonly deployed as a framework for examining broad sets of regional data (botanical, geological, and cultural) to interpret the regional manifestations of human cultural behavior in the past (Marquardt and Crumley 1990; Wilkinson 2003).

At the most elementary level, therefore, archaeologists define landscape as a unit of analysis reflecting the complex material manifestations of the relationship between humans and their environment (Crumley 1994). Importantly, however, scholars mobilizing a landscape perspective commonly argue that landscapes do not exist a priori as a natural stage upon which social processes unfold. Rather, they are *produced* by human social and cultural practice (Low and Lawrence-Zúñiga 2003), rendering palimpsests of material remains at a broad regional scale (Wilkinson 2003). As the product of cultural practice, landscapes are multivalent constructs, often defined by overlapping layers of significance which are experienced differently by members of separate ethnic, gender, economic, or political factions (Marquardt and Crumley 1990). The archaeological analysis of regional data-sets in reference to wide-ranging social and cultural processes thus characterizes a landscape approach to the archaeological record (Wilkinson 2003). We marshal the concept in this volume, therefore, as a broad and inclusive conceptual tool for understanding diverse patterns of social, economic, and political structure in West Africa's Atlantic Age. In this section, we focus on the power of landscape-scale analysis to illustrate the nature of political economy, cultural ideology, and the dynamics of power and resistance in the past.

Reflecting its roots in processual archaeology of the 1960s, identifying archaeological indices of political–economic integration has been a central focus of regionally oriented archaeological research for decades. Integrating systematic survey techniques with quantitative approaches to geographic analysis, for example, regional analysis since the 1970s has focused on using patterns in the size and regional distribution of settlement sites as a proxy for interpreting political hierarchy, market activity, trading relationships, and urban–rural economic systems in the past (Adams and Jones 1981; Crumley 1977; Earle 1976; Flannery 1998; Parsons 1972; Smith 1979; Wright 1994). Archaeologists have sought to use settlement landscapes, therefore, to generate rules of thumb for identifying periods of sociopolitical change in the past, such as the emergence of chiefdoms or the rise of the state (Flannery 1998; Wright 1994). In addition to such indices of political scale and socioeconomic relations, archaeologists commonly examine how non-settlement building activity (state facilities, agricultural works, road networks, etc.) was used in the past as a strategy to promote the political and economic agendas of centralized government institutions at the local level (Cherry 1987; Kolata 1986; Schreiber 1987; Stanish 1994; Ur 2003). Read as either indices of political–economic relationships, or as a critical component of generating those relationships, landscape stands center stage in the study of political economies in the past, a point reiterated by the chapters in this volume.

Responding to the post-processual turn taken by archaeology in the 1980s and 1990s, however, archaeologists also have made great strides in accounting for the symbolic content of ancient landscapes (Knapp and Ashmore 1999). This intellectual shift has resulted in a florescence of archaeological research examining landscapes as embedded with meaning, revealing the complex and culturally contingent ways in which landscapes anchor cultural values in place. Invested with important symbolic meaning, cultural landscapes become historical as well as symbolic constructs (Casey 1997), serving as material guides to the collective memory of evolving communities (Bender 1993; Low and Lawrence-Zúñiga 2003; C. Richards 1996; J. Richards 1999; Tilley 1994). Indeed, as Fred Inglis has suggested, landscapes become "the most solid appearance in which a history can declare itself" (Inglis 1977:489). Insofar as they shape the everyday experience of the world, landscapes thus have culturally recursive qualities (Basso 1996; Tilley 1994), providing not only memorials to the past but also roadmaps to possible futures.

Landscape-scale analysis has provided valuable perspectives on cultural meaning in the past. However, recent analyses of monumental landscapes have also emphasized the central role of such features in materializing power and authority in complex societies (DeMarrais, et al. 1996). Indeed, if landscapes are value-laden cultural constructs, monumental landscapes differentially materialize the values of elites and serve, therefore, as a potential tool of hegemonic power

(Lefebvre 1991). The power of monumental landscapes rests on their potential to shape collective perceptions of the world by providing contexts in which publics partake in the performance of power (Ashmore 1989; DeMarrais, et al. 1996; Fritz 1986; Innomata 2006; Moore 1996), thereby naturalizing historical claims to political authority in reference to deeper mythological pasts (Leone 1984; McAnany 2001; Monroe 2009). Indeed, it has been suggested that the "production and reproduction of hegemonic schemes *require* the monopolization of public spaces in order to dominate memories" (Low and Lawrence-Zúñiga 2003:22, emphasis added). Cosmologies rendered in stone and earth, thus, can serve as powerful tools for shaping the popular experience, perception, and imagination of the world (Smith 2003). The production of landscape is, therefore, at its very core a power-laden process, and one with potential to project structures of hegemonic authority (Lefebvre 1991; Smith 2003), a theme taken up by a number of contributors to this volume.

In acknowledging the power of landscape production to materialize the hegemonic strategies of political elites, however, we risk uncritically fetishizing such strategies. In even the most hegemonic political communities, for example, elites face major hurdles in reshaping non-elite perceptions of the world (Scott 1990), resulting in hidden transcripts of everyday resistance visible archaeologically (Ferguson 1992; Leone and Frye 1999; McKee 1992; Orser and Funari 2001). The abandonment of urban cores, the tearing down of walls and boundary markers, and other forms of 'vandalism' commonly noted in periods of social instability and collapse, all attest to the degree to which political subjects genuinely internalize spatially rendered elite political agendas. In a similar vein, landscape features may also form enduring barriers to the centralizing tendencies of political entrepreneurs. In societies at various scales worldwide, for example, decentralized sacred geographies and other local conceptions of landscape provide alternative narratives of social order that may be marshaled in opposition to attempts to impose centralized authority (Dyke 2004; Joyce, et al. 2001; R. J. McIntosh 2005; Robertshaw 2010; Vidal and Duwákalumi 2000; Wernke 2007). Landscape, therefore, serves as a particularly powerful source of political counter-narrative, and may play an important role in strategies to deflect hegemonic domination by aggrandizing elites. The contributors to this volume demonstrate how landscapes are contested in this way, showcasing landscape as a multivalent social construct in a broad range of societies and at different social and political scales.

Settlement archaeology and, to a lesser extent, regional approaches have a long history in West Africa (Bower 1986). Yet, until quite recently, archaeology in the region has been relatively quiet on the relations between landscape and power. Archaeological excavation at major sites since the 1930s was driven, for the most part, by historical questions focusing on issues of cultural chronology, artifact typology, and settlement history, with little attention paid towards understanding broader patterns of social and political organization at a regional level (de Barros 1990; Kense 1990). By the 1970s, mounting research allowed for large-scale syntheses of archaeological data collected from sites across broad 'regions', defined largely by modern national, rather than precolonial, political boundaries (Anquandah 1982; Davies 1961, 1967, 1970, 1972, 1976; Mauny 1961; Shaw 1978).

In this period, newly established archaeology departments across West Africa initiated regional archaeological surveys as well, often as salvage projects in response to emerging development pressures (MacEachern 2001a). Major salvage projects included the Volta Basin Research Project (Ghana) (Calvocoressi and York 1971; Davies 1971; York, et al. 1967), the Kainji Dam Project (Nigeria) (Breternitz 1968, 1969, 1975; Hartle 1970), and later, salvage archaeology in the Lower Mono Valley (Bénin) (Adande and Adagba 1988; Adande and Bagodo 1991; Adande and Dovie 1990; Bagodo 1993). The period was notable also for the initiation of a handful of problem-oriented projects of a regional nature such as the West African Trade Project (Ghana) (Posnansky 1971, 1972, 1973) and surveys in the Lake Chad region (Connah 1981), as well as for preliminary surveys and reconnaissance schemes in Liberia (Gabel, et al. 1975), Sierra Leone (Atherton 1972; DeCorse 1980; Newman 1966; Ozanne 1966), Senegambia (Evans and Beale 1966; Martin and Becker 1974; Thilmans, et al. 1980), and Togo (Posnansky and de Barros 1980). Collectively these projects provided valuable new perspectives on the potential richness and diversity of archaeological landscapes in these previously unexplored regions. Despite the fact that such studies increasingly depended on regional survey data, however, their goals largely were geared towards site inventory and description (Bower 1986; de Barros 1990; Kense 1990). The site, rather than the complex relationships

18

POWER AND
LANDSCAPE IN
ATLANTIC WEST
AFRICA

between sites, remained the primary unit of analysis, and questions of power and political organization were not a primary focus of attention.

A handful of projects initiated in the 1980s and 1990s pointed the way, however, towards a significant revision in archaeological approaches to understanding the nature of political culture in precolonial West Africa. In the Savannah and Sahel zones of West Africa, in particular, scanty vegetation cover and good archaeological visibility encouraged the use of systematic regional archaeology to address questions of sociopolitical change in the past. In particular, the trailblazing work of Susan and Roderick McIntosh in the Inland Niger Delta region of Mali (R. J. McIntosh 2005; R. J. McIntosh and S. K. McIntosh 1993; S. K. McIntosh 1995, 1999c; S. K. McIntosh and R. J. McIntosh 1980) fundamentally shifted our paradigmatic assumptions about the origins and nature of complex societies in sub-Saharan Africa and how we approach their archaeological analysis. The systematic survey of settlement mounds in this region has established the presence of a sociopolitically decentralized urban tradition in the first millennium A.D., interpreted as the regional manifestation of *heterarchical* forms of social organization in sub-Saharan Africa. Here, decentralized economies and sacred geography are read as a principle factor underwriting a social structure which resisted centralization for a millennium.

The McIntoshs' work at Jenné-Jeno was followed in the early 1980s by a handful of problem-oriented projects adopting an explicitly regional approach. Philip de Barros, for example, launched a systematic survey campaign in the Bassar region of Togo (de Barros 1985, 1986). Combining opportunist and systematic sampling strategies, de Barros incorporated data from both settlements and iron production sites to explore the changing levels of iron production in Bassar during the second millennium A.D., a process which had clear implications for political organization across the region (a topic explored by de Barros in this volume). Drawing on classic models of state formation, furthermore, archaeological surveys in the Dhar Tichitt region of Mauritania (Holl 1985, 1986) documented the presence of complex settlement hierarchies in the region as early as the second millenium B.C., providing a material basis for historical arguments regarding the origins of the Ghana Empire more than a millennium later. Following their research at Jenné-Jeno, furthermore, Susan and Roderick McIntosh initiated the first systematic survey campaigns in the tumulus zone of Senegal (S. K. McIntosh and R. J. McIntosh 1993; S. K. McIntosh, et al. 1992). In all, this period was one marked by exciting transformations in the methods employed in West Africanist research.

In the wetter zones to the south, a tradition of systematic regional archaeology had been thwarted, until recently, by the poor preservation of settlement architecture and generally dense vegetation. However, opportunistic surveys of earthwork systems associated with major historical sites dating broadly to the mid-second millenium A.D. have played a major role in our understanding of precolonial political dynamics (Connah 2000). In the Yoruba-Edo region of Nigeria, in particular, surveys have revealed extensive earthwork systems – representing the centralized control over vast quantities of labor – surrounding the urban cores at Benin City, Ife, and Old Oyo (Agbaje-Williams 1983; Connah 1975; Darling 1984; Ozanne 1969; Soper and Darling 1980). The widespread distribution of such wall systems also has been identified in the hinterlands of these cities, especially in smaller outlier communities, adding new insights into the structure of urban–rural relations in the region (Agbaje-Williams 1983, 1989; Darling 1984, 1998; Ogundiran 2002; Usman 2001, 2004). Research on the historical and archaeological landscapes of central Yorubaland has also focused on the nature of settlement cycling and intercommunity interaction, exploring the relationship between memory and landscape in the political dynamics in this region (Ogundiran 2002, 2003).

In southern Ghana, furthermore, some have attributed earthwork construction in the forest zone with Akan political expansion, reflecting either military functions or the deployment of enslaved labor for forest clearing and gold mining in the second millenium A.D. (Anquandah 1982; Kiyaga-Mulindwa 1978, 1982; Ozanne 1971), an interpretation that has been reconsidered in light of recent systematic research in the region (Chouin 2009; DeCorse and Chouin 2010). Although often interpreted essentially as fortifications, such landscape features also may have served an important symbolic role in materializing social space (Ben-Amos 1980). Earthworks in the Aja-Fon region, in particular, appear to have demarcated elite space rather than encircling urban communities entirely (Aguigah 1986; Kelly 1997a, 1997b; Norman and Kelly 2006; Posnansky 1981; Quarcoopome 1998), providing a valuable window into the materialization of power relationships in the past.

Importantly (over the last decade in particular), regional perspectives have been coupled with the emerging emphasis on social transformation in the Atlantic Era. Archaeological projects integrating historical data with extensive regional survey and targeted excavation are rapidly expanding our knowledge of West Africa in this period, reflecting a real sea change in the methods and goals of historical archaeology in the region. This research has examined the nature of settlement shifts around coastal enclaves, regional economic networks in the interior, and strategies to promote or resist political centralization in a variety of Atlantic-era cultural contexts (Chouin 2008; de Barros 2001; DeCorse 2005; DeCorse and Chouin 2010; DeCorse, et al. 2000, 2009; DeCorse and Spiers 2009; Gronenborn 2001; Holl 2001; Kelly and Norman 2007; MacEachern 1993, 2001b; McIntosh and Thiaw 2001; Monroe 2003, 2007a, 2007b; Norman and Kelly 2006). The last decade also has witnessed the completion of a number Ph.D. theses adopting explicit landscape approaches to social and political dynamics in the Atlantic Era (Chouin 2009; Monroe 2003; Norman 2008; Richard 2007; Smith 2008; Swanpoel 2004; Thiaw 1999).[4] Landscape perspectives, therefore, are increasingly redefining how we interpret the nature of West African entanglement in the Atlantic Era. This volume seeks to contribute to this emerging theme in West Africanist research.

LANDSCAPES OF POWER IN ATLANTIC WEST AFRICA

This volume is organized around the key theme of variability – variability in the types of societies engaged in the Atlantic exchange, and variability in the outcomes of that exchange. We have sought to achieve broad coverage of the region (Figure 1.2) to ensure that an emphasis on variability would emerge from this volume and that the chapters here engage the theme at three levels. The first relates to how West African societies were impacted by the overall intensity of contact. Contributors explore how some communities were forced to adapt to direct encounters with European traders, whereas others in the interior faced only the down-the-line effects of coastal trade, revealing a number of parallel responses. Second, the volume deals with communities of various scale. To be sure, the large centralized states that have generated such immense interest in scholarship are a major focus of attention. However, the volume pays due attention to intermediate-scale societies – often labeled as chiefdoms in anthropological literature (Earle 1991, 1997) or as mini-states in West African historiography (Obayemi 1985), which formed at the interstices between or on the edges of large-scale centralized polities. Third, the volume engages current archaeological debates on the nature of political centralization in African societies. Hierarchical states and chiefdoms led by entrepreneurial elites, of course, are explored throughout the volume. However, unlike the self-aggrandizers associated with the classic anthropological model of complex societies, several of the polities discussed here lacked institutionalized mechanisms for coercion. Such communities might be characterized as socially heterarchical rather than hierarchical (Crumley 1995; S. K. McIntosh 1999b). Importantly, however, in all cases a landscape approach plays an essential role in illuminating the broad sociopolitical impacts of the opening of Atlantic commerce. The case studies comprising this volume have been organized into three categories that capture the essence of this variation, which we refer to as *fragmented landscapes*, *state-generated landscapes*, and *internal frontier landscapes*, respectively.

Figure 1.2
Map of West Africa. The regions examined by authors in this volume are labeled to correspond with chapter numbers: (2) Western Lower Falemme, Senegal; (3) Siin, Senegal; (4) Central Region, Ghana; (5) Coastal Bénin; (6) Segou Toeda, Mali; (7) Abomey Plateau, Bénin; (8) Upper Osun, Nigeria; (9) Bassar, Togo; (10) Koinadugu Plateau, Sierra Leone; (11) Mandara Mountains, Cameroon/Nigeria.

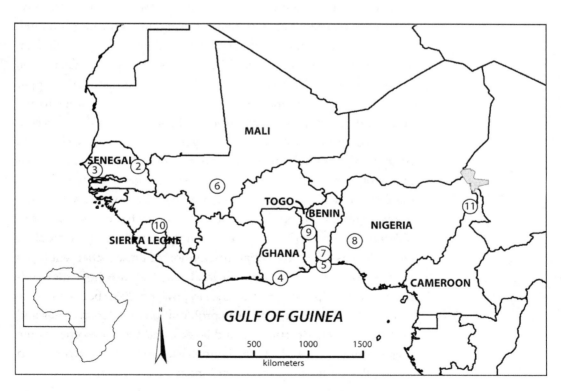

Part I explores fragmented landscapes in which the centralizing tendencies of aggrandizing elites were thwarted by factional or heterarchical tensions visible at the regional level. The chapters comprising Part I explore four case studies, from Senegambia (Falemme Valley and Siin), southern Ghana (Equafo), and southern Bénin (Hueda). In each example, trading entrepôts emerged as centers wherein local elites jockeyed for position within regional political hierarchies. In each case, however, these elites either were unable to or were uninterested in overcoming the decentralizing tendencies of political factions and heterarchies within their political spheres. Indeed, in none of the examples introduced in Part I were elites able to establish lasting centralized control over trade or sustained political authority. The result for each of these communities was a political landscape materializing social and political tension. These essays offer a cautionary note that increases in material wealth (Atlantic imports in this case) did not always result in political centralization or stability, and that the Atlantic commercial revolutions created alternative routes to power that traders and other political entrepreneurs were able to take advantage of.

In Chapter 2, Ibrahima Thiaw examines how French trading activities in the Senegambian hinterlands during the eighteenth and nineteenth centuries wrought major transformations on both settlement landscapes and power politics. Through a systematic archaeological survey along a 50-km segment of the lower Falemme River in Upper Senegal, Thiaw identifies three types of settlement dating to the eighteenth and nineteenth centuries: Indigenous defensive sites constructed of mud and stone (*tata*); Indigenous nondefensive sites with palimpsest material remains (*plages*); and European forts and settlements of mostly stone walls and cemented floors. Thiaw examines distinct characteristics in settlement type and topographic location; the *tata* and the European structures were located on escarpments, hills, and levees overlooking the Falemme River; the *plages* were sited on the levees. The differential distribution of these settlement types reveals not only the patterns of land use, but also how the landscape was manipulated in reference to power politics between European settlers and their hosts. The proliferation of defensive sites and trading posts on escarpments and levees, and the florescence of the *plages* campsites near the river channel, was a pattern which emerged during the eighteenth century and intensified throughout the nineteenth century in direct response to the integration of the Upper

Senegal into the Atlantic world. Thiaw's analysis unsettles the neat dichotomy often made in the historiography between the dominating European agencies and acquiescing Africans (Barry 1998; Rodney 1981). Instead, Thiaw shows that the landscape of the Upper Senegal was segmented according to class, wealth, and control of instruments of power during the eighteenth and nineteenth centuries.

Chapter 3 focuses on landscape transformation in the Siin Kingdom (Senegal). Here, François Richard demonstrates that in the Senegambian region, polities responded to Atlantic entanglement differently according to particular historical contingencies as well as the vagaries of the Atlantic economic system. Systematic survey of over 180 archaeological sites identified in a 36-km² area reveals an occupation sequence that spanned the period of the Late Stone Age to the twentieth century A.D., providing longitudinal depth to Richard's analysis of settlement shifts in the era of the trans-Atlantic slave trade. During the Atlantic Era, Richard documents an early phase (sixteenth to seventeenth centuries A.D.) characterized by overall decline in settlement population on the coast and a parallel pattern of settlement proliferation in the hinterlands. This phase was followed by a period (eighteenth to nineteenth centuries A.D.) marked by dramatic population realignment and resulting in large-scale settlement nucleation at coastal sites. Richard suggests that security concerns and the European demand for millet (as food for the enslaved) stimulated the growth of the large hinterland settlements in this early phase, whereas the intensification of slave raiding in the hinterland accompanied by the escalation of political conflict explains the subsequent settlement shift. The result was a fragmented sociopolitical landscape in the Siin, characterized by a segmented and decentralized political and settlement geography, all traits which the Siin carried over into the twentieth century. Ethnographic observations for the Serer and other ethnic groups of Siin in the twentieth century, therefore, seem to have been historically conditioned by the impacts of the Atlantic slave trade rather than being a feature of unchanging political tradition, a conclusion with broad implications for our understanding of the historical origins of decentralized societies in West Africa.

Chapter 4 focuses on the coastal polity of Eguafo, which emerged on the Gold Coast at the onset of the sixteenth century. Eguafo, which for several centuries was at the very margins of the regional trading networks that focused on the trans-Saharan trade, found itself at the center of lucrative commercial networks that focused on the coast within a few decades of European contact. In his chapter, Sam Spiers weaves contemporary written accounts with settlement archaeology and artifact inventories to assess the impact of new commercial opportunities on the political structures and political fortunes of Eguafo. Archaeological evidence suggests that Eguafo initially benefited from the coastal–hinterland commerce as a middleman for the export of gold and enslaved people to the coast. Spiers reveals, however, that the circulation of new wealth and novel commodities did not lead to the significant differential accumulation of wealth or social hierarchy. Indeed, in the face of the new economic opportunities, Eguafo maintained a heterarchical political system that emphasized decentralized power relations among various interest groups in the kingdom – traders, ritual specialists, corporate/lineage leaders, and other elites, who shared power with the paramount ruler at the center. The advent of European trade on the coast, therefore, created alternative sources of power for coastal elites, a process that resulted in the expansion of social networks and influence with concomitant transformations in the political and cultural landscape of Eguafo.

In Chapter 5, Neil Norman continues the fragmented landscapes theme, examining the Kingdom of Hueda on the Bight of Benin, one of the earliest centralized polities in Atlantic Africa, whose rapid growth and early demise were the twin consequences of Atlantic commercial pressures. Through a systematic regional archaeological survey, Norman is able to explore the political–economic relationships between Savi and its countryside, and, by extension, the organizational structure of the Hueda Kingdom. The study reveals a three-tier political landscape for Hueda. The capital city of Savi sat at the top of the pyramid, followed by semi-autonomous provincial towns in the middle, and small-scale villages and hamlets at the base. The power of the Hueda king ultimately rested on the extent to which he and his agents were able to centralize Atlantic commercial wealth and regulate its distribution to rural chiefs. Norman's regional survey reveals, however, that the provinces and their rural hinterlands were poorly integrated economically into the circulation of imported commodities. Thus the countryside did not share, in any significant way, in the opulence and aesthetic consumption that defined the court lifestyle at Savi. If the concentration of Atlantic wealth in the metropolitan palace was a source of power and influence for the monarchy, Norman reveals it also was a source of ambivalence of the provincial chiefs towards the center. This process laid the foundation for political fragmentation and subsequent conquest by Dahomey in 1727.

In contrast to the fragmented landscapes of Part I, Part II explores examples of state-generated landscapes rendered by political agents seeking to overcome the hurdles set up by the types of community examined in Part I. The chapters in Part II build on the question of political integration, exploring oft-cited examples of centralized states across the West African coast and interior. Essays on Segou (Mali), Dahomey (Bénin), and Oyo Empire (Nigeria), offer illustrations of the importance of the production of landscape for fostering political order and expansion in the Atlantic Era. In stark contrast to the examples provided in Part I, the polities in Part II waged relentless campaigns to institute political mechanisms for managing affairs across their respective regions. This process fundamentally depended upon the construction of regional landscapes marked by turnpike towns, colonies, palace communities, military garrisons, and villages of relocated captives. These state-generated landscapes were designed to minimize local autonomy, centralize wealth and power, and rewrite social memory across regions – strategies that underwrote the expansionist agendas of political elites and their military agents.

Analysis of the state-generated landscape of the Kingdom of Segou is the subject of Chapter 6. Segou flourished during the eighteenth and nineteenth centuries as a desert's-edge military kingdom whose expansionist project was geared primarily towards enslavement and looting. Its captives were for the most part retained in the domestic economy and resettled in agricultural–crafts villages or incorporated into elite households. Using oral interviews and archaeological survey, Kevin MacDonald and Seydou Camara examine the state-generated settlement landscape of Segou Kingdom, which included state capitals, military garrisons, and agricultural villages and hamlets. These contrast with preexisting commercial towns (*marka*) that were incorporated into the kingdom and that enjoyed some autonomy from direct state intervention. Although our understanding of the economic underpinnings of Segou society is better served by analysis of the historically rooted *marka* towns, MacDonald and Camara demonstrate that the structure of state political power and authority can be better inferred from the state-generated garrisons and agricultural–craft villages. Importantly, Chapter 6 calls for a move away from the unitary view of sociopolitical organization in the western Sudan that privileges heterarchy as a form of decentralized political system typical of Jenné-Jeno (R. J. McIntosh and S. K. McIntosh 1993), and to consider that what has been described for Jenné-Jeno may be characteristic only of commercial and spiritual centers of the region. Indeed, MacDonald and Camara argue, the settlement landscapes of states and empires in the region were decidedly hierarchical.

In Chapter 7, J. Cameron Monroe adopts a landscape perspective to examine the nature of regional power dynamics in precolonial Dahomey. Dahomey was Hueda's northern neighbor and eventual conqueror, and thrived in the eighteenth and nineteenth centuries as an example of the West African state par excellence. Dahomey seems to have learned from the failure of the Hueda monarchy to achieve regional political–economic integration. Monroe focuses on regional patterns in the construction of royal palace complexes, demonstrating that soon after Dahomey annihilated its southern neighbors, Allada and Hueda, it vigorously embarked on building an expansive bureaucratic apparatus aimed at integrating the provinces and the metropolis. It achieved this objective in two ways. First, throughout the eighteenth century, the monarchy built palaces in towns and cities along the major trade routes. In contrast, during the nineteenth century, palace complexes were constructed in rural zones at a distance from urban centers. This shift in the direction of palace building, Monroe argues, reflects a shift in the nature of African exports, from human captives to agricultural commodities (chiefly palm oil), by the second quarter of the nineteenth century. Monroe argues that this pattern represented an important transformation in the political economy of Dahomey, in which elites recast tribute-bearing rural communities into commodity-producing zones, and in which urban rural power dynamics increasingly were materialized through palace construction. The construction of palace towns in Dahomey's rural countryside was thus part of a state-generated landscape that was strategically designed to meet the ideological and economic needs of the monarchy during the two phases of commercial revolution.

In Chapter 8, Akinwumi Ogundiran examines the production of landscape as a key component of the political strategies of the Oyo Empire, the largest political formation south of River Niger. Ogundiran's chapter examines the production of colonized landscapes in particular, focusing on the way settlement features generated a conceptual landscape of imperial power and colonial identity in the Upper Osun region (central Yorubaland), a region colonized by Oyo between the late sixteenth and early seventeenth centuries. Ogundiran examines the site of Ede-Ile, which was strategically placed to control part of the commercial traffic that linked central Yorubaland to the coast, especially the eastern end of the Bight of Benin. The colony was established for the sole purpose of diverting wealth, resources, and profits to the coffers of the Oyo metropolis. It bore cultural–ritual, economic, military, and political ties to its patron, the Oyo-Ile metropolis, and was spatially and socially distinguishable from the communities in the host territory. The chapter examines the materiality of political process (colonization, in this case), emphasizing how landscape production served to materialize an Oyo colonial identity in a foreign land. The chapter thus contributes substantial insight into our understanding of the intimate relationship between landscape production and colonization in the process of building an extensive geopolitical landscape in complex societies (Smith 2003).

Whereas Parts I and II of this volume deal with societies in direct contact with Atlantic commercial agents or intermediaries, the chapters included in Part III explore the internal frontier landscapes of smaller-scale polities that emerged at the interstices of expansionist states (Kopytoff 1987). Authors contributing to this section of the volume examine such polities in the Bassar (Northern Togo), Koinadugu (Sierra Leone), and Mandara Highlands (Nigeria–Cameroon) regions. These regions often are perceived to have been the most distant – socially, economically, and geographically – from coastal commerce. As such, they often are mined by scholars seeking examples of alternate pathways towards social complexity in West Africa, 'uncontaminated' by outside influences (Stahl 1999a, 2007). The authors reveal, however, that such communities were anything but isolated from the broader impacts of Atlantic commerce. Indeed, they served as both reservoirs of captives and providers of critical resources in complex and non-linear ways, "witnessing renewed periods of migration, consolidation, and ethnic reformation" (DeCorse, this volume), and resulting in heterogeneous political landscapes across West Africa's hinterlands.

In Chapter 9, Philip de Barros engages Igor Kopytoff's original model of the Internal African Frontier to explore sociopolitical dynamics in the Bassar region of Togo during the eighteenth and nineteenth centuries. He argues that for us to understand better Kopytoff's internal frontier process as an explanatory scheme for sociopolitical changes, we need to factor in the role of ironworking specialists in re-ordering the demographic and political landscape of Bassar after the fourteenth century. Importantly, de Barros demonstrates that Bassar experienced a spectacular growth in iron production between the late sixteenth century and the end of the seventeenth century in response to the increased demands for iron weapons, horse equipment, and protective chain mail by the Dagomba, Mamprusi, Gonja, and Asante states. Population swelled due to the influx of ironworkers and the growth of market facilities, which expanded rapidly as the scale of iron production increased, and as slaves were imported to work in mines and agricultural fields. The Bassar polity thus was reconstituted into a multi-ethnic entity and organized into a regional pyramidal structure in which the Bassar metropolis wielded control and influence. Despite these transformations, power structures remained decidedly decentralized. Although chiefs operated centrally, their powers were nominal and they commanded no institutionalized political apparatus that would allow them to operate independently of the leaders of parallel corporate groups and quasi-political organizations. It was the heterarchical structure of the Bassar chiefdom that sustained the region's enormous output in iron production, until mounting pressure from the Atlantic slave trade "led to the abandonment of the Bassar peneplain between 1775 and 1825 and the regrouping of populations in mountain refuge areas" (de Barros, this volume).

In Chapter 10, Christopher DeCorse focuses on settlement patterns and material life on Koinadugu Plateau (northern Sierra Leone), which provided over 30,000 captives for the Middle Passage from the seventeenth through the early nineteenth centuries. Like de Barros, DeCorse reads changes in settlement patterns and sociopolitical organization on Koinadugu Plateau in the Atlantic Era as a local response to the Atlantic Slave trade and the inter-regional political unrest caused by predatory states in the region. European imports are scarce in the archaeological record for most of the seventeenth through the nineteenth centuries. However, as pressure from slaving states such as the Samori and Fulani polities intensified, fortified towns on hilltops and riverine plateaus increased across the region. The chief role of such towns was to provide protection for their residents and satellite communities, rather than to create political hegemonies. Indeed, the Koinadugu peoples eschewed centralizing political process, and instead developed a decentralized political system in which the power of charismatic leaders was counterbalanced by the powers of ritually sanctioned governing associations – 'secret societies' – whose members where drawn from the rank and file. Thus, despite being forced to respond to external pressures in creative ways, they remained committed to what DeCorse describes as a kinship mode of production and a decentralized, heterarchical mode of governance that cannot be boxed into a universal evolutionary typology.

In Chapter 11, which focuses on the Mandara Highlands of Nigeria and Cameroon, Scott MacEachern complements and, at the same time, provides a distinct counterpoint to the transformations witnessed in other case studies in this volume. The chapter complements, in the sense that it shows how a region even farther inland underwent political and sociocultural transformations similar to those closer to the ground zero of Atlantic commercial interaction. It serves as a valuable counterpoint, however, because the Mandara Highlands were too far removed from the magnetic pull of the Atlantic trade to have been affected directly or significantly. The area underwent dramatic political transformations over the course of the second millennium A.D., transformations marked mid-millennium by the construction of numerous massive dry-stone complexes (the DGB sites) across the region. The DGB sites required the successful mobilization of large numbers of people, yet montagnard political leadership is believed to have had very limited coercive powers and to have presided over noncentralized political systems (David 1996). In his chapter MacEachern asks what led to the emergence of massive dry-wall structures on the Mandara highlands during the mid-second millennium A.D.; from where did the builders of these structures come; and what are the political implications of the DGB sites? Many have interpreted the DGB sites as the product of externally derived rupture in the cultural history of the region, driven by the Kanuri state to the north in particular. MacEachern contends, however, that the substantial dry-stone architectural systems are better understood as the product of deeply rooted environmental, demographic, and political processes, unfolding in coordination with the external influence of Kanuri. It is not yet clear the extent to which the massive DGB constructions shaped the character of political power and authority on Mandara Highlands. MacEachern offers, however, a *longue durée* perspective which should guide future inquiries into the political, economic, and cultural processes of the Mandara Highlands.

The case studies provided in this volume reveal a diverse range of responses to Atlantic commercial encroachment in West Africa, bringing landscape to the foreground as a particularly valuable conceptual terrain in which to situate questions of power and political economy in the past. The concluding chapter by Ray Kea brings the discussion full circle to a set of issues presented in this introduction. Whereas all of the chapters speak, in one way or another, to broad anthropological discussions on the dynamics of power and political complexity, Kea places this volume squarely in the context of a revisionist historiography of the early modern world, and offers new ways of conceptualizing the historical landscapes produced by material relations engendered during West Africa's Atlantic Age. Kea challenges archaeologists to embrace historical questions of broad, regional, and global importance that impact the local levels, and tasks Africanist historians to tune in to the research findings of archaeologists. Yet, Kea's chapter makes more explicit, at the conceptual level, the necessary kinds of dialogue that need to take place between historians and archaeologists of West Africa, and he offers reflective, prescriptive, and theoretical directives for how a landscape perspective might assist in bringing the two disciplinary siblings back to a common intellectual table.

Kea views landscape as "the infrastructure of quotidian life," arguing that both historians and archaeologists must conceptualize landscape in more than just spatial terms. Landscapes emerge, in his analysis, as networks of social, political, economic, cultural, ecological, and spiritual relationships shaped by the actions of individuals, communities, societies, and polities, reflecting a general conceptual shift across the disciplines away from viewing space and landscape in absolutist terms (Lefebvre 1991; Smith 2003). For Kea, world systems analysis is particularly suited to unlocking what he calls "the global commodity chain" and "eco-historical regimes" that mediated West Africa's entanglement as a critical part of the early modern world. The chapter invokes the many levels at which West African political landscapes were entangled in the Atlantic economy– local, supra-local, regional, trans-regional, trans-oceanic, and global – as critical points of entry into this issue. Given the shared interests in landscape themes, Kea proposes that a broader theoretical and methodological perspective would allow historians and archaeologists to move beyond the question of how West Africa *responded* to Atlantic commercial encroachment, towards a more expansive understanding of West Africa's critical role in the *making* of the modern world. West African landscapes of the Atlantic Era were, after all, critical components of trans-Atlantic processes that made possible, through the enslavement of Africans, the European colonization of the New World, the rise of capitalism, and the foundations of modernity. Rather than being a peripheral factor in the global processes which led to the early modern world, the West African political landscapes examined in this volume were central to its very creation.

CONCLUDING REMARKS

In this introductory chapter we have outlined how a landscape perspective can substantially contribute to unanswered questions regarding the nature of West African entanglement within global economic processes in the Atlantic Era. Ongoing historical and archaeological research across the region has converged upon the common goal of constructing material narratives of West African cultural transition. These narratives highlight how patterns in the production, exchange, consumption, and discard of objects (drawing on a plethora of documentary and archaeological sources of data) can contribute to our understanding of the dynamic nature of material life in Atlantic West Africa. Such material narratives must be situated within broader regional contexts if the former are to be appreciated to their fullest in understanding the political economies on which power relations, political processes, and authority ultimately rested. We suggest, and the authors in this volume demonstrate, that a landscape perspective holds the power to accomplish this goal.

BIBLIOGRAPHY

Adams, J. (1966). *Remarks on the Country Extending from Cape Palmas to the River Congo: With an Appendix Containing an Account of the European Trade with the West Coast of Africa*. Frank Cass, London.

Adams, R. E. W., and Jones, R. C. (1981). Spatial patterns and regional growth among classic Maya cities. *American Antiquity* **46**, 301–22.

Adande, A. B. A., and Adagba, C. (1988). Dix années de recherches archéologiques au Benin (1978–1988). *Nyame Akuma* **30**: 3–8.

Adande, A. B. A., and Bagodo, O. B. (1991). Urgence d'une archéologie de sauvetage dans le Golfe du Bénin: cas des vallées du mono et de l'oueme. *West African Journal of Archaeology* **21**: 49–72.

Adande, A. B. A., and Dovie, A. K. (1990). Archeologie de Suavetage dans la Vallee du Mono. Equipe de Recherche Archeologieque Beninoise/ Programme Archeologique Togolaise.

Agbaje-Williams, B. (1983). *A Contribution to the Archaeology of Old Oyo*. University of Ibadan, Nigeria, Ibadan.

Agbaje-Williams, B. (1989). Archaeological reconnaissance of Ipapo-Ile, Kwara State, Nigeria: An interim report. *West African Journal of Archaeology* 19: 21–36.

Aguigah, D. (1986). La Site de Notsé: Contribution à l'Archéologie du Togo, Ph.D. dissertation, Université du Paris I, Paris.

Alpern, S. (1995). What Africans got for their slaves: A master list of European trade goods. *History in Africa* 22: 5–43.

Ammerman, A. (1981). Surveys and archaeological research. *Annual Review of Anthropology* 10: 109–43.

Anderson, D., and Rathbone, R. (2000). *Africa's Urban Past*. James Currey, Oxford.

Anquandah, J. (1982). *Rediscovering Ghana's Past*. Longman, Harlow.

Appadurai, A. (1986). *The Social Life of Things: Commodities in Cultural Perspective*. Cambridge University Press, Cambridge.

Ashmore, W. (1989). Construction and Cosmology: Politics and Ideology in Lowland Maya Settlement Patterns. In Hanks, W. F., and Rice, D. S. (eds.), *Word and Image in Maya Culture: Explorations in Language, Writing, and Representation*. University of Utah Press, Salt Lake City, pp. 272–86.

Atherton, J. (1972). Protohistoric habitation sites in northeastern Sierra Leone. *Bulletin de la Société Royale Belge d'Anthropologie et de Préhistoire* 53: 5–17.

Austen, R. (1978). African commerce without Europeans: The development impact of international trade in the pre-modern era. *Kenya Historical Review* 6: 1–21.

Austen, R. A. (1987). *African Economic History: Internal Development and External Dependency*. James Currey, London.

Bagodo, O. (1993). Archaeological reconnaissance of the Lower Mono Valley: A preliminary report. *West African Journal of Archaeology* 23: 24–36.

Barbot, J., Hair, P. E. H., Jones, A., and Law, R. (1992). *Barbot on Guinea: The Writings of Jean Barbot on West Africa, 1678–1712*. Hakluyt Society, London.

Barry, B. (1998). *Senegambia and the Atlantic Slave Trade*. Cambridge University Press, New York.

Basso, K. H. (1996). *Wisdom Sits in Places: Landscape and Language Among the Western Apache*. University of New Mexico Press, Albuquerque.

Bay, E. (1998). *Wives of the Leopard: Gender, Politics, and Culture in the Kingdom of Dahomey*. University of Virginia Press, Charlottesville.

Ben-Amos, P. (1980). *The Art of Benin*. Thames and Hudson, London.

Ben-Amos, P. (1999). *Art, Innovation, and Politics in Eighteenth-Century Benin*. Indiana University Press, Bloomington.

Bender, B. (1993). *Landscape: Politics and Perspectives*. Berg, Providence.

Bintliff, J., and Snodgrass, A. M. (1988). Off-site pottery distributions: Regional and interregional perspective. *Current Anthropology* 29: 506–13.

Bosman, W. (1967). *A New and Accurate Description of the Coast of Guinea, Divided into the Gold, the Slave and the Ivory Coasts*. Frank Cass, London.

Bower, J. (1986). A survey of surveys: Aspects of surface archaeology in sub-Saharan Africa. *African Archaeological Review* 4: 179–201.

Bradley, R. (1978). Prehistoric field systems in Britain and north-west Europe – A review of some recent work. *World Archaeology* 9: 265–80.

Breternitz, D. (1968). Interim report of the University of Colorado-Kainji Rescue Archaeology Project. *West African Archaeological Newsletter* **10**: 30–42.

Breternitz, D. (1969). Rescue archaeology at the Kainji Dam, northern Nigeria. *Current Anthropology* **10**: 136.

Breternitz, D. (1975). Rescue archaeology in the Kainji reservoirs area, 1968. *West African Journal of Archaeology* **5**: 91–151.

Brown, P. (1951). Patterns of authority in Africa. *Africa* **21**: 262–78.

Calvocoressi, D., and York, R. (1971). The state of archaeological research in Ghana. *West African Journal of Archaeology* **1**: 87–103.

Casey, E. S. (1997). *The Fate of Place: A Philosophical History.* University of California Press, Berkeley.

Champion, T. C. (1989). Introduction. In Champion, T. C. (ed.), *Centre and Periphery: Comparative Studies in Archaeology.* Unwin Hyman, London, pp. 1–19.

Cherry, J. (1987). Power in Space: Archaeological and Geographical Studies of the State. In Wagstaff, J. M. (ed.), *Landscape and Culture: Geographical and Archaeological Perspectives.* Oxford University Press, Oxford.

Cherry, J. F., Davis, J. L., and Mantzourani, E. (1991). *Landscape Archaeology as Long-Term History: Northern Keos in the Cycladic Islands from Earliest Settlement Until Modern Times.* UCLA Institute of Archaeology, Los Angeles.

Chouin, G. (2008). Archaeological Perspectives on Sacred Groves in Ghana. In Sheridan, M. J., and Nyamweru, C. (eds.), *African Sacred Groves.* James Currey, Oxford, pp. 178–94.

Chouin, G. (2009). Forests of Power and Memory: An Archaeology of Sacred Groves in the Eguafo Polity, Southern Ghana (c. 500–1900 A.D.), Ph.D. dissertation, Syracuse University.

Clapperton, H., Bruce-Lockhart, J., and Lovejoy, P. E. (2005). *Hugh Clapperton Into the Interior of Africa: Records of the Second Expedition, 1825–1827.* Brill, Leiden.

Connah, G. (1975). *The Archaeology of Benin: Excavations and Other Researches in and Around Benin City, Nigeria.* Clarendon Press, Oxford.

Connah, G. (1981). *Three Thousand Years in Africa: Man and His Environment in the Lake Chad Area of Nigeria.* Cambridge University Press, Cambridge.

Connah, G. (2000). African City Walls: A Neglected Source? In Anderson, D., and Rathbone, R. (eds.), *Africa's Urban Past.* James Currey, Oxford, pp. 36–51.

Connah, G. (2001). *African Civilizations: An Archaeological Perspective.* Cambridge University Press, Cambridge.

Coquery-Vidrovich, C. (1991). The process of urbanization in Africa (from the origins to the beginnings of independence). *African Studies Review* **34**: 1–98.

Coquery-Vidrovich, C. (2005). *The History of African Cities South of the Sahara: From the Origins to Colonization.* Markus Wiener Publishers, Princeton, N.J.

Crumley, C. L. (1977). Towards a locational definition of state systems of settlement. *American Anthropologist* **78**: 59–73.

Crumley, C. L. (1994). Historical Ecology: A Multidimensional Ecological Orientation. In Crumley, C. (ed.), *Historical Ecology: Cultural Knowledge and Changing Landscapes.* SAR Press, Santa Fe, pp. 1–16.

Crumley, C. L. (1995). Heterarchy and the Analysis of Complex Societies. In Ehrenreich, R., Crumley, C. L., and Levy, J. E. (eds.), *Heterarchy and the Analysis of Complex Societies*. American Anthropological Association, Arlington, VA, pp. 1–6.

Cruz, M. D. (2003). Shaping Quotidian Worlds: Ceramic Production and Consumption in Banda, Ghana c. 1780–1994, Ph.D. dissertation, State University of New York at Binghamton.

Curtin, P. D. (1975). *Economic Change in Precolonial Africa: Senegambia in the Era of the Slave Trade*. University of Wisconsin Press, Madison.

Curtin, P. D. (1997). *Africa Remembered: Narratives by West Africans from the Era of the Slave Trade*. Waveland Press, Prospect Heights, IL.

Curtin, P. D. (1998). *The Rise and Fall of the Plantation Complex: Essays in Atlantic History*. Cambridge University Press, Cambridge.

Daaku, K. Y. (1970). *Trade and Politics on the Gold Coast, 1600–1720: A Study of the African Reaction to European Trade*. Clarendon Press, Oxford.

Darling, P. (1998). A Legacy in Earth – Ancient Benin and Ishan, Southern Nigeria. In Wesler, K. W. (ed.), *Historical Archaeology in Nigeria*. Africa World Press, Trenton, NJ, pp. 143–98.

Darling, P. J. (1984). *Archaeology and History in Southern Nigeria: The Ancient Linear Earthworks of Benin and Ishan*. British Archaeological Reports International Series 215. 2 vols. Oxford, England.

David, N. (1996). A New Political Form? The Classless Industrial Society of Sukur (Nigeria). In Pwiti, G., and Soper, R. C. (eds.), *Aspects of African Archaeology: Papers from the 10th Congress of the Pan-African Association for Prehistory and Related Studies*. University of Zimbabwe Publications, Harare, pp. 593–600.

Davies, O. (1961). *Archaeology in Ghana*. Published on behalf of the University College of Ghana by T. Nelson, Edinburgh.

Davies, O. (1967). *West Africa Before the Europeans: Archaeology & Prehistory*. Methuen, London.

Davies, O. (1970). *Ghana Field Notes. Part 2. Northern Ghana*. Department of Archaeology, University of Ghana, Legon.

Davies, O. (1971). *The Archaeology of the Flooded Volta Basin*. Department of Archaeology, University of Ghana, Legon.

Davies, O. (1972). *Ghana Field Notes. Part 3. Ashanti*. Department of Archaeology, University of Ghana, Legon.

Davies, O. (1976). *Ghana Field Notes. Part 4. Southern Ghana*. Department of Archaeology, University of Ghana, Legon.

de Barros, P. L. (1985). The Bassar: Large Scale Iron Producers of the West African Savanna, Ph.D. dissertation, University of California, Los Angeles.

de Barros, P. L. (1986). Bassar: a quantified, chronologically controlled, regional approach to a traditional iron production centre in West Africa. *Africa* **56**: 148–74.

de Barros, P. L. (1990). Changing Paradigms, Goals & Methods in the Archaeology of Francophone West Africa. In Robertshaw, P. (ed.), *A History of African Archaeology*. James Currey, London, pp. 155–72.

de Barros, P. L. (2001). The Effect of the Slave Trade on the Bassar Ironworking Society, Togo. In DeCorse, C. R. (ed.), *West Africa During the Atlantic Slave*

Trade: Archaeological Perspectives. Leicester University Press, New York, pp. 59–80.

DeCorse, C. (1980). An archaeological survey of protohistoric defensive sites in Sierra Leone. *Nyame Akuma* **17**: 48–53.

DeCorse, C. (1992). Culture contact, continuity and change on the Gold Coast, AD 1400–1900. *African Archaeological Review* **10**: 163–96.

DeCorse, C. (1996). Documents, oral histories, and the material record: Historical archaeology in West Africa. *World Archaeological Bulletin* **7**: 40–50.

DeCorse, C. (1998). Culture Contact and Change in West Africa. In Cusick, J. G. (ed.), *Studies in Culture Contact: Interaction, Culture Change, and Archaeology.* Center for Archaeological Investigations, Southern Illinois University, Carbondale, pp. 358–77.

DeCorse, C. (2001a). *An Archaeology of Elmina: Africans and Europeans on the Gold Coast, 1400–1900.* Smithsonian Institution Press, Washington, DC.

DeCorse, C. (2001b). Introduction. In DeCorse, C. R. (ed.), *West Africa During the Atlantic Slave Trade: Archaeological Perspectives.* Leicester University Press, New York, pp. 1–13.

DeCorse, C. (2001c). *West Africa During the Atlantic Slave Trade: Archaeological Perspectives.* Leicester University Press, New York.

DeCorse, C. (2005). Coastal Ghana in the first and second millennia AD: Change in settlement patterns, subsistence and technology. *Journal des Africanistes* **72**: 43–54.

DeCorse, C., Carr, E., Chouin, G., Cook, G., and Spiers, S. (2000). Central region project, coastal Ghana – perspectives 2000. *Nyame Akuma* **53**: 6–11.

DeCorse, C., and Chouin, G. (2004). Trouble with Siblings: Archaeological and Historical Interpretation of West African Past. In Falola, T., and Jennings, C. (eds.), *Sources and Methods in African History: Spoken, Written, Unearthed.* University of Rochester Press, Rochester, NY, pp. 7–15.

DeCorse, C., and Chouin, G. (2010). Prelude to the Atlantic trade: New perspectives on southern Ghana's pre-Atlantic history (800–1500). *Journal of African History* **51**: 123–45.

DeCorse, C., Cook, G., Horlings, R., Pietruszka, A., and Spiers, S. (2009). Transformation in the era of the Atlantic world: The Central Region Project, coastal Ghana 2007–2008. *Nyame Akuma* **72**: 85–94.

DeCorse, C., and Spiers, S. (2009). A tale of two polities: Socio-political transformation on the Gold Coast in the Atlantic World. *Australasian Historical Archaeology* **27**: 29–42.

DeMarrais, E., Castillo, L. J., and Earle, T. K. (1996). Ideology, materialization and power strategies. *Current Anthropology* **37**: 15–31.

Denbow, J. (2003). Archaeology and History. In Falola, T., and Jennings, C. (eds.), *Sources and Methods in African History: Spoken, Written, Unearthed.* University of Rochester Press, Rochester, NY, pp. 3–6.

Dyke, R. M. V. (2004). Memory, meaning, and masonry: The late Bonito Chacoan landscape. *American Antiquity* **69**: 413–31.

Earle, T. K. (1976). A Nearest-Neighbor Analysis of Two Formative Settlement Systems. In Flannery, K. (ed.), *The Early Mesoamerican Village.* Academic Press, New York, pp. 196–223.

Earle, T. K. (1991). *Chiefdoms: Power, Economy, and Ideology.* Cambridge University Press, Cambridge.

Earle, T. K. (1997). *How Chiefs Come to Power: The Political Economy in Prehistory*. Stanford University Press, Stanford.

Ebert, J. I. (1992). *Distributional Archaeology*. University of New Mexico Press, Albuquerque.

Ekholm, K., and Friedman, J. (1979). Capital, Imperialism and Exploitation in Ancient World Systems. In Larsen, M. T. (ed.), *Power and Propaganda: A Symposium on Ancient Empires*. Akademisk Forlag, Copenhagen.

Eltis, D. (2000). *The Rise of African Slavery in the Americas*. Cambridge University Press, Cambridge.

Eltis, D., Behrendt, S. D., Richardson, D., Klein, H. S., and W.E.B. Du Bois Institute for Afro-American Research. (1999). *The Trans-Atlantic Slave Trade: A Database on CD-ROM*. Cambridge University Press, Cambridge.

Eltis, D., and Jennings, L. C. (1988). Trade between western Africa and the Atlantic world. *The American Historical Review* **93**: 936–59.

Evans, F. A., and Beale, P. O. (1966). The Anglo-Gambian Stone Circles Expedition, 1964/65. A report presented to the Prime Minister of the Gambia, Bathurst, Gambia.

Fage, J. D. (1969). Slavery and the slave trade in the context of West African history. *Journal of African History* **3**: 343–57.

Fallers, L. A. (1964). *The King's Men: Leadership and Status in Buganda on the Eve of Independence*. Oxford University Press, London.

Falola, T., and Jennings, C. (2003). *Sources and Methods in African History: Spoken, Written, Unearthed*. University of Rochester Press, Rochester, NY.

Ferguson, L. G. (1992). *Uncommon Ground: Archaeology and Early African America, 1650–1800*. Smithsonian Institution Press, Washington, D.C.

Flannery, K. (1998). The Ground Plans of Archaic States. In Feinman, G., and Marcus, J. (eds.), *Archaic States*. SAR Press, Santa Fe, pp. 15–58.

Foley, R. (1981). A model of regional archaeological structure. *Proceedings of the Prehistoric Society* **47**: 1–17.

Forde, C. D., and Kaberry, P. M. (1967). *West African Kingdoms in the Nineteenth Century*. Oxford University Press, London.

Fortes, M., and Evans-Pritchard, E. E. (1940). *African Political Systems*. Oxford University Press, London.

Fritz, J. (1986). Vijayanagara: Authority and meaning of a south Indian imperial capital. *American Anthropologist* **88**: 44–5.

Gabel, C., Borden, R., and White, S. (1975). Preliminary report on an archaeological survey of Liberia. *Liberian Studies Journal* **5**: 87–105.

Goody, J. (1971). *Technology, Tradition, and the State in Africa*. Oxford University Press, Oxford.

Gosden, C., and Head, L. (1994). Landscape – a usefully ambiguous concept. *Archaeology in Oceania* **29**: 113–16.

Goucher, C. (1981). Iron is iron 'til it is rust: Trade and ecology in the decline of West African iron-smelting. *Journal of African History* **22**: 179–89.

Greene, S. E. (1996). *Gender, Ethnicity, and Social Change on the Upper Slave Coast: A History of the Anlo-Ewe*. Heinemann, Portsmouth, NH.

Greene, S. E. (2002). *Sacred Sites and the Colonial Encounter: A History of Meaning and Memory in Ghana*. Indiana University Press, Bloomington.

Gronenborn, D. (2001). Kanem-Borno: A Brief Summary of the History and Archaeology of an Empire of the Central Bilad al-Sudan. In DeCorse,

C. R. (ed.), *West Africa During the Atlantic Slave Trade: Archaeological Perspectives*. Leicester University Press, New York, pp. 101–30.

Hartle, D. (1970). Preliminary report of the University of Ibadan's Kainji Rescue Archaeological Project. *West African Archaeological Newsletter* **12**: 7–19.

Holl, A. (1985). Background to the Ghana empire: Archaeological investigations on the transition to statehood in the Dhar Tichitt region (Mauritania). *Journal of Anthropological Archaeology* **4**: 73–115.

Holl, A. (1986). *Economie et Société Géolithique du Dhar Tichitt*, Mauritanie. Editions Recherche sur les civilisations, Paris.

Holl, A. (2001). 500 Years in the Cameroons: Making Sense of the Archaeological Record. In DeCorse, C. R. (ed.), *West Africa During the Atlantic Slave Trade: Archaeological Perspectives*. Leicester University Press, New York, pp. 152–78.

Hoskins, W. G. (1955). *The Making of the English Landscape*. Hodder and Stroughton, London.

Hull, R. W. (1976). *African Cities and Towns Before the European Conquest*. Norton, New York.

Inglis, F. (1977). Nation and community: A landscape and its morality. *Sociological Review* **25**: 489–514.

Inikori, J. E. (1977). The import of firearms into West Africa 1750–1807: A quantitative analysis. *Journal of African History* **18**: 339–68.

Inikori, J. E. (2001). Africans and Economic Development in the Atlantic World, 1500–1870. In Walker, S. S. (ed.), *African Roots/American Cultures: Africa in the Creation of the Americas*. Rowman & Littlefield Publishers, Lanham, MD, pp. 123–38.

Inikori, J. E. (2002). *Africans and the Industrial Revolution in England: A Study in International Trade and Development*. Cambridge University Press, Cambridge.

Inikori, J. E. (2003). The Struggle Against the Transatlantic Slave Trade: The Role of the State. In Diouf, S. A. (ed.), *Fighting the Slave Trade: West African Strategies*. Ohio University Press, Athens, Ohio, pp. 170–98.

Inikori, J. E. (2007). Africa and the globalization process: Western Africa, 1450–1850. *Journal of Global History* **2**: 63–86.

Inikori, J. E., Ohadike, D. C., and Unomah, A. C. (1992). *The Chaining of a Continent: Export Demand for Captives and the History of Africa South of the Sahara, 1450–1870*. University of the West Indies, Mona, Jamaica.

Innomata, T. (2006). Plazas, performers, and spectators: Political theaters of the classic Maya. *Current Anthropology* **47**: 805–42.

Johnson, G. A. (1977). Aspects of regional analysis in archaeology. *Annual Review of Anthropology* **6**: 479–508.

Joyce, A. A., Bustamante, L. A., and Levine, M. N. (2001). Commoner power: A case study from the classic period collapse on the Oaxaca coast. *Journal of Archaeological Method and Theory* **8**: 343–85.

Kea, R. A. (1982). *Settlements, Trade, and Polities in the Seventeenth-Century Gold Coast*. Johns Hopkins University Press, Baltimore.

Kelly, K. (1995). Transformation and Continuity in Savi, a West African Trade Town: An Archaeological Investigation of Culture Change on the Coast of Bénin During the 17th and 18th Centuries, Ph.D. dissertation, University of California, Los Angeles.

Kelly, K. (1997a). The archaeology of African-European interaction: Investigating the social roles of trade, traders, and the use of space in the seventeenth- and eighteenth-century Hueda kingdom, Republic of Bénin. *World Archaeology* **28**: 351–69.

Kelly, K. (1997b). Using historically informed archaeology: Seventeenth and eighteenth century Hueda-Europe interaction on the coast of Bénin. *Journal of Archaeological Method and Theory* **4**: 353–66.

Kelly, K. (2001). Change and Continuity in Coastal Bénin. In DeCorse, C. R. (ed.), *West Africa During the Atlantic Slave Trade: Archaeological Perspectives.* Leicester University Press, New York, pp. 81–100.

Kelly, K., and Norman, N. (2007). Historical Archaeologies of Landscape in Atlantic Africa. In Hicks, D., McAtackney, L., and Fairclough, G. J. (eds.), *Envisioning Landscape: Situations and Standpoints in Archaeology and Heritage.* Left Coast Press, Walnut Creek, CA, pp. 172–93.

Kense, F. J. (1990). Archaeology in Anglophone West Africa. In Robertshaw, P. (ed.), *A History of African Archaeology.* James Currey, London, pp. 135–54.

Kiyaga-Mulindwa, D. (1978). The Earthworks of the Birim Valley, Southern Ghana, Ph.D. dissertation, Johns Hopkins University, Baltimore, MD.

Kiyaga-Mulindwa, D. (1982). Social and demographic changes in the Birim valley, southern Ghana, c. 1450 to c. 1800. *The Journal of African History* **23**: 63–82.

Klein, M. (1992). The Impact of the Atlantic Slave Trade on the Societies of the Western Sudan. In Inikori, J. E., and Engerman, S. L. (eds.), *The Atlantic Slave Trade: Effects on Economies, Societies, and Peoples in Africa, the Americas, and Europe.* Duke University Press, Durham, pp. 25–48.

Klein, M. A. (2001). The slave trade and decentralized societies. *Journal of African History* **42**: 49–65.

Knapp, A. B. (1997). *The Archaeology of Late Bronze Age Cypriot Society: The Study of Settlement, Survey and Landscape.* University of Glasgow, Glasgow.

Knapp, B., and Ashmore, W. (1999). Archaeological Landscapes: Constructed, Conceptualized, Ideational. In Ashmore, W., and Knapp, B. (eds.), *Archaeologies of Landscape.* Cambridge University Press, Cambridge, pp. 1–32.

Kohl, P. (1987). The Ancient Economy, Transferable Technologies and the Bronze Age World System: A View from the Northeastern Frontier of the Ancient Near East. In Rowlands, M. J., Larsen, M. T., and Kristiansen, K. (eds.), *Centre and Periphery in the Ancient World.* Cambridge University Press, Cambridge, pp. 13–24.

Kolata, A. (1986). The agricultural foundations of the Tiwanaku state: A view from the heartland. *American Antiquity* **77**: 102–15.

Kopytoff, I. (1987). *The African Frontier: The Reproduction of Traditional African Societies.* Indiana University Press, Bloomington.

Lander, R., Lander, J., and Bascom, W. R. (1832). *Journal of an Expedition to Explore the Course and Termination of the Niger; with a Narrative of a Voyage Down that River to Its Termination.* J. Murray, London.

Larsen, M. (1987). Commercial Networks in the Ancient Near East. In Rowlands, M. J., Larsen, M. T., and Kristiansen, K. (eds.), *Centre and Periphery in the Ancient World.* Cambridge University Press, Cambridge, pp. 47–56.

Law, R. (1977). *The Oyo Empire, c.1600–c.1836: A West African Imperialism in the Era of the Atlantic Slave Trade.* Clarendon Press, Oxford.

Law, R. (1991). *The Slave Coast of West Africa, 1550–1750: The Impact of the Atlantic Slave Trade on an African Society.* Oxford University Press, Oxford.

Law, R. (2004). *Ouidah: The Social History of a West African Slaving 'Port', 1727–1892.* Ohio University Press, Athens, OH.

Lefebvre, H. (1991). *The Production of Space.* Blackwell, Cambridge, MA.

Leone, M. (1984). Interpreting Ideology in Historical Archaeology: Using the Rules of Perspective in the William Paca Garden in Annapolis, Maryland. In Orser, C. (ed.), *Images of the Recent Past.* AltaMira Press, Berkeley, pp. 25–35.

Leone, M. P., and Frye, G.-M. (1999). Conjuring in the big house kitchen: An interpretation of African American belief systems, based on the uses of archaeology and folklore sources. *The Journal of American Folklore* **112**: 372–403.

Lloyd, P. C. (1960). The Political Structure of African Kingdoms: An Explanatory Model. In Blanton, M. (ed.), *Political Systems and the Distribution of Power.* Tavistock, London, pp. 63–112.

Lloyd, P. C. (1971). *The Political Development of Yoruba Kingdoms in The Eighteenth and Nineteenth Centuries.* Royal Anthropological Institute, London.

Lovejoy, P. (1989). The impact of the Atlantic slave trade on Africa: A review of the literature. *Journal of African History* **30**: 365–94.

Lovejoy, P., and Richardson, D. (1999). Trust, pawnship, and Atlantic history: The institutional foundations of the old Calabar slave trade. *The American Historical Review* **104**: 333–55.

Lovejoy, P. E. (1983). *Transformations in Slavery: A History of Slavery in Africa.* Cambridge University Press, New York.

Low, S. M., and Lawrence-Zúñiga, D. (2003). Locating Culture. In Low, S. M., and Lawrence-Zúñiga, D. (eds.), *The Anthropology of Space and Place: Locating Culture.* Blackwell, Malden, MA, pp. 1–47.

MacEachern, S. (1993). Selling the iron for their shackles: Wandala – Montagnard interactions in northern Cameroon. *The Journal of African History* **34**, 247–70.

MacEachern, S. (2001a). Cultural resource management and Africanist archaeology. *Antiquity* **75**, 866–71.

MacEachern, S. (2001b). State Formation and Enslavement in the Southern Lake Chad Basin. In DeCorse, C. R. (ed.), *West Africa During the Atlantic Slave Trade: Archaeological Perspectives.* Leicester University Press, New York, pp. 131–52.

Manning, P. (1982). *Slavery, Colonialism, and Economic Growth in Dahomey, 1640–1960.* Cambridge University Press, New York.

Marquardt, W., and Crumley, C. L. (1990). Landscape: A Unifying Concept in Regional Analysis. In Allen, K. M. S., Green, S. W., and Zubrow, E. B. W. (eds.), *Interpreting Space: GIS and Archaeology.* Taylor & Francis, London, pp. 73–9.

Martin, V., and Becker, C. (1974). *Répertoire des Sites Protohistorique du Sénegal et de la Gambie.* CNRS, Kaolack.

Mauny, R. (1961). *Tableau Géographique de l'Ouest Africain au Moyen Age d'après les Sources Écrites, la Tradition et l'Archéologie.* IFAN, Dakar.

McAnany, P. (2001). Cosmology and the Institutionalization of Hierarchy in the Maya Region. In Haas, J. (ed.), *From Leaders to Rulers*. Kluwer Academic/Plenum Publishers, New York, pp. 125–48.

McCaskie, T. C. (1995). *State and Society in Pre-Colonial Asante*. Cambridge University Press, Cambridge.

McIntosh, R. J. (2005). *Ancient Middle Niger: Urbanism and the Self-Organizing Landscape*. Cambridge University Press, Cambridge.

McIntosh, R. J., and McIntosh, S. K. (1993). Cities Without Citadels: Understanding Urban Origins Along the Middle Niger. In Shaw, T., Sinclair, P., Andah, B., and Okpoko, A. (eds.), *The Archaeology of Africa: Foods, Metals, and Towns*. Routledge, London, pp. 622–41.

McIntosh, S. K. (1995). *Excavations at Jenné-Jeno, Hambarketolo, and Kaniana (Inland Niger Delta, Mali), the 1981 Season*. University of California Press, Berkeley.

McIntosh, S. K. (ed.) (1999a). *Beyond Chiefdoms: Pathways to Complexity in Africa*. Cambridge University Press, Cambridge.

McIntosh, S. K. (1999b). Modeling Political Organization in Large-Scale Settlement Clusters: A Case from the Inland Niger Delta. In McIntosh, S. K. (ed.), *Beyond Chiefdoms: Pathways to Complexity in Africa*. Cambridge University Press, Cambridge, pp. 66–79.

McIntosh, S. K. (1999c). Pathways to Complexity: An African Perspective. In McIntosh, S. K. (ed.), *Beyond Chiefdoms: Pathways to Complexity in Africa*. Cambridge University Press, Cambridge, pp. 1–30.

McIntosh, S. K. (2005). Archaeology and the Reconstruction of the African Past. In Philips, J. E. (ed.), *Writing African History*. University of Rochester Press, Rochester, NY, pp. 51–85.

McIntosh, S. K., and McIntosh, R. J. (1993). Field survey in the tumulus zone of Senegal. *African Archaeological Review* **11**: 73–107.

McIntosh, S. K., McIntosh, R. J., and Bocoum, H. (1992). The middle Senegal valley project: Preliminary results from the 1990–1991 field season. *Nyame Akuma* **38**: 47–61.

McIntosh, S. K., and McIntosh, R. J. (1980). *Prehistoric Investigations in the Region of Jenné, Mali: A Study in the Development of Urbanism in the Sahel*. B.A.R., Oxford.

McIntosh, S. K., and Thiaw, I. (2001). Tools For Understanding Transformation and Continuity in Senegambian Society: 1500–1900. In DeCorse, C. R. (ed.), *West Africa During the Atlantic Slave Trade: Archaeological Perspectives*. Leicester University Press, New York, pp. 14–37.

McKee, L. (1992). The Ideals and Realities Behind the Design and Use of 19th Century Virginia Slave Cabins. In Yentsch, A. E., and Beaudry, M. C. (eds.), *The Art and Mystery of Historical Archaeology: Essays in Honor of Jim Deetz*. CRC Press, Boca Raton, pp. 195–213.

Mitchell, P. (2005). *African Connections:An Archaeological Perspective on Africa and the Wider World*. AltaMira Press, Walnut Creek, CA.

Monroe, J. C. (2003). The Dynamics of State Formation: The Archaeology and Ethnohistory of Pre-Colonial Dahomey, Ph.D. dissertation, University of California, Los Angeles.

Monroe, J. C. (2007a). Continuity, revolution, or evolution on the slave coast of West Africa: Royal architecture and political order in precolonial Dahomey. *Journal of African History* **48**: 349–73.

Monroe, J. C. (2007b). Dahomey and the Atlantic Slave Trade: Archaeology and Political Order on the Bight of Benin. In Falola, T., and Ogundiran, A. (eds.), *The Archaeology of Atlantic Africa and the African Diaspora*. Indiana University Press, Indianapolis.

Monroe, J. C. (2009). 'In the Belly of Dan': Landscape, Power, and History in Pre-Colonial Dahomey. Excavating the Past: Archaeological Perspectives on Black Atlantic Regional Networks, Clark Library, UCLA.

Moore, J. D. (1996). *Architecture and Power in the Ancient Andes: The Archaeology of Public Buildings*. Cambridge University Press, New York.

Newman, T. (1966). Archaeological survey of Sierra Leone. *West African Archaeological Newsletter* **4**: 19–22.

Norman, N. (2008). An Archaeology of West African Atlanticization: Regional Analysis of the Huedan Palace Districts and Countryside (Bénin), 1650–1727, Ph.D. dissertation, University of Virginia.

Norman, N. (2009). Hueda (Whydah) country and town: Archaeological perspectives on the rise and collapse of an Atlantic countryside and entrepôt. *International Journal of African Historical Studies* **42**: 387–410.

Norman, N. L., and Kelly, K. G. (2006). Landscape politics: The serpent ditch and the rainbow in West Africa. *American Anthropologist* **104**: 98–110.

Northrup, D. (1978). *Trade Without Rulers: Pre-Colonial Economic Development in South-Eastern Nigeria*. Clarendon Press, Oxford.

Obayemi, A. (1985). The Yoruba and Edo-Speaking Peoples and Their Neighbours Before 1600. In Crowther, J. F. A. A. a. M. (ed.), *History of West Africa*. Oxford University Press, Oxford.

Ogundiran, A. (2001). Ceramic spheres and regional networks in the Yoruba-Edo region, Nigeria, 13th-19th Centuries A.D. *Journal of Field Archaeology* **28**: 27–42.

Ogundiran, A. (2002). *Archaeology and History in Ìlàrè District (Central Yorubaland, Nigeria) 1200–1900 A.D.* Cambridge Monograph in African Archaeology, 55.

Ogundiran, A. (2003). Chronology, Material Culture, and Pathways to the Cultural History of Yoruba-Edo Region, Nigeria, 500 B.C.–A.D. 180. In Falola, T., and Jennings, C. (eds.), *Sources and Methods in African History: Spoken, Written, Unearthed*. University of Rochester Press, Rochester, NY, pp. 33–79.

Ogundiran, A. (2007). Living in the Shadow of the Atlantic World: Material Life, History and Culture in Yoruba-Edo Hinterland, ca. 1600–1750. In Ogundiran, A., and Falola, T. (eds.), *Archaeology of Atlantic Africa and the African Diaspora*. Indiana University Press, Bloomington, pp. 77–99.

Ogundiran, A. (2009). Material life and domestic economy in a frontier of the Oyo empire during the mid-Atlantic age. *International Journal of African Historical Studies* **42**: 351–86.

Okpoko, P. U., and Obi-Ani, P. (2005). The Making of an Oligarchy in the Bight of Biafra: Perspectives on the Aro Ascendency. In Ogundiran, A. (ed.), *Precolonial Nigeria: Essays in Honor of Toyin Falola*. Africa World Press, Trenton, NJ, pp. 425–46.

Oliver, R. A., and Fage, J. D. (1962). *A Short History of Africa*. Penguin Books, Baltimore.

Orser, C., and Funari, P. P. (2001). Archaeology and slave resistance and rebellion. *World Archaeology* **33**: 61–72.

Ozanne, P. (1966). A preliminary archaeological survey of Sierra Leone. *West African Archaeological Newsletter* **5**, 31–5.

Ozanne, P. (1969). A new archaeological survey of Ife. *Odu* **1**: 28–45.

Ozanne, P. (1971). Ghana. In Shinnie, P. L. (ed.), *The African Iron Age*. Clarendon Press, Oxford, pp. 36–65.

Parsons, J. (1972). Archaeological settlement patterns. *Annual Review of Anthropology* **1**: 127–50.

Polanyi, K. (1966). *Dahomey and the Slave Trade: An Analysis of an Archaic Economy*. University of Washington Press, Seattle.

Posnansky, M. (1971). Ghana and the origins of West African trade. *African Quarterly* **11**: 110–26.

Posnansky, M. (1972). The early development of trade in West Africa – Some archaeological considerations. *Ghana Social Science Journal* **2**: 87–101.

Posnansky, M. (1973). Aspects of early West African trade. *World Archaeology* **2**: 149–63.

Posnansky, M. (1981). Notsé town wall survey. *Nyame Akuma* **18**: 56–7.

Posnansky, M., and de Barros, P. L. (1980). An Archaeological Reconnaissance of Togo, August 1979. Report prepared for H.E. the Minister of National Education and Scientific Research of the Republic of Togo.

Quarcoopome, N. O. (1998). Notse's ancient kingship: Some archaeological and art-historical considerations. *African Archaeological Review* **11**: 109–28.

Renfrew, C. (1986). Introduction: Peer Polity Interaction and Socio-Political Change. In Renfrew, C., and Cherry, J. F. (eds.), *Peer Polity Interaction and Socio-Political Change*. Cambridge University Press, Cambridge, pp. 1–18.

Richard, F. (2007). From Cosaan to Colony: Exploring Archaeological Landscape Formations and Socio-Political Complexity in the Siin (Senegal), A.D. 500–1900, Ph.D. dissertation, Syracuse University.

Richards, C. (1996). Monuments as landscape: Creating the centre of the world in late neolithic Orkney. *World Archaeology* **28**: 190–208.

Richards, J. (1999). Conceptual Landscapes in the Egyptian Nile Valley. In Ashmore, W., and Knapp, B. (eds.), *Archaeologies of Landscape*. Cambridge University Press, Cambridge, pp. 83–100.

Roberts, R. L. (1987). *Warriors, Merchants, and Slaves the State and the Economy in the Middle Niger Valley, 1700–1914*. Stanford University Press, Stanford.

Robertshaw, P. (2000). 'Sibling rivalry'? The intersection of archaeology and history. *History in Africa* **27**: 261–86.

Robertshaw, P. (2010). Beyond the segmentary state: Creative and instrumental power in western Uganda. *Journal of World Prehistory* **23**: 255–69.

Rodney, E. G. (1966). African slavery and other forms of social oppression on the upper Guinea coast in the context of the Atlantic slave trade. *Journal of African History* **7**: 431–44.

Rodney, W. (1970). *A History of the Upper Guinea Coast, 1545–1800*. Clarendon Press, Oxford.

Rodney, W. (1981). *How Europe Underdeveloped Africa*. Howard University Press, Washington, DC.

Rossignol, J., and Wandsnider, L. (1992). *Space, Time, and Archaeological Landscapes*. Plenum Press, New York.

Rowlands, M. J. (1987). Centre and Periphery: A Review of the Concept. In Rowlands, M. J., Larsen, M. T., and Kristiansen, K. (eds.), *Centre and*

Periphery in the Ancient World. Cambridge University Press, Cambridge, pp. 1–11.

Ryder, A. F. C. (1969). *Benin and the Europeans, 1485–1897.* Humanities Press, New York.

Schneider, J. (1977). Was there a pre-capitalist world system? *Peasant Studies* **6**, 20–9.

Schreiber, K. (1987). Conquest and consolidation: A comparison of the Wari and Inka occupations of a highland Peruvian valley. *American Antiquity* **52**: 266–84.

Scott, J. C. (1990). *Domination and the Arts of Resistance: Hidden Transcripts.* Yale University Press, New Haven.

Service, E. R. (1975). *Origins of the State and Civilization: The Process of Cultural Evolution.* Norton, New York.

Shaw, R. (2002). *Memories of the Slave Trade: Ritual and the Historical Imagination in Sierra Leone.* University of Chicago Press, Chicago.

Shaw, T. (1978). *Nigeria: Its Archaeology and Early History.* Thames and Hudson, London.

Smith, A. (2003). *The Political Landscape: Constellations of Authority in Early Complex Polities.* University of California Press, Los Angeles.

Smith, C. A. (1976). *Regional Analysis.* Academic Press, New York.

Smith, L. (2008). Archaeological Survey of Settlement Patterns in the Banda Region, West-Central Ghana: Exploring External Influences and Internal Responses in the West African Frontier from 1400 to 1935, Ph.D. dissertation, Syracuse University.

Smith, M. E. (1979). The Aztec marketing system and settlement pattern in the Valley of Mexico: A central place analysis. *American Antiquity* **44**: 110–25.

Snelgrave, W. (1734). *A New Account of Some Parts of Guinea, and the Slave-Trade.* Printed for P. Knapton, London.

Soper, R. C., and Darling, P. (1980). The walls of Oyo-Ile. *West African Journal of Archaeology* **10**: 61–81.

Southall, A. (1956). *Alur Society: A Study in Processes and Types of Domination.* W. Heffer, Cambridge.

Stahl, A. (2008). Slave Trade as Memory and Practice: What Are the Issues for Archaeologists. In Cameron, C. (ed.), *Invisible Citizens: Captives and Their Consequences.* University of Utah Press, Salt Lake City, pp. 25–57.

Stahl, A. B. (1999a). Perceiving Variability in Time and Space: The Evolutionary Mapping of African Societies. In McIntosh, S. K. (ed.), *Beyond Chiefdoms: Pathways to Complexity in Africa.* Cambridge University Press, Cambridge, pp. 39–55.

Stahl, A. B. (1999b). The archaeology of global encounters viewed from Banda, Ghana. *African Archaeological Review* **16**: 5–81.

Stahl, A. B. (2001). *Making History in Banda: Anthropological Visions of Africa's Past.* Cambridge University Press, Cambridge.

Stahl, A. B. (2007). Entangled Lives: The Archaeology of Daily Life in the Gold Coast Hinterlands, AD 1400–1900. In Ogundiran, A., and Falola, T. (eds.), *Archaeology of Atlantic Africa and the African Diaspora.* Indiana University Press, Bloomington, pp. 49–76.

Stahl, A. B. (2009). The archaeology of African history. *International Journal of African Historical Studies* **42**: 241–55.

Stahl, A. B., Cruz, M. d. D., Neff, H., Glascock, M. D., Speakman, R. J., Giles, B., and Smith, L. (2008). Ceramic production, consumption and exchange in the Banda area, Ghana: Insights from compositional analyses. *Journal of Anthropological Archaeology* **27**: 363–81.

Stahl, A. B., and LaViolette, A. (2009). Introduction: Current trends in the archaeology of African history. *International Journal of African Historical Studies* **42**: 347–50.

Stanish, C. (1994). The hydraulic hypothesis revisited: Lake Titicaca basin raised fields in theoretical perspective. *Latin American Antiquity* **5**: 312–32.

Swanpoel, N. (2004). Too Much Power Is Not Good: War and Trade in Nineteenth Century Sisalaland, Northern Ghana, Ph.D. dissertation, Syracuse University.

Thiaw, I. (1999). An Archaeological Investigation of Long-Term Culture Change in the Lower Falemme (Upper Senegal region) A.D. 500–1900, Ph.D. dissertation, Rice University.

Thilmans, G., Descamps, C., and Khayat, B. (1980). *Protohistoire du Sénégal: Recherches Archéologiques*. IFAN, Dakar.

Thornton, J. K. (1998). *Africa and Africans in the Making of the Atlantic World, 1400–1800*. Cambridge University Press, Cambridge.

Tilley, C. (1994). *A Phenomenology of Landscape: Places, Paths and Monuments*. Berg Publishers, Oxford.

Ur, J. (2003). CORONA Satellite photography and ancient road networks: A northern Mesopotamian case study. *Antiquity* **77**: 102–15.

Usman, A. (2000). A view from the periphery: Northern Yoruba villages during the Old Oyo empire, Nigeria. *Journal of Field Archaeology* **27**: 43–61.

Usman, A. (2004). On the frontier of empire: Understanding rampart walls in northern Yoruba, Nigeria. *Journal of Anthropological Archaeology* **23**: 119–132.

Usman, A. A. (2001). *State-Periphery Relations and Sociopolitical Development in Igbominaland, North-Central Yoruba, Nigeria: Oral-Ethnohistorical and Archaeological Perspectives*. British Archaeological Reports International Series 993, Oxford.

Vansina, J. (1995). Historians, are archeologists your siblings? *History in Africa* **22**: 369–408.

Vidal, S. M., and Duwákalumi, K. (2000). Kuwé Duwákalumi: The Arawak sacred routes of migration, trade, and resistance. *Ethnohistory* **47**: 635–67.

Wallerstein, I. M. (1974). *The Modern World-System*. Academic Press, New York.

Wernke, S. A. (2007). Negotiating community and landscape in the Peruvian Andes: A transconquest view. *American Anthropologist* **109**: 130–52.

Wilkinson, T. J. (2003). *Archaeological Landscapes of the Near East*. University of Arizona Press, Tucson.

Wilks, I. (1975). *Asante in the Nineteenth Century: The Structure and Evolution of a Political Order*. Cambridge University Press, London.

Wolf, E. R. (1982). *Europe and the People Without History*. University of California Press, Berkeley.

Wright, H. T. (1994). Pre-State Political Formations. In Stein, G., and Rothman, M. S. (eds.), *Chiefdoms and Early States in the Near East: The Organizational Dynamics of Complexity*. Prehistory Press, Madison, pp. 67–84.

Yamin, R., and Methany, K. B. (1996). *Landscape Archaeology: Reading and Interpreting the American Historical Landscape*. University of Tennessee Press, Knoxville.

York, R., Mathewson, D., Calvocoressi, D., and Flight, C. (1967). *Archaeology in the Volta Basin*. University of Ghana, Legon.

NOTES

1. This dialogue culminated in a recent symposium organized by Christopher R. DeCorse, entitled *Common Ground, Different Meanings: Archaeology, History, and the Interpretation of the African Past*, held at Syracuse University on October 8–10, 2009.

2. See Klein (1992), however, for a thorough treatment of the relationship between decentralized societies and Atlantic commercial pressures.

3. This gap is most noticeable in areas of documentary scarcity between the Sudan and the littorals, areas that either received insignificant (if any) European documentation or were not well represented in Arabic/Islamic writings during the seventeenth and eighteenth centuries.

4. Three of these theses, by Monroe, by Norman, and by Chouin, were awarded the Society for Historical Archaeology Dissertation Prize for 2005, 2007, and 2011, respectively, reflecting a growing recognition within the wider discipline of historical archaeology of the value of this approach.

PART I

FRAGMENTED LANDSCAPES

2

Atlantic Impacts on Inland Senegambia: French Penetration and African Initiatives in Eighteenth- and Nineteenth-Century Gajaaga and Bundu (Upper Senegal River)

Ibrahima Thiaw

INTRODUCTION

Senegambia is one of the regions in sub-Saharan West Africa with the longest exposure to Atlantic commercial expansion. By the mid-fifteenth century, Portuguese seafarers (and later the Dutch, French, and British) established outposts along the Atlantic coast. From there, they penetrated deep inland following navigable waterways to access the famous medieval trading towns that flourished between the Senegal and Niger rivers (Figure 2.1). In the early second millennium A.D., the towns of Silla, Gunjuru, Timbuktu, Jenné, and Gao – and their potential for trade in gold and slaves, among other products – were chronicled in the Arabic sources (Bathily 1989; Boone et al. 1990, Braudel 1946; Garrard 1982; Levtzion and Hopkins 1981; Lombard 1947; Malowist 1966; Trimingham 1962; Webb 1985). From the fifteenth through the nineteenth centuries, some of these towns still exerted a strong attraction for Europeans settled on the coast of West Africa (Bathily 1989; Becker and Martin 1980; Brunschwig 1975; Curtin 1975, 1973; Labat 1728).

Building on trans-Saharan networks, the Atlantic Era brought new opportunities for trade, connecting greater numbers of people and regions and spreading higher volumes of trade goods across most of the Senegambia. By the seventeenth century, this process was materialized by a rapid increase in the number of European fortifications along the coast, standing as symbols of Atlantic wealth and power (Lawrence 1964; Wood 1967). Some of these costal settlements grew as urban enclaves where Europeans, African elites, and emerging Afro-Europeans competed to imprint their worldview and activities in the physical landscape. From the fifteenth to the nineteenth centuries, coastal Atlantic and riverine landscapes along navigable water bodies were transformed by European forts and outposts and by the introduction of new architectural styles in stone masonry. Later in the nineteenth century, railroads funneled Atlantic material, cultures, and ideas across the Senegambian hinterland, a process with immense consequences for the distribution of settlements and centers of economic and political power.

This chapter examines the changes in the Upper Senegal drainage with particular focus on the polities of Gajaaga and Bundu (Thiaw 1999). Archaeological research in the western lower Falemme in 1996–1997 has yielded critical information on material culture and settlement. The evidence collected illuminates the emerging new political landscapes in the eighteenth and nineteenth centuries as a result of Afro-European interactions in this area, 450 km away from the shores of the Atlantic. Although historical sources emphasize the roles of trade and Islam in the regional changes that have taken place over the past 500 years, archaeological evidence demonstrates how landscape and the built environment were put into play by different groups. Control of certain topographic and geomorphological units, as well as the water routes of the Senegal and the Falemme, which were major avenues for trade, was critical in shaping intra- and intergroup relationships. Local knowledge of regional landscape and competition for control of resources, such as landforms with higher agricultural potentials, levees, and escarpments for settlement, was the major structuring force of the settlement pattern. Power was materialized and resisted in the landscape as local elites and Europeans tried to consolidate their control over these features while relegating ordinary people either to the lowlands or away from the floodplain. An archaeological perspective that focuses on how intra- and intergroup interactions were materialized in the landscape is thus well suited to examining the internal contradictions within African societies as they were incorporated into the global networks of the Atlantic system.

THE HISTORICAL AND CULTURAL CONTEXT

The development of the Atlantic system is at the root of the formation of the "modern world system" and its worldwide cultural, economic, and political interconnections (Wallerstein 1974; Wolf 1982). In this

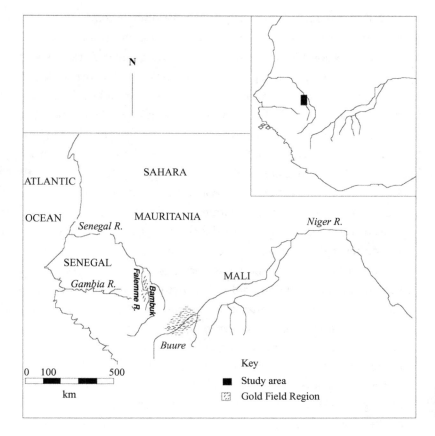

Figure 2.1
The Upper Senegal in Western Africa.

process of incipient globalization, Europe progressively assumed a hegemonic and pivotal role in world affairs, relegating non-Western societies to the margins. Nonetheless, this dynamic must not obscure the critical role played by non-Western societies in the innovations that began to emerge in the fifteenth century (Thornton 1992; Wolf 1982, 1984). The large-scale processes of post-fifteenth-century globalization mask a kaleidoscope of social, economic, and cultural worlds (Biersack 1991; O'Brian and Roseberry 1991; Thornton 1992). Both the European voyagers and the African societies with whom they interacted belonged to variable cultural settings and reacted accordingly (Decorse 1993, 1998, 2001; Kelly 1997). Consequently, the impact of Atlantic commerce on individual African societies must be evaluated with sensitivity to the particular cultural and historical contexts to understand its multiple, and often competing, dynamics.

In the Senegambia, colonial historiography and anthropology assumed that European contact caused a large-scale acculturation and assimilation of local cultures into the hegemonic colonial system (Boilat 1984; Delafosse 1972, 1927; Faidherbe 1889). This teleological perspective was aimed at maintaining the colonial status quo. That viewpoint is clearly unsatisfactory, however, African societies were neither gullible puppets nor stuck in a historical coma until Europeans intervened to accelerate, freeze, or deflect their evolutionary trajectories. Such assumptions have been dismantled by demonstrating the pervasive role played by Eurocentric ideology in the production of anthropological knowledge (Fabian 1983; Grosz-Ngaté 1988; Hammond and Jablow 1970; Trigger 1981). Postcolonial historical evaluations are no less teleological, assuming that with contact, the fate of Senegambian societies was tied to that of European nations, resulting in today's dependence and stagnation (Barry 1981, 1979; Rodney 1982). Indeed, both colonial and postcolonial perspectives grant little initiative to African societies during the contact era. Although we cannot rule out the destructive nature of Europeans on African societies, we must consider the complex strategies put into play by Africans to resist, negotiate, and adapt to the changing conditions of trade and intercultural interactions according to their own cultural, historical, and mnemonic capital.

Upper Senegal is connected to the Atlantic by the waterways of the Senegal and Gambia rivers. These were, until late in the nineteenth century, the sole commercial avenues, allowing the physical penetration of the inland regions by Europeans. The Portuguese were the first Europeans to reach Upper Senegal in the late fifteenth and early sixteenth centuries (Bathily 1989; Boulègue 1987; Hair 1984). From their bases in the Gambia, the British led several expeditions into this region from the seventeenth to the nineteenth centuries, competing with the French (Gray 1966; Hodges 1924; Jobson 1968; Park 1960). In 1659, the French established a factory in Saint Louis and progressively imposed a strict trade monopoly along the Senegal and the Falemme.

Navigational difficulties, the hostility of the Moors of the Trarza, and the rise of militant Islam in Fuuta Toro in the late seventeenth and eighteenth centuries were the major obstacles on the route to the Upper Senegal (Barry 1985, 1998). French control of the region was achieved through the construction of a ring of more than a half-dozen outposts along the Senegal and Falemme rivers that were used by chartered companies to secure inland traffic from other European competitors (Cultru 1910; Delcourt 1952; Machat 1906). The most important outposts for controlling these river trade routes were

Fort Saint Joseph de Galam on the Senegal River and Fort Saint Pierre de Kaynura near Senudebu on the Falemme (Wood 1967: 49–50) (Figure 2.2). Until the second half of the nineteenth century, most of these outposts served commercial rather than military functions and were occupied seasonally or for only a very short time (Delcourt 1952:92). The number of Europeans in the Upper Senegal, however, was quite notable for an inland region far from the shores of the Atlantic. Because navigation was restricted to the flood season from July to October, the outposts remained seasonally isolated from the headquarters at Saint Louis (Machat 1906:20–2).

The region underwent dramatic political contractions during the 500 years of Atlantic contact. Before the fifteenth century, Soninke speakers of Gajaaga controlled most of the Upper Senegal. The dynasty of Bacili Sempera is believed to have ruled over Gajaaga without interruption from the eighth to the nineteenth century (Bathily 1989). Bacili elites, including the *tunka lemmu* (royal) and the *mangu* (military retinue), operated like roaming bandits, pillaging commoner yeomen and travelers to supplement the revenue they

THE HISTORICAL AND CULTURAL CONTEXT

Figure 2.2
Major provinces and historical towns in the Upper Senegal region.

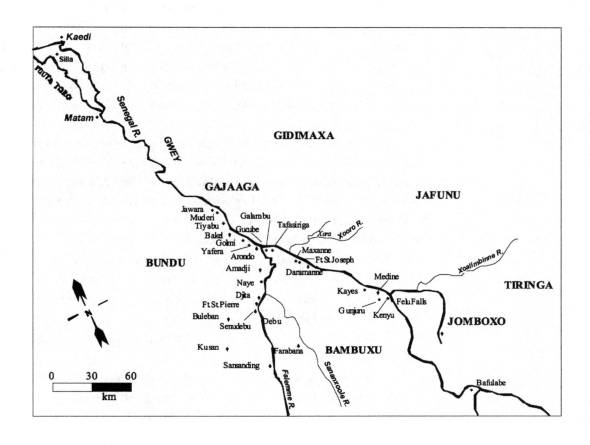

extracted from taxes (David 1974:102; Park 1960). However, Gajaaga (or Galam, as it was known in the French sources) was composed of small-scale communities dominated by factions of the Bacili Sempera dynasty. These different factions were united in theory under the leadership of the eldest Bacili member, who held the title of *tunka*, or paramount chief of Gajaaga.

Incorporation into the Atlantic system largely contributed to the reconfiguration of local polities at the regional level. In addition to the Europeans, Muslims also became a major political force in the Senegambia beginning in the seventeenth century, and Gajaaga was faced with the Almamy dynasty of Fuuta Toro in the northwest and the Malinke of Wuli in the southwest. In the late seventeenth and early eighteenth centuries, Gajaaga lost its southern frontier in Bundu to Fulbe Muslim colonists from Fuuta Toro (Gomez 1992).

War was endemic in eighteenth-century Senegambia, resulting in a recomposition of the political and ethnic map of the region. In the sixteenth century, members of the Njay dynasty of Jolof in western Senegambia were toppled from power but were granted land around Bakel by the *tunka* of Gajaaga (Bathily 1989). In the first half of the seventeenth century, Gajaaga lost its provinces of Jomboxo and Jafunu to Fulbe-speaking groups that founded the polity of Xaaso (Bathily 1972; Monteil 1915). The Bacili dynasty of Gajaaga somehow survived most of these crises, adopting a policy of peace for land; its territory became known as *leydi fergoji*, or land of immigration or exile (Bathily 1989:318).

Bundu was initially a small clerical community that settled on land donated to cleric Malik Sy by the *tunka* of Gajaaga, probably to secure the southern border against Malinke intruders (Curtin 1971; Traoré 1987). Recent historical assessments have cast doubt on the theocratic nature of the rule of the Almamy of Bundu, which is now believed to have been largely secular and pragmatic, because economic advantages and political gains superseded religious and ideological preoccupations (Clark 1996; Gomez 1992:1; 1985). It was through military conquest that Bundu colonized most of southern Gajaaga, becoming a major political player during the eighteenth and nineteenth centuries (De Lajaille 1802:55; Mollien 1967; Park 1960:44; Rançon 1898).

In the context of these political shifts, French establishments yielded both wealth and military advantages marshaled by host polities against their neighbors (David 1974:164; Boilat 1984:440).

In eighteenth-century Bambuxu, for example, local elites welcomed the erection of a French outpost in Farabana to profit from French military support in facing the raids of their Xaasonke neighbors (Boucard 1974:252). Similarly, Bundu welcomed a French garrison in Senudebu in 1845, but the installation of cannons at the outpost was opposed until 1847 by the Almamy, who maintained that he "had given permission for the establishment of a trading post, not an armed fort" (Gomez 1992:115). The Almamy feared that cannon would give the French enough power to intervene in Bundu's internal affairs. Indeed, the French did seek to use their military power to impose a trade monopoly and thwart the flourishing trade with the British, established on the Gambia River.

In 1758, France lost Saint Louis and the upriver outposts to the British. The British confined their occupation to Saint Louis, however, leaving the upper-river outposts in ruins (Dodwell 1916). During the period of British domination, Siliman, a Bacily prince from Maxanna, and his followers settled at the former fort Saint Joseph. Despite the fact that it was now occupied by a Soninke warlord and his retinue, the site was renamed Tubabunkani, or "village of Europeans," in reference to its historical origins (Bathily 1989:293). The French briefly regained control of Saint Louis and its upper-river dependencies between 1778 and 1779 and then lost them again until 1814.

Following the Napoleonic wars in 1814, French control was reinstated but not without clauses imposed by the British, including the abolition of the Atlantic slave trade and the suppression of trade monopolies that ran against the greater liberalism that accompanied the Industrial Revolution, for which Great Britain became the strongest advocate. Locally, in the Senegambia, this coincided with the rise of militant Islam, which opposed local polities that sponsored the French establishments. Nevertheless, the Upper Senegal remained critical to the commercial expansion of the French in western Sudan, as demonstrated by the creation of the Compagnie de Galam in 1824 (Bathily 1989; Saulnier 1921). Concomitantly, the French reinforced their presence, establishing fortified bases in Bakel (1818), Senudebu (1845), Medine (1855), and so forth.

French penetration in Upper Senegal had a profound impact on the organization of labor in the region. Despite high mortality rates as a result of local diseases, the French struggled to maintain control over the Upper Senegal region (Cohen 1983; Lacroix 1982; Leblanc 1822; Raffenel 1846:316). To achieve this goal, they relied largely on Africans, referred to as *laptots*, who were employed as laborers, porters, servants, and soldiers. By 1857, the contingent of the *tirailleurs senegalais* (Senegalese riflemen) was formed. Many were recruited among Soninke or Fulbe populations of the Upper Senegal, including slaves and seasonal migrant laborers. Many of them became commercial agents after France abolished slavery in Senegal in 1848 (Thompson 1990, 1992). Indigenous slavery continued until the early 1900s, well after its official abolition by the French colonial government in 1848. This contingent of *tirailleurs* even accompanied French penetration and colonization, and Africans on the French payroll were sometimes rewarded with slaves or used their wages to purchase slaves (Manchuelle 1989b; Thompson 1990, 1992).

The French penetration had dramatic ecological implications for the region. Most construction material for French outposts (largely stone and wood) was local, accelerating erosion processes and degrading the forest cover along the Senegal and Falemme riverbanks. Skyrocketing demand for charcoal to fuel steamboats, and for the growing domestic consumption by colonists and their retinues, also promoted deforestation along the major axis of French penetration (Moitt 1989:46–7; Thompson 1992: 287). Rapid urban development on the major axes of colonial penetration accelerated these processes.

Despite the long history of interaction with European powers in the Upper Senegal, colonial domination was not effective until the second half of the nineteenth century. Villages impeding French progress upriver were crushed; the small polities of the Upper Senegal provided little resistance to French penetration. By the mid-1850s, these polities signed treaties with France (Goy in 1858; Kammera in 1855; Xasso in 1855; Gidimaxa in 1855; Bundu in 1858; Bambuxu in 1858), implicitly recognizing its authority (Bathily 1989; Robinson 1988). This was a strategic move for both local elites and French colonial authorities, aimed as it was at preserving their respective domains against the *jihadi* movements, led by Al Hadj Umar Tal and Mamadu Lamiin Drame, that swept most of eastern Senegambia in the second half of the nineteenth century (Bathily 1970, 1972; Faidherbe 1863; Nyambarza 1969; Robinson 1985).

Overall, the economy of the Upper Senegal region remained healthy throughout the European contact period owing to (1) the preeminence of the Soninke *juula* in the traffic of western Sudan (Perinbam 1974); (2) the accumulation of wealth through services (labor) provided to French colonists; and (3) the reinvestment of accumulated wealth into commercial agriculture and slavery (Manchuelle 1997). Commercial continuity among *juula* traders ensured Gajaaga a central place in the economy of the Senegambia and western Sudan. The zeal and level of organization of the *juula* was such that they thwarted the authority of the local chiefs, boycotted the French factories, and negotiated prices (Bathily 1989; Bathily and Becker 1984; Becker 1983; Boucard 1974; Curtin 1975).

The fortunes of both Gajaaga and Bundu during the Atlantic Era were based on trade, commercial agriculture, and slavery. However, the two differed in that Gajaaga relied mainly on warlike societies such as the Bambara states of Kaarta and Segu for supplies in slaves (Roberts 1987), but Bundu waged wars against its smaller and weaker neighbors for booty, including numerous slaves who were put to agricultural labor and military service. Surplus agricultural products (millet, cotton cloth, tobacco, indigo) were supplied to the French and British in exchange for European goods, including firearms. The supply of grains to the Europeans' outposts was vital to the colonists, their retinues, and their slaves (Bathily 1986, 1989; David 1974; Delcourt 1952).

The centrality of trade in the economy of Upper Senegal can be evaluated archaeologically. Excavations and survey collections revealed a wide range of imported artifacts, including beads, glass, ceramics, tobacco pipes, bullets, gunflints, metal, and so forth. However, locally manufactured pottery was the most frequent artifact recorded at all sites. The quantity of imported ceramics remained extremely small throughout the contact era, most of it being associated with European outposts and local strongholds known as *tata*, suggesting that it was a prestige item. Other prestige imports included metal (Chambonneau 1898:310), cloth, carnelian beads, yellow amber, silver, black linen, gunpowder, and copper basins (Becker 1983).

Although it was dominant in all assemblages, locally manufactured pottery underwent dramatic changes after the eighteenth century. In contrast to early-second-millennium A.D. pottery with geometric motifs, appliqué, deep-red slip, finely polished surface, and, generally, grog-tempered vessels, post-eighteenth-century pottery is recognized for its extreme porosity, resulting from the abundant use of organic temper, coarse grains, nonplastic inclusions, irregular contours of the rims, high frequency of nondecorated vessels, or, when present, crudely executed motifs (Guèye 1991, 1998; McIntosh and Bocoum 2000; S. K. McIntosh and R. J. McIntosh 1993; S. K. McIntosh et al. 1992; Thiaw 1999). In northwestern Senegambia, this pottery is known as *subactuelle* and is distinguished by a decline in quality linked to the escalation of political violence and population movements, as a result of the spread of slavery and the slave trade, which began in the sixteenth century (Chavane 1985; Guèye 1998, 1991; Thilmans and Ravisé 1980). Common association between this pottery and specifically nineteenth-century occupations, however, raises the possibility that this tradition might belong largely to the latter century alone.

The nineteenth century coincided with the so-called pacification or military colonization and the beginning of legitimate and free trade. Where security was achieved, metropolitan companies, local traders, and (later in the early twentieth century) the Lebanon-Syrian merchants ensured, more than ever before, the spread of vast quantities of European goods into the Upper Senegal region, diminishing the competitiveness of many local crafts. Economic decline of Upper Senegal was also precipitated by the abolition of the slave trade and the redeployment of economic activities toward the coastal Atlantic region, forcing many Soninke and Fulbe of Gajaaga and Bundu to resort to seasonal migration as laborers in the fast-growing, cash-cropping peanuts economy beginning in the mid-nineteenth century (Brooks 1975; David 1980; Mage 1980:39–40; Swindell 1980).

ARCHAEOLOGICAL RESEARCH

During 1996–1997, I carried out a six-month archaeological research program in the western lower Falemme River, in the upper drainage of the Senegal River. The project adopted a long-term perspective to investigate the nature and the trajectory of economic, political, and social change over the past 1,000 years, without regard to the artificial boundaries of historical and prehistorical or protohistorical archaeology (Lightfoot 1995). Among the objectives of my research was the collection of data relevant to the comparison of settlement patterns, population densities, and evidence for artisanal activity and exchange throughout the second millennium A.D., representing the first regionally conceived program of archaeological research in contact-period Senegal.

Archaeological survey and excavation were conducted along a 50-km segment of the lower Falemme River. In the eighteenth and nineteenth centuries, this area was subject to the changing power relations between the polities of Gajaaga and Bundu. In contrast to the northwestern Senegambian plains, the topography of the Upper Senegal is rather complex. The Falemme stream is deeply incised and its floodplain narrowed by a rim of escarpments and hills, the altitude of which increases upstream. The survey was designed to cover all the levees bordering the Falemme channel and 25 percent of other landforms within a 3-km distance west of the river to assess the potential of each for containing abandoned settlements. Site location preference on river levees was demonstrated in the middle Senegal Valley and in preliminary reconnaissance on the Falemme, providing the rationale for this survey strategy (S. K. McIntosh et al. 1992; Thiaw 1999).

Most of the archaeological sites encountered were distributed along the river levees. Owing to past and present potential of the floodplain for settlement and recession farming, surface palimpsests of different occupations were not unusual. These account for several Late Stone Age and Iron Age sites found on the levees. Excavations were carried out near Arondo, a late-first- and early-second-millennium Iron Age site at the Senegal–Falemme confluence and at Fort Senudebu and *Tata Almamy* about 45 km upriver, both occupied in the second half of the nineteenth century. This chapter, however, focuses on the Atlantic-Era settlements identified during the regional survey, paying particular attention to Fort Senudebu and *Tata Almamy*.

TYPES OF HISTORICAL SITE

Out of a total of 154 sites, 43 were dated to the period of European contact. These can be grouped into three categories: (1) eleven indigenous defensive sites referred to as *tata*; (2) thirty indigenous nondefensive sites, often with shallow cultural deposits, referred to as *plages*; and (3) five European establishments (Figure 2.3).

Tata are sites in which the architecture and the topography suggest defensive purposes. Typically characterized by stone encirclements with stone or mud walling, they were generally built on the top of levees, hills, or escarpments (Figure 2.4). Occupations on levees have been ubiquitous phenomena in the settlement history

ATLANTIC IMPACTS ON INLAND SENEGAMBIA

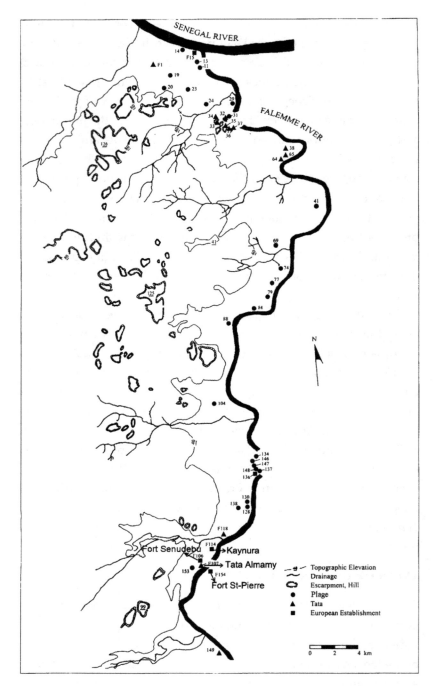

Figure 2.3
Distribution of historical sites along the Falemme River.

of the region because annual flooding there is particularly destructive. However, it was not until the eighteenth century that fortifications with a clearly military purpose were added and became widespread. Historical sources from the eighteenth and nineteenth centuries, for example, indicate that several villages in Gajaaga and

Figure 2.4
Site F32, a *tata* showing its location high above the river and stone structural features.

Bundu were protected either by city walls or by *tata* (Leblanc 1822; Park 1960; Raffenel 1846). In the mid-nineteenth century, General Faidherbe (1889:165) noted that in contrast to the Fuuta Toro, in the middle Senegal Valley, most of the villages in the Upper Senegal were fortified. In mid-eighteenth-century Bundu, for instance, Almamy Maka Jiba held three *tata* (Fena, Dara, Dyunfung) that were the bases from which he raided the neighboring provinces. In the eighteenth and nineteenth centuries, *tata* were erected in Buleban, Kusan, Djita, Senudebu, Amadji, Somsom-Tata, and Debu (Bathily 1972, 1970; Gomez 1992, Rançon 1894). It is likely that the classic *tata* was made of mud architecture. Although Mungo Park (1960:40) did not use the term *tata*, he observed that in Bundu "All the houses belonging to the king and his family are surrounded by a lofty mud wall, which converts the whole into a kind of citadel." He found similar architecture in Gajaaga, adding that the high wall that surrounded a chief's town had "a number of port holes for musketry to fire through in case of attack" (Park 1960:48).

Eleven sites matching these descriptions were found during the survey of the western lower Falemme. They were often perched atop escarpments, hills, or levees dominating the river channel. The erection of *tata* in Gajaaga and Bundu in the eighteenth and nineteenth centuries appears to correlate with the development of the Atlantic system and was a sign of wealth and prestige for the elites and traders. Many *tata* were characterized by the presence of stone pavements at surface level, but most of the architectural remains were washed out. *Tata Almamy*, a site of about 0.6 ha near modern Senudebu, was selected for excavation. The escarpment that bears the site is separated from Fort Senudebu by deep gullies that act as ravines during the wet season. One 2 m × 2 m test unit (Unit SN-3) was excavated in the central eastern region of the site. The unit was characterized by a paucity of cultural debris; architectural remains consisted of a mud floor discovered in the upper levels.

Textual sources and analysis of European imports collected at both Fort Senedebu and *Tata Almamy* situate their occupation in the second half of the nineteenth century (DeCorse et al. 2003; Thiaw 1999). The proximity of the two sites, separated by only a few dozen meters, reinforces the idea of a pragmatic Bundu state seeking to profit from the advantages of trade with the French fort and eventual logistic support during military operations. In the second half of the nineteenth century, for instance, Almamy Boubacar Saada portrayed himself as a close French ally, rallying French forces against *jihadist* Al Hadj Umar Tal (Gomez 1992).

The distribution of *tata* in the survey area shows two clusters: one near the Senegal–Falemme confluence and the other around Senudebu (Figure 2.3). This pattern is linked directly to the distribution of power within the region – Gajaaja in the north and Bundu in the south. The area in between appears to have been a "no man's land," the control of which shifted over time. The cluster of *tata* near the Senegal–Falemme confluence and south of Tiyabu, the royal capital of Gajaaga, reflects security concerns raised by the birth and growth of Bundu in the eighteenth and nineteenth centuries. Similarly, the cluster of *tata* north of Senudebu reflects the concerns of the polity of Bundu. The analysis of the distribution pattern of the *plages* campsites shows a north–south migration movement that reflects the expansion of Bundu at the expense of Gajaaga throughout the eighteenth and nineteenth centuries.

The majority (i.e., thirty) of the contact-period sites identified during the survey had only superficial cultural deposits characterized by light artifact scatters, often lacking architectural remains on the surface. These sites, referred to in Senegal as *plages*, have been interpreted as temporary short-term occupation campsites and reflect settlement instability during the Atlantic Era (Déme 1991; McIntosh and McIntosh 1993). These superficial accumulations of archaeological deposits are known locally as *gent* in Wolof, or "recently abandoned settlement." In contrast to earlier Iron Age sites, nearby populations generally retain memory about the history of these recent settlements.

In addition to *subactuelle* pottery, the assemblages of these sites generally included tobacco pipes and other European trade imports, such as glass beads. A post-fifteenth-century age has been given to these assemblages on the basis of the presence of tobacco pipes, which are believed to have been introduced into the region no earlier than that time (Mauny 1961:59). Analysis of European trade imports from both eastern and coastal Senegal has permitted narrowing this chronology. Although historical documentary sources unambiguously indicate that Afro-European contacts were initiated in the Senegambia in the fifteenth century, available archaeological chronologies inferred from analysis of European trade imports indicate that these became significant only after the eighteenth century (DeCorse et al. 2003; Richard 2007; Thiaw 2003).

The fact that archaeological deposits on *plages* sites are very superficial (and the rarity or absence of architectural remains on their surfaces) suggests that either the activities of their occupants did not generate significant accumulation of domestic debris or that these sites largely may have been temporary settlements. When found within the floodplain, the sites are subject to erosion processes, contributing to the superficial aspects. Here, occupation was at best seasonal, depending on the length and intensity of the flood – annual flooding would have made the sites difficult for habitation for at least a certain time of the year. This explains why these sites have been interpreted in terms of agriculturist–pastoralist interactions, climate change, and the annual availability of water and pasture resources (Guèye 1991, 1998; S. K. McIntosh and R. J. McIntosh 1993). This interpretation holds in the present, but its projection into the past is less convincing because it does not take into account the other forces at play during the era of the Atlantic slave trade.

It must also be pointed out that many *plages* were recorded away from floodplains (Déme 1991; S. K. McIntosh and R. J. McIntosh 1993; Thiaw 1999). In these contexts, an interpretation that takes into account historical linkages with nearby modern settlements seems appropriate. Mobility within the context of the political violence of the Atlantic slave trade is consistent with social memories of site occupation and abandonment that are often contingent on political and social forces. In this light, distribution patterns of *plages* can be

63

TYPES OF
HISTORICAL SITE

analyzed in terms of a horizontal stratigraphy that resembles a shifting internal frontier according to the model proposed by Kopytoff (1987).

Population mobility may have been ancient in the region, but large-scale migration during the contact era was unprecedented. Certain communities in the region still retain a memory of their itinerary. Oral memories in the village of Jimbe, for instance, indicated that their ancestors initially settled at an unknown time at a site referred to as Jagy (site 74) (Thiaw 1999). From there, they migrated to a site known as Seno (site 69) and then to Jimbe, their current location, situated about 1.2 km to the northeast. Jagy and Seno were located approximately 1 km and 1.4 km away from the Falemme stream, respectively. Both are *plages* campsites, but Jimbe is situated on a levee on the banks of the Falemme. The pattern of this three-step migration outlines south–north and westward movement away from the river, from Jagy to Seno, and then a northeast move back toward the Falemme, from Seno to the current settlement at Jimbe. Today, Jimbe is mainly a Pulaar-speaking community. It is likely that these short-distance migrations coincided with the growth of the polity of Bundu and the erosion of the power of the *tunka* (paramount chief) of Gajaaga. It is not clear whether the village of Jimbe was occupied prior to this migration, but the name of the site is mentioned in eighteenth-century maps.

Archaeological data confirm that the number of short-term settlements grew rapidly during the eighteenth and nineteenth centuries. Additionally, the overall increase in the frequency of *plages* campsites beginning in the eighteenth century coincided with increased European presence and the development of the Atlantic economy. This pattern can be interpreted as a logical response to the slave trade and the political violence that developed along with it. Indeed, migration would have become one of the most effective responses to the stress and crisis imposed by the slave trade.

Bundu grew out of Gajaaga at about the same time period, competing with Gajaaga for control of the Falemme banks and the Atlantic networks (Gomez 1992). These successive short-term migrations from south to north support historical indications that the polity of Bundu developed out of small clerical communities that expanded by progressively nibbling lands from neighboring Soninke communities of southern Gajaaga. The advantages for trade offered by European outposts would have only exacerbated such conflicts. This analysis of settlement mobility outlines the complexity of relationships between Gajaaga and expanding Muslim clerical communities in Bundu beginning in the eighteenth century within the context of the Atlantic slave trade.

In addition to Fort Senudebu and Kaynura, three additional European outposts were located during the survey (Figure 2.3). These sites were characterized by cemented floors, stone architecture, and a variable quantity of European imports that included ceramics, glass, beads, and metals. Documentary sources indicate that the first French establishment in the Falemme was Fort Saint Pierre de Kaynura, erected in 1714. A site with this toponym was located about 1.5 km north of Fort Senudebu. Neither the architecture (which probably was made of mud) nor the imported goods (the presence of which was relatively small) differentiated this site from other indigenous settlements referred to as *plages*. Yet, this does not rule out the possibility that Kaynura was Fort Saint Pierre. Indeed, documentary evidence indicates that the earliest French establishments in the region, including Fort Joseph and Fort Saint Pierre, were built almost entirely with mud (Wood 1967).

Modern inhabitants of Senudebu are unclear about the exact locations of Fort Senudebu and Fort Saint Pierre. Textual sources are more precise about Fort Senedubu than about Fort Saint Pierre. Confusion in local memories must have resulted from the proximity of the two sites and the absence of standing architectural ruins in the abandoned settlement of Kaynura. It is also possible that Fort Saint Pierre was located on the eastern bank of the Falemme, opposite Fort Senudebu, where a site that local informants referred to as *cimetiere des toubab*, or "white men's cemetery," was found.

Fort Senudebu was a small outpost established on a small levee overlooking the Falemme stream. It was erected on a small piece of land of about 0.4 ha, purchased by the French in 1845 for 5,000 francs in merchandise and an annual royalty of 1,200 francs (Flize 1857:176) (Figure 2.5). Portions of the western and eastern walls and the rooms in each corner of the main structure are still in place. The western and northeastern sections are better preserved than the eastern and southeastern sides. The wall that surrounded the fort was about 4 m high in the western and eastern part of the site. The northern and southern walls had completely collapsed, but the foundations revealed a 2-m-wide structure. The western and eastern walls, and the northeastern and southwestern rooms, had a number of ramparts suited to protecting the building in case of attack. Both the wall that surrounded the fort and the rooms in the corners were built with local stone and lined with cement mixed with shell fragments and sand. A better mix was achieved for the rooms than for the wall surrounding the fort, which had crumbled. Fired red bricks were used to define the openings, including the windows, the ramparts, and the entrances. The fact that Mungo Park (1960:48) noted similar architecture for *tata* and indigenous city walls in Bundu and Gajaaga is significant, and it perhaps indicates the mixing of African and European traditions in eighteenth- and nineteenth-century African military architecture.

Other structures were found outside the walls of the fort. One that caught my attention is a 44 × 37 m cattle enclosure immediately adjacent to the northern wall of the fort. Other rectangular and circular mud and stone structures were found outside the northeastern, eastern, and southeastern walls separating the fort from the Falemme stream. Most of these structures are badly eroded and deeply cut by gullies. It is likely that some of these structures were the houses of the French indigenous domestics and retinues.

Two units, including one 3 m × 3 m (SN-1) and one 2 m × 2 m (SN-4), were opened in the area within the walls of Fort Senudebu. A third 2 m × 2 m unit (SN-2) was sunk in the southern region of the cattle enclosure adjacent to the northwestern wall of the fort. SN-1 was set about halfway along the western wall near a cemented floor. Unit SN-4, about halfway along the southern wall, was established in one of several structures with tumbled fired red bricks and stones within the walls of the fort. Large quantities of building material with traces of firing were uncovered in all three units, perhaps representing the violent attacks on the site during the wars against Al Hadj Umar Tal in the early second half of the nineteenth century and against Mamadu Lamiin in 1885–1886.

Architectural remains unearthed in units SN-1 and SN-4 consisted of mud, stones, and fired red bricks consistent with the history of the site. Like some other early European-contact sites in the Senegambia, the architecture of Fort Senudebu combined both local and European raw material and was fundamentally Creole in that it relied mainly on local masons and artisans, often of slave origin, who added their own cultural input to the instructions of colonial engineers and officials who were not necessarily architects (Hinchman 2006; Wood 1967). The local elite occupied the fort after its evacuation by the French in the early 1860s and contributed once more to the "creolisation" of the architecture as new features were added to the settlement. In contrast to SN-1 and SN-4, unit SN-2 yielded relatively large amounts of domestic debris that were excavated as fill in several refuse pits, perhaps suggesting that the enclosure was also used for that purpose.

Of the five European outposts recorded in the study area, four were located in the southern end of the survey area near Senudebu in Bundu and only one nearby the Senegal–Falemme confluence. This suggests that Bundu funneled most of the trade along the Falemme River in the eighteenth and nineteenth centuries. At the time of chartered companies from early contact to the nineteenth century, Europeans sought protection from African polities to secure the trade. The establishment of outposts and the development of trade in this area remote from the Atlantic coast required security clearance that could be ensured with efficiency only by centralized polities like Bundu. The structure of Gajaaga that was composed of small-scale competing factions could only favor the newly founded state of Bundu.

The mid-nineteenth century was characterized by the militarization of European establishments and the imposition of French imperial domination. At this time, weakened African monarchs struggled to maintain their trading advantages under the protection of the European machine gun. Paradoxically, however, although the guns protected the monarchs against their other African competitors, the guns also considerably eroded their power. This explains the proximity of Fort Senudebu and *Tata Almamy* and the complex historical relationships between the French and the local elite in Bundu.

Figure 2.5 Nineteenth-century drawing of Fort Senudebu (right) and *Tata Almamy* (left) (Vernoll 1859).

SETTLEMENT DYNAMICS

Archaeological data suggest that pre-European settlement in the region favored the high levees along the Falemme River as a response to the destructive nature of annual flooding. Rapid occupation of the escarpments and hills with clear military concerns is, however, an eighteenth-century phenomenon (Thiaw 1999). The most stunning aspect of the settlement dynamics during the period of the French contact is the rapid appearance and growth of the *tata* and *plages* camps. The time when local populations began erecting *tata* strongholds is uncertain, but their rapid multiplication parallels the European penetration. At the same time, the growth of campsites known as *plages* is directly linked to the greater mobility of the defenseless populations as a result, in part, of the political violence imposed by the Atlantic system.

The rise of militant Islam in the Senegambia beginning in the seventeenth century caused the displacement of several thousand people from their homelands, either as followers or as victims. The French–Umarian wars of the early second half of the nineteenth century, for example, generated wide-scale population movements and the relocation of over 40,000 persons, mostly Pulaar speakers from the middle and Upper Senegal regions (Mage 1980; Robinson 1985, 1987). The *jihad* of Mamadu Lamiin (1885–1887) was more ephemeral, but it also caused wide-scale population movements. In contrast to Umar Tal's movement, which relied mostly on Fulbe-speaking populations, the Soninke-speaking people and the Jakhanke predominantly supported the Mamadu Lamiin *jihad*. This caused the depopulation of the region within the triangle formed between the communities of Bakel, Arondo, and Senudebu, areas directly exposed to the French colonial rule.

Following the abolition of the slave trade in 1848, this pattern would have been accelerated by the imposition of the head tax, the census, and forced labor (e.g., for railroad construction). Indeed, many populations migrated away from the zones of direct French control as a result of these impositions (Clark 1994). Ex-slaves headed toward the *villages de liberté* (freedom villages) and their former masters moved away from areas under direct French control to found new settlements. The arrival of migrants in previously unoccupied areas and the clearing of forest for agriculture and settlements were important sources of environment degradation (Becker 1985, 1986; Chastanet 1983; Clark 1994, 1995).

These settlement dynamics reflect transformations caused by incorporation into Atlantic networks. The types of site identified yield important insights into the social and political cleavages between traders, Muslim clerics and their followers, the political elite and their retinues, European colonists and their free and enslaved personals, free ordinary peasants, and slaves. The wealth and prestige of the local elites, clerics, and traders allowed them to compete for the control of trade, to settle on higher elevations that are more easily defensible sites, and, at the same time, to impose their domination on a defenseless population of peasants and slaves who constantly sought refuge from ceaseless exactions.

Tatas and European forts appear as centers of economic and political power, but the lowland or *plages* were relegated to defenseless populations. These strongholds had paradoxical meanings. They offered protection, but at the same time they exploited the ordinary peasants and slaves who lived in the lowlands or *plages*. The regional settlement pattern shows very little evidence of political centralization, power being seemingly dispersed among independently operating, small-scale polities. This interpretation is consistent with our understanding of socioeconomic and political organization in the region during the Atlantic Era.

CONCLUSION

Because of its geographical location and its long-term implication in global trade, Senegambia is an ideal laboratory for investigating how landscape contributed to attempts to construct, regulate, resist, or negotiate political position in the new geography of power resulting from the Atlantic expansion. From the fifteenth century onward, European, African, Afro-European, and Islamic worldviews collided in the region. Both the Atlantic commercial expansion and the spread of Islam contributed to restructuring and redistributing regional political power in response to these new forces. The archaeology of Atlantic contact in Upper Senegal yields critical information on such processes. Although initial contact with the Europeans is historically situated in the fifteenth century, it was not until the eighteenth century that Atlantic impact had clear archaeological visibility both in the landscape and in material culture. Over the past decades, historical studies have emphasized the attraction of Upper Senegal for the Europeans beginning in the fifteenth century and the critical role this region played in the Atlantic economy of the Senegambia (Bathily 1989; Clark 1996; Gomez 1992; Manchuelle 1997). The merit of this archaeological research has been to show how these processes were imprinted in the landscape and settlement patterns in the region and the implications this had on political, social, and economic organization.

Prior to European contact, inhabitants of this region favored high levees bordering the Falemme River. By the eighteenth and nineteenth centuries, however, escarpments and hills were occupied in addition to levees. It was on these elevated landforms that local strongholds, or *tata*, and European outposts were established. Both types of settlement reflected the wealth and prestige of Europeans and local elites and traders, along with the rise of political violence in the region.

The predominance in the eighteenth and nineteenth centuries of superficial short-term occupation sites or *plages* (where domestic slaves and ordinary peasants typically were confined) signals social cleavage between local elites and European traders on the one hand and slaves and ordinary peasants on the other. Additionally, the greater frequency of *plages* in the eighteenth and nineteenth centuries is linked to greater population mobility, reflecting relative regional instability in this period that was accelerated by the decomposition of the local political and social systems from rising competition for trade and resources. The decentralized polity of Gajaaga shrank considerably, but other polities such as Bundu grew at its expense. However, Gajaaga managed to maintain its role via trade thanks to its dynamic class of *juula* traders and plunder by a divided elite dependent on Atlantic resources. Bundu relied on tax, plunder, and the competition beween the French and the British to maximize its profits in trade. The Europeans and the elite of the newly founded state of Bundu largely benefited from these conditions. In both cases, African initiatives were a key component in the operation of the Atlantic system as a whole until the imposition of the colonial government late in the nineteenth century. Ultimately, the advantages of trade, and the political weakness of Gajaaga, created a situation of unregulated competition that accentuated local cleavages that, in the long term, eased the conquest and the imposition of the colonial government.

The shift of commercial avenues from the rivers to land routes (e.g., railroads) and the post-1850 success of groundnut cash farming in the coastal regions profoundly impacted the Upper Senegal economy. In response to this redeployment of economic activities, Soninke and Fulbe populations of the Upper Senegal initiated a massive seasonal labor migration toward the Senegambian peanut basin on the coast from the mid-nineteenth century onward. These changes precipitated the marginalization of the Upper Senegal. As a result, today this region has one of the lowest population densities (five inhabitants per km^2) and the highest emigration rate (60 percent of the active male population) (Manchuelle 1989a, 1989b; Weigel 1982) in the Senegambia.

BIBLIOGRAPHY

Barry, B. (1979). The Subordination of Power and the Mercantile Economy: The Kingdom of Waalo, 1600–1831. In O'Brian, R.C. (ed.), *The Political Economy of Underdevelopment. Dependence in Senegal*, Sage Publications, Beverly Hills, CA, 39–63.

Barry, B. (1981). Economic Anthropology of Precolonial Senegambia from the Fifteenth through the Nineteenth Centuries. In Colving, L. G. (ed.), *The Uprooted of the Western Sahel: Migrants' Quest for Cash in the Senegambia*, Praeger, New York, 27–57.

Barry, B. (1985). *Le Royaume du Waalo: Le Sénégal avant la Conquête*. Éditions Karthala, Paris.

Barry, B. (1998). *Senegambia and the Atlantic Slave Trade*. Cambridge University Press, Cambridge.

Bathily, A. (1970). Mamadou Lamine et la résistance anti-impérialiste dans le haut Sénégal (1885–1887). *Notes Africaines* **125**: 20–32.

Bathily, A. (1972). La conquête Française du Haut-Fleuve (Sénégal) 1818–1887. *Bulletin de L'Institut Fondamental d'Afrique Noire*, T. XXXIV, série B, **1**: 67–112.

Bathily, A. (1986). La traite Atlantique des esclaves et ses effets économiques et sociaux en Afrique: Le cas du Galam, royaume de l' hinterland Sénégambien au dix-huitième siècle. *Journal of African History* **27**: 269–93.

Bathily, A. (1989). *Les Portes De l'Or: Le Royaume de Galam (Sénégal) de l'ère des musulmanes au temps des négriers (VIII–XVIIIe siècles)*. Editions l'Harmattan, Paris.

Bathily, A., and Becker C., eds. (1984). Mémoires de Sr Charpentier, Comm. de ST Joseph en Galam Pendant l'Année 1725. Dakar: Faculté des Letrres et Sciences Humaines.

Baum, R. M. (1999). *Shrines of the Slave Trade: Diola Religion and Society in Precolonial Senegambia*. Oxford University Press, Oxford.

Becker, C. (1983). *Mémoire sur le Commerce de la Concession du Sénégal (1752)*. Publié et commenté par C. Becker. CNRS, LA. 94.

Becker, C. (1985). Notes sur les conditions écologiques en Sénégambie aux 17e et 18e siècle. *African Economic History* **14**: 167–216.

Becker, C. (1986). Conditions écologiques, crises de subsistances et histoire de la population à l'époque de la traite des esclaves en Sénégambie (17e–18e siècle). *Canadian Journal of African Studies* **20** (3): 357–76.

Becker, C., and Martin, V. (1980). Mémoires d'Adanson sur le Sénégal et l'île de Gorée (1763). *Bulletin de l'Institut Fondamental d'Afrique Noire*, T. 42, série B, 4: 722–79.

Biersack, A., ed. (1991). 1. Introduction: History and Theory in Anthropology. In Biersack, A. (ed.), *Clio in Oceania: Toward a Historical Anthropology*. Smithsonian Institution Press, Washington, DC, 1–36.

Boilat, D. (1984). *Esquisses Sénégalaises*. Éditions Karthala, Paris.

Boone, J. L., et al. (1990). Archaeological and Historical Approaches to Complex Societies: The Islamic States of Medieval Morocco. *American Anthropologist* **92**: 630–46.

Boucard, C. (1974). Relation de Bambouc (1729). Introduction et annotations par P. D. Curtin avec la collaboration de J. Boulègue. *Bulletin de L'Institut Fondamental d'Afrique Noire*, T. XXXVI, 2: 246–75.

Boulègue, J. (1987). *Les Anciens Royaumes Wolof (Sénégal): Le Grand Jolof (XIII-XVIè siècle)*. Éditions Façades, Paris.

Braudel, F. (1946). Monnaies et civilisations: De l'or du Soudan à l'argent de l'Amérique, un drame Méditerranéen. *Annales* **1**: 9–22.

Brooks, G. E. (1975). Peanuts and Colonialism: Consequences of the Commercialization of Peanuts in West Africa, 1830–70. *Journal of African History* **16** (1): 29–54.

Brooks, G. E. (1993). *Landlords and Strangers: Ecology, Society, and Trade in Western Africa, 1000–1630*. Westview, Boulder, CO.

Brooks, G. E. (2003). *Eurafricans in Western Africa: Commerce, Social Status, Gender and Religious Observance from the Sixteenth to the Eighteenth Century*. Ohio University Press, Athens.

Brunschwig, H., (1975). Le docteur Colin, l'or du Bambouk et la "colonisation moderne." *Cahiers d'Etudes Africaines* **58**, XV-2: 166–88.

Chambonneau (1898). Relation du Sr Chambonneau, commis de la compagnie de Sénégal, du voyage par luy fait en remontant le Niger (Juillet 1688). *Bulletin de Géographie Historique et Descriptive* **2**: 308–21.

Chastanet, M. (1983). Les crises de subsistances dans les villages Soninke du Cercle de Bakel de 1858 à 1945: Problémes méthodologiques et perspective de recherche. *Cahiers d'Etudes Africaines* **89**–90, XXIII-1–2: 5–36.

Chavane, B. A. (1985). *Villages de l'Ancien Tekrour: Recherches archéologiques dans la moyenne vallée du fleuve Sénégal*. Éditions Karthala, Paris.

Clark, A. F. (1994). Internal Migrations and Population Movements in the Upper Senegal Valley (West Africa), 1890–1920. *Canadian Journal of African Studies* **28** (3): 399–420.

Clark, A. F. (1995). Environmental Decline and Ecological Response in the Upper Senegal Valley, West Africa, from the Late Nineteenth Century to World War I. *Journal of African History* **36**: 197–218.

Clark, A. F. (1996). The Fulbe of Bundu (Senegambia): From Theocracy to Secularization. *International Journal of African Historical Studies* **29** (1): 1–23.

Cohen, W. B. (1983). Malaria and French Imperialism. *Journal of African History* **24**: 23–36.

Cultru, P. (1910). *Les Origines de l'Afrique Occidentale: Histoire du Sénégal du XVe Siècle à 1870*. Larose, Paris.

Curtin, P. D. (1971). Jihad in West Africa: Early Phases and Inter-Relations in Mauritania and Senegal. *Journal of African History* **12** (1): 11–24.

Curtin, P. D. (1973). The Lure of Bambuk Gold. *Journal of African History* **14** (4): 623–31.

Curtin, P. D. (1975). *Economic Change in Precolonial Africa: Senegambia in the Era of the Slave Trade*. University of Wisconsin Press, Madison.

Daniel, F. (1910). Étude sur les Soninkés ou Sarakolés. *Anthropos* **5**: 27–49.

David, P. (1974). *Journal d'un Voiage fait en Bambouc en 1744*. Publié par Delcourt, A. Société française d'Histoire d'Outre-Mer. Paris.

David, P. (1980). *Les Navétanes: Histoire des migrants saisonniers de l'arachide en Sénégambie des origines à nos jours*. Les Nouvelles Editions Africaines, Dakar.

DeCorse, C. R. (1993). The Danes in the Gold Coast: Culture Change and the European Presence. *The African Archaeological Review* **11**: 149–73.

DeCorse, C. R. (1998). Culture Contact in West Africa. In Cusick, J. G. (ed), *Studies in Culture Contact: Interaction, Culture Change, and Archaeology*. Center for Archaeological Investigations, Occasional Paper No. 25, Southern Illinois University, Carbondale, 358–77.

DeCorse, C. R. (2001). *An Archaeology of Elmina: Africans and Europeans on the Gold Coast, 1400–1900*. Smithsonian Institution Press, Washington, DC.

DeCorse, C. R., et al. (2003). Toward a Systematic Bead Description System: A View from the Lower Falemme, Senegal. *Journal of African Archaeology* **1** (1): 81–105.

Delafosse, M. (1927). *Les Négres*. Les éditions RIEDER, Paris.

Delafosse, M. (1972). *Le Haut Sénégal Niger*. 3 vols. Maisonneuve and Larose, Paris.

De Lajaille, G. (1802). *Voyage au Sénégal Pendant les Années 1784 et 1785, d'aprés les mémoires de Lajaille*. P. Labarthe, Paris.

Delcourt, A. (1952). *La France et les etablissements Français au Sénégal entre 1713 et 1763. Mémoire de l'IFAN*, 17. Paris.

Déme, A. (1991). *Evolution Climatique et Processus de Mise en Place du Peuplement dans L'Île de Morphil*. Mémoire de Maîtrise, Département Lettres et Sciences Humaines, UCAD.

Dodwell, H. (1916). Le Sénégal sous la domination Anglaise. *Revue d'Histoire des Colonies Française* **4**: 267–300.

Fabian, J. (1983). *Time and the Other: How Anthropology Makes Its Objects*. Columbia University Press, New York.

Faidherbe, L. C. (1863). L'Avenir du Sahara et du Soudan. *Revue Maritime et Coloniale* **8**: 221–48.

Faidherbe, L. C. (1889). *Le Sénégal: La France dans l'Afrique Occidentale*. Librairie Hachette et Cie, Paris.

Flize, L. (1857). Le Boundou (Sénégal). *Revue Coloniale* **17**: 175–78.

Garrard, T. F. (1982). Myth and Metrology: The Early Trans-Saharan Gold Trade. *Journal of African History* **23**: 443–61.

Gomez, M. A. (1985). The Problem with Malik Sy and the Foundation of Bundu. *Cahiers d'Études Africaines* **100**, XXV-4: 537–53.

Gomez, M. A. (1992). *Pragmatism in the Age of Jihad: The Precolonial State of Bundu*. Cambridge University Press, Cambridge.

Gray, J. M. (1966). *A History of the Gambia*. Frank Cass, London.

Grosz-Ngaté, M. (1988). Power and Knowledge: The Representation of the Mande World in the Works of Park, Caillé, Monteil, and Delafosse. *Cahiers d'Études Africaines* **111–112**, XXVIII-3–4: 485–511.

Guèye, N. S. (1991). L'Étude de la Céramique Subactuelle et de ses Rapports avec la Céramique de Cuballel. Unpublished Mémoire de maîtrise, Faculté des Lettres, Université de Dakar.

Guèye, N. S. (1992). Les Pipes de la Moyenne Vallée du Fleuve Sénégal: Approche Typologique. Unpublished Mémoire de DEA, Faculté des Lettres, Université de Dakar.

Guèye, N. S. (1998). Poteries et Peuplement de la Moyenne Vallée du Fleuve Sénégal du XVIe au XXe: Approches Ethnoarchéologique et Ethnohistorique. Ph.D. dissertation, University of Paris X, Nanterre.

Hair, P. E. H. (1984). The Falls of Félou: A Bibliographical Exploration. *History in Africa* **11**: 113–30.

Hammond, D., and Jablow, A. (1970). *The Africa That Never Was: Four Centuries of British Writing about Africa*. Twayne, New York.

Hinchman, M. (2000). African Rococo: House and Portrait in Eighteenth-Century Senegal. Ph.D. dissertation, University of Chicago.

Hinchman, M. (2006). House and Household on Gorée, Sénégal, 1758–1837. *Journal of the Society of Architectural Historians* **65** (2): 66–187.

Hodges, C. (1924). The Journey of Cornelius Hodges in Senegambia, 1689–90. Published by G. Stone. *English Historical Review* **39**: 89–95.

Jobson, R. (1968). *The Golden Trade. London 1623. Or a Discovery of the River Gambia, and the Golden Trade of the Aethiopians*. Da Capo, Amsterdam.

Kelly, K. G. (1997). The Archaeology of African-European interaction: Investigating the Social Roles of Trades, Traders, and the Use of Space in the Seventeenth- and Eighteenth-Century Hueda Kingdom, Republic of Benin. *World Archaeology* **28** (3): 351–69.

Kopytoff, I., ed. (1987). The Internal African Frontier: The Making of African Political Culture. In Kopytoff, I. (ed.), *The African Frontier: The Reproduction of Traditional African Societies*. Indiana University Press, Bloomington, 3–84.

Labat, J. B. (1728). *Nouvelle Relation de l'Afrique Occidentale*. 5 vols. Paris.

Lacroix, J. B. (1986). *Les Français au Sénégal au Temps de la Compagnie des Indes de 1719 à 1758*. Service Historique de la de la Marine, Vincennes.

Lawrence, A. W. (1964). *Trade Castles and Forts in West Africa*. Stanford University Press, Stanford, CA.

Leblanc (1822). Voyage à Galam. *Annales Maritimes et Coloniales* **1**: 133–59.

Levtzion, N., and Hopkins, J. F. P., eds. (1981). *Corpus of Early Arabic Sources for West African History*. Cambridge University Press, Cambridge.

Lightfoot, K. G. (1995). Culture Contact Studies: Redefining the Relationship between Prehistoric and Historical Archaeology. *American Antiquity* **60** (2): 199–217.

Lombard, M. (1947). Les bases monétaires d'une suprématie économique: L'Or Musulman du VIIe au XIe siècle. *Annales Economies, Sociétés, Civilisations* **2**: 143–60.

Machat, J. (1906). *Documents sur les Établissement Français d'Afrique Occidentale au XVIIIe siècle*. Librairie maritime et coloniale, Paris.

Mage, E. (1980). *Voyage dans le Soudan Occidental, Sénégambie, Niger, 1863–1866*. Karthala, Paris.

Malowist, M. (1966). Le commerce d'or et d'esclave du Soudan. *Africana Bulletin* **4**: 49–72.

Manchuelle, F. (1989a). Slavery, Emancipation and Labour Migration in West Africa: The Case of the Soninke. *Journal of African History* **30**: 89–106.

Manchuelle, F. (1989b). The "Patriarchal Ideal" of Soninke Labor Migrants: From Slave to Employers of Free Labor. *Canadian Journal of African Studies* **23** (1): 106–25.

Manchuelle, F. (1997). *Willing Migrants: Soninke Labor Diasporas, 1848–1960*. Ohio University Press, Athens.

Mauny, R. (1961). *Tableau Géographique de l'Ouest Africain au Moyen Âge: D'après les sources écrites, la tradition et l'archéologe*. Mémoire de L'IFAN, 61, Dakar.

McIntosh, S. K., and Bocoum, H. (2000). New Perspectives on Sincu Bara, a First Millennium Site in the Senegal Valley. *African Archaeological Review* **17** (1): 1–43.

McIntosh, S. K., and McIntosh, R. J. (1993). Field Survey in the Tumulus Zone in Senegal. *African Archaeological Review* **11**: 73–107.

McIntosh, S. K., McIntosh, R. J., and Bocoum, H. (1992). The Middle Senegal Valley Project: Preliminary Results from the 1990–91 Field Season. *Nyame Akuma* **38**: 47–61.

Moitt, B. (1989). Slavery and Emancipation in the Senegal's Peanut Basin: The Nineteenth and Twentieth Centuries. *International Journal of African Historical Studies* **22** (1): 27–50.

Mollien, G. (1967). *Travels in the Interior of Africa. To the sources of the Senegal and Gambia. Performed by command of the French Government in the year 1818*. Edited by T. E. Bowdich. Frank Cass, London.

Monteil, C. (1915). *Les Khassonke, Monographie d'une Peuplade du Soudan Français*. Ernest Leroux, Paris.

Nyambarza, D. (1969). Le marabout El Hadj Mamadou Lamine d'aprés les archives Françaises. *Cahiers d'Études Africaines* **9**, XXXIII: 124–45.

O'Brian, J., and Roseberry, W. (1991). Introduction. In O'Brian, J., and Roseberry, W. (eds.), *Golden Ages, Dark Ages: Imagining the Past in Anthropology and History*. University of California Press, Berkeley, 1–18.

Park, M. (1960). *Travels of Mungo Park*. Edited by R. Miller. J. M. Dent and Sons, London.

Perinbam, M. B. (1974). Notes on Dyula Origins and Nomenclature. *Bulletin de l'Institut Fondamental d'Afrique Noire*, série B, **36** (4): 676–90.

Raffenel, A. (1846). Le haut Sénégal et la Gambie en 1843 et 1844. *Revue Coloniale* **8**: 309–40.

Rançon, A. (1894). Le Boundou: Étude de géographie et d'histoire Soudaniennes de 1681 à nos jours. *Bulletin de la Société de Géographie de Bordeaux* **7**: 433–63.

Richard, F. G. (2007). From Cosaan to Colony: Exploring Archaeological Landscapes Formations and Socio-Political Complexity in the Siin (Senegal), AD 500–1900. Ph.D. dissertation, Syracuse University.

Roberts, R. (1987). *Warriors, Merchants, and Slaves: The State and Economy in the Middle Niger Valley, 1700–1914*. Stanford University Press, Stanford, CA.

Robinson, D. (1985). *The Holy War of Umar Tal: The Western Sudan in the Mid-Nineteenth Century*. Clarendon, Oxford.

Robinson, D. (1987). The Umarian Emigration of the Late Nineteenth Century. *International Journal of African Historical Studies* 20 (2): 245–70.

Robinson, D. (1988). French "Islamic" Policy and Practice in Late Nineteenth-Century Senegal. *Journal of African History* 29: 415–35.

Rodney, W. (1982). *How Europe Underdeveloped Africa*. Howard University Press, Washington, DC.

Ross, S. E. (2005). *Villes Soufies du Sénégal: Réseaux Urbains Religieux dans la Longue Durée*. Institut des Études Africaines, Rabat, Série: Conférence 20.

Santoir, C. (1990). Le conflit Mauritano-Sénégalais: La Genèse. Le cas de la Haute Vallée. *Cahiers Sciences Humaines* 26 (4): 553–76.

Santoir, C. (1994). Décadence et résistance du pastoralisme : Les peuls de la Vallée du Fleuve Sénégal. *Cahiers d'Études Africaines*, **133**–135, XXXIV-1-3: 231–63.

Saulnier, E. (1921). *Une Compagnie à privilège au XIXe siècle: La Compagnie de Galam au Sénégal*. Gouvernement Général de l'Afrique Occidentale Française, Publications du Comité d'Etudes Historique et Scientifiques, Paris Ve, Emile Larose.

Schmitz, J. (1990). Les peuls: Islam, pastoralisme et fluctations du peuplement. *Cahiers Sciences Humaines* 26 (4): 499–504.

Searing, J. F. (1993). *West African Slavery and the Atlantic Commerce: The Senegal River Valley, 1700–1860*. African Studies Centre, Cambridge.

Searing, J. F. (2002). *"God Alone Is King": Islam and Emancipation in Senegal. The Wolof Kingdoms of Kajoor and Bawol, 1859–1914*. Social History of Africa. James Currey, Oxford.

Swindell, K. (1980). Serawoollies, Tillibunkas and Strange Farmers: The Development of Migrant Groundnut Farming along the Gambia River, 1848–95. *Journal of African History* **21**: 93–104.

Thiaw, I. (1999). An Archaeological Investigation of Long-Term Culture Change in the Lower Falemme (Upper Senegal Region) A.D. 500–1900. Ph.D. dissertation, Rice University.

Thiaw, I. (2003). The Gorée Archaeological Project (GAP): Preliminary Results, *Nyame Akuma* **60**: 27–35.

Thiaw, I. (2008). Every House Has a Story: The Archaeology of Gorée Island, Sénégal. In Sansone, L., Soumonni, E., and Barry, B. (eds.), *Africa, Brazil and the Construction of Trans-Atlantic Black Identities*. Africa World Press, Trenton, NJ, 45–62.

Thiaw, I. (2010). "A small pot behind every big man": Faith and Settlement Dynamics in the Late Atlantic Period in Bawol (Western Senegambia). 13th PanAfrican Archaeological Congress and the 20th Meeting of the Society of Africanist Archaeologists. University Cheikh Anta Diop, Dakar.

Thilmans, G., and Ravisé, A. (1980). *Protohistoire du Sénégal. Recherches archéologiques. Tome 2, Sincu Bara et les sites du Fleuve*. Mémoires de l'Institut Fondamental d'Afrique Noire, No. 91.

Thompson, M. (1990). Colonial Policy and the Family Life of Black Troops in French West Africa, 1817–1904. *International Journal of African Historical Studies* **23** (3): 423–53.

Thompson, M. (1992). When the Fires Are Lit: The French Navy's Recruitment and Training of Senegalese Mechanics and Stokers, 1864–1887. *Canadian Journal of African Studies* **26** (2): 274–303.

Thornton, J. (1992). *Africa and Africans in the Making of the Atlantic World, 1400–1680*. Cambridge University Press, Cambridge.

Traoré, S. (1987). Le Système foncier Soninké du Gajaaga. *Bakel Discussion Paper Series*, No. 4F. Land Tenure Center, University of Wisconsin, Madison.

Trigger, B. G. (1981). Archaeology and the Ethnographic Present. *Anthropologica* **23**: 3–17.

Trimingham, J. S. (1962). *A History of Islam in West Africa*. Oxford University Press, London.

Vernoll, M. (1859). Les Nouveaux Etablissements Français au Sénégal. *L'Illustration*.

Wallerstein, I. (1974). *The Modern World System: Capitalist Agriculture and the Origins of the European World Economy in the Sixteenth Century*. Academic Press, New York.

Webb, J. L. (1985). The Trade in Gum Arabic: Prelude to French Conquest in Senegal. *Journal of African History* **26**: 149–68.

Weigel, J. Y. (1982). *Migration et Production des Soninké du Sénégal*. Travaux et Documents de l'ORSTOM, No. 146. ORSTOM, Paris.

Wolf, E. (1982). *Europe and the Peoples without History*. University of California Press, Berkeley.

Wolf, E. (1984). Culture: Panacea or Problem? *American Antiquity* **49** (2): 393–400.

Wood, R. W. (1967). An Archaeological Appraisal of Early European Settlements in the Senegambia. *Journal of African History* **8** (1): 39–64.

3

Political Transformations and Cultural Landscapes in Senegambia during the Atlantic Era: An Alternative View from the Siin (Senegal)?

François Richard

INTRODUCTION: MINDING POLITICAL LANDSCAPES

Landscape perspectives have enjoyed meteoric popularity in the past twenty years in archaeology. While there are many reasons behind the archaeological turn to landscape (and while the latter is, indeed, not without precedents), the attractiveness of the concept partly rests on the fact that it provides a link between theory and data, mind and matter, past and present, and archaeological remains and the physical world in which they are embedded. Landscapes involve material settings and the ways in which they are experienced, perceived, and imagined by different social actors (cf. Lefèbvre 1991; Moore 2005; Smith 2003). These settings, however, are not just physical givens – mere stages on which humans move and act. Rather, landscapes are socially produced and rendered meaningful by the people who inhabit them. At the same time, while agents work to construct their landscapes, material worlds recursively act back to create the people who belong to them. Landscapes, then, materialize long, cross-cutting histories of social, political, economic, environmental, and semiotic relations; they are, to evoke Gosden and Head (1994:114–15), "both the locus of past action and the medium within which evidence of the past is preserved or destroyed."

This juxtaposition presents archaeologists with three enticing implications: (1) An engagement with landscapes can usefully assist historical reconstruction precisely because landscapes bear traces of the various processes that went into their creation; (2) Landscapes are not just assemblages of space, place, and practice – they compel attention to temporality. It is important to inscribe transformations at various points in longer histories of change, just as it is essential to situate archaeological analyses in the evolving landscape (milieu, politics, representations) of the present; and (3) Lastly, as a "concrete abstraction," which combines real-world referents and analytical remove, the landscape provides a powerful interface between archaeology's units of analysis (regional survey, sites, artifacts, etc.), the past cultural environments we seek to understand, and the historical agencies that shaped them.

In sum, it seems particularly apposite that archaeology openly welcomed the landscape concept in that it capitalizes on two of the discipline's most critical vantages – its attention to materiality and its grasp of multiscalarity (Marquardt 1992). These two dimensions seem particularly crucial to the study of the African past because they conjure qualities and levels of experience that often evade the scope of the documentary record and oral traditions – the empirical cornerstones for most of what we know of African history, especially during the Atlantic Era. Investigating African life through the lens of materiality can shed light on the constellation of object-oriented or spatial practices (consumption, production, exchange, subsistence, technology, residential logics, and political configuration) that mediated Africans' interactions with the broader world and variably transformed in response to changes in Atlantic circulations. These practices, incidentally, often receive sparse coverage in archival records, in which remarks often are confined to panoramic treatments of political and economic conditions near the coasts and along navigable rivers. Moreover, the kinds of social phenomena captured archaeologically seldom amount to discrete events, intentional actions, or conscious decisions, which generally are the province of documented history; rather, they represent the aggregated effects of these shorter-term processes and the longer-term dispositions that framed past courses of action, and were themselves reshaped in the entanglement with outside people, objects, and ideas (Dietler and Herbich 1998). Concurrently, archaeology's ability to plumb social and material expressions at a variety of scales, from the humble artifact to settlement systems and region-wide exchange networks, permits us to monitor how the effects of Atlantic forces might have been felt and negotiated on different planes of human experience. Rather than portraying Atlantic forces as a monolithic process equally impacting all aspects of African life, archaeology can show that change at one level of social relations did not necessarily entail similar changes at other scales, complicating the temporality, agency, and causality of global encounters in Africa.

As with other contributors in this volume, my objective is to use the lessons of landscape archaeology to complicate existing readings of Atlantic encounters in coastal Senegambia. Again, mirroring most chapters in this book, my interest lies particularly in the twinned questions of power and political architecture and using archaeological information to revisit their expressions in Atlantic-Era Senegal, with focus on the Siin polity. In this chapter, I engage with "politics" on two related fronts, in reference to (1) the (shifting) assemblage of institutions, structures, and practices involved in the making of governance, authority, and power relations in the past – in contexts in which history often privileges the deeds of elites and states, and (2) the legacies of the Atlantic past in contemporary narratives of the nation or, more specifically, how historical representations forged in the cauldron of global encounters have assisted the fashioning of difference and exclusion in present-day Senegal.

In the course of this chapter, I use archaeological information to shed alternative light on past politics to rethink the position of marginalized groups in the political arena of Senegal. With regard to the former, the chapter draws inspiration from recent scholarly attention to the distinctive cultural logic animating African modes of power (S. K. McIntosh 1999; Monroe and Ogundiran, this volume) to examine how elites and nonelites took part in the construction of state authority and how the material properties of the Siin social world may have partly constrained the operation of governance in the region (cf. R. J. McIntosh 2005). In this sense, this chapter seeks to present political landscapes once described as state dominated and hermetically centralized in a more ambiguous light – or in a more "fragmented" state, as the editors propose in their introduction. The internal dynamism emerging from the analysis seems to challenge popular perceptions of the Siin (and its historical residents) as a backwater mired in pristine, age-old tradition and aversion to change. Instead, the province and its dominant ethnic population, the Serer, can be moved from the historical backseat to which they have been consigned and recuperated as bona fide actors in and contributors to regional history, who can, in turn, reclaim a legitimate place in the space of Senegal's political modernity.

Finally, this chapter also is indebted to developments in the archaeological literature of Senegal, which, for some years now, has certainly been mindful of landscape, albeit more in its commitment to track archaeological and geoenvironmental expressions at multiple scales and over the long term (e.g., S. K. McIntosh and R. J. McIntosh 1993) than in an explicit concern with landscape as conceptual framework. Drawing on this tradition of region-wide research, recent archaeological work in Senegal has mounted an appreciative critique of earlier historical scholarship (S. K. McIntosh 2001; see Richard 2009 for a review), driven by the pursuit of "small narratives" that relentlessly supplement the "master narratives" of the nation – in other words, the sidelined material histories of underrepresented groups (ethnic and religious minorities, slaves, women) and geographic peripheries that simultaneously undermine the certitudes of canonical history while forming the necessary underside to the making of Senegal's past, present, and future.

ATLANTIC TURBULENCES AND SENEGAMBIAN HISTORY

The past 500 years mark a turbulent period in the political–economic history of Senegambia, one defined by the collapse and emergence of regional polities, the lures of the Atlantic trade, gradual immersion into the world economy, Islamic revolutions, and incorporation into colonial empires. This period, traditionally, has been examined through the lens of large coastal or riverine polities deeply enmeshed with oceanic commerce and historically well documented, such as the Wolof kingdoms of Waalo and Kajoor, the Soninke state of Gajaaga in Senegal, or the Mandinka polities lining the Gambia River (Barry 1972; Bathily 1989; Becker and Martin 1975; Klein 1977; Wright 1997). Sifting through European accounts and oral traditions, historians have written compellingly about the disruptive effects of Atlantic and colonial interactions on local African societies caught in a spiral of social disintegration, chronic warfare, slave raiding, political upheavals, and ecological crises (Becker 1986). The eighteenth and nineteenth centuries are often viewed as corresponding with the ascendance of strong, predatory kingdoms – feasting on peasant populations, growing rich from the proceeds of the slave trade, yet increasingly dependent on foreign commodities for their reproduction (Klein 1992). In this light, some of the scholarly literature has equated Atlantic contacts with Senegambia's irreversible economic dependency on the outside and its crumbling political autonomy, underdevelopment, and loss of historical agency (e.g., Barry 1998; Curtin 1975; Rodney 1982; Searing 1993).

Against this broad historical backdrop, it is nevertheless possible to discern a more nuanced picture of Atlantic encounters by looking at the experiences of smaller polities that played a secondary role in oceanic transactions. One such more distant participant was the coastal kingdom of Siin in Senegal, which witnessed firsthand the momentous changes that reshaped the political geography of the region. Once a vibrant frontier on the margins of Sahelian empires and powerful regional states (Figures 3.1, 3.2), the Siin appears to have oscillated between a variety of political arrangements throughout its history, from loosely integrated village communities to centralized polity (Galvan 2004; Gravrand 1983). Oral traditions are rife with narratives of sweeping population movements, tracing the

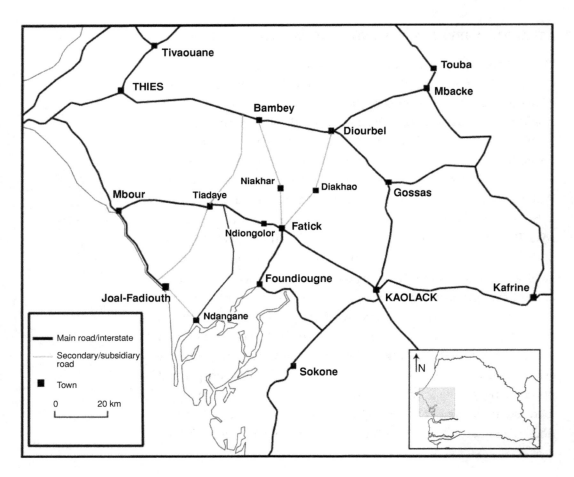

Figure 3.1
The Siin-Saalum region of Senegal.

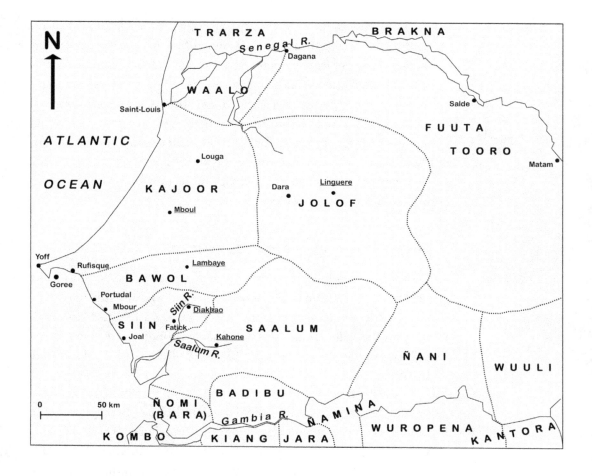

Figure 3.2
Precolonial kingdoms of northern Senegambia (c. 1850s).

kingdom's origin to Mandinka migrations in the mid-fourteenth century (e.g., N. Diouf 1972; Sarr 1986–1987). From the 1450s onwards, historic accounts pick up the storyline and depict the Siin as a modest participant in Atlantic commerce but one increasingly affected by the region's deteriorating political climate and dependence on imported goods (e.g., Klein 1992; Mbodj 1978). By the nineteenth century, this corpus of documents grows into a rich, if uneven, database for studying the local impact of the colonial conquest or probing the more distant past (Klein 1968, 1979).

Although rich in cultural detail, oral and documentary narratives afford a portrait of local histories painted only in the broadest of strokes. Oral traditions are frequently obscured by uncertain chronologies, factual license, and stylized presentations of the past (Henige 1974, 1982; Lentz 1994, 2000; but see Barber 1991; Baum 1999; Schmidt 2006; Shaw 2002). Oral memory tends to gloss the complexities of historical change and process behind a façade of

84

POLITICAL
TRANSFORMATIONS
AND CULTURAL
LANDSCAPES IN
SENEGAMBIA
DURING THE
ATLANTIC ERA

sweeping population movements (Wright 1985). Although textual sources are more specific on the timing of events and processes, the settings they depict were perceived through the filter of cultural distance and can only be known reliably for the European trading posts and their close perimeter (Becker 1985, 1987). Collectively, existing sources shed meager light on precolonial social structures and political trajectories, especially for the more remote past. They leave the dynamics of population encounters and cultural contact unspecified, and they offer a very spotty coverage of the impact of outside forces on the cultural fabrics of local societies.

WRITING THE SIIN FROM THE MARGINS OF HISTORY

Despite its seemingly dynamic history, curiously, the Siin has been portrayed as a cultural backwoods, moored to a timeless past and shackled to the rock of custom. This historical discourse has roots deep in the colonial imaginary. Very early on, indeed, Siin's Serer people came to be seen as primitive agriculturalists barely touched by contacts with the outside (Boilat 1853; Galvan 2004:33–71).

In 1879, two years after the creation of the Siin protectorate, amateur ethnologist and colonial administrator Bérenger-Féraud described local rural villagers in the following terms: "The Sérères are peaceful, [they] live off the soil to which they are extremely attached," and have little "taste for migration," before concluding that their "lack of industry failed to trigger sustained relations with the outside" (Bérenger-Féraud 1879:279, 274). Unlike the French political reports and correspondence of the 1860s, which had focused on the alcoholism, degeneracy, and tyranny of the local political elite, military pacification now afforded a picture of Siin painted in the colors of reified tradition, trapped between the twin poles of social conservatism and cultural isolationism. It is in the crucible of France's colonial racial imagination, in effect, that subsequent images of the Siin and Serer populations congealed. The myth of the "typical peasant," held back by the burden of traditions, became one of the cornerstones of the colonial reflection on the Serer. This view is echoed by Aujas, who in 1931 wrote that "[d]espite the blending, unions, alliances with neighboring tribes, the Serer constitutes today for the foreign observer a very primitive individuality which has jealously retained its customs, beliefs, language, and religion. He did not let civilization cut into him a lot. His local evolution itself has varied little throughout the centuries. There is then in him a type of humanity whose originality is undeniable" (Aujas 1931:293–94). Two years later, Geismar (1933:23) branded the Serer as the "very model of the Black peasant." Senegal's "colonial library" abounds with such references (e.g., Bourgeau 1933; Carlus 1880; Corre 1883; Dulphy 1939).

These perceptions, however, did not stop at the colonial offices in Dakar or Saint-Louis. Indeed, the colonial discourse on the Serer continued to frame subsequent writings on the region well into the postindependence period. Thus, they recur with surprising resonance in Paul Pélissier's monumental and authoritative study of Senegalese agrarian societies, which describes precolonial Siin as "the very model of egalitarian and anarchic peasantry" (Pélissier 1966:198). Linking past and present, he conjures up nostalgic evocations of a people wedded to land and cattle, industrious, respectful of the environment, fearful of the ancestors and earth spirits, tradition bound, culturally conservative, adverse to change and movement, and so forth. This remarkable "geographic patriotism" is praised as the natural expression of "a society which up to now has derived its strength and persistence from its fidelity to the past, from an essentially defensive political organization, from eminently conservative social structures" (Pélissier 1966:224).

These views are problematic on several levels, of course, if only for their flickering attention to the play of history, power, and discourse in the fashioning of colonial identities and the African past. And yet, the notion of "generic peasant" cannot be easily dismissed, insofar as it has broadly set the terms in which Siin's history has been interpreted, from colonial reports to the ethnographic and geographic work conducted in the decades following independence. Pélissier's views on rural Africa have been critical in this regard, both in providing a juncture with colonial perspectives and in influencing the development of later research on Siin's economy and society. Subsequent cultural geographers have drawn a sharp line between the precolonial era and its immobile institutions, and the post-peanut era, roughly the late nineteenth century, which in essence brought the Siin within the stream of history, world economy, and modernity (e.g., Dupire et al. 1974; Gastellu 1975). To be sure, some historians have been more sensitive to historical dynamism in the Serer past, drawing from oral traditions and written documents to trace deep-time population movements and recent political history (e.g., Klein 1968, 1992; cf. Galvan 2004). Yet, they have also stressed that

POLITICAL
TRANSFORMATIONS
AND CULTURAL
LANDSCAPES IN
SENEGAMBIA
DURING THE
ATLANTIC ERA

Siin's moderate involvement in the slave trade largely sheltered Serer populations from the rampant instability experienced by neighboring polities. In doing so, they have tended to map *political* changes against a rather placid *cultural* background, left relatively unmoved for centuries before colonial contact. In tacit ways, culture – the stuff of tradition – is accepted as a conservative force that endures through time and precedes politics – the stuff of history, motion, and change (see Dirks 1996 for a related point).

Although often ostensibly couched in the longue durée and material processes, archaeological research should recognize the salience of social contexts in understanding the recent and more remote past. In this light, historical construction, discourse, power, and the social landscape ought to form a critical scaffold for any exploration of the African past (Comaroff and Comaroff 1992). Here, I follow the lead of recent scholarship, which has pleaded very cogently for the need to consider history as a *process* blending both reality and narration (Trouillot 1995; also Cooper 2005; Stahl 2001; Stahl et al. 2004). In the process of disentangling these threads, David Cohen (1994:xxii) urges us to examine what he calls the "folds and the layers of [historical] production that join the past and the present" – the making of historical memories, the contradictions between different models of the past, the discordant voices, the silences of history, and the broader discourses framing the whole (Moore and Roberts 1990).

The image of the typical peasant – with its implications of social stubbornness and stagnancy – has had a complex "social life." The concept has combined and recombined with a variety of parallel discourses, keeping or losing some of its elements, but leaving a distinct imprint on the production of Serer history and the experiences of contemporary populations. Assumptions of the Serer peasant, pagan and backward looking, have trickled into popular consciousness. The trope has also framed how the region has been incorporated into national narratives and pushed to the marginalia of Senegal's history and modernity. Today, one finds a palpable sense of malaise across the Serer countryside with regard to its position in the national community – the feeling of being left out of state programs, a sentiment of marginalization and discrimination, and a sense of disempowerment when it comes to controlling local history (Faye 2003). These concerns can be seen as structural offshoots of what Momar-Coumba Diop and Mamadou Diouf (1990:46–47) have called the Islamo–Wolof model. The model refers to the long-term processes of political peripheralization and cultural exclusion that have shaped Senegal's social landscape since the opening of the Atlantic frontier.

Over the past 500 years, Senegal's interactions with the world economy have increasingly privileged coastal areas dominated by Wolof populations, which have become the uncontested political–economic hub of the country and the center of gravity of national sensibilities. These material processes have been articulated and legitimated in a broader discourse, which accords a preponderant place for Islam, the Wolof language, urban lifestyle, and the Wolof way of life in the national imagination, while downplaying the importance of the pre-Muslim past, non-Wolof groups, and rural settings in national narratives. As a result, culturally and economically stigmatized groups like the Serer of Siin, or the Joola of Casamance, have been increasingly estranged from Senegal's imagined community. Another consequence has been the rewriting of the country's recent history as a tale of Wolof and Muslim achievements, focusing on the resistance to the forces of colonialism (M. Diouf 1990), a process amply assisted by state cultural politics in the post-independence era (Thioub 2002). In this narrative, the Serer and other peoples serve as a ready-made foil for the historic élan and success of Wolof populations, occupying what Michel-Rolph Trouillot (2003:7–28) names the "savage slot" in Senegal's national ethnic imagination.[1]

In his recent examination of Senegal's history, Mamadou Diouf (2001:9–10) urges us to offset accounts of the Islamo–Wolof past with alternative visions of history produced and experienced at the periphery of Wolof hegemony. He makes the valid point that Senegal's past is an ensemble of pluralities sharing a common field of historical experience; as such, it cannot be captured adequately without reference to the past of its peripheries, which were integral parts of the process of history. As spaces where social processes often are in a state of *becoming* (and thus acquire particular salience), margins, frontiers, peripheries, and interstitial settings provide alternative windows into regional trajectories. Juxtaposed over broader patterns, these settings reveal unseen textures and variability in historical experience and expose silences that haunt historical discourse, while stressing that different peoples are part of a common history and geography of exchanges.

This is one such alternative history that I propose to explore in the rest of this chapter, an alternative that navigates between archaeology and history, between experience and representation, and between the past and present to retrieve the distinctive qualities of Siin's past without losing sight of its inscription within the broader stream of Senegambian history. Because of its ability to confront material culture with more "logocentric" lines of evidence (Stahl 2002), archaeology is well positioned to expose the contradictions between *lived* history and historical *representations* (Trouillot 1995), thus promising fresh understandings of the past (Pauketat and DiPaolo Loren 2005; Schmidt 2006; Schmidt and Patterson 1995). Recent work has shed increasing light into Africa's past by revisiting established historical scenarios and expanding our understanding of political economy, trajectories of complexity, and social variability across the continent (DeCorse 2001; Ogundiran 2001; Ogundiran and Falola 2007; Stahl 2001, 2002, 2005).

In many respects, Siin is an ideal case study for investigating these issues because it provides a number of epistemic vantages into the Senegambian past: (1) The region appears to have exhibited a broad range of political forms – spanning the heterarchy–hierarchy spectrum during its history; (2) It was embedded in different scales of economic and social networks; and (3) It is described as a political frontier in the pre-Atlantic Era and remained an influential, if secondary, player in Atlantic exchanges. These characteristics clearly resonate with recent anthropological advocacy for grappling with complexity through the more de-centered angle of rural hinterlands and political peripheries (Amselle 1998; Kopytoff 1987; LaViolette and Fleisher 2005; MacEachern 2005; Schwartz and Falconer 1994; Stahl 2001; Stein 2002), a trend also emergent in Senegambian history (Baum 1999; Hawthorne 2003; Klein 2001; Linares 1987; Searing 2002). These characteristics are also consistent with the broader project to re-think African political change outside of the canons of evolutionist thought, in a light attentive to history, political economy, landscape, and alternative social logic.[2] In other words, the region shows clear potential for illuminating the diversity and broader contours of historical developments on this stretch of the African coast.

THE SIIN LANDSCAPE ARCHAEOLOGY PROJECT: METHOD AND EVIDENTIAL ARCHIVES

Recent archaeological research conducted in Siin in 2003 and 2004 offers independent evidence for assessing conventional historical scenarios of complexity (Richard 2007). Initial results from regional survey, excavations, and extensive archival work provide a suggestive *entrée* into different scales of social and material existence that can be brought to bear on questions of historical experience. Research was framed in broad geographic terms, a strategy motivated by the need to develop an initial archaeological database for the region,which could guide subsequent research and be revised by the acquisition of new data and perspectives.

The large-scale survey was designed to retrieve surface information on settlement patterns and archaeological variability across the region (Figure 3.3). Three 200-km^2 survey zones were defined around the villages of Fatick, Diakhao, and Mbissel, which oral and documentary traditions associate with political formation and commercial activity. A 6 percent sample was drawn from each survey region and examined in full through a pedestrian survey. Over 180 sites or loci were identified and surface-collected, which exhibited a diverse array of assemblages, ranging from late Neolithic materials to recent historic and contemporary deposits. Sites also showed considerable size variation, from single finds and thinly spread surface scatters to large site complexes and areas of densely interconnected deposits covering several hectares. Several classes of sites were identified, the majority of which were habitation sites, characterized by widespread surface scatters of cultural materials and mound accumulations varying in size, number, and density. Survey material was complemented by limited excavations at seven locales, spanning the past two millennia. Although modest in scale, excavations were aimed at retrieving clues about settlement chronology (which is difficult to access through surface archaeological evidence), landscape history, as well as village life and cultural economy.

The final research component included the examination of available archival collections. This work aimed at gaining a clearer understanding of historical dynamics in the precolonial and colonial Siin, diversifying the repertoire of evidence and creating an ethnographic baseline to compare archaeological patterns. Extensive original research was conducted in the Archives Nationales du Sénégal (ANS) in Dakar and the Archives Françaises d'Outre-Mer (ANF) in Aix-en-Provence. This work focused largely on political, commercial, and military reports covering the 1850–1900 period and on original company records, letters, travel accounts, and correspondence spanning the late seventeenth through the early nineteenth centuries. Prior to the 1860s, these documents tend to focus on commercial transactions (with some references to political intrigues and conflict between the coastal kingdoms), but they provide rather anemic descriptions of cultural practices. While preliminary, these archaeological baselines can be used to examine the impact of Atlantic entanglements on past political economy in Siin. Archaeological signatures offer proxy measures of change in past cultural and spatial fabrics, providing an empirical ground for interrogating the course and forces of Siin's social history over the past 500 years. In tandem with other lines of evidence, the material record promises to contribute critical readings of long-term political dynamics in Senegambia and finer insights into Siin's historical encounter with global forces.

ATLANTIC TRANSFORMATIONS: SETTLEMENT LANDSCAPES AND POLITICAL ECONOMY IN SIIN (1400–1900)

Survey evidence suggests relative stability in Iron Age occupations during the few centuries that preceded the Atlantic Era (c. 600–1400 A.D.) (Figure 3.4). Siin's coastal façade seems to have supported the bulk of human occupations, although we see the emergence of a few hamlets and smaller sites in the interior, particularly along dessicated tidal channels and the low-rising plateau overlooking the dried-out bed of the erstwhile Siin River. Aside from a handful of large coastal sites, the picture is one of a dispersed habitat made up of small-scale, shifting communities leaving relatively impermanent traces in the landscape and no significant long-term accumulation (S. K. McIntosh and R. J. McIntosh 1993). While the region was connected to the Saharan economy (Garenne-Marot 1993; Thilmans et al. 1980), material assemblages are conservative and relatively homogeneous across the sites. They show some trade in regional ceramics and marine resources (e.g., Fernandes 1951) but little evidence of long-distance exchanges (e.g., Almada 1984; Brooks 1993; Cadamosto 1937 [1456]).

Following the advent of oceanic contact, settlements underwent a clear shift manifested by a sharp decline in human densities along the Petite Côte, yet village remains are present in the vicinity of Joal, Siin's principal trading post during the Atlantic Era (Figures 3.5, 3.6). Concurrently, the social habitat seems to have been reoriented towards a new sphere of interaction centered on the Siin heartland. Interior areas witnessed a demographic explosion, perhaps in

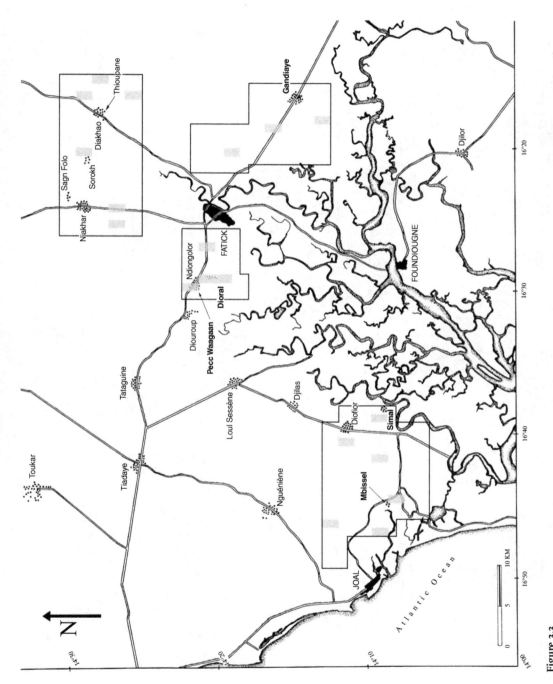

Figure 3.3
Siin Landscape Archaeology Project: 2003 fieldwork. The polygons represent survey regions; the grey rectangles refer to survey quadrats; the place names in bold typeface indicate excavated sites.

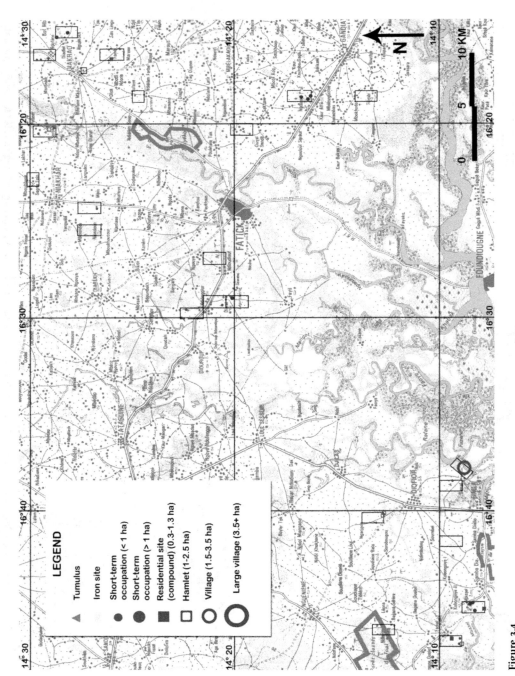

Figure 3-4
Siin settlement map (mid-first to mid-second millennium A.D.).

ATLANTIC
TRANSFORMATIONS:
SETTLEMENT
LANDSCAPES AND
POLITICAL ECONOMY
IN SIIN (1400–1900)

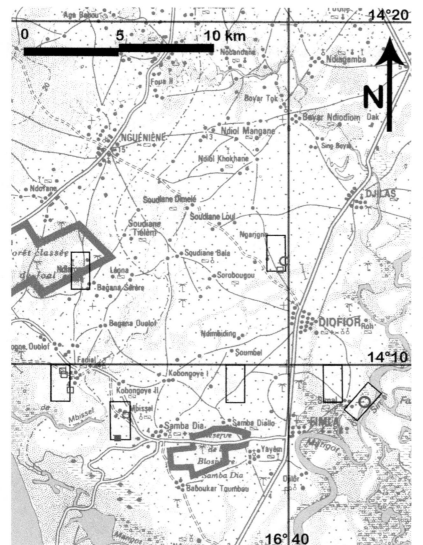

Figure 3.5
Petite Côte: Settlement map, ca. fifteenth (?) to seventeenth century. Legend follows that of Figure 3.4, namely dot (short-term occupation); solid square (residential site, probably compound size); empty square (hamlet); circle (village). The size of the symbols is commensurate with actual site size.

relation to the organization of the Siin kingdom and the growth of the Atlantic slave trade. Oral traditions associate this period with a wave of demographic shifts that accompanied the migration of the kingdom's political center towards the interior after the fifteenth century, when Diakhao became the capital (e.g., Becker and Mbodj 1999; Diouf 1972). At the same time, no major urban center or rigid settlement hierarchies stand out from the archaeological landscape. The few European testimonies we have on the capitals of coastal kingdoms lend support to this picture because they describe small villages that departed from neighboring settlements only in their

POLITICAL
TRANSFORMATIONS
AND CULTURAL
LANDSCAPES IN
SENEGAMBIA
DURING THE
ATLANTIC ERA

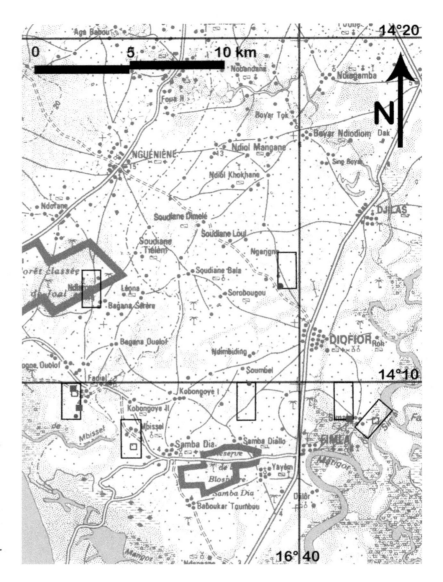

Figure 3.6
Petite Côte: Settlement map (eighteenth to nineteenth century).

more defensive and partitioned internal organization (Boilat 1984 [1853]:143–45; Cadamosto 1937 [1456]; Desmenager 1766; Diouf 1879:349; Durand 1802:56; de Repentigny 1785 and Sauvigny 1822, in Marty (n.d.):11–12, 43–44; Mollien 1967 [1818]:40–2; Noirot 1890).

Settlement organization in Siin experienced another change during the eighteenth century. Between 1500 and the early 1700s, sites on average were larger, more concentrated, and occupied for longer periods of time. Although the eighteenth century brought another demographic increase, habitations normally were smaller and formed

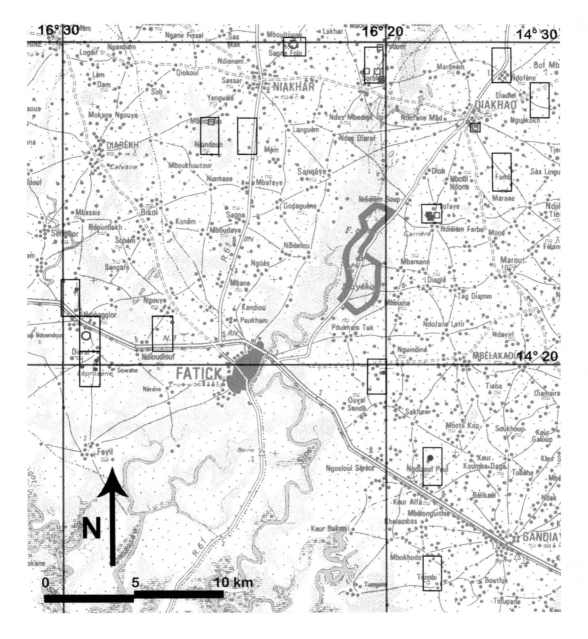

Figure 3.7
Siin interior (Fatick and Diakhao): Settlement map, c. fifteenth (?) to seventeenth century.

a more dispersed landscape (Figures 3.7, 3.8). This subtle change may have coincided with the intensification of Atlantic exchanges, a period generally portrayed in European accounts as struck by famines, rising military conflict, and subsistence crises. The European correspondence between Gorée and Joal suggests frequent conflicts and skirmishes between Siin and its powerful neighbor in Kajoor and alludes to frequent but low-intensity military violence along border villages (Clarkson 1789, in Thèsée 1988; Dapper 1971:541; Labat 1728:4:243; Lamiral 1789; Loyer 1714:134–35). Exactions by slave warriors on farming communities also appear to have intensified, particularly during the nineteenth century (Boilat 1853).[3]

The constellated spatial arrangement could reflect responses to the escalation of instability, in particular a move away from border areas exposed to political conflict and towards the more insulated center. Small-scale skirmishes appear to have been frequent on political frontiers, turning interstitial areas into desolate no-man's lands marking fluctuating borders between the warring kingdoms (Doumet 1974:60–61; Mateo de Anguiano 1646–1647, in de Moraes 1995:352; de Sainct-Lô 1637). The virtual absence of surface archaeological evidence from fringe areas examined during the survey seems to support documentary mentions. Archaeological patterns of disaggregation seem to indicate that new settlements splintered away from earlier villages and resettled a short distance away. The larger habitation sites of the fifteenth and sixteenth century may have represented obvious targets for raidings; spatial dispersal may have offered a viable defensive strategy or may have been a product of the rising political economy of violence.

This pattern stands in sharp contrast to previous arguments that the rise of the Atlantic slave trade caused massive depopulation and site abandonment in coastal kingdoms (Diop 1997, 2000). Instead, we observe a demographic increase involving smaller, hamlet-sized sites, a pattern documented archaeologically in the Falemme region of Senegal (Thiaw 1999). Also striking is the near absence of overt signs of militarization, such as gunflints or fortified sites, while these frequently turn up in neighboring regions (Lawson 2003; Thiaw 1999). Although the presence or absence of evidence offers meager insight into the materialization of violence, it is tempting to see this trend as supporting the suggestion that political instability in Siin never approached the disruptive proportions reached in neighboring polities (Barry 1998:88; Klein 1968:26).

More interestingly, these changes in settlement landscape suggest that the dispersed habitat, which reminded one colonial observer of the "immense *communes* [municipalities] rounding up an infinity of minuscule hamlets, not to mention isolated habitations, that one still encounters in many parts of France" (Reynier 1933:2–3) and which is believed to be an intrinsic long-term feature of Serer cultural repertoires, may actually be a fairly recent phenomenon associated with

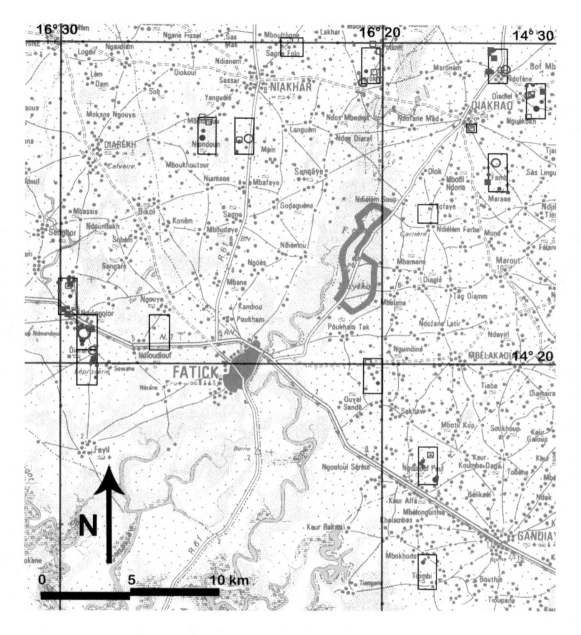

political degradation and social violence (Anonymous 1936:9; Noirot 1892:168; Rousseau 1928:38–39). By extension, it is quite possible that other features of the Serer social landscape long thought to be "traditional" – the system of land tenure, agro-pastoral management, or residential mobility expressed in the documented practice of moving to a new piece of lineage-controlled land when the soils under cultivation became exhausted (Guigou 1992) – took shape during this period.

Figure 3.8
Siin interior (Fatick and Diakhao): Settlement map (eighteenth to nineteenth century).

Settlement transformations also appear to reflect changes in social organization. The new habitation sites largely gravitate towards the orbit of political centers at Ndiongolor and Diakhao and could represent small satellite settlements associated with retainers and craft specialists working for the monarchy (M. Faye 2002:48–75). These spatial reconfigurations can be read in part as material echoes of an increasing concentration of authority and power in the hands of the monarch documented by contemporary observers (Doumet 1974; Le Brasseur 1776). More broadly, however, material landscapes present few if any signatures of political centralization, spatial hierarchy, or strategies of economic accumulation. Indeed, the maintenance of a scattered, relatively undifferentiated rural habitat, with consistent artifact inventories across the region, invokes the possibility that a more subtle power arrangement might have been at play.

Similar ambiguity arises from documentary records in the form of an uneasy dialogue between the hints and passing mentions given by traders and coastal visitors and the narratives espoused in official correspondence. There, we can discern a more nuanced picture involving variations in political power, with central authority contracting or expanding depending on the individual king's age, ability, kin relations, social networks, and political alliances. Historically, royal armies appear to have kept relatively firm control over the hinterland, but villagers along the Petite Côte seem to have enjoyed a greater degree of autonomy at various periods in time. In the mid-fifteenth century, for instance, Cadamosto (1937:54–55) observed that the Siin possessed no formal structure of government – a puzzling admission to many historians, since the Siin kingdom supposedly had been in existence for at least a century. Similar allusions to the sovereignty of coastal populations intermittently recur in European writings (Golberry 1802:2:111; Paris 1976:25), culminating in Aumont's description in 1850 of Joal as an independent republic on the eve of colonial penetration (Aumont 1850). By contrast, other accounts portray local monarchs as strong, centralizing figures holding a tight grip over the whole kingdom (Barbot 1992; Dapper 1971:533, 541;) and whose most faithful and docile subjects were the very coastal populations that appear so rebellious in other descriptions (Demanet 1767:111).

This cycling between control and autonomy seems to suggest a fundamental dynamism built into the cultural logic of the Siin state

(Richard 2007: chap. 6 and 10). The juxtaposition of an ideology of centralized rule at the regional level over a more dispersed authority at the local level created a certain imbalance in political power in which concentration and decentralization were at once mutually reinforcing, integrative, and destabilizing. The changing configuration of events and political economic conjectures could tilt the system either one way or the other while reshaping the conditions of power and autonomy of the state in the process.

The endurance of a relatively unstratified village landscape throughout the Atlantic Era could indicate that royal power did, indeed, work through, or parallel to, local social structures and spatial forms, even as monarchies and their enslaved warriors were becoming more consolidated and politically centralized. However, because Siin's settlement patterns lend themselves to a variety of possible interpretations, more robust material correlates are needed to pin down convincingly the dynamics and anatomies of political power during the Atlantic Era and define their enmeshment with past social landscapes (e.g., Smith 2003).

The limited diversity in trade imports and the homogeneity in material distributions during this period perhaps suggest Siin's ancillary position in European commercial circuits and regional trading networks, though the concrete traces of certain pivotal items of exchange (cloth, gunpowder, paper) unfortunately remain beyond archaeological reach. Regional distribution of spindle whorls appears to show some specialization of activities, particularly as these concentrate in "satellite" villages surrounding former capitals or in coastal settlements. A number of early documentary references signal that local cloth may have embodied forms of social differentiation in the seventeenth century (Barbot 1992:85; De Marees 1602, in de Moraes 1993:54; Fr. Gaspar de Sevilla 1647, in de Moraes 1995:363; Villault de Bellefond 1666–1671, in Thilmans and de Moraes 1976), raising the possibility that ideas of social distinction in Siin were reframed by the introduction of imported textiles (Hendrickson 1996; Stahl 2001). Regional variation in classes of prestige items may indicate uneven access to trade imports and differentiated consumption patterns – certain objects tend to turn up in political centers or land concessions controlled by ruling classes, though they never do so exclusively. Higher concentrations of toiletry and cosmetic glass were found in the surface and in excavated assemblages of two aristocratic residences (Thioupane and Pecc Waagaan), for instance, and these

POLITICAL
TRANSFORMATIONS
AND CULTURAL
LANDSCAPES IN
SENEGAMBIA
DURING THE
ATLANTIC ERA

sites also revealed a much richer variety and quantity of beads and European ceramics.

Overall, however, the same objects – beads, glass, and tobacco pipes – largely turn up on sites across the region, and no major disparities in wealth emerge in the regional settlement system. A letter by Le Brasseur (1776) suggests one possible reason for this homogeneity, namely the opening of commodity circuits to peasants and commoners. He observed, "Almost all the women on the continent have obtained [the right] to sell millet, so they could request that the [trading] assortment contain all the baubles that they need. Have we ever traded such large quantity of millet without being obliged to give in exchange all the necessary merchandise?" (Le Brasseur 1776). Earlier European descriptions of women villagers' bead paraphernalia hint that the sphere of Atlantic commodities was not a de facto royal monopoly but also could encompass Serer commoners (see DeCorse et al. 2003:79–80). The congruence of documentary and material patterns lends credence to Searing's (1993:90) suggestion that Senegambia's engagement with the Atlantic economy was structured by a "dual seller's market, one dominated by consumption goods valued by the peasants, the other by aristocratic prestige goods." French trading posts relied heavily on coastal kingdoms for provisioning, an economic domain that remained in peasants' control and lay beyond royal regulation (Desmenager 1765; Dubellay 1723, 1724; Le Brasseur 1776; Searing 1988). While the realities of political violence in the eighteenth and nineteenth century are inescapable, the convertibility between peasant goods and foodstuffs and commodities acquired through the sale of slaves ensured the widespread circulation of trade imports in the local economies and the participation of peasants in external exchange on an unprecedented scale (Klein 1992; Mbodj 1978).

The threat posed by the creation of new consumer markets to traditional spheres of sumptuary consumption may have prompted uneven patterns of response on the part of notables and other elites. One such strategy may have involved the political manipulation of imported objects to reshape and retrench old spheres of social distinction. It is interesting to note that the bulk of the bottle glass assemblage (close to 80%) in Siin consists of fragments of gin and brandy bottles (*alcool de traite*), which are found in great numbers all over the region. Excavations at Pecc Waagaan, an early capital which apparently was reused periodically as such over the centuries (Almada 1984; Diouf 1972), stumbled upon a feasting pit that contained a large glass assemblage. Unlike the expected high numbers of gin and liquor bottles, the pit yielded a majority of wine bottles, which are associated directly with aristocratic practices of conspicuous consumption. Perhaps we can see here an instance of "diacritical feasting" (Dietler 2001), in which the display and consumption of selected valuables serve to mark and refashion social distance (Lesure 1999; Stahl 2002). It is possible that as local access to Atlantic circuits became more porous and less circumscribed, political elites gradually appropriated wine as an emblem of distinction, publicly singling out elite consumption practices from those of commoners (see also Dietler 1990; Hamilakis 1999).

This being said, European trade goods (e.g., bottle glass and ceramics) do not become a significant material presence until the second half of the eighteenth century and more generally during the nineteenth century – which raises questions regarding the extent and timing of European impact on local cultural practices (Thiaw 2003). This suggests that local societies retained considerable initiative during that period and remained relatively peripheral to the Atlantic economy. Tobacco pipes combine local forms and the red-slipped, molded elbow bend pipes mass produced by the French in the late nineteenth century. Bead assemblages are dominated by Venetian beads and nineteenth-century Czech beads, but they also include a few local clay specimens. Glass is seen mostly in wine and gin bottles, joined in the 1870s by *alcool de menthe* flacons and mineral-water bottles.

We should be careful, however, not to homogenize the influence of Atlantic processes on local regimes of production, exchange, and consumption. Different classes of artifact in Siin have different social histories (Appadurai 1986; Myers 2001) entailing different entanglements with various spheres of domestic and political economies (Richard 2010; Thomas 1991). Here again, homogeneity at one scale may conceal finer nuances at more intimate levels of existence, affording partial glimpses of the manifold trajectories intentionally or accidentally caught in the ambit of Atlantic history.

It is only in the late nineteenth century that colonial imposition truly began to be felt in local consumption patterns and the restructuring of social space towards French commercial outposts (Galvan 2004; Guigou 1992). For instance, we note a palpable increase of post-1870s deposits in the Fatick region, which seems to support isolated archival references to rural migrations as the town became an important colonial commercial crossroads in the last quarter of the nineteenth century (Rabourdin 1888a, 1888b; "Letter . . . to the Governor" 1889). However, even in the second half of the nineteenth century, European ceramics remain few in number and are generally limited to utilitarian earthenwares or stonewares and white-bodied earthenware plate fragments. By contrast, the sheer abundance of liquor bottles recovered during the survey offers a potent memento of the role of alcohol in processes of Atlantic and colonial entanglements (cf. Dietler 2006:237–41; Dietler and Herbich 2001) and provides undeniable support for the portrait of the rampant alcoholism that eighteenth- and nineteenth-century documents paint for the region.

"ROOTED IN THE SOIL": MAKING ALTERNATIVE HISTORIES OF SENEGAMBIA'S PAST?

My first visit to the Siin in May 2001 highlighted very salient issues in the production of local history. Upon our arrival in Diakhao (the former capital), we were greeted with undisguised animosity by one of the village elders who was defiantly brandishing an old issue of Senegal's iconic scholarly journal, the *Bulletin de l'IFAN*. With fiery animus, the man launched into a passionate condemnation of "those" historians who practice history from the comfort of their urban offices without ever setting foot in the regions whose past they purport to study. Siin's real past, he contended, did not flow from the pens of Dakar academics; instead, it was "rooted in the soil" and declaimed by the sons of the land and heirs of tradition.[4] We defused the tension by mentioning that we were interested in the more remote past, before the Gelwaar royals, and managed to walk away from the confrontation.

Many other anecdotes could be parsed out from memory that provide many illustrations of the intersection of past and present in the making of Siin's past and the layers of power plays framing this process. All, however, would be linked by the same underlying message – the salience of the past in the present and the role of the landscape as the contested terrain where this dialectic plays itself out (Bender 2002; Dietler 1994; Shackel 2003). Designed as a short reconnaissance, my initial visit to the Siin transcended the requisite exposure to field conditions and archaeological remains. More unexpectedly, this trip and subsequent ones brought me face to face with the "underside" of Siin's history – its social context, politics, and hidden economy (Roseberry 1991:22). In this light, the ethnographic vignette we experienced condenses a number of critical themes in the making of Serer history.

First, local inhabitants, whatever their stations, often care deeply about their history. The past flashes in and out of sight in a variety of social contexts, giving shape and meaning to political interactions. Second, the production of history is not a democratic or an innocent business – it is a complex machinery of struggles over who owns and makes the past. Multiple versions compete, histories are reworked to suit the political moods du jour, and the geometry of power influences what is known of Siin's past and how it is told and remembered. Last, archaeological research is not immune to the play of political forces. As we set out to study the history of a landscape, we also become part of that landscape as subjects and architects caught in the web of social processes, power relations, and multiple levels of discourse framing the production of the past. Clearly, how history is made and remade matters a great deal. Material realities and historical discourses cannot be understood in isolation from each other.

I began this chapter with a brief excursus into the ideological architecture of historical discourse in Senegal, particularly as it has affected the perception of cultural minorities, such as those inhabiting the Siin. Scholars, unwillingly or not, have at times been complicit with these images and have relied on unquestioned assumptions in their narratives of the Serer past. These dynamics provide a powerful reminder that the past is a power-laden process blending reality and narration and that successful historical understanding must address the silences, mentions, and incongruities produced in the encounter between social experiences and representations (Hall 2000; Reid and Lane 2004; Schmidt 2006; Stahl 2001; Trouillot 1995, 2003).

The labor of African history is complicated by the partiality of sources and the ideological fields in which they were produced and used. Yet, as Jane Guyer recently reminded us (in Stahl 2004:258, 268), it is also haunted by the specter of those innumerable social strategies that fell prey to the process of "turbulence and loss" unleashed by the Atlantic trade. While a widening political economical field introduced new possibilities, it also foreclosed others and erased still more that have left no presence in the ethnographic or ethnohistoric records. Using preliminary information on settlements and artifacts from the Siin, I have tried to show that a landscape-minded archaeology can combine with more traditional sources to reveal alternative histories that can shed fresh light on local historicities and their linkages to regional and global political economic fields. Such research aims to promote fairer portrayals of the past that do justice to local historical expressions, or at least to those once-cardinal dispositions and tempos of change, social possibilities, and limitations embodied in material culture. It also encourages us to be accountable for the pasts we write and to be relevant in the present by being alert to how our writings are shaped by broader forces and how they impact our host communities.

While the nascent archaeological record of Siin raises many more questions than it answers, initial outcomes from the survey and excavations quickly dispel assumptions of direct continuities between the ethnographic past of the region and its more remote periods and help us ward off historical accounts written in the idiom of cultural inertia. At the same time, though there is indisputable evidence that the Atlantic Era ushered in a period of social turbulence, the archaeological record brings many shades of nuance to earlier scenarios of catastrophic devolution and political–economic subordination. More saliently, it underscores the need to recast our conventional assumptions of change and continuity in the African past – not as antinomial processes but as inseparable moments of a dialectic. Sometimes change serves the interests of stability and continuity, and aspirations of permanence or tradition can be powerful vehicles of transformation and hybridity (e.g., Pauketat 2001; Silliman 2005). Preliminary results point to tensions between and within our various archives and generate new questions and paths of inquiry. These considerations in turn can orient future research and guide our steps into more nuanced and complex visions of the African past, its political landscapes, and their entanglement with the broader world.

ACKNOWLEDGEMENTS

The research reported in this chapter received financial support from the Wenner-Gren Foundation, National Science Foundation, Syracuse University Graduate School, Maxwell School of Citizenship and Public Affairs, Patrick Moynihan Institute of Global Affairs, and Bremen Stiftung für Sozialanthropologie. The ideas presented here developed as part of my doctoral work, and I am indebted to Christopher DeCorse, Martin Klein, Doug Armstrong, and Theresa Singleton for their help and suggestions at various stages of the project. I also wish to thank J. Cameron Monroe and Akin Ogundiran for inviting me to contribute to this volume and the other participants for their comments. Naturally, I am responsible for the errors that may have escaped their careful scrutiny or those left in place by my own stubbornness. Final words of thanks must go to the team of students, led by Mor Faye, who expertly carried out the fieldwork, and to the friends, families, and municipalities in Dakar, Ndiongolor, Diakhao, Fatick, and Diofior that supported our stay in 2002–04.

BIBLIOGRAPHY

Almada, A. A. de (1984) [c. 1594]. *Brief Treatise on the Rivers of Guinea*. University of Liverpool, Liverpool.

Amselle, J.-L. (1998). *Mestizo Logics: Anthropology of Identity in Africa and Elsewhere*. Stanford University Press, Stanford, CA.

Anonymous (1936). Coutumes Sérères – Région du Sine. ANS, 1 G 26/104.

Appadurai, A., ed. (1986). *The Social Life of Things*. Cambridge University Press, New York.

Aujas, L. (1931). Les Sérères du Sénégal (moeurs et coutumes de droit privé). *Bulletin du Comité d'Études Historiques et Scientifiques de l'A.O.F.* **14**: 293–333.

Aumont, P. (1850). Report to the Governor, 10 October 1850. ANS, 13 G 23.

Barber, K. (1991). *I Could Speak Until Tomorrow: Oriki, Women, and the Past in a Yoruba Town*. Smithsonian Institution Press, Washington, DC.

Barbot, J. (1992). *Barbot on Guinea: The Writing of Jean Barbot on West Africa, 1678–1712*. Edited by P. Hair, A. Jones, and R. Law. Hakluyt Society, London.

Barry, B. (1972). *Le Royaume du Waalo: Le Sénégal Avant la Conquête*. Maspéro, Paris.

Barry, B. (1998). *Senegambia and the Atlantic Slave Trade*. Cambridge University Press, New York.

Bathily, A. (1989). *Les Portes de l'Or: Le Royaume de Galam (Sénégal) de l'Ère Musulmane au Temps des Négriers (VIIIe–XVIIIe Siècle)*. Éditions l'Harmattan, Paris.

Baum, R. (1999). *Shrines of the Slave Trade: Diola Religion and Society in Precolonial Senegambia*. Oxford University Press, New York.

Bayart, J.-F. (2006). *L'état en Afrique: La Politique du Ventre*. Fayard, Paris.

Becker, C. (1985). Histoire de la Sénégambie du XVe au XVIIIe siècle: Un bilan. *Cahiers d'Études Africaines* **25** (2): 213–42.

Becker, C. (1986). Conditions Écologiques, Crises de Subsistance et Histoire de la Population à l'époque de la Traite des Esclaves en Sénégambie (17e–18e siècle). *Canadian Journal of African Studies* **20** (3): 357–76.

Becker, C. (1987). Réflexions sur les Sources d'histoire de la Sénégambie. In Heintze, B., and Jones, A. (eds.), *European Sources for Sub-Saharan Africa Before 1900: Use and Abuse*. Frobenius-Institut E.V., Frankfurt, 147–65.

Becker, C., and Martin, V. (1975). Kayor et Baol: Royaumes sénégalais et traite des esclaves au XVIIIe siècle. *Revue Française d'Histoire d'Outre-Mer* **62**: 270–300.

Becker, C., and Mbodj, M. (1999). La Dynamique du Peuplement Sereer: Les Sereer du Sine. In Lericollais, A. (ed.), *Paysans Sereer: Dynamiques Agraires et Mobilités au Sénégal*, Éditions de l'IRD, Paris, 40–73.

Bender, B. (2002). Landscape and Time. *Current Anthropology* **43**: S103–S112.

Bérenger-Féraud, L.-J.-B. (1879). *Les Peuplades de la Sénégambie: Histoire – Ethnographie – Moeurs et Coutumes – Légendes, etc.* Ernest Leroux, Paris.

Boilat, P.-D. (1984) [1853]. *Esquisses Sénégalaises, Physionomie du Pays – Peuplades – Commerce – Religions – Passé et Avenir – Récits et Légendes.* Karthala, Paris.

Bourgeau, J. (1933). Note sur la coutume des Sérères du Sine et du Saloum. *Bulletin du Comité d'Études Historiques et Scientifiques de l'A.O.F.* **16**: 1–65.

Brooks, G. E. (1993). *Landlords and Strangers: Ecology, Society, and Trade in Western Africa, 1000–1630.* Westview, Boulder, CO.

Cadamosto, A. (1937) [1456]. *The Voyages of Cadamosto, and Other Documents on Western Africa in the Second Half of the Fifteenth Century.* Translated and edited by G. R. Crone. Hakluyt Society, London.

Carlus, J. (1880). Les Sérères de la Sénégambie. *Revue de Géographie* **6**: 409–20; **7**: 30–37, 98–105.

Chouin, G., and DeCorse, C. R. (2010). Prelude to the Atlantic Trade: New Perspectives on Southern Ghana's Pre-Atlantic History. *Journal of African History* **51**: 123–45.

Cohen, D. W. (1994). *The Combing of History.* University of Chicago Press, Chicago.

Comaroff, J. L. (1998). Reflections on the Colonial State, in South Africa and Elsewhere: Factions, Fragments, Facts, and Fictions. *Social Identities* **4** (3): 321–61.

Comaroff, J. L., and Comaroff, J. (1992). *Ethnography and the Historical Imagination.* Westview, Boulder, CO.

Cooper, F. (2005). *Colonialism in Question: Theory, Knowledge, History.* University of California Press, Berkeley.

Corre, Dr. A. (1883). Les Sérères de Joal et de Portudal (côte occidentale d'Afrique): Esquisse ethnographique. *Revue d'Ethnographie* **2**: 1–20.

Curtin, P. D. (1975). *Economic Change in Precolonial Africa: Economic Change in the Era of the Slave Trade.* University of Wisconsin Press, Madison.

Dapper, O. (1971) [1664]. Le Sénégal dans l'oeuvre d'Olfried Dapper. Edited by Guy Thilmans. *Bulletin de l'IFAN*, série B, **33** (3): 508–63.

DeCorse, C. R. (ed.) (2001). *West Africa during the Atlantic Slave Trade: Archaeological Perspectives.* Continuum, New York.

DeCorse, C. R., Richard, F. G., and Thiaw, I. (2003). Toward a Systematic Bead Description System: A View from the Lower Falemme, Senegal. *Journal of African Archaeology* **1** (1): 77–109.

Demanet, M. (1767). *Nouvelle Histoire de l'Afrique Françoise.* 2 vols. Lacombe, Paris.

de Moraes, N. I. (1993). *À la Découverte de la Petite Côte au XVIIe Siècle. Tome I: 1600–1621.* Université Dakar – IFAN, Cheikh Anta Diop, Dakar.

de Moraes, N. I. (1995). *À la Découverte de la Petite Côte au XVIIe Siècle. Tome II: 1622–1664.* Université Dakar – IFAN, Cheikh Anta Diop, Dakar.

de Sainct-Lô, R.-P. A. (1637). *Relation du Voyage du Cap-Verd.* François Targa, Paris.

Desmenager (1765). Letter to the Duke of Choiseul, 13 June 1765. ANF, C[6] 15.

Desmenager (1766). Letter to Duc de Choiseul, June 1765. ANF, C[6] 15.

Dietler, M. (1990). Driven by Drink: The Role of Drinking in the Political Economy and the Case of Early Iron Age France. *Journal of Anthropological Archaeology* **9**: 352–406.

Dietler, M. (1994). "Our Ancestors the Gauls": Archaeology, Ethnic Nationalism, and the Manipulation of Celtic Identity in Modern Europe. *American Anthropologist* **96**: 584–605.

Dietler, M. (2001). Theorizing the Feast: Rituals of Consumption, Commensal Politics, and Power in African Contexts. In Dietler, M., and Hayden, B. (eds.), *Feasts: Archaeological and Ethnographic Perspectives on Food, Politics, and Power*. Smithsonian Institution Press, Washington, DC, 65–114.

Dietler, M. (2006). Alcohol: Anthropological/Archaeological Perspectives. *Annual Review of Anthropology* **35**: 229–49.

Dietler, M., and Herbich, I. (1998). Habitus, Techniques, Style: An Integrated Approach to the Social Understanding of Material Culture and Boundaries. In Stark, M. T. (ed.), *The Archaeology of Social Boundaries*. Smithsonian Institution Press, Washington, DC, 232–63.

Dietler, M., and Herbich, I. (2001). Feasts and Labor Mobilization: Dissecting a Fundamental Economic Practice. In Dietler, M., and Hayden, B. (eds.), *Feasts: Archaeological and Ethnographic Perspectives on Food, Politics, and Power*. Smithsonian Institution Press, Washington, DC, 240–64.

Diop, B. (1997). Traite Négrière, Désertions Rurales, et Occupation du sol dans l'arrière-pays de Gorée. In Samb, D. (ed.), *Gorée et l'Esclavage*. IFAN, Cheikh Anta Diop, Dakar, 137–53.

Diop, B. (2000). L'impact de la traite négrière sur l'habitat en pays Wolof. In Samb, D. (ed.), *Saint-Louis et l'Esclavage*. IFAN, Cheikh Anta Diop, Dakar, 177–95.

Diop, M.-C., and Diouf, M. (1990). *Le Sénégal sous Abdou Diouf: État et Société*. Karthala, Paris.

Diouf, M. (1990). *Le Kajoor au XIXe Siècle: Pouvoir Ceddo et Conquête Coloniale*. Karthala, Paris.

Diouf, M. (2001). *Histoire du Sénégal: Le Modèle Islamo-Wolof et ses Périphéries*. Maisonneuve & Larose, Paris.

Diouf, N. (1972). Chronique du royaume du Sine. *Bulletin de l'IFAN*, série B, **34** (4): 702–32.

Diouf, R.-P. L. (1879). Une excursion dans le Sine et le Saloum. *Les Missions Catholiques* **11**: 324–26, 346–49, 360–62, 371–73.

Dirks, N. (1996) Is Vice Versa? Historical Anthropologies and Anthropological Histories. In McDonald, T. J. (ed.), *The Historic Turn in the Human Sciences*. University of Michigan Press, Ann Arbor, 17–51.

Doumet, J. (1974). Mémoire inédit de Doumet (1769), publié et commenté par C. Becker and V. Martin. Le Kayor et les pays voisins au cours de la seconde moitié du XVIIIe siècle. *Bulletin de l'IFAN*, série B, **36** (1): 25–92.

Dubellay, J. (1723). Letter to the Council of the Indies, 18 December 1723. ANF, C^6 7.

Dubellay, J. (1724). Letter to the Director, 18 December 1724. ANF, C^6 8.

Dulphy, M. (1939). Coutumes Sérère de la Petite Côte (1936). In *Coutumiers Juridiques de l'Afrique Occidentale Française, Tome I (Sénégal)*. Librarie Larose, Paris, 237–321.

Dupire, M., Lericollais, A., Delpech, B., and Gastellu, J.-M. (1974). Résidence, Tenure Foncière, Alliance dans une Société Bilinéaire (Serer du Sine et du Baol, Sénégal). *Cahiers d'Études Africaines* **14** (3): 417–52.

Durand, J.-B.-L. (1802). *Voyage au Sénégal*. Henri Agasse, Paris.

Ekeh, P. (1990). Social Anthropology and Two Contrasting Uses of Tribalism in Africa. *Comparative Studies in Society and History* **32**: 660–700.

Faye, M. (2002). La Résidence Royale de Jaxaw Siin: Histoire et Archéologie. Masters thesis, Université Cheikh Anta Diop de Dakar.

Faye, P. J. (2003). Les Sérères sont-ils Encore des Sénégalais à Part Entière? *Walfadjri*, **16** September.

Fernandes, V. (1951) [1506–1510]. *Description de la Côte Occidentale d'Afrique (Sénégal au Cap de Monte, Archipels)*. Translated, edited, and annotated by T. Monod, A. Teixeira da Mota, and R. Mauny. Centro de Estudos da Guiné Portuguesa, Bissau.

Galvan, D. C. (2004). *The State Must Be Our Master of Fire: How Peasants Craft Culturally Sustainable Development*. University of California Press, Berkeley.

Garenne-Marot, L. (1993). Archéologie d'un Métal: Le Cuivre en Sénégambie entre le Xe et le XIVe Siècle. Ph.D. dissertation, Université de Paris I, Panthéon-Sorbonne.

Gastellu, J.-M. (1975). L'autonomie locale des Serer du Mbayar. In Balans, J.-L., Coulon, C., and Gastellu, J.-M. (eds.), *Autonomie Locale et Intégration Nationale au Sénégal*. Éditions A. Pedone, Paris, 111–60.

Geismar, L. (1933). *Recueil des Coutumes Civiles des Races du Sénégal*. Imprimerie du Gouvernement, Saint-Louis.

Golberry, S. M. X. (1802). *Fragments d'un Voyage en Afrique*. 2 vols. Treuttel et Würtz, Paris.

Gosden, C., and Head, L. (1994). Landscape: A Usefully Ambiguous Concept. *Archaeology in Oceania* **29**: 113–16.

Gravrand, R.-P. H. (1983). *La Civilisation Sereer. "Cosaan," Les Origines*. Les Nouvelles Éditions Africaines, Dakar.

Guèye, M. (1999). Koumba Ndoffène, roi du Sine de 1853 à 1871. *Historiens-Géographes du Sénégal* **7**: 14–22.

Guyer, J. I. (1993). Wealth in People and Self-Realization in Equatorial Africa. *Man* **28**: 243–65.

Guyer, J. I. (2004). *Marginal Gains: Monetary Transactions in Atlantic Africa*. University of Chicago Press, Chicago.

Guyer, J. I., and Eno Belinga, S. M. (1995). Wealth in People as Wealth in Knowledge: Accumulation and Composition in Equatorial Africa. *Journal of African History* **36**: 91–120.

Guigou, B. (1992). Les Changements du Système Familial et Matrimonial: Les Sérères du Sine (Sénégal). Ph.D. dissertation, École des Hautes Études en Sciences Sociales, Paris.

Hall, M. (2000). *Archaeology and the Modern World: Colonial Transcripts in South Africa and the Chesapeake*. Routledge, New York.

Hamilakis, Y. (1999) Food Technologies/Technologies of the Body: The Social Context of Wine and Oil Production and Consumption in Bronze Age Crete. *World Archaeology* **31** (1): 38–54.

Hawthorne, W. (2003). *Planting Rice and Harvesting Slaves: Transformations along the Guinea-Bissau Coast, 1400–1900*. Heinemann, Portsmouth, NH.

Hendrikson, H., ed. (1996). *Clothing and Difference: Embodied Identities in Colonial and Post-Colonial Africa.* Duke University Press, Durham, NC.

Henige, D. P. (1974). *The Chronology of Oral Traditions: Quest for a Chimera.* Clarendon, Oxford.

Henige, D. P. (1982). *Oral Historiography.* Longman, New York.

Klein, M. A. (1968). *Islam and Imperialism in Senegal: The Sine-Saloum, 1847–1914.* Stanford University Press, Stanford, CA.

Klein, M. A. (1977). Servitude among the Wolof and Sereer of Senegambia. In Miers, S., and Kopytoff, I. (eds.), *Slavery in Africa: Historical and Anthropological Perspectives.* University of Wisconsin Press, Madison, 335–64.

Klein, M. A. (1979). Colonial Rule and Structural Change. In Cruise O'Brien, R. (ed.), *The Political Economy of Underdevelopment: Dependence in Senegal.* Sage Publications, Inc., Beverly Hills, 65–99.

Klein, M. A. (1992). The Impact of the Atlantic Slave Trade on the Societies of the Western Sudan. In Inikori, J., and Engerman, S. L. (eds.), *The Atlantic Slave Trade: Effects in Economies, Societies, and Peoples in Africa, the Americas, and Europe.* Duke University Press, Durham, NC, 25–47.

Klein, M. A. (2001). The Slave Trade and Decentralized Societies. *Journal of African History* **42**: 49–65.

Kopytoff, I. (1987). The Internal African Frontier: The Making of African Political Culture. In Kopytoff, I. (ed.), *The African Frontier: The Reproduction of Traditional African Societies.* Indiana University Press, Bloomington, 3–84.

Kus, S., and Raharijaona, V. (1998). Between Earth and Sky There Are Only a Few Large Boulders: Sovereignty and Monumentality in Central Madagascar. *Journal of Anthropological Archaeology* **17**: 53–79.

Kus, S., and Raharijaona, V. (2000). House to Palace, Village to State: Scaling Up Architecture and Ideology. *American Anthropologist* **102** (1): 98–113.

Kus, S., and Raharijaona, V. (2006). Visible and Vocal: Sovereigns of the Early Merina (Madagascar) State. In Inomata, T., and Coben, L. (eds.), *Archaeology of Performance: Theaters of Power, Community, and Politics*, AltaMira, New York, 303–29.

Labat, J.-B. (1728). *Nouvelle Relation de l'Afrique Occidentale.* 4 vols. Guillaume Cavelier, Paris.

Lamiral, M. (1789). *L'Affrique et le Peuple Affriquain.* Dessenne, Paris.

LaViolette, A., and Fleisher, J. (2005). The Archaeology of Sub-Saharan Urbanism: Cities and Their Countrysides. In Stahl, A. B. (ed.), *African Archaeology: A Critical Introduction*, Blackwell, Malden, MA, 327–52.

Lawson, A. (2003). Megaliths and Mande States: Sociopolitical Change in the Gambia Valley over the Past Two Millennia. Ph.D. dissertation, University of Michigan.

Le Brasseur, J. A. (1776). Mémoire pouvant servir de réponse à la lettre de Monseigneur de Sartines . . . (1776). ANF, C⁶ 17.

Lefèbvre, H. (1991). *The Production of Space.* Blackwell, Cambridge.

Lentz, C. (1994). A Dagara Rebellion against Dagomba Rule? Contested Stories of Origin in the North-Western Ghana. *Journal of African History* **35**: 457–92.

Lentz, C. (2000). Of Hunters, Goats, and Earth-Shrines: Settlement Histories and the Politics of Oral Traditions in Northern Ghana. *History in Africa* **27**: 193–214.

Lesure, R. (1999). On the Genesis of Value in Early Hierarchical Societies. In Robb, J. (ed.), *Material Symbols: Culture and Economy in Prehistory*. Center for Archaeological Investigations, Carbondale, IL, 23–55.

"Letter from the Jarafs of Fatick and Fayil to the Governor," 15 October 1889. ANS, 13 G 321.

Linares, O. F. (1987). Deferring to Trade in Slaves: The Jola of Casamance, Senegal in Historical Perspective. *History in Africa* **14**: 113–39.

Loyer, R.-P. G. (1714). *Relation du Voyage du Royaume d'Issyny, Côte d'Or, Païs de Guinée en Afrique*. Arnoul Seneuze, Paris.

MacEachern, S. (2005). Two Thousand Years of African History. In Stahl, A. B. (ed.), *African Archaeology: A Critical Introduction*, Blackwell, Malden, MA, 441–66.

Marquardt, W. (1992). Dialectical Archaeology. *Archaeological Method and Theory* **4**: 101–40.

Marty, P. (n.d.). *Études Sénégalaises (1725–1826)*. Éditions Leroux, Paris.

Mbembe, A. (2001). *On the Postcolony*. University of California Press, Berkeley.

Mbodj, M. (1978). *Un Exemple d'Économie Coloniale: Le Sine-Saloum et l'Arachide, 1887–1940*. 2 vols. Ph.D. dissertation, Université de Paris VII.

McCaskie, T. C. (1995). *State and Society in Pre-Colonial Asante*. Cambridge University Press, New York.

McIntosh, R. J. (2005). *Ancient Middle Niger: Urbanism and the Self-Organizing Landscape*. Cambridge University Press, New York.

McIntosh, S. K. (ed.) (1999). *Beyond Chiefdoms: Pathways to Complexity in Africa*. Cambridge University Press, New York.

McIntosh, S. K. (2001). Tools for Understanding Transformation and Continuity in Senegambian Society: 1500–1900. In DeCorse, C. R. (ed.), *West Africa during the Atlantic Slave Trade: Archaeological Perspectives*, Continuum, New York, 14–37.

McIntosh, S. K., and McIntosh, R. J. (1993). Field Survey in the Tumulus Zone of Senegal. *African Archaeological Review* **11**: 73–107.

McIntosh, S. K., McIntosh, R. J., and Bocoum, H. (1992). The Middle Senegal Valley Project: Preliminary Results from the 1990–91 Field Season. *Nyame Akuma* **38**: 47–61.

Mitchell, P. (2005). *African Connections: Archaeological Perspectives on Africa and the Wider World*. Altamira, Walnut Creek, CA.

Mollien, G. T. (1967) [1818]. *L'Afrique Occidentale Vue par un Explorateur Français, Gaspard Théodore Mollien*. Presented by Hubert Deschamps. Calmann-Lévy, Paris.

Monroe, J. C. (2007). Continuity, Revolution, or Evolution on the Slave Coast of West Africa? Royal Architecture and Political Order in Pre-Colonial Dahomey. *Journal of African History* **48**: 349–73.

Moore, D. (2005). *Suffering for Territory: Race, Place, and Power in Zimbabwe*. Duke University Press, Durham, NC.

Moore, D., and Roberts, R. (1990). Listening for Silences. *History in Africa* **17**: 319–25.

Myers, F. R., ed. (2001). *The Empire of Things: Regimes of Value and Material Culture*. School of American Research Press, Santa Fe.

Noirot, E. (1890). Letter to the Governor, No. 67 bis, May-June 1890. ANS, 13 G 321.

Noirot, E. (1892). Notice sur le Sine-Saloum. *Journal Officiel du Sénégal* **1892**: 28–29, 141–42, 153–54, 167–68, 176, 184–86.

Norman, N., and Kelly, K. G. (2004). Landscape Politics: The Serpent Ditch and the Rainbow in West Africa. *American Anthropologist* **106** (1): 98–110.

Ogundiran, A. (2001). Factional Competition, Sociopolitical Development, and Settlement Cycling in Ìlàrè District (ca. 1200–1900): Oral Traditions of Historical Experience in a Yorùbá Community. *History in Africa* **28**: 203–23.

Ogundiran, A., and Falola, T., eds. (2007). *Archaeology of Atlantic Africa and the African Diaspora*. Indiana University Press, Bloomington.

Paris, F. de (1976). La relation de François de Paris (1682–1683). Edited by G. Thilmans. *Bulletin de l'IFAN*, série B, **38** (1): 1–51.

Pauketat, T. R., ed. (2001). *The Archaeology of Traditions: Agency and History before and after Columbus*. University of Florida Press, Gainesville.

Pauketat, T. R., and DiPaolo Loren, D. (2005). Alternative Histories and North American Archaeology. In Pauketat, T. R., and DiPaolo Loren, D. (eds.), *North American Archaeology*. Blackwell, Malden, MA, 1–21.

Pélissier, P. (1966). *Paysans du Sénégal: Les Civilisations Agraires to Cayor à la Casamance*. Imprimerie Fabrègue, Saint-Irieix.

Piot, C. D. (1999). *Remotely Global: Village Modernity in West Africa*. University of Chicago Press, Chicago.

Rabourdin, L. (1888a). Rapport politique, 10 May 1888. ANS, 13 G 321.

Rabourdin, L. (1888b). Rapport sur la Situation Politique et Économique, 18 November 1888. ANS, 13 G 321.

Reid, A., and Lane, P. (2004). African Historical Archaeologies: An Introductory Consideration of Scope and Potential. In Reid, A., and Lane P. (eds.), *African Historical Archaeologies*. Kluwer Academic/Plenum, New York, 1–32.

Reynier, M. (1933). Rapport politique annuel (1933). ANS, 2 G 33/70.

Richard, F. G. (2007). From *Cosaan* to Colony: Exploring Archaeological Landscape Formation and Socio-Political Complexity in the Siin (Senegal), A.D. 500–1900. Ph.D. dissertation, Syracuse University.

Richard, F. G. (2009). Historical and Dialectical Perspectives on the Archaeology of Complexity in the Siin-Saalum (Senegal): Back to the Future? *African Archaeological Review* **26** (2): 75–135.

Richard, F. G. (2010). Re-Charting Atlantic Encounters: Object Trajectories and Histories of Value in the Siin (Senegal) and Senegambia. *Archaeological Dialogues* **17** (1): 1–27.

Roberts, R. (2000). History and Memory: The Power of Statist Narratives. *International Journal of African Historical Studies* **33** (3): 513–22.

Rodney, W. (1982). *How Europe Underdeveloped Africa*. Howard University Press, Washington, DC.

Rousseau, R. (1928). Notes sur l'habitat rural du Sénégal (1928). ANS, 1 G 23/104.

Roseberry, W. (1991). Potatoes, Sacks, and Enclosures in Early Modern England. In O'Brien, J., and Roseberry, W. (eds.), *Golden Ages, Dark Ages: Imagining the Past in Anthropology and History*. University of California Press, Berkeley, 19–47.

Sarr, A. (1986–1987). Histoire du Sine-Saloum. Introduction, bibliographie, et notes par Charles Becker. *Bulletin de l'IFAN*, série B, **46** (3–4): 211–83.

Schmidt, P. R. (2006). *Historical Archaeology in Africa: Representations, Social Memory, and Oral Traditions*. Kluwer Academic, New York.

Schmidt, P. R., and Patterson, T. C., eds. (1995). *Making Alternative Histories: The Practice of Archaeology and History in Non-Western Settings*. School of American Research Press, Santa Fe.

Schwartz, G. M., and Falconer, S. E., eds. (1994). *Archaeological Views from the Countryside: Village Communities in Early Complex Societies*. Smithsonian Institution Press, Washington, DC.

Searing, J. F. (1988). Aristocrats, Slaves and Peasants: Power and Dependency in the Wolof States, 1700–1850. *International Journal of African Historical Studies* **21** (3): 475–503.

Searing, J. F. (1993). *West African Slavery and Atlantic Commerce: The Senegal River Valley, 1700–1860*. Cambridge University Press, New York.

Searing, J. F. (2002). "No kings, no lords, no slaves": Ethnicity and Religion among the Sereer-Safèn of Western Bawol, 1700–1914. *Journal of African History* **43**: 407–29.

Sèye, A. (2001). Iba der Thiam face à la presse: Les régions sont maintenues. *Le Soleil*, **17** Juillet 2001.

Shackel, P. (ed.) (2003). Remembering Landscapes of Conflict. *Historical Archaeology* **37** (3): 1–148.

Sharpe, B. (1986) Ethnography and a Regional System: Mental Maps and the Myth of States and Tribes in Central Nigeria. *Critique of Anthropology* **6** (3): 33–65.

Shaw, R. (2002). *Memories of the Slave Trade: Ritual and Historical Imagination in Sierra Leone*. University of Chicago Press, Chicago.

Silliman, S. (2005). Culture Contact or Colonialism? Challenges in the Archaeology of Native North America. *American Antiquity* **70** (1): 55–74.

Smith, A. (2003). *The Political Landscape: Constellations of Authority in Early Complex Polities*. University of California Press, Berkeley.

Stahl, A. B. (2001). *Making History in Banda: Reflections on Historical Anthropology and the Construction of Africa's Past*. Cambridge University Press, New York.

Stahl, A. B. (2002). Colonial Entanglements and the Practices of Taste: An Alternative to Logocentric Approaches. *American Anthropologist* **104** (3): 827–45.

Stahl, A. B. (2004). Comparative Insights into the Ancient Political Economies of West Africa. In Feinman, G., and Nicholas, L. (eds.), *Archaeological Perspectives on Political Economies*. University of Utah Press, Salt Lake City, 253–70.

Stahl, A. B. (ed.) (2005). *African Archaeology: A Critical Introduction*. Blackwell, Malden, MA.

Stahl, A. B., Mann, R., and DiPaolo Loren, D. (2004). Writing for Many: Interdisciplinary Communication, Constructionism, and the Practices of Writing. *Historical Archaeology* **38** (2): 83–102.

Stein, G. (2002). From Passive Periphery to Active Agents: Emerging Perspectives in the Archaeology of Interregional Interaction. *American Anthropologist* **104**: 903–16.

Sud Quotidien (2000). Grand serigne de Dakar, "Bour Sine," Roi d'Oussouye.... 21 April 2000.

Thèsée, F. (1988). Au Sénégal, en 1789. Traite des Nègres et société africaine dans les royaumes de Sallum, de Sin et de Cayor. In Daget, S. (ed.), *De la Traite à l'Esclavage. Actes du Colloque International sur la Traite des Noirs, Nantes 1985. Tome II: XVIIIe–XIXe Siècles*. Société Française d'Histoire d'Outre-Mer, Paris, 223–45.

Thiaw, I. (1999). An Archaeological Investigation of Long-Term Culture Change in the Lower Falemmé (Upper Senegal Region), A.D. 500–1900. Ph.D. dissertation, Rice University.

Thiaw, I. (2000). L'impact de la traite des noirs dans le Haut Fleuve du Sénégal: Archéologie des interactions afro-européennes dans le *Gajaaga* et le *Buundu* aux XVIIIe et XIXe siècles. In Samb, D. (ed.), *Saint-Louis et l'Esclavage*. IFAN, Cheikh Anta Diop, Dakar, 129–37.

Thiaw, I. (2003). The Gorée Archaeological Project (GAP): Preliminary Results. *Nyame Akuma* **60**: 27–35.

Thilmans, G., and de Moraes, N. I. (1976). Villault de Bellefond sur la côte occidentale d'Afrique. Les deux premières campagnes de l'Europe (1666–1671). *Bulletin de l'IFAN*, série B, **38** (2): 257–99.

Thilmans, G., Descamps, C., and Khayat, B. (1980). *Protohistoire du Sénégal. Recherches Archéologiques. Tome I. Les Sites Mégalithiques*. IFAN, Mémoire de l'Institut Fondamental d'Afrique Noire, Dakar.

Thioub, I. (2002). L'école de Dakar et la production d'une écriture académique de l'histoire. In Diop, M.-C. (ed.), *Le Sénégal Contemporain*. Karthala-Sephis, Paris-Amsterdam, 109–53.

Thomas, N. (1991). *Entangled Objects: Exchange, Material Culture and Colonialism in the Pacific*. Harvard University Press, Cambridge, MA.

Trouillot, M.-R. (1995). *Silencing the Past: Power and the Production of History*. Beacon, Boston.

Trouillot, M.-R. (2003). *Global Transformations: Anthropology and the Modern World*. Palgrave Macmillan, New York.

Wright, D. R. (1985). Beyond Migration and Conquest: Oral Traditions and Mandinka Ethnicity in Senegambia. *History in Africa* **12**: 335–48.

Wright, D. R. (1997). *The World and a Very Small Place in Africa*. M. E. Sharpe, Armonk, NY.

NOTES

1. The state has a long history of involvement in the construction of national culture and history in Senegal dating at least back to the days of President Léopold Sédar Senghor. Senghor fancied himself a bit of a mythmaker and crafted a "symbolic" genealogy, which combined African and European elements rather than drawing on specific ethnic pasts, to serve as the "historical" foundation for the Senegalese nation-state. Subsequent presidents have moved away from Senghor's vision towards a less consistent national project, a more decentralized and performative yet no less authoritative cultural politics articulated on the figure of the *griot* (Diop and Diouf 1990; Thioub 2002). This project has increasingly gravitated around Wolof heritage and historical memory. More recently, the government of Abdoulaye Wade has taken more direct and controversial steps in

favor of a Wolof- and Islam-centric politics (M. Diouf 2000). Witness, for instance, the ill-fated – and largely unpopular – attempt to redefine the country's administrative subdivisions in the image of putative "historical provinces," or the effort to "alphabetize" governmental bureaucrats and functionaries in Wolof, one of the six national languages (Sèye 2001). For a more general examination of the power of statist narratives in shaping history and memory, see Roberts (2000).

2. It would be impossible to draw a comprehensive list of this vast literature. For a short selection of historical and anthropological analyses grounded in Africa, see Bayart (2006), Comaroff (1998), Guyer (1993, 2004,) Guyer and Eno Belinga (1995), Mbembe (2001), McCaskie (1995), Moore (2005), Piot (1999), and Shaw (2002). For important examples in African archaeology, see Chouin and DeCorse (2010), Kus and Raharijaona (1998, 2000, 2006), Mitchell (2005), R. J. McIntosh (2005), S. K. McIntosh (1999), Monroe (2007), Norman and Kelly (2004), and Stahl (2004a).

3. Official correspondence between the military post in Joal and Gorée, and between the governor and metropolis during the 1860–1890 period, contains numerous documents lamenting the escalation of violence and tensions between commoners and the military aristocracy. See, in particular, archival series ANS 4 B 51; 4 B 63; 13 G 23; 13 G 314; 13 G 319; 13 G 321; and 13 G 329.

4. As became clear during the conversation, this resentment had been triggered by a short article from a historian at the University of Dakar that presented a somewhat unflattering portrait of king of Siin Koumba Ndofeen and his victorious military campaign against jihadist Maba in 1867 (M. Guèye 1999). Our interlocutor found much to disagree with in Guèye's interpretations and repeatedly urged us to refer to Niokhobaye Diouf's (1972) seminal synopsis of Serer traditions, featured in the journal he was carrying. There, he implied, we would find Siin's "authentic" history. In effect, unlike Guèye – an urban, Wolof outsider – Diouf has impeccable credentials – not only is he Serer and a relative of our interlocutor, but he is also a member of the royal family and thus close to what can be seen as the "dominant" or "official" ideological strand of historical memory. In other words, our host equated a particular kind of pedigree – *both* grassroots *and* royal, namely – as the condition of true knowledge. Such forms of strategic maneuvering have gained much purchase among Siin's royal family as it seeks to stake out the ground of its legitimacy in a historical arena where local pasts are increasingly contested and encroached upon, from within and without (e.g., Sud Quotidien 2000; Galvan 2004).

4

The Eguafo Polity: Between the Traders and Raiders

Sam Spiers

INTRODUCTION

Eguafo was one of several African polities that began trading with the Portuguese in the 1470s on the former Gold Coast, West Africa. For the coast and its immediate hinterland, this maritime contact directed the focus of trade away from trans-Saharan routes. Eguafo, once at the periphery, was now on the front lines of this new Atlantic economy (Cook and Spiers 2004:17; DeCorse 2001:9). Initial European trading interests were in gold, though this became supplanted in importance by the transatlantic slave trade, especially during the seventeenth and eighteenth centuries. Although documentary records give an indication of the types of imported goods being traded in Eguafo – cloth, beads, copper, iron, ceramics, firearms, and alcohol – we have a limited understanding from historical records alone as to how daily life was structured for the inhabitants of the town and of the nature of the political organization of the polity itself. In the following discussion I argue that there was a transformation in the political economy of Eguafo in response to the increasing volume of trade passing through the polity's borders and that this transformation can be seen in changes in the settlement pattern of the town of Eguafo itself, and more broadly in the surrounding landscape. In a sense, a regional approach highlights what J. Cameron Monroe and Akinwumi Ogundiran (this volume) refer to as the creation of a politically "fragmented landscape" in the coastal hinterland of central Ghana: a mosaic of weakly centralized polities where centers of economic and political power do not necessarily coincide.

THE EGUAFO POLITY:
BETWEEN THE
TRADERS AND
RAIDERS

My investigation into the Eguafo polity is part of the broader Central Region Project, which seeks to understand transformations that occurred along this portion of the Gold Coast in the wake of the dramatic increase in trade with the opening up of the Atlantic world in the late fifteenth century (Carr 2001; Chouin 2002a, 2002b, 2008, 2009; Cook and Spiers 2004; DeCorse 1987, 1992, 1998, 2001, 2005, 2008; DeCorse et al. 2000; DeCorse et al. 2009; DeCorse and Spiers 2009; Spiers 2007). Here I focus mostly on change in the settlement pattern of Eguafo, the capital of the polity, and how this transformation in the landscape reflects changes in the political organization of the polity in precolonial times (DeCorse and Spiers 2009; Spiers 2002, 2007). The modern town of Eguafo, and the associated archaeological site, is located approximately 12 km northwest of the coast town of Elmina in the central region of Ghana (Figure 4.1). The site is larger than the contemporary town and incorporates a large forested hill to the northwest (Figure 4.2). This hill, known as the Dompow, is a prominent sacred grove for the traditional Eguafo state and can be seen from the coast (Chouin 2002a, 2002b, 2008, 2009; Cook and Spiers 2004; DeCorse and Spiers 2009; Spiers 2007). The town is also bordered on the north, east, and southeast sides by several cemeteries, some of which date to the eighteenth century. Unfortunately,

Figure 4.1
Study area (illustration by S. Spiers).

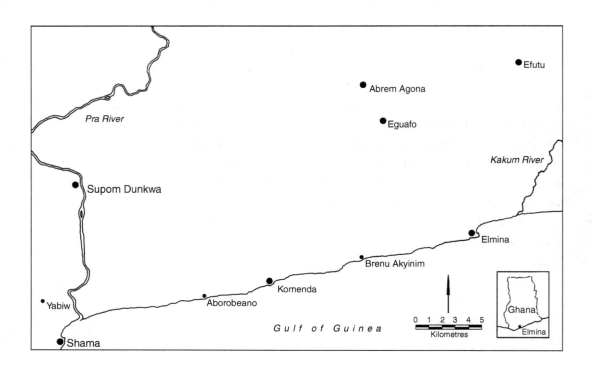

Figure 4.2
The Dompow, from the edge of the town, facing northwest. Note the shrine, Acomani, is also located in the valley (photograph by S. Spiers).

much of these areas have been disturbed by small-scale gold mining, locally known as *galamsey*, which makes an assessment of their significance difficult (Kankpeyeng and DeCorse 2004; Spiers 2007).

CHARTING TRANSFORMATIONS IN THE POLITICAL LANDSCAPE

Over the last few decades there has been a reassessment of the archaeology of landscapes and the investigation of the intangible heritage values they embody (Ashmore and Knapp 1999; Bender 1993; Bender et al. 1997, 2007; Bender and Winer 2001; Crumley 1994a; Fisher and Thurston 1999; Harrison 2004; Hicks et al. 2007; Smith and Gazin-Schwartz 2008; Thurston and Fisher 2007; Ucko and Layton 1999). Though varied, these approaches generally view the environment as being a culturally constructed and maintained entity. Landscape, and people's attachment to it, can be understood as being produced through human relations and social interactions (Lefebvre 1991). The material traces of past lifeways, however, may not indicate the complete picture of how people perceived and lived in their surroundings. Common examples of this in sub-Saharan Africa are sacred groves, often considered to be stands of relic natural forest in an otherwise cultivated landscape. Such groves and associated shrines, however, are often both actively created and maintained (Chouin 2008:179; Fairhead and Leach 1996:6; Fortes 1945:80; Greene 2002:9–10; Sheridan 2008:13). They are often associated with myths of origin or the residence of gods or spirits, but more often than not they have no obvious material signature (DeCorse 2001:181). Hence, even though for practical purposes I define site boundaries of Eguafo as those observed physically, I take an overall landscape approach that tries to encompass the spaces in between, which situates Eguafo in a broader network of social, political, and economic relations with neighboring towns, polities, and trade networks (a similar approach can be found in Marquardt and Crumley 1987; Deetz 1990).

In this approach, landscape is defined as being the socially constructed relationship between people and their physical environment (Marquardt and Crumley 1987). Settlement or polity boundaries are seen as both barriers and fields of opportunity, either political or economic. For example, the reuse of a portion of the former settlement of Eguafo as a sacred grove marks an important transformation in the landscape, whereby a defensive settlement becomes recontextualized as shrine of great authority and power. Thus we can move from observed material traces of settlement patterns toward the interpretation of the political landscape and the relationships that constitute and challenge it. Such scalar modeling between components of the settlement does not necessarily imply hierarchical ranking between them, for example between coast and hinterland or the sacred and profane, but it may also represent a factional, heterarchical system of organization that may even defy political centralization (Brumfiel 1992; Crumley 1994b). The implication of this for our understanding of the organization of society is to allow for the possibility of a more intricate net of counterpoised power relations – what some have referred to in different contexts as nested landscapes (Bender et al. 2007:34). This can lead to a certain degree of flexibility in the negotiation of power relations between different interest groups, be they secular or religious (Crumley 1994b:187; McIntosh 1999:4).

One of the challenges to traditional authority was the growth in trade with the opening up of the Atlantic world. The impact this had on local coastal polities is reflected in changes in the landscape itself. It could be argued that a generalized concept of an African kingdom is one that is superimposed on the structure of agricultural life. Power was vested in aristocratic or privileged groups that were often viewed as absolute monarchs by the Europeans, though this was not always the case (DeCorse 2001:40; Spiers 2007:32). Yet trade itself has also been viewed as a force of production (Marx 1973:277). Maurice Godelier defined a generalized African mode of production in terms of the presence of a minority who "dominates and exploits the communities intervening in their conditions of production not directly, but indirectly" through the control and taxation of interregional trade in rare commodities rather than investing in public works that might improve surplus agricultural production (Godelier 1978:242). On the former Gold Coast trade also allowed for independent merchants to become increasingly powerful (Daaku 1970:115–43; Kea 1982:176–77; Law 2007). Catherine Coquery-Vidrovitch (1977:83) argues that it "seems excessive to seek the only motive for this development of African societies in the productive forces of a subsistence economy." Rather, she favors the use of trade as a mechanism to accumulate surplus. In this way a minority can exploit their neighbors (through warfare and dominating trade routes) rather than their subjects (through the direct extraction of agricultural surplus). It must be noted, however, that such generalizations do not always fit well with archaeological evidence from different regions of sub-Saharan Africa (Kusimba and Kusimba 2007:220–21). Further, it must also be noted that the connection between long-distance trade and the centralization of power is not always appropriate where economic and political hegemony can operate separately within two different social groups (Bloch 1978; Terray 1974:317–18). This point helps to illustrate the challenges faced by the coastal polities along the Gold Coast and may also help to explain the shift in settlement pattern of Eguafo.

The elite may not have had complete control over trade, but they could demonstrate control indirectly through the exclusive consumption of foreign or rare goods. Thus elites could exclude their subjects from the symbolic trappings of power by restricting access to exotic trade goods, thereby maintaining a source of symbolic capital (Ekholm 1972:103; Terray 1974:324; Yoffee 2005:36). Because such transformation was partly brought about by increases in regional trade, it becomes necessary to investigate how new social relations were maintained and validated. I argue it is not the mere possession of objects that is of interest but the transformation of the broader landscape setting that informs on social processes of identity construction. Just as material culture can be used to express, reinforce, and challenge aspects of social relationships that are related to economic and political strategies, so too can the physical landscape (Hodder 1977, 1979:448; Miller 1995:146, 154; Yoffee 2005:36).

The changing nature of trade on the West African coast after the arrival of European traders and companies in the late fifteenth century led to a transformation within the Eguafo polity. This may have provided the means for alternative networks of power to emerge within its own diffuse political structure. Although the era of the gold trade was marked by a population increase, and a growing number and variety of trade goods and locally produced items, these seem to be evenly distributed (though this is difficult to assess with the high level of *galamsey* at the site). The structure of governance of Eguafo drawn from historical sources would suggest that the nature of political control was relatively diffuse, whereby several interest groups including the royal family, heads of matrilineages, traders, religious experts, military leaders, and tax officers acted as checks and balances against strong centralization (Arhin 1966:67). Such forces greatly weakened Eguafo's ability to wrest effective control of the bourgeoning slave trade from the more powerful and increasingly centralized states in the forest zone.

EQUAFO

Documentary references to Eguafo during the early contact period are limited and more commonly relate to the coastal settlements of Shama, Komenda, and Elmina. Eustache de la Fosse noted that by 1480 there were only two places to trade on the coast: the towns of Shama and Elmina, both of which he referred to as "la minne" (Foulché-Delbosc 1897:181–82; Hair 1994a:43n3). Whether these marked the borders of Eguafo in the fifteenth century is unclear. By the close of the fifteenth century, Pacheco Pereira wrote that midway between the villages of Shama and Elmina was the "village of Torto," referring to the coastal town of Komenda, an important port for Eguafo that later had French, Dutch, and British trading posts and forts (Fage 1980:54–55; Pacheco 1937:119). Rui de Pina, who was on the coast in the late fifteenth century (Hair 1994a:6), wrote of a war started in 1490 between two men who lived near Elmina. One of the protagonists tricked the other "king" into thinking that he had garnered the support of the Portuguese. Instead of standing his ground, the tricked "king" fled, much to the detriment of his forces (as cited in Blake 1967 [1942]:86). If this somewhat ambiguous anecdote were true, as Hair (1994a:39) cautiously argues, then it may refer to the rulers of the two polities surrounding Elmina: Eguafo and Efutu (Vogt 1979:87). Certainly, by 1503 we have reference to a king of Eguafo who "came hither with all his people... in order to clear the roads... and to permit the merchants to come" (cited in Blake 1967 [1942]:94; see also Hair 1994a, 1994b; Vogt 1979:87). Most of these early references, however, relate to European and African interaction on the immediate coast rather than the hinterland where the settlement of Eguafo is located.

Given the nature of available documentary sources, it is very difficult to get a sense of the nature of political organization in Eguafo at this time. In his discussion of kingship at Elmina, DeCorse (2001:40) points out how a somewhat biased, late-sixteenth-century Portuguese document suggested that it was misleading to call African leaders kings, where it is unlikely that "being King of Cumani [Eguafo] or King of Afuto [Efutu], which are villages of not more than one hundred huts or shacks, is the same as being King of Portugal, which is a kingdom worthy of the name" (see also Teixeira da Mota and Hair 1988:74). In European terms, the coastal polities of this part of the former Gold Coast were on a smaller scale. The title of king, applied to a single ruler of Elmina, does not appear in the Dutch documents until 1732, and the Dutch seemed to have been unfamiliar with the title with regard to Elmina until that time (DeCorse 2001:39–40; Hair 1994a:55n37; Henige 1974a:503).

According to a 1629 Dutch map, in the early seventeenth century Eguafo was bordered by several other polities, including Efutu to the east, Abrem to the northeast, Adom (and later Wassa) to the northwest, and Yabiw and Ahanta to the west (Daaku 1970:199; Daaku and van Dantzig 1966; Kea 1982:27). This western border was linguistic and political (Daaku 1970: 182–184; Daaku and van Dantzig 1966; Kea 1982:23–28; Hair 1969:229). These polities competed for trade and were at various times opposed or aligned with each other. This general description of the relative position of polities seems to hold for most of the seventeenth century (Roussier 1935:10). Along the coast, the port town of Elmina became independent early on, and Komenda followed after the Komenda wars in the late seventeenth century (Chouin 2009:232; Daaku 1970:81; Daaku and van Dantzig 1966:15; DeCorse 2001:39; DeCorse and Spiers 2009; Henige 1974b, 1977; Law 2007: 140–41; Spiers 2007). This marked a shift in the settlement hierarchy of Eguafo, in which its two major port towns had both become independent by the end of the seventeenth century.

Although we have numerous European references to warfare, trade, and political boundaries, it is difficult to get a clear sense of how Eguafo was organized and how much power rested in the hands of its rulers. It is not surprising that the early travel accounts do give pertinent information on taxation within the coastal polities, which was a major concern of trading companies. Inland African traders, such as the Akani, were obliged to pay tolls to the tax collectors in order to pass through a polity. De Marees (1987 [1602]:58) wrote that "the traders who come from the Interior have to pay the King of the Port where they want to do business the weight of one *Testoen* of Gold for passing through the King's Land. Whether they want to buy much or not, they must all pay the same amount" (see also van Dantzig 1978: 5). Once on the coast, the traders then had to hand over one-quarter of their goods to the tax collector of the port. If the remainder was over a certain value, then they paid further duty (de Marees 1987 [1602]:59). This rate decreased toward the late seventeenth century, though they would have to hand over one-third of their goods at the coast rather than a quarter (Kea 1982:259). For example, the Dutch around 1690 stated that "about half a mile to the East-North-East of Elmina town is a hamlet situated behind a mountain in which there is a cleft, which the Dutch call the Commanise Pass because one has to pass through it when going from Elmina to Aguaffo. In this hamlet lives the Marinie or toll-master of the King of Aguaffo, who levies tolls on all goods which are brought to and from Aguaffo" (as cited in van Dantzig 1978:64; see also de Marees 1987 [1602]:58–59; Ulsheimer cited in Jones 1983:32). There was further reference in 1703 to a prominent merchant broker of an Akani king who lived in a small town between Elmina and Eguafo (Kea 1982:268).

European companies trading along the Gold Coast were also levied with similar taxes. For example, in 1687 when the British Royal African Company (RAC) was building its fort at Komenda, the king of Eguafo demanded that the RAC "pay the kinge two peize per month till the house be build, and when build one bendy per month for ground rent." If this was met the king would "take us into his protection and endeavour the advancement of the Royall Affrican Companys interest, as he has done allready without any consideration from them by granting the merchants of all countreys a free passage through his [land] and in sending them down with their money to our Factory" (as cited in Law 2001:114). Such meetings were often undertaken in the town itself. For example, Ulsheimer wrote in the following account regarding his 1603–1604 voyage that with regards to government, the inhabitants of the Gold Coast would meet in "a special house for the purpose" (as cited in Jones 1983:31). Similarly Barbot (1992:511) wrote there was a "large space empty in the middle, where people hold their market and their meetings" in most towns.

The main group of hinterland traders was often referred to as the Akanists. Their place of origin, referred to by the Europeans as Akani, remains somewhat of a mystery (Boahen 1974). Kea (1982:249) argues that the history of the Akani trade network predates 1600. They appear frequently in the European sources of the seventeenth and early eighteenth centuries as traders in gold, coming from the hinterland to ports along the coast between Axim and Accra, though it is doubtful that there was a political entity or state associated with them until the beginning of the eighteenth century (van Dantzig 1990:205). For example, Michael Hemmersam (as cited in Jones 1983:115–16) published in 1663 that traders would "set off, and the way to Ackania is very narrow, so that they can only go in single file . . . these Akomist Moors bring the most gold for sale." And the English factor William Cross wrote in 1686 that he "found my old customers the Arcania merchants weighting my comeing" in Komenda (as cited in Law 2001:95). Certainly to access the coast, they had to pass through several polities, which involved paying certain taxes to keep the paths open and "free" (Kea 1982:259).

Historians have described the organization of this hinterland trade network in the seventeenth century in several ways – as a single kingdom (such as Assin or Adansi), a loose confederacy of hinterland polities, or city-states drawn together with kinship ties (Boahen 1974b:105–7; Daaku 1970:146; Kea 1982:33; van Dantzig 1990: 205). From the coast, the Akani traded in local and imported goods, some directly from overseas trade and the coastal trade (Kea 1982:250). The traders would deal through a broker or captain (Müller cited in Jones [1983:247], with regard to Efutu) in the coastal town who would then sell the goods to the Europeans on their behalf (Kea 1982:52). Such captains were usually men of high regard and would settle in the coastal town. William Cross, for example, wrote in 1686–1687 that "here are lately come down the Arcania merchants with a new Captain, they having given and taken hostage of the king of Aguaffo for a trade and safe passage" (as cited in Law 2001:103). Goods were generally transported using enslaved persons, and Kea (1982:253) hypothesizes that while Assin may have been producing gold in the sixteenth century, by the seventeenth century enslaved persons used in gold mining would have been pulled by traders and speculators from gold production to portage, thus transforming Assin into a gold-trading rather than gold-producing polity. It remains to be seen if this can be extrapolated to other polities in the Akani "confederacy."

By the late seventeenth century, we get a description of a visit to Eguafo that outlines this process of taxation further and illustrates the importance of controlling trade routes to the coast. William Cross (Law 2001:97), the English factor at Komenda, wrote in 1686 that he had a meeting with the Eguafo tax collector who collected gifts for the king, his officer, his cousin, and their respective wives. The next day, Cross met with the king and various officials in Eguafo about the construction of the British trade post at Komenda. The king demanded a down payment and an annual levy, which included brandy (Law 2001:97; 117). This would suggest that the king of Eguafo would decide on issues affecting the polity in the presence of the royal household and officials, presumably with their support.

With the end of the British Atlantic slave trade in 1806–1807, Europeans pursued more legitimate trade, though some illicit slave trading occurred, and domestic slavery continued, especially with the new interest in the production of cash crops (Miers 2003). The Gold Coast became a British Crown colony in 1874; hence domestic slavery was still legal up until that time, though discouraged by the British after their abolition of the slave trade. The merchant class that had emerged in the eighteenth century once again acted as middlemen between the traditional polities and, by this time, principally British traders (Dumett 1971:79; Kaplow 1978:20). A series of ordinances were passed between 1878 and 1910 regarding Native Jurisdiction in the Gold Coast to provide a framework for local rulers in the new British colony (Henige 1973:10; Metcalfe 1964:390–93). Under this system, the political power of the traditional leaders was greatly lessened. Arhin (1983:13) has argued, however, that it was the earlier differential acquisition of wealth among the coastal Fante through access to trade that "undermined the state and considerably modified the normal Akan rank system," which perhaps fits the material from Eguafo.

Between the early eighteenth and nineteenth centuries the Eguafo polity moved from a position of prominence among the coastal polities to an increasingly marginalized status. Initially, Eguafo was able to benefit from the increase in population that European demand for trade brought to the coast (DeCorse and Spiers 2009). Toward the end of the seventeenth and the beginning of the eighteenth century, however, a series of local wars and internal political crises weakened Eguafo's role as "middleman" in facilitating trade between the interior and the coast. Further, the rise of powerful, centralized polities in the forest zone began to encroach upon Eguafo's northern borders (van Dantzig 1978:72, 106–7). This led to several short-lived alliances between coastal polities and further blockades of the trade routes by the mid-eighteenth century, causing trade to stagnate on the coast (Boahen 1974a; Yarak 1977). This strategy, however, led to the weakening of an already diffuse system of governance because towns such as Elmina began to trade directly with forest states, such as Asante, bypassing Eguafo altogether. Thus we are faced with an interesting conundrum. During the late seventeenth and eighteenth centuries we observe the accumulation of wealth and a diverse array of trade goods appearing in Eguafo at the height of the Atlantic slave trade, yet this is also a time of marked political instability within the polity. This change is also reflected in the settlement pattern of the capital itself.

ARCHAEOLOGY AT EGUAFO

In 1993, the Central Region Project undertook preliminary archaeological survey and excavation in Eguafo (DeCorse 2001:20). This survey was expanded by Gérard Chouin and me in 1998 (Cook and Spiers 2004; DeCorse et al. 2000; Spiers 2002, 2007). From this preliminary work I undertook excavation in several areas of the site (Figure 4.3). The following discussion is organized around three periods in the settlement history of Eguafo that relate to the political economy of the polity. These periods can be summarized as follows. The first is marked by the pre- and early contact site located on the Dompow and the surrounding lowland to the sixteenth century. The second period broadly covers Eguafo's involvement in the transatlantic slave trade during the seventeenth and eighteenth centuries. The final period marks the decline of the Eguafo polity during the nineteenth century.

Although I use radiometric dates where possible, much of this chronology is based on locally produced, low-fired ceramics and the appearance of European manufactured goods. These local ceramics fall into two broadly distinctive ware types that are chronologically sensitive (DeCorse 2001:116; 2005; Spiers 2007). Ware Paste 1 is common in southern Ghanaian Iron Age sites right up to the period dominated by Portuguese trade to the early seventeenth century (Figure 4.4). Associated radiometric dates from Eguafo (Cook and Spiers 2004; Spiers 2007), along with the coastal sites of Brenu Akyinim

(DeCorse 2001:228n57) and Coconut Grove (DeCorse 2005), indicate that this ware type extends back to the first millennium A.D. Ware Paste 2 is more compact, less eroded, generally darker in color, and distinctive in form and decoration (Figure 4.5). This style is associated with European trade materials and generally appears during or after the seventeenth century. This transition is well documented in the Eyim locus at Eguafo (Spiers 2007).

Period one: Pre-contact to the sixteenth century

During the first period, the population was small, though it gradually grew during the sixteenth century as the gold trade began to attract more settlers to the coast (Daaku 1970:4; DeCorse 2001:112; Fynn 1971:26; 1974:11; Wilks 1993:42). The people were probably subsistence farmers, and there is limited archaeological evidence for long-distance trade, even during the early contact period. We cannot be certain of the nature of the political organization, but it is unlikely that the settlement was strongly centralized, and it was probably organized around a charismatic leader or successful matriclan.

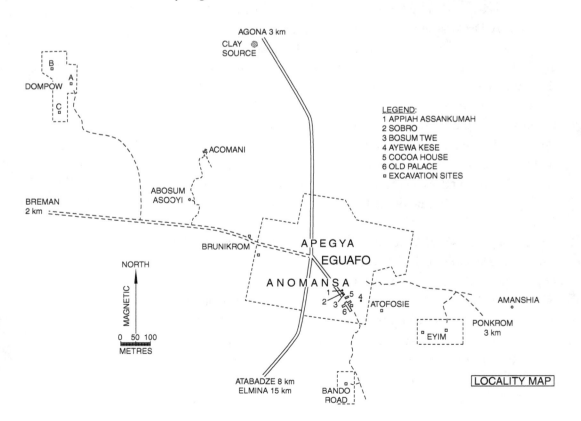

Figure 4.3
Locus map of Eguafo (illustration by S. F. Spiers).

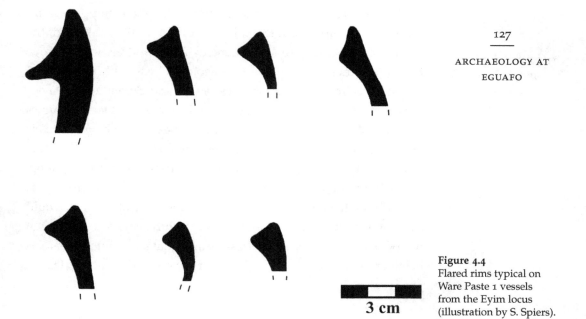

Figure 4.4
Flared rims typical on Ware Paste 1 vessels from the Eyim locus (illustration by S. Spiers).

The technology used in farming remained fairly consistent during the precolonial period, and without the use of draught animals, much of this process was labor intensive. It is likely that farmers used extended family to clear the land and then were obliged to feed the laborers (de Marees 1987 [1602]:111; Müller cited in Jones 1983:220–21; McCaskie 1995:26; Villault 1670:262).

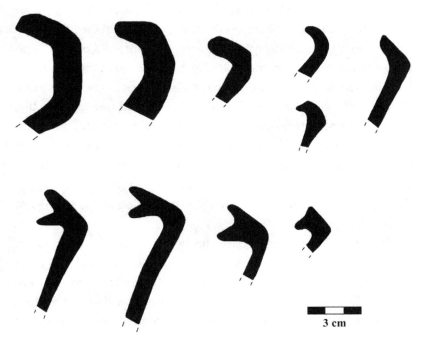

Figure 4.5
Everted rims typical on Ware Paste 2 vessels from the Eyim locus (illustration by S. Spiers).

Archaeologically, this period is typified by the Dompow assemblage. The Dompow is a large, forested hill to the northwest of the contemporary town. Today it remains an important sacred grove for the traditional polity. The archaeological assemblage is typical of the Late Iron Age hilltop sites (Cook and Spiers 2004; Davies 1961; DeCorse 2005; Nunoo 1948), and the majority of local ceramics belong to Ware Paste 1. The presence of stone beads and *nyame akuma* (ground stone celts) from lower levels, along with associated production sites (Figure 4.6), suggest a pre-European contact occupation. At the upper range, the presence of seventeenth-century slipware at Locus B, and the fifteenth-century Portuguese ceitil at Locus C, would suggest abandonment during the seventeenth century, which is not out of keeping with the historical records that still depict Eguafo as being on or near a mountain in the early eighteenth century (Daaku 1970:202).

Period two: Seventeenth century to the late eighteenth century

The second occupation period in Eguafo is marked by the growth of the settlement in the lower valley and the eventual abandonment of the Dompow during the seventeenth century. During this transformation, Eguafo appears as a historical polity, covering a broad territory (Daaku and van Dantzig 1966). There is also an increasing diversity in the artifact assemblage at the site, especially in the late seventeenth and eighteenth centuries. Clearly, segments of the population were able to benefit from, and manipulate to their advantage, the gold and slave trade passing through Eguafo's borders to get to the coast. This is nicely illustrated by the presence of a gold bead shaped like a pair of shackles recovered from an eighteenth-century context by *galamsey*, now housed in the Cape Coast Museum (Kankpeyeng and DeCorse 2004:119). This economic prosperity is matched, however, with an increasing political instability and increased warfare during the eighteenth century leading to the latter period of the settlement history (Spiers 2007).

This period is best typified archaeologically by the Eyim locus. The archaeological deposits excavated at Eyim span at least 900 years and chart the change in ceramic paste types from Ware Type 1 to Ware Type 2. The lower levels of the 1993 excavations are dated to the first half of the second millennium A.D., and the presence of European

Figure 4.6
Grinding grooves associated with the production of *nyame akuma*, near Locus B, the Dompow (photograph by S. Spiers).

trade goods show a continuous occupation sequence until the mid- to late nineteenth century. Stratigraphically, the early Ware Paste 1 ceramics dominate the assemblage between 2.72 and 3.40 m deep in Unit 8. Above this Ware Type 2 dominates. A specific everted rim treatment, with an exterior ridge at, or below, the lip, appears just after this transformation in paste types, from the generally flared rims of Ware Type 1 pots to the everted rims common on Ware Type 2 globular pots (Figure 4.5). This distinctive rim treatment wanes in popularity by 1.6 m in Unit 8. In the shallower Unit D to the west of Unit 8, this distinctive rim form appears in Levels 16 and 17 between a depth of 1.2 and 1.6 m. This is associated with a piece of Rhenish stoneware with cobalt blue decoration probably dating to the late seventeenth to early eighteenth century. The raised band or ledge on many of the Ware Type 1 vessels found in coastal Ghanaian sites in the central region, such as at Coconut Grove, Brenu Akyinim, or Komenda, may have become a decorative element in the early Ware Type 2 ceramics in the late seventeenth to early eighteenth century (DeCorse 2001, 2005; DeCorse et al. 2009; DeCorse and Spiers 2009; Spiers 2007). This would also help to date the transition in ceramic paste type to some point in the early to mid-seventeenth century. The small fragments of nondiagnostic tin-enameled earthenware recovered between 2.2 and 2.4 m also support this date.

During this period, we see the introduction of cemeteries at Eguafo. At Atofosie, for example, the cemetery was in use from the late seventeenth century. Several near-complete Rhenish stoneware vessels, dating to the early eighteenth century, were recovered from contemporary disturbed *galamsey* excavations. The gold weights recovered would fit within its use during the late seventeenth and early eighteenth centuries (Garrard 1980:281), and the presence of nineteenth-century beads and tobacco pipes would suggest continued use to this time. The burial shafts exposed by the gold miners in both the Atofosie and Bando Road loci varied greatly in both depth and shape, while some also had a small niche at the bottom of the shaft, presumably for the placement of the corpse. Surface artifacts collected from disturbed contexts included local ceramics and pipes, *forowa* (containers made from sheet brass), and one example of a *kuduo* (a cast copper-alloy vessel) (Garrard 1980:186; Ross 1974:42), gold weights, gold and glass beads, and various forms of imported ceramics, notably Rhenish stoneware dating to the early part of the eighteenth century, and tobacco pipes.

Period three: The nineteenth century

By the late eighteenth century and nineteenth centuries, we not only see a decline in the size of the Eguafo settlement, but also in the territory of the polity itself, which was gradually reduced to a nucleus of core villages that defines the traditional polity today (Fynn 1974). In part this was caused by the pressures exerted by the Asante along the northern borders of the polity in the eighteenth century. Yet it was also exacerbated by Eguafo's inability to control the trade passing through its borders. Eguafo ceases to be a political power on the Gold Coast during the nineteenth century. Kofi Intuah, the paramount chief of Eguafo at the time, lamented in the early twentieth century that the capital of Eguafo had "been treated as a bush Country hence the advantage of the coast people to ignore this memorable city" (ADM 11/1/485). After independence in 1957, Eguafo reemerged as a traditional authority along the coast. Along with Komenda, Edina, and Abrem, it forms part of the traditional council of the K.E.E.A. district in the Central Region.

The chronology outlined above suggested that the oldest portions of the site were located in what is now an important sacred grove for Eguafo, the Dompow and the lower excavation levels of the area known locally as Eyim. In the case of the Dompow B locus, we have two calibrated radiocarbon dates (A.D. 450–570 and A.D. 650–770), which place the occupation in the early second half of the first millennium A.D. From the excavations at Eyim carried out in 1993, we have thermoluminescence dates between 1161 and 1392 A.D. for the lower deposits associated with Ware Type 1. Between European contact and the seventeenth century, it would appear that the settlement in the Dompow was in the process of being abandoned and that by the end of the century the settlement around Eyim grew in size and scope, including several cemeteries and other loci, including sections of the contemporary town.

This spatial transformation denotes a change in spatial practice or the way in which people used the landscape. The abandonment of this settlement with the natural defense that existed in the Dompow also implies an increase in the population during the seventeenth century so as to make such a settlement untenable, and a reorganization of defensive strategies during that time that might make such a refuge unnecessary (Spiers 2007). Certainly both had occurred by the early eighteenth century, when the population had increased and there were organized armies, possibly based on the arrangement of satellite villages (DeCorse and Spiers 2009; Sanders 1975; Spiers 2007). The trade in firearms also became more common during the eighteenth century, which also may have allowed for different offensive and defensive strategies (Barbot 1992:349; Kea 1982:182); but note that limited archaeological evidence of the use of firearms was found in Eguafo (Spiers 2007).

Though we do not know how long ago the Dompow took on sacred functions (Chouin 2002a, 2002b, 2008, 2009), we can suggest that the creation of the Dompow helped to physically anchor Eguafo at a time of economic and political instability – the northern borders were being threatened and its coastal ports had become independent. Following Lefebvre (1991), this shift in the representation of space with the transformation of a hilltop settlement to a sacred grove gave the Eguafo polity a sense of permanence and ritual empowerment in a changing political landscape.

DISCUSSION

The coastal political system of which Eguafo was a part has been described as consisting of a diffuse authority, where the power of individual leaders was kept in balance by traditional authority and a new trading elite (Arhin 1966:67). Historian Kwame Arhin (1966:68) locates the origins of this political system in the post-European contact, but still precolonial, period of interaction. During

THE EGUAFO POLITY:
BETWEEN THE
TRADERS AND
RAIDERS

this time, traders gained political independence and presented a challenge to the traditional authority of the coastal polities from the late seventeenth century, especially in the port towns like Elmina and Komenda. The success of coastal traders indicated to traditional rulers the need for diplomacy, both between and within polities, in order to benefit from the external economy (Boahen 1974a; Henige 1977; Law 2007; McCaskie 1990; Yarak 2003).

In the seventeenth century we know Eguafo had a defined territory that could be defended with military force. The polity could levy taxes on trade and initially had flourishing satellite port towns. Yet Eguafo's leaders had limited power in practice, and there is a continuous cycle of rulers during the seventeenth and eighteenth centuries (Chouin 1998, 2009; Spiers 2007). Materially, there does not appear to be an obvious differential accumulation of wealth among sectors of society that would indicate the clear emergence of classes, though this may be skewed by the heavy looting of the site. If we can begin to understand the production of the Eguafo's social spaces and the routines of its inhabitants, however, perhaps we can begin to tease out this conundrum, which, I think, was both fueled and exacerbated by the control over trade and the shift from the gold trade to the growing slave trade, commodities that Eguafo did not possess in great numbers.

The majority of people living in Eguafo probably practiced some form of subsistence farming and possibly traded any surplus with local villages. There were limited gold resources within the polity, and slaving was discouraged on a large scale. Thus the main source of income was through the external trade passing through its borders. During the seventeenth century there was a system of taxation for any traders passing through the polity, and de Marees (1987 [1602]:112) also suggests that some form of tax was paid by farmers to their chiefs. It is difficult to know, however, when this system of taxation and rents developed or how systematic was the collection of this form of tribute, and if it was carried out by the polity or simply by the heads of matriclans. Another source of income was to collect a tax from the European traders posted on the coast in return for maintaining trade routes to the coast (Law 2001:114).

Most of the seventeenth-century references we have for the location of such tax collectors, however, were often in towns or villages outside of the capital itself on major trade routes to the coast (de Marees 1987 [1602]:58–59; Ulsheimer cited in Jones 1983:32;

van Dantzig 1978:64). Further, it is not clear if they were also involved in the trade themselves as merchants (Kea 1982:268). During the seventeenth century, therefore, we see that the rulers of Eguafo attempted to control, and benefit from, the trade between Europeans and African traders. Yet, it is not always clear how successful they were. In Eguafo, succession was often challenged where there was a shift from matrilineal descent to patrilineal descent of the royal succession in the mid-seventeenth century, where an infraction in the usual matrilineal succession occurred (Chouin 1998:66; 1999:170; Feinberg 1989:11; Michael Hemmersam cited in Jones 1983:123).

Information regarding African religious practices drawn from the archaeological record is difficult, but suggestive, in Eguafo and is drawn from transformations in the landscape itself, with the creation of a major grove and the formation of several cemeteries. The abandonment of the Dompow as a settlement in the seventeenth century, as evidenced by the local and trade goods found in excavated contexts, and its maintenance as a grove since this time is suggestive of creating a ritualized space, yet we have little documented evidence that it had always been considered of sacred significance until the mid-nineteenth century (Chouin 2002a:180). However, it is important to note that even in the twentieth century it is very clear that the religious significance of the grove is tied to the political stability of Eguafo (Chouin 2002a). We do not know exactly when formal burials grounds were first established along the Gold Coast or how their use differed between ethnic groups (DeCorse 2001:187). Our partial historical information comes from the early seventeenth century or later. It is more than likely that practices varied greatly; for example, individuals could be interred in house-floors as Isert (1992) described in the late eighteenth century for the Ga inhabitants of Accra, where every person "is buried in the room of his house where he died" (1992:132). Second, they may have been buried in burial grounds associated with an extended family network or matriclans or for other specific use, such as with Atofosie (Chouin 2002a:187– 88). In a very general sense de Marees (1987:180–82) wrote of the complex mortuary rituals that an individual undergoes in the early seventeenth century prior to burial on the Gold Coast during the process of interment and the following obsequies (Jones 1985:186; Villaut 1760:190–92). According to de Marees, the ceremony varied depending on the social status of the individual (Dapper 1670:457). Grave goods might have included utilitarian objects such as pottery vessels, jugs, *forowa*, or implements used by the deceased in his or her lifetime. What is interesting to note is that items of status included in the burial seem to occur from the seventeenth century onwards, yet we have little information regarding the interment of individuals prior to this time (DeCorse 2001:188).

It would seem that an actively maintained sacred landscape was created in Eguafo during the eighteenth century, and possibly earlier, where the maintenance of sacred groves, personal shrines, ancestor's burial grounds and house burials, and specific-purpose sites for those who had died violently helped to define both the spiritual and political landscape of the capital and thereby its relationship with neighboring polities, such as Abrem to the north, and with former parts of the old polity, such as the port towns of Elmina and British and Dutch Komenda (Chouin 2002a, 2002b; DeCorse 2001; DeCorse and Spiers 2009). Thus, as the Eguafo polity began to contract, these areas probably became increasingly important in delineating family land and political boundaries in the nineteenth century.

CONCLUSION

It has often been thought that the maintenance of the political stability of any complex society has been its ability to control a segment of the economy in order to create enough wealth to sustain its political structure, usually through taxes or tribute (Earle 1987). Yet it has become clear in the preceding discussion that Eguafo could not effectively capture this external economy passing through its boundaries. Recall that Eguafo had little in the way of key resources used in the trade: gold and enslaved persons. Certainly, the polity could (and often did) threaten to cut off access to the coast unless suitable conditions were met, but this was far more disruptive to the economy of Eguafo than the amounts gained. Further, this inability to control the trade allowed for the creation of opportunities for groups, such as the traders themselves, to accumulate wealth and positions of influence. Thus, the inability to control the external economy provided an important challenge to existing power structures. This would suggest that the economic and political "central places" did not spatially coincide in the polity creating a single settlement hierarchy (Bender et al. 2007:34–35; Crumley 1994a; Marquardt and Crumley 1987:4–9). Rather, alternatives emerged, certainly on the immediate coast in places such as Elmina and Komenda where it would have been easier to profit directly from the trade with Europeans. It may be possible to suggest that the change in settlement pattern observed archaeologically in the Eguafo site may have been a response to this development, whereby the polity was able to claim ritual control over a section of the settlement in order to authenticate its sovereignty.

In the early contact period there is reference to persons of importance within the coastal communities, such as Caramansa at Elmina (DeCorse 2001), but it is not until the early sixteenth century that we see the distinction between various political roles for hinterland polities, though the use of these terms is somewhat unclear. In the early seventeenth century, Eguafo stretched from Elmina and Efutu on the east, to the Pra River on the west, and was to remain fairly stable until the early eighteenth century, though by this time many of the coastal ports had become independent of Eguafo. The main source of revenue for the polity came through the taxation of external trade in gold and enslaved persons. With the shift to an increasing slave trade in the seventeenth century, a decline in the gold trade, and the rise of expansionist states deep in the hinterland, we see a change in settlement organization in Eguafo at this time. This highlights the tensions between the accumulation of wealth associated with the decline of the gold trade and the apogee of the slave trade in the coast, and the diffuse system of government that led to the political instability of Eguafo in the eighteenth century and its subsequent decline. By invoking a landscape approach we can begin to place the site of Eguafo in a broader network of social, political, and economic relations at the local, regional, and global levels.

ACKNOWLEDGEMENTS

This chapter is dedicated to Michael Freedman, in fond memory of many conversations. Work conducted at Eguafo would not have been possible without the generous support of the Wenner-Gren Foundation for Anthropological Research, the Earthwatch Institute, and Syracuse University. I would like to thank the Ghana Museums and Monuments Board, in particular Deputy Director Raymond Agbo for his continued support of this project. Further, I received much logistical help from the Archaeology Department, University of Ghana, in particular from Ben Kankpeyeng and Bossman Murey. I would also like to thank the director of the Central Region Project, Chris DeCorse, who has given much needed support and advice over the years. Thanks also to other members of the project, including Ed Carr, Gérard Chouin, Greg Cook, Rachel Horlings, and Drew

Pietruszka, whose work has informed so much of my own. I would also like to thank Joseph Jones, Ernest Quayson, Stuart Spiers, Natalie Swanepoel, and many other volunteers who assisted in the field and in the laboratory at Eguafo. Most important, I would like to thank the people of Eguafo, especially the Paramount Chief of the Eguafo Traditional Area, Nana Kwamina Ansah IV, who has supported this work from the beginning, and local crew members, including Joe Dadze, Ransford Kofi Egyir, Francis Quayson, and Kwesi Nibah. Thanks also to the Ntwaa and Yankson families in Eguafo for letting me excavate on their family land. The work presented here was conducted for my doctoral thesis, and the advice and suggestions of my committee members at the time, including Chris DeCorse, Doug Armstrong, Michael Freedman, Ken Kelly, and Theresa Singleton, continue to inform my work. Thanks also to Samuel Amartey, the editors of this volume, and two anonymous reviewers for their very helpful comments on an earlier draft of this chapter.

BIBLIOGRAPHY

ADM 11/1/485. Eguafo Native Affairs. Public Records and Archives Administration Department (PRAAD), Accra, Ghana.

Arhin, K. (1966). Diffuse Authority Among the Coastal Fanti. *Ghana Notes and Queries* **9**: 66–70.

Arhin, K. (1983). Rank and Class Among the Asante and Fante in the Nineteenth Century. *Africa* **53** (1): 2–22.

Ashmore, W. A., and Knapp, A. B., eds. (1999). *Archaeologies of Landscape: Contemporary Perspectives*. Basil Blackwell, Oxford.

Barbot, J. (1992). *Barbot on Guinea: The Writings of Jean Barbot on West Africa, 1678–1712*. 2 vols. Edited by P. E. H. Hair, A. Jones, and R. Law. Hakluyt Society, London.

Bender, B., ed. (1993). *Landscape: Politics and Perspectives*. Berg, Oxford.

Bender, B., Hamilton, S., and Tilley, C. (1997). Leskernick: Stone Worlds, Alternative Narratives, Nested Landscapes. *Proceedings of the Prehistoric Society* **63**: 147–78.

Bender, B., Hamilton, S., and Tilley, C. (2007). *Stone Worlds: Narrative and Reflexivity in Landscape Archaeology*. Left Coast Press, Walnut Creek, CA.

Bender, B., and Winer, M., eds. (2001). *Contested Landscapes: Movement, Exile and Place*. Berg, Oxford.

Blake, J. W., ed. (1967) [1942]. *Europeans in West Africa, 1450–1560*. 2 vols. Hakluyt Society, London.

Bloch, M. (1978). The Disconnection Between Power and Rank as a Process: An Outline of the Development of Kingdoms in Central Madagascar. In Friedman, J., and Rowlands, M. J. (eds.), *The Evolution of Social Systems*. Duckworth, London, 303–40.

Boahen, A. (1974a). Fante Diplomacy in the Eighteenth Century. In Ingham, K. (ed.), *Foreign Relations of African States*. Butterworths, London, 25–49.

Boahen, A. (1974b). Arcany or Accany or Arcania and the Accanists of the Sixteenth and Seventeenth Centuries' European Records. *Transactions of the Historical Society of Ghana* **14** (1): 105–12.

Brumfiel, E. M. (1992). Distinguished Lecture in Archaeology: Breaking and Entering the Ecosystem – Gender, Class, and Faction Steal the Show. *American Anthropologist* N.S. **94** (3): 551–67.

Carr, E. (2001). "They Were Looking for White Jobs": The Archaeology of Postcolonial Capitalist Expansion in Coastal Ghana. Ph.D. dissertation, Syracuse University.

Chouin, G. L. (1998). *Eguafo: Un royaume africain "au coeur françois" (1637–1688): Mutations socio-économiques et politique européenne d'un État de la Côte de l'Or (Ghana) au XVIIe siècle*. Afera éditions, Paris.

Chouin, G. L. (1999). Tentation patrilinéaire, guerre et conflits lignagers en milieu akan: Une contribution à l'histoire de la transmission du pouvoir royal en Eguafo (XVII–XXème siècles). In Valsecchi, P., and Viti, F. (eds.), *Mondes Akan/Akan Worlds: Identitè et pouvoir en Afrique occidentale/Identity and power in West Africa*. L'Harmattan, Paris, 169–85.

Chouin, G. L. (2002a). Sacred Groves as Historical and Archaeological Markers in Southern Ghana. *Ghana Studies* **5**: 177–96.

Chouin, G. L. (2002b). Sacred Groves in History: Pathways to the Social Shaping of Forest Landscapes in Coastal Ghana. *IDS Bulletin* **33** (1): 39–46.

Chouin, G. L. (2008). Archaeological Perspectives on Sacred Groves in Ghana. In Sheridan, M. J., and C. Nyamweru (eds.), *African Sacred Groves: Ecological Dynamics and Social Change*. James Currey, Oxford, 178–94.

Chouin, G. L. (2009). Forests of Power and Memory: An Archaeology of Sacred Groves in the Eguafo Polity, Southern Ghana (c. 500 – 1900 A.D.). Ph.D. dissertation, Syracuse University.

Coquery-Vidrovitch, C. (1977). Research on an African Mode of Production. In Gutkind, C. W., and Waterman, P. (eds.), *African Social Systems: A Radical Reader*. Monthly Review Press, New York, 77–92.

Cook, G., and Spiers, S. (2004). Central Region Project: Ongoing Research on Early Contact, Trade and Politics in Coastal Ghana, AD 500–2000. *Nyame Akuma* **61**: 17–28.

Crumley, C. (1994a). Historical Ecology: A Multidimensional Ecological Orientation. In Crumley, C. (ed.), *Historical Ecology: Cultural Knowledge and Changing Landscapes*. School of American Research Press, Sante Fe, 1–16.

Crumley, C. (1994b). The Ecology of Conquest: Contrasting Agropastoral and Agricultural Societies' Adaptations to Climatic Change. In Crumley, C. (ed.), *Historical Ecology: Cultural Knowledge and Changing Landscapes*. School of American Research Press, Sante Fe, 183–201.

Crumley, C. (1995). Heterarchy and the Analysis of Complex Societies. In Ehrenreich, R. M., Crumley, C., and Levy, J. E. (eds.), *Heterarchy and the Analysis of Complex Societies*. American Anthropology Association Papers, Arlington, 1–5.

Daaku, K. Y. (1970). *Trade and Politics on the Gold Coast 1600–1720: A Study of the African Reaction to European Trade*. Oxford University Press, London.

Daaku, K. Y., and van Dantzig, A. (1966). Map of the Regions of the Gold Coast in Guinea. *Ghana Notes and Queries* **9**: 14–15.

Dapper, O. (1967) [1670]. *Beschreibung von Afrika*. Johnson Reprint Corporation, New York.

Davies, O. (1961). Excavations at Kokobin and the Entrenchments in the Oda Area. In Davies, O. (ed.), *Archaeology in Ghana: Papers by O. Davies*. Thomas Nelson and Sons, Edinburgh, 14–26.

DeCorse, C. R. (1987). Excavations at Elmina, Ghana. *Nyame Akuma* **28**: 15–18.

DeCorse, C. R. (1992). Culture Contact, Continuity, and Change on the Gold Coast, AD 1400–1900. *African Archaeological Review* **10**: 163–96.

DeCorse, C. R. (1998). The Europeans in West Africa: Culture Contact, Continuity and Change. In Connah, G. (ed.), *Transformations in Africa: Essays on Africa's Later Past*. Leicester University Press, London, 219–44.

DeCorse, C. R. (2001). *An Archaeology of Elmina: Africans and Europeans on the Gold Coast, 1400–1900*. Smithsonian Institution Press, Washington, DC.

DeCorse, C. R. (2005). Coastal Ghana in the First and Second Millennia AD: Change in Settlement Patterns, Subsistence and Technology. *Journal des Africanistes* **75** (2): 43–54.

DeCorse, C. R. (2008). Varied Pasts: History, Oral Tradition and Archaeology on the Mina Coast. In Brooks, J. F., DeCorse, C. R., and Walton, J. (eds.), *Small Worlds: Method, Meaning and Narrative in Microhistory*. School for Advanced Research, Santa Fe, 76–96.

DeCorse, C. R., Carr, E., Chouin, G. L., Cook, G., and Spiers, S. (2000). Central Region Project, Coastal Ghana – Perspectives 2000. *Nyame Akuma* **53**: 6–11.

DeCorse, C. R., Cook, G., Horlings, R., Pietruszka, A., and Spiers, S. (2009). Transformation in the Era of the Atlantic World: The Central Region Project, Coastal Ghana, 2007–2008. *Nyame Akuma* **72**: 85–94.

DeCorse, C. R., and Spiers, S. (2009). A Tale of Two Polities: Socio-Political Transformation on the Gold Coast in the Atlantic World. *Australasian Historical Archaeology* **27**: 29–42.

Deetz, J. (1990). Prologue: Landscapes as Cultural Statements. In Kelso, W. M., and Most, R. (eds.), *Earth Patterns: Essays in Landscape Archaeology*. University Press of Virginia, Charlottesville, 1–7.

de Marees, P. (1987) [1602]. *Description and Historical Account of the Gold Kingdom of Guinea*. Translated and edited by A. van Dantzig and A. Jones. Oxford University Press, Oxford.

Dumett, R. E. (1971). The Rubber Trade of the Gold Coast and Asante in the Nineteenth Century: African Innovation and Market Responsiveness. *Journal of African History* **12** (1): 79–101.

Earle, T. (1997). *How Chiefs Come to Power: The Political Economy of Prehistory*. Stanford University Press, Stanford, CA.

Ekholm, K. (1972). *Power and Prestige: The Rise and Fall of the Kongo Kingdom*. Skriv Service AB, Uppsala.

Fage, J. D. (1980). A Commentary on Duarte Pacheco Pereira's Account of the Lower Guinea Coastlands in his Esmeraldo de Situ Orbis, and on Some Other Early Accounts. *History in Africa* **7**: 47–80.

Fairhead, J., and Leach, M. (1996). *Misreading the African Landscape: Society and Ecology in a Forest-Savanna Mosaic*. Cambridge University Press, Cambridge.

Feinberg, H. M. (1989). *Africans and Europeans in West Africa: Elminans and Dutchmen on the Gold Coast during the Eighteenth Century*. American Philosophical Society, Philadelphia.

Fisher, C. T., and Thurston, T. L., eds. (1999). Dynamic Landscapes and Socio-Political Process: The Topography of Anthropogenic Environments in Global Perspective. *Antiquity* **73** (281): 630–88.

Fortes, M. (1945). *The Dynamics of Clanship Among the Tallensi*. Oxford University Press, London.

Foulché-Delbosc, R. (1897). Voyage a la Côte Occidentale d'Afrique en Portugal et en Espagne (1479–1480). *Revue Hispanique*. Alphones Picard and Sons, Paris, 174–201.

Fynn, J. K. (1971). *Asante and its Neighbours, 170–1807*. Longman and Northwestern University Press, Evanston, IL.

Fynn, J. K. (1974). *Eguafo, Oral Traditions of the Fante States 2. Unpublished manuscript, copy on file at the Institute of African Studies*. University of Ghana, Legon.

Garrard, T. F. (1980). *Akan Weights and the Gold Trade*. Longman, London.

Godelier, M. (1978). The Concept of the "Asiatic Mode of Production" and Marxist Models of Social Evolution. In Seddon, D. (ed.), *Relations of Production: Marxist Approaches to Economic Anthropology*. Frank Cass, London, 209–57.

Greene, S. E. (2002). *Sacred Sites and the Colonial Encounter: A History of Meaning and Memory in Ghana*. Indiana University Press, Bloomington.

Hair, P. E. H. (1969). An Ethnolinguistic Inventory of the Lower Guinea Coast before 1700: Part II. *African Language Review* **8**: 225–56.

Hair, P. E. H. (1994a). *The Founding of the Castelo de São Jorge da Mina: An Analysis of the Sources*. African Studies Program, University of Wisconsin, Madison.

Hair, P. E. H. (1994b). Early Sources on Guinea. *History in Africa* **21**: 87–126.

Harrison, R. (2004). *Shared Landscapes: Archaeologies of Attachment and the Pastoral Industry in New South Wales*. University of New South Wales Press, Sydney.

Henige, D. P. (1973). Abrem Stool: A Contribution to the History and Historiography of Southern Ghana. *International Journal of African Historical Studies* **6** (1): 1–18.

Henige, D. P. (1974a). Kingship in Elmina before 1869: A Study in "Feedback" and the Traditional Idealization of the Past. *Cahiers d'Études Africaines* **14** (3): 499–520.

Henige, D. P. (1974b). Komenda Fort in 1778: Commentary on a Document. *Transactions of the Historical Society of Ghana* **15** (2): 241–45.

Henige, D. P. (1977). John Kabes of Komenda: An Early African Entrepreneur and State Builder. *Journal of African History* **18** (1): 1–19.

Hicks, D., McAtackney, L., and Fairclough, G., eds. (2007). *Envisioning Landscape: Situations and Standpoints in Archaeology and Heritage*, Left Coast Press, Walnut Creek, CA.

Hodder, I. (1977). The Distribution of Material Culture Items in the Baringo District, Western Kenya. *Man* (n.s.) **12**: 239–69.

Hodder, I. (1979). Economic and Social Stress and Material Culture Patterning. *American Antiquity* **44** (3): 446–54.

Isert, P. E. (1992). *Journey to Guinea and the Caribbean Islands in Columbia* (1788). Translated by S. A. Wisnes. Oxford University Press, Oxford.

Jones, A., ed. and trans. (1983). *German Sources for West African History, 1599–1669*. Franz Steiner, Wiesbaden.

Jones, A., ed. and trans. (1985). *Brandenburg Sources for West African History, 1680–1700*. Franz Steiner, Wiesbaden.

Kankpeyeng, B., and DeCorse, C. R. (2004). Ghana's Vanishing Past: Development, Antiquities, and the Destruction of the Archaeological Record. *African Archaeological Review* **21** (2): 89–128.

Kaplow, S. B. (1978). Primitive Accumulation and Traditional Social Relations on the Nineteenth Century Gold Coast. *Canadian Journal of African Studies* **12** (1): 19–36.

Kea, R. A. (1982). *Settlements, Trade, and Polities in the Seventeenth-Century Gold Coast*. Johns Hopkins University Press, Baltimore.

Kusimba, S. B., and Kusimba, C. M. (2007). Intensification and Protohistoric Agropastoral Systems in East Africa. In Thurston, T. L., and Fisher, C. T. (eds.), *Seeking a Richer Harvest: The Archaeology of Subsistence Intensification, Innovation, and Change*. Springer, New York, 217–33.

Law, R. (2001). *The English in West Africa 1685–1688: The Local Correspondence of the Royal African Company of England, 1681–1699, Part 2*. Oxford University Press, Oxford.

Law, R. (2007). The Komenda Wars, 1694–1700: A Revised Narrative. *History in Africa* **34**: 133–68.

Lefebvre, H. (1991). *The Production of Space*. Blackwell, Oxford.

Marquardt, W. H., and Crumley, C. L. (1987). Theoretical Issues in the Analysis of Spatial Patterning. In Crumley, C. L., and Marquardt, W. H. (eds.), *Regional Dynamics: Burgundian Landscapes in Historical Perspectives*. Academic Press, San Diego, 1–18.

Marx, K. (1975). *Capital, Vol. 1: A Critical Analysis of Capitalist Production*. Translated and edited by Engels. F. International, New York.

McCaskie, T. C. (1990). Nananom Mpow of Mankessim: An Essay in Fante History. In Henige, D., and McCaskie, T. C. (eds.), *West African Economic and Social History: Studies in Memory of Marion Johnson*. African Studies Program, Madison, WI, 133–50.

McCaskie, T. C. (1995). *State and Society in Pre-Colonial Asante*. Cambridge University Press, Cambridge.

McIntosh, S. K. (1999). Pathways to Complexity: An African perspective. In McIntosh, S. K. (ed.), *Beyond Chiefdoms: Pathways to Complexity in Africa*. Cambridge University Press, Cambridge, 1–30.

Metcalfe, G. E. (1964). *Great Britain and Ghana: Documents of Ghana History 1807–1957*. University of Ghana, Thomas Nelson and Sons, London.

Miers, S. (2003). *Slavery in the Twentieth Century: The Evolution of a Global Problem*. Altamira, Oxford.

Miller, D. (1995). Consumption and Commodities. *Annual Review of Anthropology* **24**: 141–61.

Nunoo, R. B. (1948). A Report on Excavations at Nsuta Hill, Gold Coast. *Man* **48**: 73–76.

Pacheco Pereira, D. (1937). *Esmeraldo de Situ Orbis*. Edited and translated by G. H. T. Kimble. Hakluyt Society, London.

Ross, D. H. (1974). Ghanaian Forowa. *African Arts* **8**: 40–49.

Roussier, P. (1935). *L'Établissment d'Issiny: 1687–1702*. Larose, Paris.

Sanders, J. (1975). Warfare and Village Location in Elmina and Eguafo. *Asante Seminar* **2**: 16–17.

Sheridan, M. J. (2008). The Dynamics of African Sacred Groves: Ecological, Social and Symbolic Processes. In Sheridan, M. J., and Nyamweru, C. (eds.), *African Sacred Groves: Ecological Dynamics and Social Change*. James Currey, Oxford, 9–41.

Smith, A., and Gazin-Schwartz, A., eds. (2008), *Landscapes of Clearance: Archaeological and Anthropological Perspectives*. Left Coast Press, Walnut Creek, CA.

Spiers, S. (2002). Struggling Pasts: A Commentary. *International Journal of Historical Archaeology* **6** (3): 217–24.

Spiers, S. (2007). The Eguafo Kingdom: Investigating Complexity in Southern Ghana. Ph.D. dissertation, Syracuse University.

Terray, E. (1974). Long Distance Exchange and the Formation of the State: The Case of the Abron Kingdom of Gyaman. *Economy and Society* **3** (3): 315–45.

Thurston, T. L., and Fisher, C. T., eds. (2007). *Seeking a Richer Harvest: The Archaeology of Subsistence Intensification, Innovation, and Change*. Springer, New York.

Teixeira da Mota, A., and Hair, P. E. H. (1988). *East of Mina: Afro-European Relations on the Gold Coast in the 1550s and 1560s, an Essay with Supporting Documents*. University of Wisconsin, Madison.

Ucko, P., and Layton, R., eds. (1999). *The Archaeology and Anthropology of Landscape: Shaping Your Landscape*. Routledge, London.

van Dantzig, A. (1978). *The Dutch and the Guinea Coast, 1674–1742: A Collection of Documents from the General State Archive at The Hague*. Ghana Academy of Arts and Sciences, Accra.

van Dantzig, A. (1990). The Akanists: A West African Hansa. In Henige, D., and McCaskie, T. C. (eds.), *West African Economic and Social History: Studies in Memory of Marion Johnson*. African Studies Program, University of Wisconsin Press, Madison, 205–16.

Villault, N. (Sieur de Bellefond) (1670). *Relation of the Coasts of Africk Called Guinee*. English Translation, 2nd ed. John Starkey, London.

Vogt, J. (1979). *Portuguese Rule on the Gold Coast, 1469–1682*. University of Georgia Press, Athens.

Wilks, I. (1993). *Forests of Gold: Essays on the Akan and the Kingdom of Asante*. Ohio University Press, Athens.

Yarak, L. (1977). The Dutch-Elmina Peace Initiative of 1754–1758. *Asantesem* **7**: 26–31.

Yarak, L. (2003). The Kingdom of Wasa and Fante Diplomacy in Eighteenth-Century Ghana. In Falola, T. (ed.), *Ghana in Africa and the World*. Africa World Press, Trenton, NJ, 141–53.

Yoffee, N. (2005). *Myths of the Archaic State: Evolution of the Earliest Cities, States and Civilizations*. Cambridge University Press, Cambridge.

5

From the Shadow of an Atlantic Citadel: An Archaeology of the Huedan Countryside

Neil L. Norman

> From the fifteenth century [A.D.], as sailors of the Iberian peninsula began to take their ships around the coast of Africa, we begin to find an accumulation of written European sources on African towns . . . [in the areas they visited] we find some of Africa's most deeply rooted and enduring urban cultures. (Anderson and Rathbone 2000:3)

> Europeans are but little acquainted with the inland parts of *Whidah*, their Knowledge of the Country being almost wholly confined to the Road, which lies between the Port of *Whidah* and the capital Town [of Savi]. (Astley 1745–7:9; italics in original)

INTRODUCTION

These passages highlight a tension in the investigation of Atlantic African urban cultures. In their review of recent historical and archaeological research, David Anderson and Richard Rathbone (2000) conclude that established coastal West African *towns* served as the backdrop for major exchanges and moments of discovery. In generating these urban histories, researchers from most academic traditions draw heavily on documentary accounts generated by Western European traders, travelers, and explorers. This is nowhere more true than with the narrative history of Savi, a major seventeenth- to eighteenth-century trading entrepôt along the West African coast and the palatial capital of the Hueda kingdom. Thomas Astley[1] notes, however, that Europeans living and trading at Savi (Figure 5.1) had little knowledge of the scope of this major West African urban culture beyond the palace and the road linking it to the Atlantic Ocean. As European chroniclers peered from the palace and queried Huedan elites on the extent of the kingdom, they recorded Savi as a densely settled town with international markets, state-supported temples, and a hierarchical political structure with a king and vast elite class at its apex (Bosman 1705; Phillips 1732; Smith 1967 [1744]).

These evocative documents focus on the centrality of Savi at local and international levels. However, few accounts characterize life outside of the royal court at Savi. Despite the historically opaque content of the broader Savi settlement system, researchers make strong arguments that Savi sat amid a functionally differentiated countryside with goods and services flowing from rural areas to urban ones (Manning 1989; cf. Fox 1977; Law 1990, 1991). This chapter offers an evaluation of such propositions by specifically addressing the secondary palace complexes and rural settlements surrounding Savi – the sites that heretofore have been presented in the shadow of Savi's Atlantic-era fluorescence. By refocusing the investigative gaze on the broader Hueda settlement system and highlighting the often conflicting interests of countryside residents, a new perspective is put forward on the rise and collapse of Hueda. The internal divisions and occasional outright warfare between Huedan political factions are long-standing research topics (Akinjogbin 1967; Law 1990). Indeed, the inability of Huedan elites to parlay Atlantic

Figure 5.1
Project area with major cities and approximate political boundaries c. 1700; adapted from Law (1991:232).

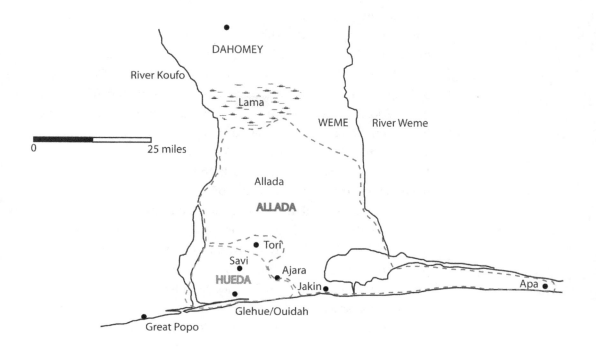

riches into a sustainable polity and regional preeminence causes some to question what real impact the Atlantic world had on shaping Huedan political and economic developments (Eltis 2000:184). This chapter offers an archaeological perspective on the emergence, political operation, and factionalism of the Hueda polity and foregrounds entanglement within Atlantic commercial systems in these processes. It presents an example of an immensely prosperous, yet politically tenuous, coalition of urban and rural dwellers. In so doing, it builds on a growing body of scholarship that challenges archaeologists to isolate and compare the conflicting needs and strategies of the constitutive groups in complex societies, rather than seeing these civilizations as adaptive wholes (cf. Brumfiel 1995; Schwartz and Falconer 1994; Smith 2010). This chapter addresses the issue of urban rural dynamics within the human landscape surrounding Savi and argues that the residues of the performance of power, the creation of political legitimacy, and exercise of authority are inscribed on that landscape (Fleisher and Wynn-Jones 2010; Monroe 2010; Smith 2003).

ATLANTIC CITADELS AND THEIR COUNTRYSIDES

The investigation of urban forms is a growing concern in West Africa archaeology. Early archaeological research on urbanism, notably in Southwest Asia and Mesoamerica, defined cities in terms of a series of characteristic traits, such as density of settlement, literacy, monumentality, and evidence of science and astronomy (Childe 1950; Sjoberg 1960). Early settlement centers in sub-Saharan Africa were often lacking in one or more of these characteristics, however. Hence the continent was largely omitted from these early discussions (LaViolette and Fleisher 2005; S. K. McIntosh 1997, 1999). Susan and Roderick McIntosh (S. K. McIntosh and R. J. McIntosh 1984, 1995) have demonstrated the need to move beyond trait-list approaches to urbanism. Rather than focusing on what a city "is" in terms of its internal qualities, the McIntoshes insist, following Trigger (1972:577), that "whatever else the city may be, it is a unit of settlement which performs specialized functions in relation to a broader hinterland." This functional approach defines a city in terms of its purpose to a larger region and emphasizes the dynamic relationship between various elements operating within a settlement system (Blanton 1976;

Hodder and Orton 1976). Such an approach demands that the investigation of urbanism not use hinterlands to simply provide a fuller understanding of the city proper, but recognize the inexorable intellectual connection between the parallel and often coeval processes of urbanism and ruralization (cf. Yoffee 1997:260).

Archaeological approaches that examine material culture and architectural evidence to contextualize settlement centers and evaluate the political, economic, and social ties that interrelate centers to countrysides are long-standing (Adams 1965; Flannery 1972; Willey 1953). Acknowledging the strength of archaeological methods and theories for addressing such issues, researchers repeatedly call for the archaeology of the early African Atlantic to move beyond fort- and palace-centric research paradigms (DeCorse 2001b; Kelly 2004; Posnansky and DeCorse 1986; Stahl 2001b). In coastal West Africa, countrysides and towns surrounding palaces often contained the demographic majority of settlement systems. Thus focused research in these contexts offers real challenges to external historic narratives focused on European traders and conventionally elite-focused narratives replete with named African kings and the actions of entitled political leaders (cf. LaViolette and Fleisher 2005). Accordingly, the countryside has emerged as a locale worthy of research in its own right (Stahl 2001a). Yet, the archaeology of regions surrounding major trading centers involved in Atlantic exchanges is in its earliest stages (DeCorse 2001a; DeCorse et al. 2000; Kelly 1995, 2003; Monroe 2003, 2007; cf. Ogundrian 2002; Richard 2005; Stahl 2001b; Usman 2001).

In advancing such research in West Africa, Ann Stahl (1999:47–48) calls for archaeologists to extend into hinterlands with methodologies that include a "regional approach that is sensitive to variability within regions through time." A major facet of this research agenda has been to explore the active role played by Africans in the emerging Atlantic system (Mitchell 2005). Through such research, we have come to realize that integrating local political and economic networks into the Atlantic world often had the effect of intensifying and centralizing these structures – European contact and interaction did not necessarily spawn novel structures or networks (Kelly 1995). As Christopher DeCorse (2001b:2) describes, the expanding Euro-centric economic system is simply one variable in a complex local "intricately textured mosaic of interactions" that integrated novel

European players into a deep history or transregional political and economic exchange (cf. Brooks 1993). Scholarship at major trading centers thus refutes a long line of research conducted within a "colonial paradigm" (Sinclair et al. 1995:22–23) that stressed outside trade and influences as the primary stimulus for African urban complexes, state formation, and novel political and economic innovations (Clark, 1962; Hopkins 1973).

Such biases are compounded by the fact that the predominate source used for interpreting the cities of the African Atlantic are travel logs, ship manifests, and published traveler accounts, all of which contain the concerns, bias, and misunderstandings of their authors and compliers. As for the Hueda example, such documents have been used to argue that functionally differentiated countrysides supported the palace center (Law 2000; Manning 1989). Despite the presumably urban nature of these politically, socially, and economically centralized settlement systems, historical accounts of rural countrysides remain incomplete. The unevenness of documentary sources calls into question the degree to which hinterland settlements were integrated into a broader settlement system or operated as autonomous entities.

Andrew Reid and Paul Lane (2004) call for historical archaeologies of Africa to be mindful of the utility of historical techniques applied to very early sites previously considered beyond the interpretive reach of documentary or oral sources (cf. R. McIntosh 2005). Expanding, and in some cases establishing, common intellectual territory for addressing sites once considered disparate by their designation as either historic or prehistoric is a laudable goal. Building on such hybrid vigor, archaeologists of sites firmly embedded in the historical Atlantic world should be mindful of the utility of techniques and theories used by our colleagues on sites where urbanism or regional integration cannot be assumed or implied through documentary sources. This chapter forwards systematic regional survey as a means of foregrounding the smaller-scale sites that remain in the shadow of major Atlantic centers and institutions (cf. Ogundrian 2007) and archaeologically testing rather than taking for granted urban–rural relations (S. K. McIntosh and R. J. McIntosh 1984). The research builds directly on previous archaeological research at Savi itself by Kelly (1995, 1997a, 1997b, 2001, 2002) and presents new data from the surrounding countryside to illustrate a more holistic view of the content and connectivity of the Savi settlement system.

THE SAVI COUNTRYSIDE FROM THE CITADEL LOOKING OUT

The prevailing historical narrative for the Savi region concerns political transformation and conflict, economic exchange between local and foreign groups, and demographic intensification and fluctuation, particularly as these events and processes related to elite Africans negotiating the emergent Atlantic world (Bay 2001:42). In order to open the aperture as widely as possible on the region beyond the Huedan palace at Savi, this section engages previous research and works from inside the dominant historic narrative and thus from perspectives that highlight palace dwellers and their built spaces, outward into the Huedan countryside.[2]

By the mid-sixteenth century, African elite groups from the palace-centered polity of Allada dominated trade with Europeans in the Bight of Benin. Fueled by New World demands for labor, competition among European traders for captured Africans reached a fever pitch in the mid- to late seventeenth century. New African players emerged, as European traders in search of relief from monopolistic trading relations with Allada built economic ties with the kingdoms of Hueda and, somewhat later, Dahomey. These three palace-based polities were the political and economic juggernauts of the Bight of Benin from about 1600–1890. Hueda was first mentioned by name in European accounts in 1671, when the French established a trading factory within the bounds of the kingdom (Law 1990:211). The 1670s mark a watershed for European–African interactions in the area and the start of a period of significant written documentation.

At approximately the same time that Hueda entered the historic record, Huedan elites wrested political independence from Allada (Akinjogbin 1967:36–53; Law 1990:213). From the 1670–80s, political relations in the region spiraled downward as competition between Hueda and Allada over trade and war captives grew (Law 1991). Huedan kings and their associates administered political economies oriented towards funneling war captives to the sea and taxing traders moving through their territories. Huedan trade in war captives peaked in the early eighteenth century, amounting to approximately 10,000 people being spirited across the Atlantic per year (Law 1991:165–80). In contrast, the local Huedan economy was oriented around indigenous markets, the largest of which took place near the palace at Savi every four days (Phillips 1732:221–22). Savi markets were large affairs that drew thousands. Every second market cycle, traders from throughout Hueda and neighboring regions visited Savi to exchange both local and imported items (Law 1991:48–49). Astley (1745–7:11) recounts other travelers' descriptions to note the vast range of items available for sale:

> The Markets are surrounded with little Booths occupied by Cooks, or Sutlers, who sell the People Victuals: But they can only sell Meat, wither Beef, Pork, Goat's Flesh, or Dog's, there being other Booths, where Women sell Bread, Rice, Millet, Maize, and *Kûskûs*: others sell *Pito*, (or *Pitow*) which is a kind of refreshing Beer, well tasted, and not heady. In other booths are sold Palm-Wine and Brandy ... *European* Cloth of all Sorts; Linen and Woolen, printed Calicos, Silks, Grocery-Ware, China, Gold in Dust, or Bars; Iron in Bars, or wrought: In a Word, all sorts of *European* Goods, as well as the Produce of *Africa* and *Asia* ... Their chief Wares to sell, are *Whidah*-Cloths, Mats, Baskets, Jars for *Pito*, Kalabashes of all Kinds, wooden Bowls and Cups, red and blue Pepper, *Malaghetta*, Salt, Palm-Oil, *Kanki*, and the like. (Astley 1745–7:11; italics in original)

Huedan farmers and artisans were the driving force of the local economy and provided the foodstuffs and wares sold in the king's market. Conservative population estimates for Hueda as a whole (approximately 100,000 people during the early eighteenth century) suggest that there was a high degree of production capacity for the kingdom (Law 1991:59). Although prices were subject to state regulation, they were largely driven by market fluctuations (Law 1992). Thus by around 1690, the Huedan kingdom was clearly well integrated into a variety of regional and international commercial networks and maintained a highly commercialized domestic economy.

In addition to evidence for a central market, the historical record suggests that the palace was a central place for judicio-political deliberations (Law 1991:89) and a key locale for the celebration of Huedan ancestral deities and the tutelary python deity *Dangbe*. The various kings of Hueda often presided, sometimes alongside the high priest to *Dangbe*, over ceremonies that venerated the python deity, thought to bring material wealth and provide physical protection against enemies. During the main ceremony dedicated to *Dangbe*, scheduled annually but held sporadically, the king paraded from the palace to the temple bestowing largess on elites who administered regional governorships (Law 1991:94–96). This enormous capital outlay made holding the parade a financial burden on Huedan royalty. Because large numbers Huedans attended the parade, contemporary

European travelers were probably correct in suggesting this carnival-like atmosphere helped to bolster the legitimacy of Huedan kings (Norman and Kelly 2004). Nonetheless, it is apparent that the parade became a burdensome responsibility of elite Huedans and a right demanded by the populace (Norman 2010).

Given the centrality of *Dangbe* in public spheres, it is notable that the three last kings of an expansive Hueda (Agbangala d. 1703, Aysan reign 1703–1708, and Huffon reign 1708–1727, d. 1733) each attempted to distance themselves from participation in the annual parade to the temple of *Dangbe* (Law 1990). Tension resulting from the king neglecting these ceremonies was symptomatic of larger internal problems between rebelling secondary regional administrators and the crown. As internal factions grew during the reign of Huffon in the 1720s, the Dahomean king Agaja took advantage of the contentious situation in Hueda and annexed the Huedan kingdom to his own. In the resulting Huedan/Dahomean war of 1727, the Hueda army was humbled. Thousands of Huedans were killed or sold into slavery, tens of thousands more displaced, and the royal palace at Savi was burned to the ground. The former palace at Savi would be reintroduced sporadically into the historical record by Europeans visiting its ruins in the late eighteenth (Norris 1789) and mid-nineteenth centuries (Burton 1966:92–94). However, it would await sustained scholarly investigation until the 1990s.

Kenneth Kelly (1995) was the first to use archaeological and ethnohistorical techniques to investigate the former Huedan palace at Savi. In this investigation, Kelly used single survey (i.e., one test in width) transects from the center of a concentration of collapsed architectural features identified by local residents as a possible location of the palace. The survey crew team conducted a 6-m-diameter "dogleash" surface collection and a shovel test pit every 100 m along the transects and extended transects in each cardinal direction for a total of 5 km coverage north–south by 4.8 km coverage east–west. Artifact drop-off at the end of these transects led Kelly to interpret the cluster of architecture and artifacts, the point of origin for the survey, as a portion of the former palace. Excavations immediately surrounding the palace, particularly Kelly's House Areas 1–2 and 4–6, which were presumably nonelite areas, revealed a concentric series of densely packed structures. Although these outlying structures also contained many similar riches imported from across the Atlantic (e.g., Dutch trade pipes, wine bottles, and trade beads), they did not contain the high diversity of types nor the extraordinary quantities found inside the palace itself.

Based on this work inside and outside the palace, Kelly posited that Savi stretched approximately 5 km north–south/east–west. With the population of the modern village of Savi as a guide (3,000 residents) (1995:213–14), Kelly cautiously offered a population estimate for the circa 1727 town and palace of between 75,000 and 80,000 people. Given that these figures amount to approximately 75 percent of the population recorded by European visitors for the entire polity, however, Kelly noted that this was an improbably high number.

Yet, these archaeological findings are in general agreement with contemporary eighteenth-century historical accounts, which unanimously describe the Kingdom of Hueda as exceedingly populous. By the late seventeenth century, for example, travelers noted that the kingdom is "so populous, and close[ly] inhabited" that the area had reached its carrying capacity and large wild animals were difficult to be found (Bosman 1705:390). Indeed, in the late seventeenth century it appears that most arable land in the kingdom was under agriculture. Bosman (1705:339) recorded that "the [people] of this country are so covetous, that no place which is thought fertile can escape planting, though even within the Hedges which enclose their Villages and Dwelling-places." Snelgrave added that the greater Savi region was so populated that it resembled one large agricultural complex:

the land was become so stock[e]d with people, that the whole country appeared full of towns and villages: and being a very rich soil, all well cultivated by the inhabitants, it looked like an [e]ntire garden. (Snelgrave 1734:3)

Despite clear references to a vast and densely populated urban complex, we know little of the Huedan countryside or its political boundaries. Bosman expressed frustration in attempts to define the limits of the Hueda polity:

During my stay here, I used all possible means to discover the length and breadth of the Kingdom but could never obtain a farther satisfactory account than that its Extent along the Sea-shore is about nine or ten miles; and in the middle is reaches six or seven miles inland: after which it extends like two Arms; and in some places is ten or twelve Miles broad, and in other much narrower. (Bosman 1705:338)

Based on extrapolation from earlier traveler's accounts, Astley (1745–47:8) suggested that there were twenty-six Huedan provinces "given" to prominent men of the kingdom, each with a "Chief Town" or secondary administrative center at its center. Phillips added that "on the road to the king's town [at Savi] are several little villages, or parcels of houses" (Philips 1732: 216–17), indicating a third tier of the Huedan settlement system, beyond the center at Savi and the secondary administrative centers.

This historical and archaeological evidence strongly suggests that during the period of the emergence of Hueda ca. 1650 until the collapse of the polity in 1727, Savi served the surrounding countryside as a center for religious, political, economic, and judicial processes. As such a center for deliberations that would resonate through economic networks at local, regional, and international levels, profits from exchanges poured into the palace. The next section tracks the movement of these goods throughout the Hueda coalition to evaluate the integration of the polity and posit the local political dynamics that lay behind its collapse.

FROM THE SAVI COUNTRYSIDE LOOKING INTO THE CITADEL

The main body of data for this project was collected in two-month summer field seasons (2003 and 2004) and an extended research program of a year and a half (2005–2006). During this fieldwork, project members[3] conducted archaeological and architectural survey within a 10-km block surrounding the palace at Savi and conducted over one hundred ethnohistoric interviews throughout southeastern Bénin (Figure 5.2). The size of the survey universe was chosen based on J. Cameron Monroe's (2003:204–44) argument that major service centers on the Abomey Plateau (100 km to the north) were, in the precolonial period, an average of 10.75 km from their nearest neighbor (cf. Hodder and Orton 1976:57). It was assumed, therefore, that a survey universe extending approximately 5 km outwards from Savi would include the vast majority of sites politically and economically associated with the center.

The survey methodology depended on two survey strategies: transects up to 1.5 km long placed to sample high-probability areas identified in Landsat V satellite imagery (Transects 1–8) and systematically placed 0.5-km transects (Transects 9–54). In both phases of the survey, 6-m-diameter "dogleash" surface collection was conducted at 100-m intervals along transects. In total, the project team conducted

54 survey transects covering 35 km and containing 407 surface collection tests, representing 2.8 percent coverage of the survey universe. Three hundred and seventeen (78%) of the tests were positive for at least one artifact. Indeed, the survey universe was so densely scattered with artifacts, particularly locally produced ceramics, that it proved impossible to identify the limits of distinct "sites" using crosscutting transects or other techniques.[4] The vast majority of the survey-recovered ceramics were similar in paste type and surface treatment to the seven ware types identified by Kelly (1995), suggesting these outlying archaeological deposits and the palace center were contemporary.[5] What appears to have been continuous regional ceramic scatter, however, should not be considered one large residential zone but several concentrated primary living areas. These were connected by productive zones, mostly agricultural, where rural inhabitants used, broke, and discarded ceramics and other artifacts.

This survey identified twenty-one loci of deflated architecture, such as half-meter-thick exterior earthen walls melted by torrential seasonal rains into low mounds.[6] Time constraints, dense vegetation, survey restrictions, and the density of architectural features did not allow firm boundaries to be established at these features, and future research will be geared towards identifying connections between these loci. Nonetheless, these loci were classified based on the size of the architectural elements, the density and richness of artifacts, and evidence for the types of productive activity taking place therein (e.g., agricultural village, secondary administrative center). The densest concentration of architectural loci form two major axes: a southwest–northeast zone surrounding the modern road between Abomey and the sea and an east–west trending area surrounding the banks of Lake Toho (Figure 5.3).

Seven of these twenty-one loci (Figure 5.4), all of which contained deposits contemporary with Savi, were chosen for excavation and further exploration: three villages (Loci 1, 5, 6), three secondary administrative centers (Loci 2, 4, 7), and one smelting center (Locus 3).[7] Fifty excavation units ranging from 1 m × 1 m tests to 3 m × 2 m blocks were placed judgmentally throughout these loci to test different architectural zones (e.g., ditches, rooms, courtyards, middens). At least 12 m^2 of material were excavated at each locus, for a total of 123 m^2 (269 m^3), and all soil was sifted through 0.13-cm screen. Some general trends can be highlighted from these initial excavations. One of the more interesting discoveries was the presence of clear and distinct stratigraphy between Hueda-era and earlier deposits at all loci except 2 and 3. Lower levels typically contained friable coarse local ceramics and local stone tools and debitage.[8] These strata were overlain by levels containing Hueda-era material (early-seventeenth- to early-eighteenth-century imported material and local ceramics with mostly hard-pastes). Radiocarbon dates for these sites are pending, but it is likely that these earlier strata represent Late Stone Age (LSA) occupation in the area. It is possible, therefore, that these units identified a transition, between LSA and iron-using groups.

When viewed in concert, loci with heavy concentrations of presumably LSA material near Lake Toho and loci with heavy Savi-era material, but lacking LSA materials away from the lake but near

FROM THE SAVI COUNTRYSIDE LOOKING INTO THE CITADEL

Figure 5.2
Archaeological survey transects.

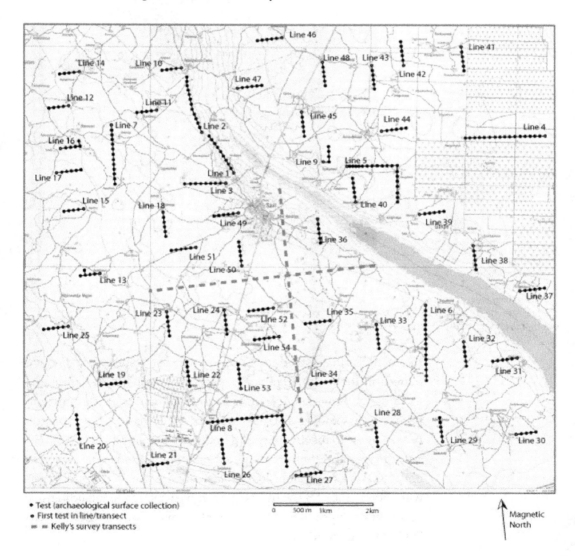

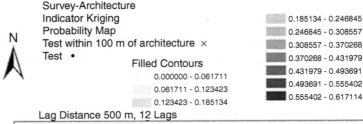
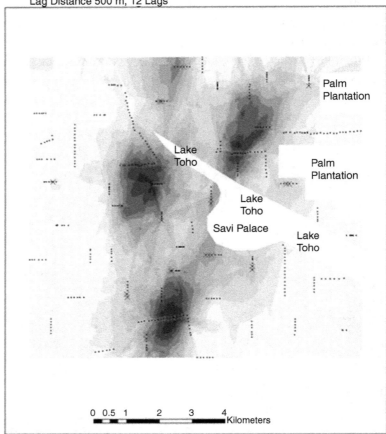

Figure 5.3
Krigged density map of architectural features. *Note:* The white zones on the eastern half of the map are the zones omitted from the survey.

the main north–south trade corridor, suggest a shifting settlement pattern in the early Atlantic Era away from aquatic resources and towards the economic resources of international trade. When comparing the assemblages of the two periods, there is an order of magnitude increase in the diversity and frequency of material between LSA assemblages and those for Savi-era material. For example, whereas only two types of friable coarse earthenware and two vessel forms were defined for LSA assemblages, eight ware types, including five highly fired types, and fifteen vessel forms were recorded for the Savi-era countryside loci.

There is remarkable similarity in the ware types and vessel forms recorded in the Savi countryside and those recorded by Kelly (1995: 139–57) within the palace. Likewise, distinctive ceramic decoration, such as rouletting, stamping, incising, and composites of these three recovered in the palace, were recorded at sites in Savi's countryside. Overall, similarity in size, form, and the decorative techniques applied to ceramics recovered from Savi and sites in its hinterland, and scarce evidence for ceramic production (4 wasters out of 98,386 sherds) from countryside sites, suggests ceramics were centrally produced and sold through the Savi markets. Historical references suggest the "wives" of Huedan kings held royal monopolies on particular activities in the market. These included beer brewing and special

FROM THE SAVI COUNTRYSIDE LOOKING INTO THE CITADEL

Figure 5.4 Excavation Loci.

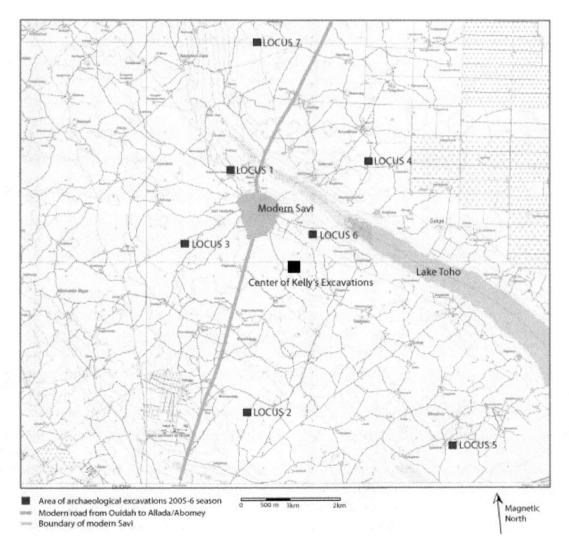

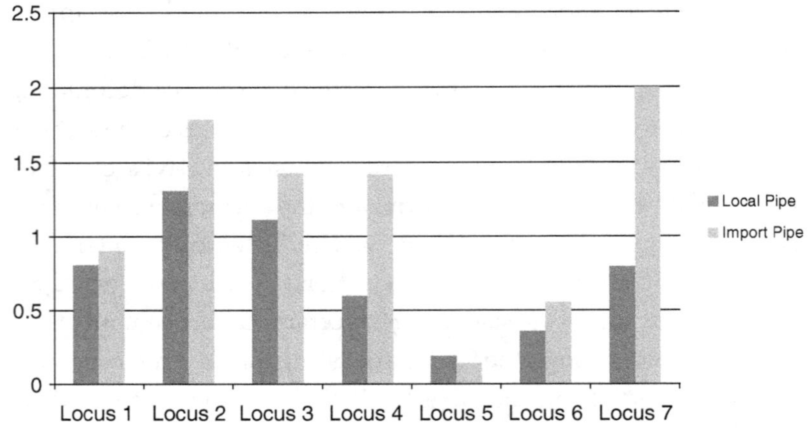

Figure 5.5
Artifact counts divided
by cubic meters of mate-
rial excavated.

trading status in such items as fiber "basketware" (Law 1991:81) and presumably other containers. Perhaps this archaeological pattern resulted from the efforts of these royal women. The relative frequencies of these vessel types and other artifact types are notable in that they speak to the political organization of the Hueda coalition. Fragments of large (up to a meter in height) storage jars are more frequent in larger scale sites (Loci 2, 3, 4, and 7) than they are in smaller ones (Loci 1, 5, and 6). In contrast, there is a high concentration of Hueda-era grinding stones and cooking vessels at smaller-scale sites (Figure 5.5). This artifact distribution appears to have resulted from a socioeconomic system where staple grains grown and processed in the hinterland were transferred to larger-scale sites for storage and consumption.

SMOKE AND ASHES

One of the clearest indications that dwellers of the Huedan countryside were economically integrated into the early Atlantic world is the presence of imported European white clay and locally produced tobacco pipes at sites across the region around Savi. The regional distribution of pipes identified through survey and excavation suggests a countryside with many smokers. The distribution of these pipes, however, was not even (Figure 5.6). Measured in terms of cubic material excavated per site, the secondary administrative centers and the smelting center had a much higher frequency of imported pipes than did the village sites and a slightly higher frequency of local pipes. This regional pattern in itself suggests central

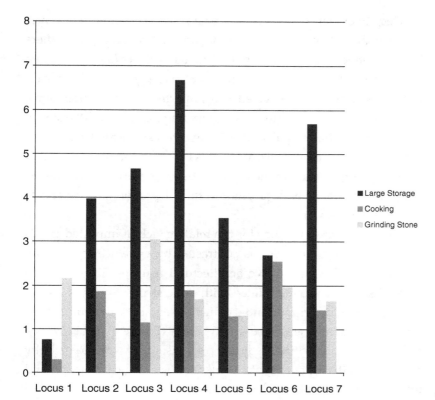

Figure 5.6
Smoking pipe counts divided by cubic meters of material excavated.

distribution, with pipes concentrated in markets and storehouses associated with elite areas. Presumably, the imported pipes, and the tobacco that charged them, were filtered through markets at Savi because the trade in international items was administered by the Huedan king and his seconds. Both local and imported tobacco pipes allowed rural Huedans to wield a symbol that is often associated with Huedan, and later Dahomean, elite status. Historical evidence (Skertchly 1874:25, 396) suggests elite women in Dahomey controlled the production and sale of pipes in this kingdom (Bay 1998:210), and the same may have been true for Hueda.[9] For example, Phillips (1737:216) records that during his visit the king at Savi "was smoking tobacco in a long wooden pipe, the bole [sic] of which, I dare say, would hold an ounce, and rested on his throne" (Phillips 1737:216). It is possible that countryside people acquired these pipes through purchase at the Savi markets or through the complex systems of redistribution that linked elites and nonelite Huedans (Law 1991). In either case the pipes are visible symbols of wealth and prosperity found throughout the settlement Hueda settlement system.

Despite evidence that the Savi palace served as a market center and a possible source of local and imported tobacco pipes, there was a relative lack of fine imported items in the countryside when compared to the heavy concentration of these goods in the palace. Kelly (1995:139–256) recovered 946 imported ceramics fragments, 3,276 import pipe fragments, 4,878 glass fragments, and 258 beads in excavations within the palace district. In contrast, the total quantity of material recovered from *all* excavations in the countryside amounted to merely 9 imported ceramics fragments, 372 import pipe fragments, 83 glass fragments, and 34 beads – thus a pronounced difference emerges (Figure 5.7).

Archaeological evidence for the relative lack of imported goods in rural contexts, however, is contrasted by evidence for a countryside packed with massive architectural features. These include palatial secondary centers filled with large structures (25 × 15 m), often surrounded with boundary ditches segments similar to those identified around the palace at Savi itself (Figure 5.4). Elsewhere, Kelly and I (Norman and Kelly 2004; see also Blier 1998:104–5; Kelly 1997a) argue that ditches evoked Huedan cosmological elements and follow a general pattern observed across West Africa where architectural features are used to materialize social distance between elite and nonelite members of the community. The presences of ditches and massive structures in and around secondary centers throughout indicate the presence of a powerful elite class in the Savi countryside. These rural Huedan elites were able to command surplus labor and create symbols of political authority that rivaled those of the palace. Furthermore, the presence of secondary administrative sites with imposing structures encircled by boundary ditches suggests that these regional administrators, although lacking the quantity of imported items commanded by the king, nonetheless held a high degree of political autonomy (Norman 2009a).

Quite possibly Huedan kings, and especially King Huffon, were more concerned with channeling the riches of the Atlantic world into their palace than they were in maintaining a regional coalition. When viewed in terms of a social system predicated on redistribution, in which kings dispensed largess to maintain the social ties necessary to muster wealth in attached and affiliated people (cf. Bay 1998:119–65; Guyer and Belinga 1995), the pooling of sumptuary artifacts in the palace could represent a blockage in the flow items used to secure goodwill – an ultimately catastrophic political strategy. Snelgrave, in

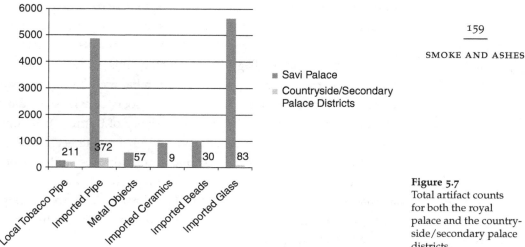

Figure 5.7
Total artifact counts for both the royal palace and the countryside/secondary palace districts.

his oft-quoted summary of the Huedan political world under Huffon, foreshadowed this interpretation when he commented:

> For the great men [of Hueda] played the petty tyrants, often falling out, and pursuing their particular interests, without regarding the good of their king or country. By this means the common people were divided, and such parties arose among them, as, added to their fears, rendered them prey to their neighbors. (Snelgrave 1734:5)

Historic accounts suggest that such political stress reached a high point during the later reign of Huffon where John Atkins (1737:110), who visited Savi in 1721, noted that Huffon had not left his palace for several years. Atkins suggests that one reason for the seclusion was a large "Dole" he owed to the people.

Hueda could not weather the divisions that emerged in its countryside over the long term. In 1727, Dahomean troops invaded Hueda, seized Savi, and razed the palace by fire. This moment of massive wholesale displacement, death, and the sale of Huedan peoples across the Atlantic is considered one of the defining moments in the consolidation of African polities in the early African Atlantic (Akinjogbin 1967; Law 1991). Yet, heretofore little has been known about the extent of destruction across Hueda. Excavations in Savi's countryside yielded evidence for burning at Loci 1, 3, 4, 5, and signs of catastrophic burning were recorded at Loci 2, 6, 7. Notably, these latter sites were all classified as secondary administrative centers. Although there is a long history in the region of razing house compounds with fire after the death of a patriarch or matriarch, such destruction is, and was, almost always followed by a period of rebuilding (Blier 2005). Only Locus 1 exhibited signs of sustained habitation after the eighteenth century, and this site was located adjacent to a modern village. Taken together, this evidence suggests that these sites were destroyed during combat and that Dahomean troops specifically targeted the structures associated with secondary Huedan administrators. In addition, evidence of burning from one secondary administrative center and one village site each at least 4 km from the palace core suggest many, perhaps most, of the structures surrounding Savi were put to the torch (Norman 2009a). Thus just as the nonelite Huedan shared in the riches of Atlantic commerce, so did they share in the disastrous results of regional strife that often rode in the wake of European traders.

CONCLUSION

The emerging Atlantic world and the global systems of interaction that connected it did not end at the major palaces and trading centers of the West African coast. Nonelite Huedans were integral members of polities that are largely known through their major settlement centers bristling with cannons and brimming with massive structures. In the Savi area, nonelite Huedans sustained the kingdom through agricultural production and constructed many of the monumental edifices considered synonymous with royal authority. In turn, nonelite Huedans used local markets at Savi to participate in an international consumer revolution. As the Atlantic world unfolded and Huedan prosperity rose, people poured into and around the Savi area, particularly near the major trade corridor that connected Savi to the sea. At a general level, these archaeological findings are in strong agreement with the historical record. Yet, the socioeconomic integration of Hueda belies the factiousness that worked against the fragile Huedan political coalition. Secondary administrators pursued their own interests and sought to create their own architectural legacies. Arguably, the pooling of Atlantic resources inside the Savi palace added to political tensions as Huedan kings in general and Huffon in particular pursued a policy of amassing and centralizing wealth, rather than redistributing it across the polity. Quite possibly, such political intrigue and stifling demands for labor by elites were contributing factors to the fact that nonelite Huedans did not take up arms when Dahomey raided in 1727 (Bay 1998:56–63). Just as the Savi countryside was critical to the development of one Savi, so were divisions emanating from this countryside fundamental to its disintegration. Archaeological investigations provide the lines of evidence necessary to draw the town and countryside surrounding Savi out of the shadow of one of the best documented Atlantic African urban citadels (Ogundiran 2007).

By contextualizing Savi within the network of relations that linked it to the surrounding countryside, we arrive at a more holistic view of the economic and social dynamics that encouraged integration and the political pressures that forced it apart. Archaeologists, who engage in comparative theory building for the global phenomenon of urbanism, have long recognized the need to address such connectivity and stress. It is hoped that archaeologists addressing emerging social complexity will be mindful of both the unique forms of urbanism present on the African continent (S. K. McIntosh and R. J. McIntosh 1984, 1995) and of examples such as the Savi urban settlement system where similar processes can be identified and explored vis-à-vis other sites separated by time and space. In so doing, we forward not only the comparative project of anthropological archaeology, but also highlight the historical issue that many Africans entering the diaspora lived in, or passed through, fully urban places before entering the horrors of the Middle Passage. Africa, and Africans, were fundamentally involved in "making" the Atlantic world (Thornton 1998), and moreover, they were also instrumentally involved in shaping the character of Atlantic urbanism.

ACKNOWLEDGEMENTS

Kenneth Kelly first introduced me to the archaeology of the Hueda and continues to generously support my research and academic development. Intellectually, this project was forged through coursework at the University of Virginia with Adria LaViolette, Jeffery Hantman, Joseph Miller, Steve Plog, and Fraser Neiman. I offer special thanks to Adria LaViolette, who through numerous conversations and frequent review brought clarity to muddled thoughts and attempted to untangle my mangled prose. I would like to thank Prof. Alexis Adandé and Constance Nouanti for guidance and logistical support in Bénin. During the project, I enjoyed the archaeological insights of J. Cameron Monroe, Jeff Fleisher, and Didier N'dah. The project would not have been possible without funding from the National Science Foundation, Fulbright-Hays, Explorers Club Washington Group, Embassy of the Netherlands to Cotonou, University of

Virginia Graduate School of Arts and Sciences, the American Council of Learned Societies, and the Dean of the Faculty of Arts and Sciences at the College of William and Mary.

BIBLIOGRAPHY

Adams, R. McC. (1965). *Land Behind Baghdad*. University of Chicago Press, Chicago.

Akinjogbin, I. A. (1967). *Dahomey and Its Neighbors 1708–1818*. Cambridge University Press, Cambridge.

Astley, T. (1745–47). *A New General Collection of Voyages and Travels: Consisting of the most Esteemed Relations, which have been Hitherto Published in any Language*. vol. 3. London.

Anderson, D. M., and Rathbone, R. (2000). Urban Africa: Histories in the Making. In Anderson, D. M., and Rathbone, R. (eds.), *Africa's Urban Past*. James Currey, Oxford, 1–17.

Bay, E. (1998). *Wives of the Leopard: Gender, Politics, and Culture in the Kingdom of Dahomey*. University of Virginia Press, Charlottesville.

Bay, E. (2001). Protection, Political Exile, and the Atlantic Slave-Trade: History and Collective Memory in Dahomey. In Mann, K., and Bay, E. (eds.), *Rethinking the African Diaspora: The Making of a Black Atlantic World in the Bight of Benin and Brazil*. Frank Cass, London, 42–60.

Blanton, R. E. (1976). Anthropological Studies of Cities. *Annual Review of Anthropology* **5**: 249–64.

Blier, S. P. (1998). *The Royal Arts of Africa: The Majesty of Form*. Abrams, New York.

Bosman, W. (1705). *A New and Accurate Description of the Coast of Guinea, Divided into the Gold, the Slave, and the Ivory Coasts*. London.

Brooks, G. E. (1993). *Landlords and Strangers: Ecology, Society and Trade in Western Africa, 1000–1630*. Westview, Boulder, CO.

Brumfiel, E. M. (1995). Heterarchy and the Analysis of Complex Societies: Comments. In Ehrenreich, R. M., Crumley, C. L., and Levy, J. E. (eds.), *Heterarchy and the Analysis of Complex Societies*. Archaeological Papers of the AAA, Washington, DC, 125–31.

Burton, R. (1966) [1864]. *A Mission to Gelele, King of Dahome*. Routledge and Kegan Paul, London.

Childe, V. G. (1950). The Urban Revolution. *Town Planning Review* **21**: 9–16.

DeCorse, C. R. (1992). Culture Contact, Continuity, and Change on the Gold Coast: AD 1400–1900. *African Archaeological Review* **10**: 163–96.

DeCorse, C. R. (2001a). *An Archaeology of Elmina: Africans and Europeans on the Gold Coast, 1400–1900*. Smithsonian Institution Press, Washington, DC.

DeCorse, C. R. (2001b). Introduction. In DeCorse, C. R. (ed.), *West Africa during the Atlantic Slave Trade: Archaeological Perspectives*. Leicester University Press, London, 1–13.

Eltis, D. (2000). *The Rise of African Slavery in the Americas*. Cambridge University Press, Cambridge.

Flannery, K. V. (1972). The Origins of the Village as a Settlement Type in Mesoamerica and the Near East: A Comparative Study. In Ucko, P. J.,

Tringham, R., and Dimbleby, D. E. (eds.), *Man, Settlement, and Urbanism*. Duckworth, London, 23–49.

Fleisher, J., and Wynn-Jones, S. (2010). Authorization and the Process of Power: The View from African Archaeology. *Journal of World Prehistory* **23**: 177–93.

Fox, R. G. (1977). *Urban Anthropology: Cities in Their Cultural Settings*. Prentice-Hall, Englewood Cliffs, NJ.

Hodder, I., and Orton, C. (1976). *Spatial Analysis in Archaeology*. Cambridge University Press, Cambridge.

Kelly, K. G. (1995). *Transformation and Continuity in Savi, a West African Trade Town: An Archaeological Investigation of Cultural Change on the Coast of Bénin during the Seventeenth and Eighteenth Centuries*. Ph.D. dissertation, University of California at Los Angeles.

Kelly, K. G. (1997a). The Archaeology of African-European Interaction: Investigating the Social Roles of Trade, Traders, and the use of Space in the Seventeenth and Eighteenth Century Hueda Kingdom, Republic of Bénin. *World Archaeology* **28** (3): 77–95.

Kelly, K. G. (1997b). Using Historically Informed Archaeology: Seventeenth and Eighteenth Century Hueda/European Interaction on the Coast of Bénin. *Journal of Archaeological Method and Theory* **4** (3/4): 353–66.

Kelly, K. G. (2001). Change and Continuity in Coastal Bénin. In DeCorse, C. R. (ed.), *West Africa During the Atlantic Slave Trade: Archaeological Perspectives*. Leicester University Press, London, 81–100.

Kelly, K. G. (2002). Indigenous Responses to Colonial Encounters on the West African Coast: Hueda and Dahomey from the 17th through 19th Centuries. In Lyons, C. L., and Papadopoulos, J. (eds.), *The Archaeology of Colonialism*. Getty Research Institute, Los Angeles, 96–120.

LaViolette, A., and Fleisher, J. (2005). The Archaeology of Sub-Saharan Urbanism: Cities and Their Countrysides. In Stahl, A. B. (ed.), *African Archaeology: A Critical Introduction*. Blackwell, Malden, MA, 327–52.

Law, R. (1990). The Common People Were Divided: Monarchy, Aristocracy, and Political Factionalism in the Kingdom of Whydah, 1671–1727. *International Journal of African Historical Studies* **23** (2): 201–29.

Law, R. (1991). *The Slave Coast of West Africa, 1550–1750: The Impact of the Atlantic Slave Trade on an African Society*. Clarendon, Oxford.

Law, R. (1992). Trade, Economy and the West African Coast: Posthumous Questions for Karl Polanyi: Price Inflation in Pre-Colonial Dahomey. *Journal of African History* **33** (3): 387–420.

Law, R. (2000). *Ouidah*: A Precolonial Urban Centre in Coastal West Africa, 1727–1892. In Anderson, D. M., and Rathbone, R., *Africa's Urban Past*. James Currey, Oxford, 85–97.

McIntosh, R. J. (2005). *Ancient Middle Niger and the Self-Organizing Landscape*. Cambridge University Press, Cambridge.

McIntosh, S. K. (1997). Urbanism in Sub-Saharan Africa. In Vogel, J. O. (ed.), *Encyclopedia of Precolonial Africa*. AltaMira, Walnut Creek, CA, 66–79.

McIntosh, S. K. (1999). Pathways to Complexity: An African Perspective. In McIntosh, S. K. (ed.), *Beyond Chiefdoms: Pathways to Complexity in Africa*. Cambridge University Press, Cambridge, 1–30.

McIntosh, S. K., and McIntosh, R. J. (1984). The Early City in West Africa: Towards an Understanding. *African Archaeological Review* **2**: 73–98.

McIntosh, S. K., and McIntosh, R. J. (1995). Cities without Citadels: Understanding Urban Origins along the Middle Niger. In Shaw, T., Sinclair, P. J., Andah, B., and Okpoko, A. (eds.), *The Archaeology of Africa: Food, Metals, and Towns*. Routledge, New York, 622–41.

Manning, P. (1989). Coastal Society in the Republic of Bénin: Reproduction of a Regional System. *Cahiers d'Études Africaines* **114** (XXIX): 239–57.

Monroe, J. C. (2003). *The Dynamics of State Formation: Archaeology and Ethnohistory of Pre-Colonial Dahomey*. Ph.D. dissertation, University of California at Los Angeles.

Monroe, J. C. (2007). Dahomey and the Atlantic Slave Trade: Archaeology and Political Order on the Bight of Benin. In Ogundiran, A., and Falola, T. (eds.), *Archaeology of Atlantic Africa and the African Diaspora*. Indiana University Press, Bloomington, 100–21.

Monroe, J. C. (2010). Power by Design: Architecture and Politics in Precolonial Dahomey. *Journal of Social Archaeology* **10**: 347–66.

Norman, N. L. (2009a). Hueda (Whydah) Country and Town: Archaeological Perspectives on the Rise and Collapse of an African Atlantic Kingdom. *International Journal of African Historical Studies* **43** (3): 387–410.

Norman, N. L. (2009b). Powerful Pots, Humbling Holes, and Regional Ritual Processes: Toward an Archaeology of Huedan Vodun. *African Archaeological Review* **26** (3): 187–218.

Norman, N. L. (2010). Feasts in Motion: Archaeological Views of Parades, Ancestral Pageants, and Socio-Political Process in the Hueda Kingdom, 1650–1727. *Journal of World Prehistory* **23**: 239–54.

Norman, N. L., and Kelly, K. G. (2004). Landscape Politics: The Serpent Ditch and the Rainbow in West Africa. *American Anthropologist* **106** (1): 98–110.

Norris, R. (1789). *Memoirs of the Reign of Bossa Ahadee, King of Dahomey*. London.

Ogundiran, A. (2002). Filling a Gap in the Ife–Benin Interaction Field (Thirteenth–Sixteenth Centuries AD): Excavations in Iloyi Settlement, Ijesaland. *African Archaeological Review* **19** (1): 27–60.

Ogundiran, A. (2007). Living in the Shadow of the Atlantic World: History and Material Life in the Yoruba-Edo Hinterland, ca. 1600–1750. In Ogundiran, A., and Falola T. (eds.), *Archaeology of Atlantic Africa and the African Diaspora*. Indiana University Press, Bloomington, 77–99.

Phillips, T. (1732). *A Journal of a Voyage Made in the Hannibal of London, Ann. 1693, 1694*. In Churchill, J. (ed.), *A Collection of Voyages*. London.

Merrick, P., and DeCorse, C. R. (1986). Historical Archaeology in Sub-Saharan Africa: A Review. *Historical Archaeology* **20**: 1–14.

Mitchell, P. (2005). *African Connections: Archaeological Perspectives on Africa and the Wider World*. AltaMira, Walnut Creek, CA.

Reid, A., and Lane, P. J. (2004). African Historical Archaeologies: An Introductory Contribution of Scope and Potential. In Reid, A., and Lane, P. J. (eds.), *African Historical Archaeologies*. Kluwer, New York, 1–32.

Schwartz, G. M., and Falconer, S. E. (1994). Rural Approaches to Social Complexity. In Schwartz, G. M., and Falconer, S. E. (eds.), *Archaeological Views from the Countryside: Village Communities in Early Complex Societies*. Smithsonian Institution Press, Washington, DC, 1–9.

Sinclair, P. J., Shaw, T., and Andah, B. (1995). Introduction. In Shaw, T., Sinclair, P., Andah, B., and Okpoko, A. (eds.), *The Archaeology of Africa: Food, Metals and Towns*. Routledge, New York, 1–31.

Sjoberg, G. (1960). *The Preindustrial City*. Free Press, Glencoe, IL.

Smith, A. (2003). *The Political Landscape: Constellations of Authority in Early Complex Societies*. University of California Press, Berkeley.

Smith, M. (2010). *A Prehistory of Ordinary People*. University of Arizona Press, Tucson.

Smith, W. (1967) [1744]. *A New Voyage to Guinea: Describing the Customs, Manners, Soil*. Frank Cass, London.

Snelgrave, W. (1734). *A New Account of Some Parts of Guinea and the Slave Trade*. Knapton, London.

Stahl, A. B. (1999). Perceiving Variability in Time and Space. In McIntosh, S. K. (ed.), *Beyond Chiefdoms: Pathways to Complexity in Africa*. Cambridge University Press, Cambridge, 39–55.

Stahl, A. B. (2001a). Historical Process and the Impact of the Atlantic Trade on Banda, Ghana, c. 1800–1920. In DeCorse, C. R. (ed.), *West Africa During the Atlantic Slave Trade: Archaeological Perspectives*. Leicester University Press, London, 38–58.

Stahl, A. B. (2001b). *Making History in Banda: Anthropological Visions of Africa's Past*. Cambridge University Press, Cambridge.

Thornton, J. (1998). *Africa and Africans in the Making of the Atlantic World, 1400–1800*. Cambridge University Press, Cambridge.

Trigger, B. (1972). Determinations of Growth in Pre-Industrial Societies. In Ucko, P. J., Tringham, R., and Dimbleby, D. E. (eds.), *Man, Settlement, and Urbanism*. Duckworth, London, 575–99.

Usman, A. (2001). *State-Periphery Relations and Sociopolitical Development in Igbominaland, North-Central Yoruba, Nigeria: Oral-Ethnohistorical and Archaeological Perspectives*. British Archaeological Reports, Archaeopress, Oxford.

Willey, G. (1953). *Prehistoric Settlement Patterns in the Virú. Bulletin 155*. Bureau of American Ethnology, Washington, DC.

Yoffee, N. (1997). The Obvious and the Chimerical: City-States in Archaeological Perspectives. In Nichols, D. L., and Charlton, T. H. (eds.), *The Archaeology of City-States: Cross-Cultural Approaches*. Smithsonian Institution Press, Washington, DC, 255–63.

NOTES

1. Astley was a compiler of traveler accounts rather than a traveler/trader, and thus this statement should be read as an early historiographical note.

2. There is a long tradition of research into the emergence and historical dynamics of the Hueda kingdom, and it is beyond the scope of this section to summarize this body of research. For recent historiographies of research in the area of the Bight of Benin, see Law (1991), Bay (2001), Mann and Bay (2001, and chapters therein), Kelly (1995), and Monroe (2003).

3. I was fortunate to have been aided by students of the University of Abomey-Calavi, who participated in three archaeological field schools, and twelve field technicians from the Savi area.

4. Ninety-five percent of the artifacts recovered are locally produced coarse earthenware ceramics. All other categories of artifacts (e.g., trade pipe, local tobacco pipe, glass) represented less than 1 percent of the total survey assemblage.

5. For the survey, 99 percent of the ceramics recovered fit within Kelly's ware type nomenclature for late-seventeenth- to early-eighteenth-century ceramics, with less than 1 percent identified as Brown Ware associated with the Chevron and Lozenge rouletted wares that Monroe (2003:270–300) recovered in late-eighteenth- to nineteenth-century deposits on the Abomey plateau.

6. Architectural features ranged from small deflated structures of less than 3 m in circumference to 1.5-km ditch segments. Here "loci" is defined as a test, or collection of contiguous tests, with architectural features within 100 m of the center of the test without a break of 100 m surrounding the test negative for architecture. In total, architectural features were recorded within 100 m of sixty-eight tests: seventeen loci contained multiple tests near, or within, architectural features, and four loci contained one test with closely related architecture.

7. Radiocarbon dates are pending on all of these loci and will further clarify the evolution of the urban complex in and around Savi. At the smelting center (Locus 3) no firmly datable artifacts (e.g., trade pipe with maker's mark) were recovered from the primary smelting context (i.e., Units 2 and 7, Layer 3), although numerous artifacts contemporary with Savi were recovered at other units throughout the locus. Hence, it is impossible to say with certainty that the smelting context was contemporary to the main settlement at Savi. However, local ceramics recovered from the primary smelting context are tantalizingly similar to those found in Savi-era contexts.

8. Most local lithics were quartz, microblades, and related debitage, most likely traded from near the Mono River valley. Other lithic artifacts recovered were constructed from local flint from north of the Abomey plateau. I thank Béninese archaeologist Didier N'dah for reviewing these artifacts.

9. See image of the representative of the King's Mother smoking a European-style pipe during the annual procession to the Temple of *Dangbe* in Astley (1745–7: plate 7 facing p. 42). Later, King Behanzin of Dahomey was rarely photographed without a long reed-and-stem local pipe.

PART II

STATE-GENERATED LANDSCAPES

6

Segou, Slavery, and Sifinso

Kevin C. MacDonald and Seydou Camara

INTRODUCTION

Slavery formed a fundamental element in the economic production systems of many historic African states. Such economies, which include documented West African cases, such as the Sokoto Caliphate, Songhai, and Segou, appear to have relied upon an enslaved workforce, derived from warfare, for agricultural production (Lovejoy 2005; Meillassoux 1991; Roberts 1987). The settlement landscape of Segou (c.1700–1861) was populated largely by individuals who have been categorized, by both contemporary observers and historians of oral tradition, as slaves (e.g., Park 2000 [1799]; Roberts 1997). Whether cultivators or soldiers, the "ownership" of groups of individuals by ruling elites and their emplacement within the state's core landscape appears to have been a major attribute of the Segou state. The present study deals with new enquiries into both the oral history and archaeology of Segou's social landscape, considering it in contrast to the mercantile "eternal landscape" of Marka urban centres. Ultimately, it is hoped that this historical archaeological study will be of relevance to the archaeology of other African polities and will inform approaches to the earlier slave economies of the West African Sahel.

The extent to which state-level systems of enslavement existed prior to the sixteenth century is a question fraught with difficulties of definition and perception. As Lovejoy (2000:21) states, "that slavery probably existed in Africa before the diffusion of Islam is relatively certain . . . its characteristics are not." Some scholars, such as Kopytoff and Miers (1977), have portrayed African slavery as an indigenous development out of a sliding scale of "rights in persons," ranging from bride-price, to indenture, to actual chattel slavery. Such indigenous systems of obligation and caste may have played a role in the advent of social complexity on the continent. Others, such as Meillassoux (1991), have challenged hypotheses of indigenous slavery, arguing that the "slave mode of production" was a contagion spread by contact between the Islamic world and arid West Africa in the ninth century.

Early Arabic written accounts, depending on their translation, can provide support for both camps. First, there is Al-Yakūbī, writing about Sahelian polities such as Kawkaw and Ghana in A.D. 889: "I have been informed that the kings of the Sūdān [the West African Sahel] sell their people without any pretext or war" (Levtzion and Hopkins 2000 [1981]:22). This statement is made in the context of the acquisition of slaves by Muslim trading intermediaries at Zawīla for trans-Saharan commerce. Yet, interestingly, it registers surprise on the part of the chronicler at the nature, or perhaps the scale, of enslavement in Sahelian polities, potentially indicating the pre-existence of a slave caste within these societies.

Then there is Al-Zuhri writing in A.D. 1137 who, in Cuoq's translation, infers that the slave economy of the Sahel began as a response to slave raiding by Muslim (presumably Arabo-Berber) populations: "The people of Ghāna fight in the lands of the Barbara, the Anima, and seize the inhabitants as others had seized them in the past, when they were pagans" (Cuoq 1975:120, as translated into English via Meillassoux 1991:45–46). Alternatively, Levtzion and Hopkins (2000 [1981]:98) translate this ambiguous passage differently, with the consequence that it conforms to the earlier statement by Al-Yakūbī: "The people of Ghāna make raids on the land of the Barabara and Anima and capture their people as they used to do when they were pagans." The resolution of such historical ambiguities, and the archaeological evaluation of the origins of state-controlled slave agricultural production in West Africa, has major consequences for broader sociopolitical models.

In recent years, archaeologist Roderick McIntosh (1998, 2005) has passionately argued that the indigenous political system of the Middle Niger and adjoining regions was a noncoercive heterarchical one, only succumbing to militarism and hierarchy with the acceptance of an "Islamic imperial tradition" after the time of the Ghana Empire. Such heterarchical systems are characterized as being reliant upon the division of authority between multiple crosscutting associations (earth priests/autochthonous groups, metallurgists, mercantile federations, etc.), which discourage the formation of centralized elites (R. J. McIntosh 1998:8–10). Similarly, the seminal edited volume *Beyond Chiefdoms: Pathways to Complexity in Africa* (S. K. McIntosh 1999) has attempted to turn archaeological investigations of social complexity in Africa away from issues of labor control and elite/non-elite dichotomies in favor of models prioritizing the role of ideology and ritual in cementing "horizontal" cooperative alliances between diverse groups. Although such nonhierarchical complex social systems hold great research promise and have undoubtedly been underinvestigated, one cannot sweep under the carpet centuries of historically recorded Sahelian hierarchical and coercive societies. The previously prevailing paradigm (cf. Goody 1971; Kopytoff 1987) – that relatively low population densities in a continent with masses of arable land necessitate a means of acquiring and controlling agricultural labor – has not yet been displaced. One must *demonstrate* that socioeconomic elements such as enslaved or indentured agricultural workforces are only of relatively recent date, and to do so, one needs an understanding of what the "slave mode of production" might look like in the archaeological record.

To this end, and for the construction of broader Middle Range models for undertaking archaeologies of statehood in Africa, the Leverhulme Trust-sponsored *Patterns of African Statehood* project was initiated by K. C. MacDonald and D. A. M. Reid in 2003. This project sought to synthesize existing data on precolonial African social formations and produce new ethnoarchaeological and historical data on eighteenth- and nineteenth-century states in Mali and Uganda. In the present work, we will limit our focus to information derived on slavery as visible in the landscape of Segou, a polity used by scholars such as Roberts (1987) and Meillassoux (1991) as an exemplar of the militarized and enslaving Sudanic state.

SEGOU 2005–2010

Segou (c. 1712–1861) is one of West Africa's best documented historical states, with a formidable array of recorded oral traditions, explorer accounts, French colonial records, and historical syntheses dating from the colonial era onward. However, until the present study, Segou had not been analyzed from a geographic perspective – via its settlement system. Nor has the path blazed by Jean Bazin, one of Segou's foremost ethnographers, been followed to its logical conclusion. Bazin (1970) stressed that a systematic village-level collection of local oral histories, coupled with corresponding archaeological investigations, was the only way to understand the origins of Segou and develop its critical history – subjects heretofore oversimplified and obscured by the hegemony of griotic accounts. Such griotic accounts, supplied by this "bardic" caste of Mande society, generally paint with a broad brush, focusing on central heroic figures and editing out lesser and controversial ones (and events in the provinces and most aspects of social history). Thus, we chose to collect Segou's local traditions primarily from councils of village elders. Of course, this too, is not without its dangers; personal bias, village pride, and the "best interests" of a lineage can easily come into play in such interviews. However, multiple informants questioned on identical topics, sometimes even at the same locality, can serve as a counterbalance or furnish an instant self-critique of oral narratives. Additionally, we used a comparative approach when considering individual historical themes or events by contrasting multiple interviewee responses with pre-existing written records and griotic accounts.

Over five months of fieldwork, undertaken between 2005 and 2010, we visited, interviewed, and surveyed at forty-four of the eighty-nine historic settlements of the Segou *Toeda* or heartland as identified by Bazin and Meillassoux (1977:418–19; an area approximately between Nyamina and Sansanding) (Figure 6.1). Interviews were normally coupled with a walked (about 2 km) archaeological radius survey around each ruin or settlement and the GPS mapping of each locality. We were always guided by local elders who showed us the remains of town walls, boundary markers, and other points of historical interest. The folk taxonomy of sites was derived from multiple interviews within continuously occupied towns and the characterization of ruins or settlements by informants from neighboring localities. There was relatively little dissonance regarding the role of particular settlements at the time of Segou, the exception being occasional attempts at deflection regarding the origins of agricultural slave settlements. All interviews were conducted in Bamana and tape recorded. Transcripts (SEGOU 2005, SEGOU 2006, SEGOU 2010) exist in French. From these data we will distill some useful observations about Segou, its spatial organization, and slavery.

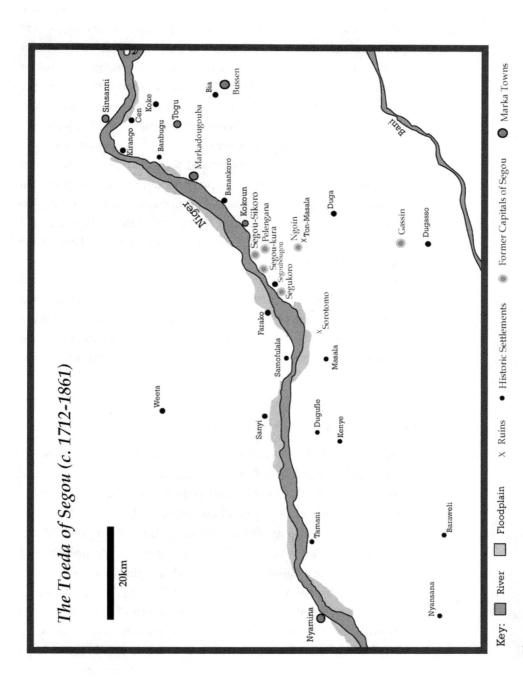

Figure 6.1
The *Toeda* (or core) of Segou.

SLAVERY AND SEGOU'S SETTLEMENT SYSTEM

Segou was established at the beginning of the eighteenth century by the Coulibaly Dynasty, which suppressed the preexisting Mande agricultural gerontocracy, replacing it with a militarized meritocracy driven economically by warfare and its consequent plunder (Roberts 1987). Or, as Meillassoux (1991:59) succinctly wrote, the state of "Segu's function was war and the capture of men." Slavery in Segou was a complex phenomenon consisting of at least two classes of enslaved peoples: a *jon* class of private or state captives used largely for agricultural labor and the *ton jon*, the state's military captives who had a degree of personal autonomy and potential upward mobility (Bazin 1974). Yet, despite the centrality of slavery to the sociopolitical structure of Segou, relatively little has been learned about how this slave system of production was organized across the Segovian landscape.

Geographically, Segou exhibits the "bull's-eye" structure typical of many historic West African states. There was a consciously defined and well-protected core (in this case of approximately 120 x 60 km diameter, referred to as the *Toeda*) with rings of diminishing political domination and tribute beyond it, giving way to peripheral areas exploited by raiding (Figure 6.1).

Marka towns and the "eternal landscape"

As many states before it had done, Segou extended autonomy to the ancient Soninke commercial centers within its boundaries, which had become known by this time as the Marka towns. The term "Marka" is a loose ethnonym given to and embraced by Islamicized Soninke and other allied Moslem Mande, meaning "those who pray" (Bazin 1972). This signifier was a conscious contrast to the eighteenth- and nineteenth-century Bamana, who as a rule practiced and advocated their own traditional religion (Bazin 1985). Serving partially as a protection device, most Marka towns have assumed two roles as (1) "eternal cities" ancestral to all Mande civilization, and (2) as "holy cities," which to differing degrees mix Islamic scholarship (large Koranic schools and ancient mosques) and traditional sorcery. Their supernatural status has served as protection from attack because most Marka towns never had defences or standing armies. Few were used as major colonial centers, notionally because they rejected the colonial presence, though their reputation as inviolable spiritual centres may have also played a role. Marka towns were thus ancient islands of Islam – although often robustly syncretized with elements of indigenous beliefs. Partially as a consequence of this, and because of their long established agricultural hinterlands, they appear to have been relatively free of the slave system of economic production until late in the Segovian period.

The origins of the Marka towns of the region of Segou extend well beyond the historical record. Certainly in size, and according to oral tradition in age as well, they are comparable to the well-known Inland Niger Delta tell complexes of Jenné (Jenné-Jeno) (McIntosh 1995) and Dia (Bedaux et al. 2001, 2005), both of whose foundation reaches back to the first millennium B.C. The two Marka towns about which we were able to collect the richest oral traditions were Markadougouba (literally, "Big Marka Town") and Bussen. In the words of Bussen town elder Abin Sanogo, aged 104, "The old men used to say that only a few towns are older than Bussen: Jenné, Dia, and [Marka]Duguba. The fourth is Bussen. No one knows how long ago they were founded" (SEGOU 2005, transcript 4:1:5). Today, both Markadougouba and Bussen are greatly reduced in size from their extent during the epoch of Segou. Both are surrounded by clusters of abandoned tells, reminiscent of the archaeological landscapes around Jenné and Dia. Markadougouba is flanked by an arc of at least fourteen discrete abandoned settlement mounds ranging from 5 to 7 m in height. The total area of the modern town and its ruins comprise approximately 60 ha. Bussen's twelve historic quarters, which we suspect were originally discrete settlement mounds, have now united beneath the modern town, which covers 45 ha. Numerous abandoned tells that we have not yet been able to record in detail litter its hinterland.

An illuminating Bamana-centric perspective on the nature of Marka towns, and Markadougouba in particular, is provided by Zoumana Coulibaly, local historian of Dugukuna:

Q = What power installed them there at Markadougouba?

ZC = Ah! We [the Bamana] had much power but we could not have done it! They had power themselves. But to say that their power went along way, that they were real kings, no! But their town was very big. They had a great deal of power and resources. But to say that they made war to found villages, or indeed made war to conquer, is to make too much of them! They did not make such wars.

Q = Then what did they do?

ZC = Their work was *maraboutism* [the teaching of Islam, the issuing of blessings, and the making of *gris gris* or sacred charms]...They were the Marabouts of all Segou those people there. It was the largest Maraboutic centre.

(SEGOU 2005, transcript 10:24–25)

The landscape of the Segovian state was thus a blend of "eternal" preexisting urban settlements, such as Markadougouba, Bussen, and their hinterlands, overlain by a new layer of settlements expressly created by the state. The "eternal" landscape is defined here as the Marka towns or *Markadugu* combined with the scattered agricultural villages of Mande freemen or *horon*, known as *Horondugu*.

Traditionally, Marka towns do not appear to have been centres of large-scale enslavement, although slaves were undoubtedly held by individual families within the towns. Only at the apogee of Segou, with the increase of captives due to the successes of the *ton jon*, did fundamental changes occur. At a few Marka towns, wealthy merchants began to amass large holdings of slaves at the end of the eighteenth century. In particular, Roberts (1987:47) cites a merchant of Sinsani (a.k.a. Sansanding) as personally owning 3,000 slaves. Likewise, Bazin (1974:121) cites nineteenth-century Sansanding as a center of enslavement, with many slave plantations (or *cikebugu*) established in its orbit; slaves were employed en masse in the spinning and weaving of cotton and exploited as porters in long-distance commerce. However, in our research at Markadougouba and Bussen we found no oral memory of such plantations or of a comparable local, large-scale exploitation of slave labor. For example, citing once again Abin Sanogo of Bussen:

Q = Around Bussen were there villages where you kept slaves?

R = They had such things around Banankoro [a nearby royal Bamana town]. Our slaves resided right here, in the quarter of the Sanogo.

(SEGOU 2005, transcript 4:3)

It may be that such a large-scale exploitation of slaves was unique to Sansanding, a Marka town located at the northern periphery of the Segou *Toeda*, which was more oriented towards commerce than religion and made moves towards regional economic hegemony during the first half of the nineteenth century. Indeed, such slave hamlets (*cikebugu*) as we were able to document were rare in the central, relatively urbanized core of the Segou *Toeda* but widely dispersed around its margins, both north and south of the Niger.

The state-generated landscape: *Fadugu, Dendugu,* and *Cikebugu*

In contrast to the "eternal landscape," the state-generated landscape included three settlement types. The most important of these are the *Fadugu*, towns of the king or *Fama*, being either capitals or locations of secondary royal courts. For Segou's century-and-a-half existence, we have been able to identify – via oral tradition, colonial documentation, and archaeological remains – six capitals. Each marks a rupture in either ideology or dynasty. As to secondary royal courts, there are at least two from the Diara dynasty, with those from earlier periods being more difficult to confidently define.

Next, there are *Dendugu* – literally "son's villages" – towns created by the king either to house his sons or to hold military garrisons commanded by the nobility. Finally, there are the *Cikebugu*: agricultural hamlets, normally founded by the state. The inhabitants of such hamlets were, notionally, resettled captives taken either in battle or in raids. Although termed slaves by outsiders, theirs was not a chattel status; rather they were more like serfs who were tied to a village and obliged to provide the *Fama* (ruler) with a disproportionate quantity of their produce.

Cikebugu are deserving of special consideration, given the theme of this chapter. Bazin (1974) quite rightly notes that the Bamana use of slave labor at *Cikebugu* was unique in that it normally comprised a combined unit of production (termed *Gwa*) with military supervision and both free and enslaved workers, sometimes in clustered or paired village localities. He cites the example of Banankozo:

At Banankozo, Da-ye-ma-cen (Kulubali) important warrior chief of the *Fama* Da, leads a production and consumption unit (*Gwa*) of about 200 people ... There are no individual fields (at least for the men). Subsistence is mainly based on war loot (cowry), gifts from the *Fama*, and production ... of the *Fama's* captives who are assigned essentially to agricultural tasks and settled in neighbouring villages dependent on Banankozo. The captives produced by the group are concentrated in the hands of the *gwatigi* [head of the collective unit]. (Bazin 1974:124)

Such *Gwa* and their satellite hamlets rarely exist as discrete entities today and are often either abandoned or combined into a single settlement. The more isolated examples that continue to exist have their positive identification blurred by the stigma of slavery. Modern inhabitants may either try to deflect questions about their origins or state that they were "placed here by Segou to cultivate" without making reference to social status. Sometimes the slave status of *Cikebugu* can only be confirmed by interviews at neighboring villages. Despite these difficulties, we believe that we have been able to identify a number of *Gwa/Cikebugu* at the periphery of the Segou *Toeda*.

At Kenye we found a situation very much resembling that described at Banankozo. Here there are actually clear remains of a *Gwa* pairing, with a fortified village of the *ton* (Segovian army) twinned with a similarly sized, small agricultural village (Figure 6.2). The untangling of the history of this settlement, however, was a delicate process, as the transcriptions of our discussions with the elders of Kenyé (Djara Quartier) demonstrate:

Q = So the Samaké [lineage] are here too?

R = They come from near Sanankoroba.

Q = The Samaké from near Sanankoroba? They were taken from over there?

R = No, it is not us who took them, it is the [state] power that brought them here.

Q = Yes, we understand it was the [state] power.

R = The Samaké, they are the ancestors of this place.

Q = They are your ancestors, how do you explain that?

R = How do we explain it? As we said before it was the time of slavery. The slaves, certain ones were taken in war. The others, if you had the money, you purchased people so that they would work for you. Those were the two types of slavery, no? The slaves of war and the slaves of purchase.

(SEGOU 2005, transcript 19:10–11)

The relationship of the military garrison, installed and led by the commander Tiema Coulibaly, to the agricultural laborers was explained in different ways:

Q = Were there any agricultural hamlets outside of the current settlements of Kenyé in that [Segovian] époque?

R = One could not have agricultural hamlets during that period!

Q = Why?

R = If you went to cultivate, if you did not have armed guards, others would come and take you by force. You are in the fields. There are muskets in front of you. You cultivate in this way. The muskets are never left behind you . . . When your [mid-day] meal is prepared there is a person with a

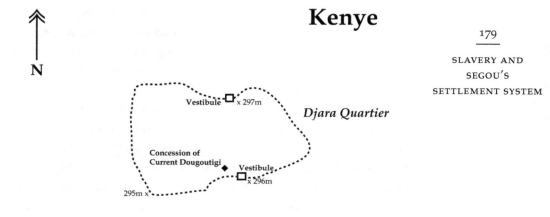

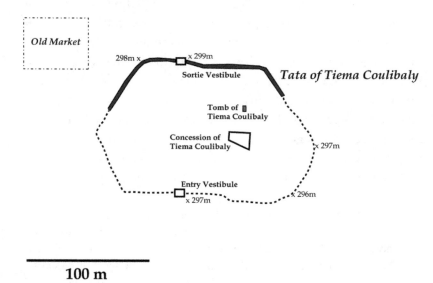

Figure 6.2
Plan of the Historic Kenyé, a *Gwa* (slave agricultural production unit) including traces of the eighteenth- to nineteenth-century *Tata* (fortified walled settlement) of the military garrison of Tiema Coulibaly and the limits of the slave quarter. Both are still occupied today.

musket who comes and brings you your meal and that of the other cultivators.

(SEGOU 2005, transcript 19: 8)

Q = If the garrison was called to war by the demand of someone, how were they provisioned wherever they went?

R = The ruler of here, it is he that provided fresh supplies from here. Their food left from here.

Q = Those who called them did not feed them?

R = No [laughs]!

(SEGOU 2005, transcript 19:12)

Clearly, there was a closely linked relationship between the cultivators of the Djara Quartier and the soldiers from the *Tata* (walled settlement) of Tiema Coulibaly. The pairing of *Cikebugu* and military detachments into *Gwa* seems to have been a widespread phenomenon and may explain both the means of provisioning of the widespread units of the *ton jon* (army) and the means of collecting tribute from captive cultivators. They also served as military outposts or frontier forts. For example, the military garrison of Kenyé was said to have consisted of 600 men, and the cultivators of a roughly equivalent number are said to have farmed millet and groundnuts. The place name Kenyé seems to derive from its historic role as a Segovian military emplacement, meaning in Bamana "you will stop them."

Another example is that of Dugasso, said to have been founded during the reign of Monzon Djara (c. 1787–1808) both to serve as a military outpost and to cultivate millet and herd cattle for the *ton jon*. Our informants tell us that there were roughly 740 slaves supervised by or linked with a garrison of only 100 soldiers (Figure 6.3). Dugaso may represent an unpaired village, because only one ruin was visible in the area. Alternatively, and more likely, the emplacement of the Segovian military garrison may rest beneath the recently rebuilt modern village. This would certainly seem to be implied in our interview with the current *dugutigi* (village head), a descendent of the Segovian garrison commander Namba Mengoro:

This place was given to us by Monzon in saying "we are of the same family, go there [to the edge of the Bani] and see where you would like to install yourselves"...Beside the place where he wanted to install the settlement [Namba Mengoro] found a small Peulh camp. He took these Peulh as slaves. Thus our slaves are the descendents of these Sangaré Peulhs. Their place [ruins] can be found just to the east of our village. It is the ancient site of Ba Dougoutigi Sangaré, one of our slaves. (SEGOU 2005, transcript 12:2–3)

An interesting aspect of Dugasso is that it has an explicitly pastoral connection. One usually does not speak of the "captive pastoralists" of Segou, but such a phenomenon appears to have existed in the region of Dugasso, which lies upon the northern banks of the Bani. According to Malamine Coulibaly, *dugutigi* of Dugasso, the cattle of the *Fama* were termed *Fourouba Fula*, and "they were generally entrusted to Bamana [the *ton*] who in turn gave these cattle to the Peulhs to raise" (SEGOU 2005, transcript 12:1). This adds a new dimension to our understanding of the diverse roles of *cikebugu*

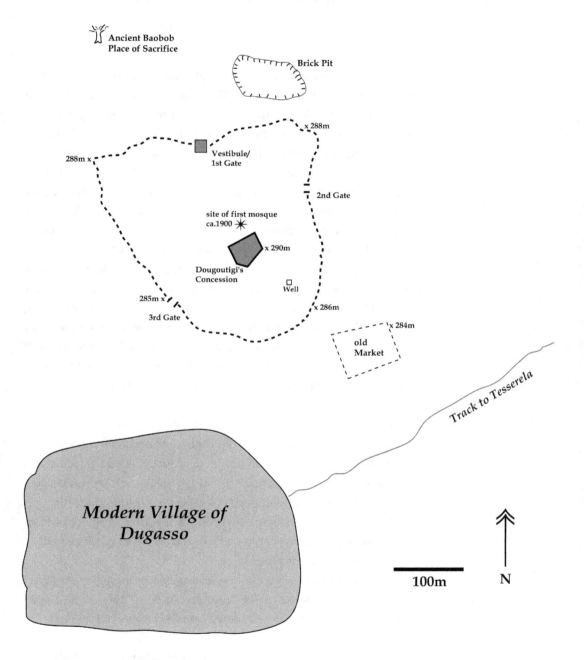

Figure 6.3
Plan of Old Dugasso in relation to the modern village of that name. Dotted lines represent a putative town wall, claimed by oral tradition, but not visible on the ground.

and the productive unit, or *Gwa*, of which they form a part. Regarding the toponym of Dugasso, it is like Kenyé similarly evocative of things military: "the place where vultures rest." It seems such colorful toponyms may provide a predictive key to *Gwa* complexes.

Sifinso

During our fieldwork we also encountered the term *Sifinso*, meaning "place of the black hair" in Bamana, or less literally "place or school of youth." This term has only been referred to in passing in the historical literature on Segou. For example, Kamara and Ndiaye (1978:473–74) note that a *Sifinso* was a walled area maintained beside the *Fama*'s court in which youths lived. Griotic traditions often place a *Sifinso* near the town of Banankoro (e.g., Conrad 1990: footnote 2900). Through interviews and archaeological surveys, we have been able to make a new contribution to our knowledge about *Sifinso* and to potentially associate them with the slave economy of Segou.

We located two *Sifinso* during our survey, one to the east of Banankoro, another near the town of Ngoin. Details about these sites in oral traditions were, of course, strongest at villages surrounding these localities. All informants agreed about the basic elements of *Sifinso*: they were walled settlements that housed youths of both sexes, in other words no "grey hairs." However, explanations as to their purpose revolved around three different narratives:

1. They were established for the entertainment of the *Fama*, who enjoyed this artificial town of eternal youth and would bring forth youths from it to entertain him at his court. Such an emphasis on youth is of course particularly suited to the anti-gerontocratic, almost "Cultural Revolutionary" aspects of the Segou state.
2. They were particularly for the keeping of young women to whom the *ton jon* (the army) could have sexual access to produce further offspring for the *ton jon*.
3. They were places of schooling and indoctrination for enslaved and pawned youths or for "orphans of war," who would later join the *ton jon* (if male) or marry into the *ton jon* (if female).

Of course, these three functions are not contradictory, and the *Sifinso* could have served all of these purposes. One particularly telling explanation for their origin was given to us by Macoma Dembélé of the council of elders at Banankoro:

> After the war against Toto, when they were conquered, Dah [Monzon] brought their children here. His griots had told him that he had better be careful with those children because they were of good family . . . They were afraid that if they left them there in Toto that the idea of vengeance would come to them. The griots counselled him to raise them in a way which would change their mentality, and that if they were well indoctrinated they could be of use to him later on. Over time they assembled around 8,000 youths here: 4,000 young men and 4,000 young women, virgins. (SEGOU 2005, transcript 7.1:1–2)

Our evidence suggests that such Sifinso probably began before the time of Dah Monzon Diara (who reigned 1808–27), because they are also associated with Ton Mansa, who reigned for an uncertain number of years between 1750 and 1760. Thus, at Ngoin we were asked by the elders to accompany them to the *Sifinso* of Ton Mansa, which they said was some kilometres away through acacia scrub to the east. At first we were dubious, but upon arrival we were stunned to find the ruins of an untouched triple-walled city, with the outline of each mud house foundation still clearly visible (Figure 6.4). Subsequent oral historical investigations have suggested that this heretofore unknown site was the short-lived capital of Ton Mansa, constructed for him by the *ton jon* after he had eliminated or exiled the remaining claimants of the Couilibaly Dynasty and abandoned the old capital of Segoukoro in the 1750s or 1760s. According to tradition, this site was abandoned after the death of Ton Mansa, and so it would have been occupied for less than ten years.

Ton Masala features a central, double-walled concession of limited access, which it is tempting to identify as a palace area. Another walled area in the northwest quadrant of the town has direct access to the exterior and controlled access to the interior. This is said to have been the place of the *Sifinso*. If this is true, it contains only thirty structures, which despite their substantial size (most being round houses of 5 to 8 m diameter) are unlikely to have housed more than a few hundred youths. This may represent a *Sifinso* prototype. However, this is only speculative – excavations may eventually supply further indications.

The *Sifinso* at Banakoro appears to have been far more substantial and is certainly the *Sifinso* most often cited in oral testimonies (in each instance where our informants knew about the *Sifinso* phenomenon, they cited Banankoro as a *Sifinso*). Unfortunately, the site has been truncated by a modern military base destroying anywhere from half to two-thirds of its longest axis. From the wall stumps remaining it seems to have been designed for at least two segregated quarters (presumably male and female?) with a reception area and internal round gatehouse (Figure 6.5). Its internal dimensions are unlikely to have exceeded 8 ha. There may well have been other *Sifinso* near the six capitals of the Segou state. Continued interviews and planned future excavations may shed valuable light on the function and distribution of these sites.

DISCUSSION: SETTLEMENT TYPE AND SETTLEMENT SIZE

In the course of our study we were able to map the historic boundaries, tell topographies, and/or city wall-lines of twenty-five Segovian settlements from within the *Toeda*. Despite this relatively small

Figure 6.4
Plan of Ton Masala.

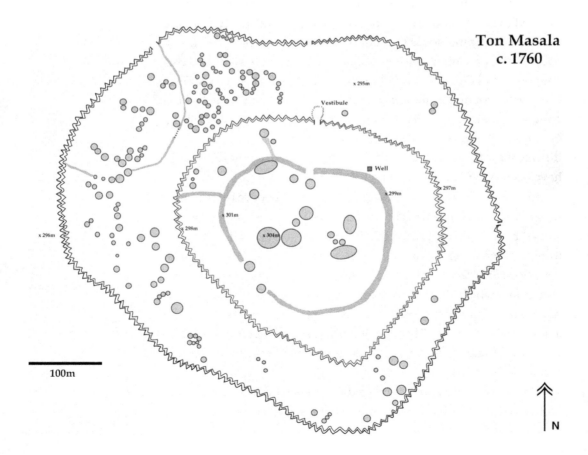

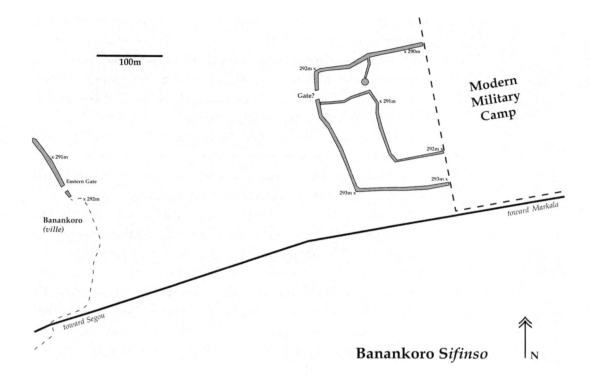

Figure 6.5
Plan of the remnants of Banankoro Sifinso.

sample, if we look at these sites' size ranges and medians, there are some informative patterns (Figure 6.6). The state-created sites form three nonoverlapping size classes. Meanwhile, the "eternal" Markadugu equate in area with the Segovian capitals, with the towns of freemen overlapping in size the *Cikebugu/Gwa* complexes and *Dendugu* of the state. It is worth noting that of the seven *Cikebugu/Gwa* complexes, five fall within the 4.75 to 5.25 ha size range. This suggests that a standard number of garrison troops and supporting captive cultivators, or herders, were emplaced at each (total founding populations of between about 800 to 1200 persons are claimed for these sites).

There are also some noticeable trends in settlement mound height and tell clustering. The Marka towns were heavily stratified, rising 5 to 7 m above the surrounding plain, whereas few of the state-generated settlements can boast a stratigraphy of more than a meter, and most show no visible relief. This clearly equates to the relatively short-lived nature of political capitals versus mercantile cities, and it may explain the relative "invisibility" of Sahelian capitals archaeologically (see, e.g., Conrad 1994, concerning the difficulty of locating the capital(s) of Mali). Indeed, the heavily stratified Malian urban centres that have seen major excavation in past decades such as Jenné-Jeno (S. K. McIntosh 1995) and Dia (Bedaux et al. 2001, 2005) are, essentially, Marka towns. As such, perhaps it is not surprising that they evince little in the way of state organization, given their historic role as semiautonomous spiritual and market centres (cf. R. J. McIntosh 2005). Also like Jenné-Jeno and Dia, *Markadugu* and *Horondugu* usually feature multiple clustered mounds – from two to fourteen of them, whereas few state-generated settlements that we visited possess more than two settlement mounds (with paired mounds appearing to be the norm for *Cikebugu/Gwa*).

In sum, our data suggest that site size, order of settlement, length of occupation, and clustering may have predictive value for modeling state-generated as opposed to organic settlements. Particularly, for all their importance at a given time, settlements that grow up only to fulfill the needs of a specific state are likely to be less apparent on an archaeological landscape. However, one must bear in mind that a certain quantity of one polity's state-generated settlements may be incorporated into the "eternal" landscape of its successor, potentially obscuring their initial role.

CONCLUSIONS

The histories of place that we have collected within the *Toeda* of Segou have surprised us by their richness and clarity. In addition to providing fresh materials for a geographic reconstruction of the Segovian state, we believe our research also has important implications for archaeological work in and around the Middle Niger. Heretofore regional archaeology has concentrated on well-known trading cities, usually of the Soninke diaspora, and not on centers of political power or wider state-led settlement networks. This has been a bit like using a study of selected cities of the Hanseatic League to understand the political history of medieval northern Europe, and it can just as easily lead to false conclusions. In general there has been a lack of consideration of the larger political systems that ancient cities like Jenné-Jeno and Dia existed *within* – such as those of Ghana/Wagadu and Mali. This is in part because the notion of statehood is more intangible, less archaeologically visible, than the notion of the city. In this work we are beginning to give a notion of both the possible function and appearance of the critical, if transitory, state-generated settlements that surround these more durable mercantile cities.

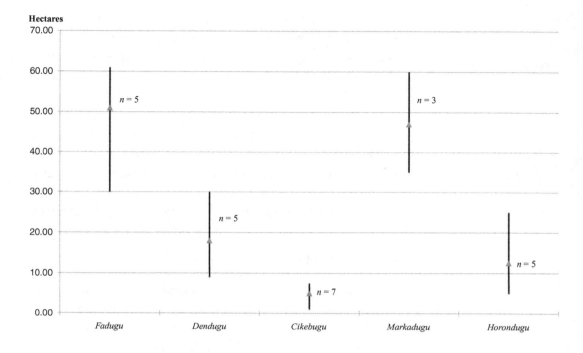

Figure 6.6
Site size ranges with medians for Segovian settlement types. Site sizes include the sum of all contiguous settlement mounds associated with the settlement. Only those settlements for which clear landmarks and limits of eighteenth and nineteenth century were available are included in this sample.

As to the predicative value of the foregoing regarding slave systems of economic production, there remain unresolved questions as to whether or not state-generated landscapes are inextricably linked to the control of populations. The ability of ruling elites to coerce – or merely convince – populations to act as units of agricultural production is a complex issue (Goody 1971, Kopytoff 1987), and there exists the option that large-scale redeployments of population could take place without enslavement. Yet, there is reason to believe – based on textual evidence – that enslavement and the exploitation of captives existed in the Western Sahel from at least the ninth century A.D. Therefore elements of the state settlement structure encountered by our study may be detectable in earlier portions of the Middle Niger archaeological record. Additionally, we have recourse to other evidence germane to the perception of the "slave mode of production" in the archaeological landscape, notably warfare, raiding, and their impact: settlement network collapse and refugia (Folorunso 2006; Kusimba 2004; Usman 2007). Although we deal with issues of warfare and settlement abandonment in the Segou region elsewhere (MacDonald and Camara, 2011), suffice it to say, moments of rupture – the creation of new polities – and the warfare attached to acquisition of captives lead to substantive horizons both of settlement abandonment and the creation of fresh settlement networks. Indeed, factors such as warfare and enslavement should be accorded as serious a consideration as environmental change, ideological change, or disease for the explanation of well-documented regional abandonments around the Middle Niger in the thirteenth and fourteenth centuries (McIntosh 1998:246–50).

Further work will be necessary to explore the extension of the concept of state-generated landscapes back in time. It is hoped that our multidisciplinary program of research will gradually extend from the Segovian landscape to the Empire of Mali and to even earlier time periods. In this manner we may eventually build a narrative of social change as reflected by the remaking of regional patterns of settlement.

ACKNOWLEDGEMENTS

The fieldwork described in this chapter was principally funded by the Leverhulme Trust, London, with additional funding from the British Academy (via the British Institute in Eastern Africa) in 2006, and the Bremer Stiftung für Kultur- und Sozialanthropologie in 2009/2010. Our research was facilitated by Dr. Klena Sanogo, Director of the Malian Institut des Sciences Humaines (ISH), and by Mr. Mammadou Keita, Malian Division of Cultural Heritage representative at Segou. Particular thanks go to Dr. Moussa Sow of the ISH and to our two British colleagues, Renata Walicka Zeh and Sean McDonald, who were an important part of the Segou team in 2005 and 2006.

BIBLIOGRAPHY

Bazin, J. (1970). Recherches sur les Formations Socio-Politiques Anciennes en pays Bambara. *Études Maliennes* **1**: 29–40.

Bazin, J. (1972). Commerce et Prédation: l'état Bamabara de Segou et ses Communautes Marka. *Proceedings of the [First] Conference on Manding Studies, volume 2b*. School of Oriental and African Studies, London, 1–26.

Bazin, J. (1974). War and Servitude in Segou. *Economy and Society* **3**: 107–44.

Bazin, J. (1985). A Chacun son Bambara. In J.-L. Amselle and E. M'Bokolo, (eds.), *Au Couer de l'Ethnie: ethnies, tribalisme et l'état en Afrique*. Éditions la Découverte, Paris, 87–127.

Bazin, J., and Meillassoux, C. (1977). Notes. In C. Monteil, *Les Bambara du Segou et du Kaarta*. G. P. Maisonneuve et Larose, Paris, 403–27.

Bedaux, R., MacDonald, K., Person, A., Polet, J., Sanogo, K., Schmidt, A., and Sidibé, S. (2001). The Dia Archaeological Project: Rescuing Cultural Heritage in the Inland Niger Delta (Mali). *Antiquity* **75**: 837–48.

Bedaux, R., Polet, J., Sanogo, K., and Schmidt, A., eds. (2005). *Recherches Archéolgiques à Dia dans le Delta Intérieur du Niger (Mali): bilan des saisons de fouilles 1998–2003*. CNWS, Leiden.

Conrad, D. C., ed. (1990). *A State of Intrigue: The Epic of Bamana Segu according to Tayiru Banbera*. British Academy and Oxford University Press, London.

Conrad, D. C. (1994). A Town Called Dakalajan: The Sunjata Tradition and the Question of Ancient Mali's Capital. *Journal of African History* **35**: 355–77.

Cuoq, J. M. (1975). *Recueil des Sources Arabes Concernant l'Afrique Occidentale du 8e au 16e siècle*. CNRS, Paris.

Folorunso, C. A. (2006). The Trans-Atlantic Slave Trade and Local Traditions of Slavery in the West African Hinterlands: The Tivland Example. In Haviser, J., and MacDonald, K. C. (eds.), *African Re-Genesis: Confronting Social Issues in the Diaspora*. UCL, London, 237–45.

Goody, J. (1971). *Technology, Tradition and the State in Africa*. Cambridge University Press, Cambridge.

Kamara, C. M., and Ndiaye, M. (1978). Histoire de Ségou. *Bulletin de l'IFAN*, séries B, **40** (3): 458–88.

Kopytoff, I., ed. (1987). *The African Frontier: The Reproduction of Traditional African Societies*. Indiana University Press, Bloomington.

Kopytoff, I., and Miers, S. (1977). African "Slavery" as an Institution of Marginality. In Miers, S., and Kopytoff, I. (eds.), *Slavery in Africa: Historical and Anthropological Perspectives*. University of Wisconsin Press, Madison, 3–81.

Kusimba, C. (2004). Archaeology of Slavery in East Africa. *African Archaeological Review* **21**: 59–88.

Levtzion, N., and Hopkins, J. F. P., eds. (2000) [1981]. *Corpus of Early Arabic Sources for West African History*, 2nd ed. Markus Wiener, Princeton, NJ.

Lovejoy, P. E. (2000). *Transformations in Slavery: A History of Slavery in Africa*, 2nd ed. Cambridge University Press, Cambridge.

Lovejoy, P. E. (2005). *Slavery, Commerce and Production in the Sokoto Caliphate of West Africa*. Africa World Press, Trenton, NJ.

MacDonald, K. C., and Camara, S. (2011). Segou: Warfare and the Origins of a State of Slavery. In Lane, P. J., and MacDonald, K. C. (eds.), *Slavery in Africa: Archaeology and Memory*. The British Academy and Oxford University Press, Oxford, 25–46.

McIntosh, R. J. (1998). *The Peoples of the Middle Niger*. Blackwell, Oxford.

McIntosh, R. J. (2005). *Ancient Middle Niger: Urbanism and the Self-Organizing Landscape*. Cambridge: Cambridge University Press.

McIntosh, S. K., ed. (1995). *Excavations at Jenné-Jeno, Hambarketolo, and Kaniana (Inland Niger Delta Mali), the 1981 Season*. University of California Press, Berkeley.

McIntosh, S. K., ed. (1999). *Beyond Chiefdoms: Pathways to Complexity in Africa*. Cambridge University Press, Cambridge.

Meillassoux, C. (1991). *The Anthropology of Slavery: The Womb of Iron and Gold*. Translated by A. Dasnois. Athlone, London.

Park, M. (2000) [1799]. *Travels in the Interior Districts of Africa*. Edited by K. Ferguson Marsters. Duke University Press, Durham, NC.

Roberts, R. L. (1987). *Warriors, Merchants, and Slaves: The State and the Economy in the Middle Niger Valley, 1700–1914*. Stanford University Press, Stanford, CA.

SEGOU 2005. *Project Archives*. Transcripts of taped interviews in Bambara, translated to French, held at the Institute of Archaeology, London, and the Institut des Sciences Humaines, Bamako.

SEGOU 2006. *Project Archives*. Transcripts of taped interviews in Bambara, translated to French, held at the Institute of Archaeology, London, and the Institut des Sciences Humaines, Bamako.

SEGOU 2010. *Project Archives*. Transcripts of taped interviews in Bambara, translated to French, held at the Institute of Archaeology, London, and the Institut des Sciences Humaines, Bamako.

Usman, A. (2007). The Landscape and Society of Northern Yorubaland during the Era of the Atlantic Slave Trade. In Ogundiran, A., and Falola, T. (eds.), *Archaeology of Atlantic Africa and the African Diaspora*. Indiana University Press, Bloomington, 140–59.

7

Building the State in Dahomey: Power and Landscape on the Bight of Benin

J. Cameron Monroe

INTRODUCTION

At the dawn of the Atlantic Era, numerous polities were distributed across the Aja-Yoruba region of West Africa, which spanned the modern nations of Togo, Bénin, and Nigeria. Ethnohistorical sources indicate that many of the kings of these polities migrated across this region in a series of royal dispersals from the Yoruba urban centers Ile-Ife, Oyo, and later Ketu, subjugating local communities and founding centralized kingdoms wherever they went (Adediran 1994; Akinjogbin 1967:10). The centrifugal diffusion of elites across this region yielded a political landscape integrated by complex tributary and ritual obligations that cemented interpolity ties between royal families within this far-flung Aja-Yoruba *oecumene*. Within the western Aja region, the dominant polities by the seventeenth century A.D. were Allada and its tributary kingdoms, Hueda, and Dahomey (Akinjogbin 1967:11) (Figure 7.1). Founded sometime in the sixteenth century, Allada was the preeminent kingdom of the three (Law 1997). Allada exacted regular tribute from Dahomey and Hueda and legitimized these tributary relationships through various ritual obligations, reflecting the broad pattern of Aja-Yoruba political order in this period.

As Atlantic commerce intensified in the late seventeenth and early eighteenth centuries, this regional system was upset by the rise of the Kingdom of Dahomey, oft-cited example of a centralized state par excellence (Akinjogbin 1967). Following nearly a century of Dahomean expansion and consolidation across the Abomey Plateau,

Dahomey marched south and conquered Allada (1724) and Hueda (1727). Dahomey thus formally severed the tributary and ceremonial obligations demanded by Allada, established Dahomean hegemony across the region, and initiated unfettered commerce with European merchants on the coast. Dahomey continued to expand in the nineteenth century, despite an economically destabilizing shift in Atlantic commerce away from slave trading in favor of the export of agricultural products.

The strategies employed by kings of Dahomey to maintain and extend political order until its eventual conquest by French colonial forces between 1892 and 1894 have been the source of much historical research (Akinjogbin 1967; Polanyi 1966). Broadly speaking, war and Atlantic commerce have been seen as catalyzing factors in the emergence of a revolutionary militaristic, and increasingly bureaucratic, ideology that differed dramatically from the ritually based principles of political order established across the Aja-Yoruba cultural sphere (Akinjogbin 1967; Polanyi 1966). In recent analyses of Dahomean political organization, however, scholarly attention has largely shifted away from questions exclusively focused on the revolutionary qualities of Dahomean political order in favor of recognizing both change and continuity within a diverse set of fields of economic, ideological, and political power in Dahomean society (Bay 1998; Law 1991, 1997).

This perspective has added significantly to our understanding of Dahomean society in the precolonial period. Importantly, however, these interpretations have been based almost exclusively on historical descriptions of, or oral traditions from, major Dahomean urban centers, most notably Abomey and Whydah. Because of the limited number of documentary references relating to areas in the hinterlands of such urban centers, secondary centers and rural communities have been, in fact, largely removed from the equation. Unfortunately this has resulted in significant gaps in our understanding of the way this polity distributed power and authority across its broader territorial holdings.

Archaeological perspectives on landscape have demonstrated that political centralization is closely tied to elite construction campaigns across regions, linking urban centers and rural hinterlands in innovative and historically contingent ways (Schwartz and Falconer 1994; Smith 2003; Wilkinson 2003). Indeed, landscapes can be used to cement elite-centric cosmological orders (Ashmore

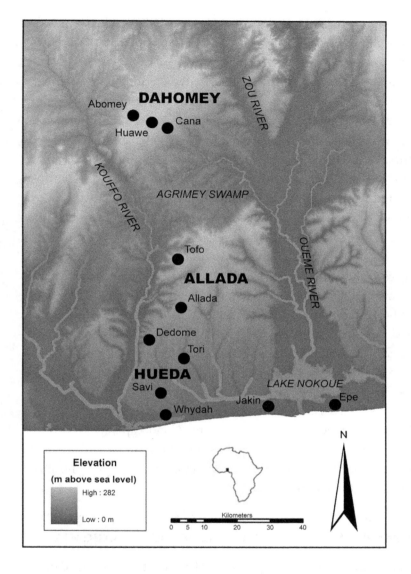

Figure 7.1
Political map depicting important polities in the Aja-Fon region of the Bight of Benin in the seventeenth century.

1989; DeMarrais, Castillo, and Earle 1996; Fritz 1986; Leone 1984), economically integrate vast territories (Schreiber 1987; Stanish 1994; Ur 2003; Wilkinson 2003), and define both the historical perception and daily experience of the world in elite terms (Monroe 2010; Smith 2003; Tilley 1994). In the process, however, landscape features designed to cement vertical and horizontal economic relationships carve out and define specific spheres of social interaction between leaders and followers, a centrally important process in the creation of *legible*, and thus exploitable, subjects within territories (Scott 1999). Landscapes thereby create spatial fields of power for agents participating in the broad and unequal dynamics of civic life. As tools for promulgating the economic, ideological, and political agendas of the elite, landscapes emerge as a central component of state-level political economies (Monroe and Ogundiran, this volume).

In this chapter a landscape perspective is adopted to explore the dynamics of Dahomean political economy over time. Drawing from both archaeological and historical evidence, I will outline the manner with which Dahomean elites remade the regional landscape over the course of three centuries. Patterns in the distribution of Dahomean royal palace sites identified archaeologically are examined in relation to available historical evidence for regional construction campaigns of various kinds. These construction campaigns reveal dramatic transformations in the expression of political authority across Dahomey's rural hinterlands over the course of three centuries, processes linked inextricably to the changing dynamics of Atlantic commerce. I will chart a broad shift from a relatively decentralized political economic apparatus, in which regional networks and urban–rural ties were expressed along ritual and tributary lines, towards a political landscape that integrated urban centers and rural countrysides in new ways. This resulted in intensifying levels of economic integration and new conceptual frameworks that recast rural hinterlands from "tribute-bearing" to "commodity-producing" zones. This process rendered a dynamic regional landscape, which fostered the centralized control over the flow of people and goods throughout Dahomey's territory and resulted in an increasingly centralized political order over time.

ROYAL PALACES AND POLITICAL POWER IN DAHOMEY

Historically and archaeologically, royal palace structures stand out as the best documented material statements of royal power and authority in precolonial Dahomey. Indeed, if Abomey was the political center for Dahomey as a whole, the royal palace was the center of political discourse within Abomey itself. At a fundamental level these structures served as residences for the king and his dependents, who may have numbered from 2,000 to 8,000 at Abomey alone (Dalzel 1793:xi; Le Hérissé 1911:27–31). Indeed, according to some observers, the palace formed a "true city" within Abomey (Le Hérissé 1911:27). The broader importance of Dahomean palace structures to the kingdom as a whole, however, lies in their symbolic meaning and political functions.

These buildings played a major role, for example, in the promulgation of a militaristic royal ideology that emerged in Dahomey in the eighteenth century. Royal palaces, in fact, were presented as material manifestations of state violence (Blier 2005). According to dynastic oral traditions, for example, the Dahomean royal line was born of a dynastic dispute that erupted between princes of Allada in the early seventeenth century. One of these princes, Dakodonu, abandoned Allada in search of political opportunities on the Abomey Plateau to the north. Arriving first at Cana, and then at Wawe sometime in the 1620s, he was granted permission to settle by the Guedevi, a confederacy of ethnically Yoruba chiefdoms that dominated the region.

According to some oral accounts, sometime in the 1650s Dakodonu's son Wegbaja demanded additional territory from a local chief named Dan. According to oft-cited royal traditions, Dan exclaimed to Wegbaja: "What! Have I given you so much land and yet you want more? Must I open my belly for you to build your house upon?" (Skertchly 1874:86–87). Wegbaja responded by skewering Dan with a pole and building his royal palace over his exposed entrails. Wegbaja thereby proclaimed that his kingdom would forever rest "in the belly of Dan." It is from this architectonic event that the kingdom purportedly earned its name *Dan-xo-me*, *Dan* for the victim, *xo* meaning "stomach," and *me* meaning "inside" in Fongbe, the branch of the Gbe language cluster spoken by Dahomeans (Blier 2005).

This initial symbolic act of political violence was creatively materialized in later palace construction efforts at Abomey as well. Historical accounts suggest blood from sacrificial victims was mixed with the earth used to build royal palace walls, which were decorated with bas-reliefs depicting symbols of state power, and were often lined with the heads of enemy soldiers slain in battle (Pique and Rainer 1999). Indeed, in the mid-eighteenth century, referring to the tradition of lining the palace gates with the heads of fallen enemies, King Tegbesu purportedly informed his general, "his house wanted thatch," indicating it was time to go to war (Norris 1789:18).

During the eighteenth and nineteenth centuries, the symbolic association between royal architecture and state violence was accentuated annually during the *Xwetanu*. These ceremonies were a centrally important part of the Dahomean annual ritual cycle. They served to venerate the royal ancestor cult, which involved the sacrifice of hundreds to thousands of human captives and the ceremonial distribution of wealth, much of which was acquired through Atlantic trade (Figure 7.2). Additionally, they served as an important context in which taxes were collected from subjects, "from the Ningan [*sic*; Migan] in the capital to the lowest free man in the villages" (Skertchly 1874:180). Historical accounts attest to the fact that the royal palace at Abomey served as the primary locus for activities associated with the *Xwetanu*. Additionally, however, Abomey was home to seven palaces of the *vidaho*, or heir apparent, each of which played important ceremonial roles leading up to the major events of the *Xwetanu*. In all, the royal palaces of Abomey were part of a dynamic ritual landscape in which historical claims to political authority were materialized (Blier 2005).

In addition to these symbolic reminders of state power, however, the Abomey palaces served important administrative functions in Dahomey. Indeed, many of the royal wives who lived behind their walls were important officials themselves. Referred to as *Begani*, these women played central roles in the management of state affairs and are thought to have balanced the power of the *Bonugan*, or male officials of the "outside" (Bay 1998). Additionally, the interior courtyards of the palaces at Abomey were central places for discussions of great legislative, judicial, and military consequence for the state. In all, the inner courtyards of these structures were stages upon which all the notable dignitaries of the day (both male and female) vied to tip the balance of royal favor in their direction (Monroe 2010).

Residential structures, administrative centers, and vessels for the symbolic authority of kings, Dahomean palace complexes fit into a general West African pattern in which critically important components of the political economy were played out behind and before palace walls (Kelly 1995, 1997a, 1997b, 2002; Nast 1996, 2005; Norman 2010; Ojo 1966). However, despite the overwhelming attention the Abomey palaces have received from both contemporary observers and historical scholarship, these structures made up only a small fraction of total palace construction efforts of the kings of Dahomey. Indeed, available historical accounts point towards the presence of lesser-known palace structures across the Dahomean landscape. During his brief captivity in the palace of King Agaja at Great Ardra, Bulfinche Lambe wrote, "He likewise very often adjournes to some other of his palaces, which are some miles distant hence; and I am told in number eleven" (B. Lambe in Forbes 1851, 1:186). Those structures at a distance from Abomey, often called *country palaces* in later

Figure 7.2
Period depiction of the *Xwetanu* performed before the royal palace walls at Abomey (Dalzel 1793, facing p. 55).

sources, were devoted to the production of manufactures or agricultural products, served as waypoints along major routes through the kingdom and housed large contingents of soldiers. Many housed princes and princesses, dignitaries, soldiers, and, on occasion, the king himself. Although never investigated by scholars at the same level of intensity as the royal palaces at Abomey, these structures served as central places in the symbolic and practical 'management' of the state. They grounded the royal family's economic and political interests in the countryside and provide an ideal context in which to explore the changing nature of Dahomean regional authority over time.

Integrating data collected from local informants, historical sources, aerial photography, and archaeological field survey, the *Abomey Plateau Archaeological Project* has documented as many as twenty-eight palace structures on or immediately around the Abomey Plateau itself since the year 2000 (Figure 7.3) (Monroe 2003, 2004, 2007a, 2007b). Surface collection and excavation, used in coordination with relevant oral and documentary data, dated each of these structures to within a century, at minimum, and often to within the reign of a particular Dahomean king (Monroe 2003, 2010) (Figure 7.4). Together these dates place the tradition of royal palace construction squarely within the period from the seventeenth through nineteenth centuries (Monroe 2003, 2010). Palace construction on the Abomey Plateau is thus an Atlantic-era phenomenon associated with the rise of the Dahomean state. In the following discussion, these structures serve as anchors for the examination of broader rural landscape transformations over three centuries. This discussion will reveal the dynamic processes involved in the transformation of a regional landscape defined by ritual and tributary obligations into one conceptualized as a commodity producing hinterland. This process involved various transformations in the economic, ideological, and political underpinnings of the state itself.

The seventeenth century

Ethnohistorical sources indicate that soon after its arrival on the Abomey Plateau in the early seventeenth century, the Fon dynasty expanded quickly across the region (Le Hérissé 1911:295). Oral sources suggest that this expansion was geared towards gaining control over interplateau and coastal–inland trade in various luxury commodities (Monroe 2003:93–98). Like those of their southern neighbors Allada and Hueda, Dahomean kings in this period appear

Figure 7.3
Aerial photograph (courtesy of l'Institute Géographique Nationale du Bénin) and views of the ruins of a nineteenth-century palace complex at Cana-Mignonhi (photographs by J. Cameron Monroe).

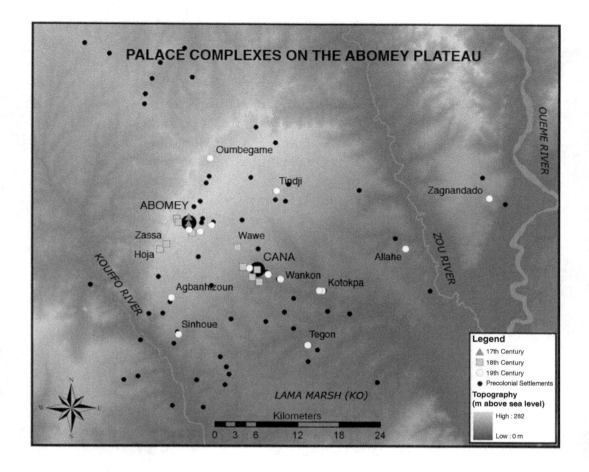

Figure 7.4
Palace sites identified by the Abomey Plateau Archaeological Project.

relatively uninterested in centralizing control over their immediate countryside, depending instead on local elites to govern rural conquests (Le Hérissé 1911:73). They were deeply concerned with ensuring the regular flow of tribute from these chiefs to Abomey, however, and political authority was largely established along ceremonial lines.

For example, a central component of Dahomean political strategies in the seventeenth century was the strategic deployment of material resources in ceremonial contexts in order to cement tributary relationships with rural elites. According to some oral traditions, Wegbaja adopted public feasting and the distribution of wealth precisely in order to curry political favor with subordinate chiefs:

The Aladahonou [sic; Fon Dynasty]... offered many gifts to tribal heads in the region in which they had come to live, and he made them good friends... Ouêgbadja [sic; Wegbaja], in lavishing food upon the tribal chiefs, knew that he had bound them, since one loves he who pleases his belly, and the Dahomean came running to those who fed him. (Le Hérissé 1911:82)

In holding such redistributive events, Wegbaja created a debt relationship between himself and subordinate chiefs, which could only be repaid with loyalty and tribute (Le Hérissé 1911:86).[1] These sources hint at the presence of a tributary system in which local surplus was used to fund palace subsistence and public feasting.[2] Rural elites were thus tied to the capital by the performance of redistributive ceremonies centered on public feasts and royal distribution of wealth. These sumptuary events doubtlessly provided the foundation for more elaborate ceremonies, such as the *Xwetanu* of later periods.

Reflecting the relatively loose nature of regional authority in this period, the seventeenth century was a period of relatively few royal construction efforts across Dahomey. Dahomean traditions indicate that Wegbaja (1650–80) began the construction of the royal palace complex proper at Abomey, which includes both the *Agrigonmey* and *Dahomey* palace structures (Figure 7.5). The *Agrigonmey* palace was initiated by Wegbaja at its northernmost corner. He granted his heir, Akaba (1680–1718), the palace of the conquered King Da, which stands to the north of the *Agringomey* palace and which later became known as the *Dahomey Palace*. These structures clearly served important political functions in this period. Oral accounts indicate that the ceremonial activities outlined above took place within and before the walls of these structures (Herskovits and Herskovits 1958:359; Le Hérissé 1911:276–79), thereby materializing Dahomean political strategies in this period (DeMarrais, Castillo and Earle 1996).

Palace construction on the Abomey Plateau, therefore, was limited to Abomey itself, standing in notable contrast to the pattern of extensive regional conquest on the Abomey Plateau in the seventeenth century and closely paralleling our understanding of the nature of political and economic organization in this period. Indeed, if these structures can be read as an index of relative political integration, direct royal control was focused within a core royal zone wherein Dahomean authority was particularly salient. Within this zone, the royal palaces at Abomey were integral to the ritual-economic strategies of Dahomean elite in this period and stand as material testimonies to a political system wherein direct administrative authority was essentially limited to the capital and relatively absent in the countryside. Abomey emerged in this period, therefore, as the central node in a regal-ritual (Fox 1977) political landscape broadly similar to those of neighboring polities in the region.

The eighteenth century

The eighteenth century was a period of sweeping change on the Slave Coast. Early in this period Dahomey's King Agaja (1718–1740) marched south. Conquering his principal coastal rivals, he established Dahomean hegemony across the region and opened unfettered trade with European powers. What followed was an era of political expansion and centralization, characterized by experiments in building an expansive bureaucratic apparatus geared towards controlling

Figure 7.5
Ground plan of the royal palace at Abomey identifying construction phases by king (after Antongini and Spini 1995).

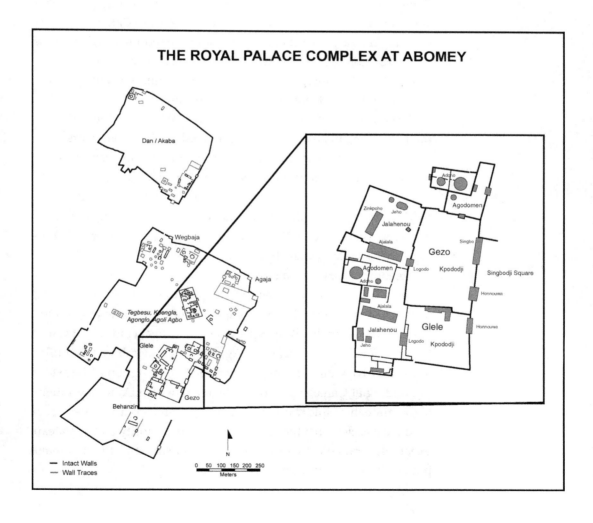

the traffic in human captives. This involved three processes designed to foster political authority across the regional landscape: the expansion and intensification of ritual strategies established in the seventeenth century, the integration of urban centers along the major coastal–interior trade route, and an increasingly bureaucratic conceptualization of state territory.

Palace construction continued, for example, within the core royal zone. The *Agringomey* palace at Abomey was expanded significantly towards the southwest (Figure 7.5), and secondary palaces were initiated by kings Tegbesu (1740–1775), Kpengla (1775–1789), and Agongolo (1789–1797) across Abomey (Figure 7.6). Oral sources suggest that Agaja built a palace structure at Zassa, 4 km southwest of Abomey, and that King Kpengla constructed an enclosure at nearby Hoja (Nondichao Bachalou, personal communication, Abomey, Bénin, 2000).[3] Additionally, documentary evidence suggests that Tegbesu built a royal enclosure at nearby Wawe (Dakodonu's second stop on the plateau) to commemorate Dakodonu's arrival in the region (Burton 1864, 1:285). Most notably, Cana, located 11 km southeast of Abomey, emerged as the major site of building activity on the plateau in the eighteenth century (Figure 7.6).

Cana originated as a Guedevi settlement prior to the arrival of the Fon on the plateau and is remembered as Dakodonu's first stop following his arrival in the region. Cana served as a major node in the dominant trade route to the coast in the eighteenth century (Fakambi 1993) and a crucial link in a chain of cities leading eastwards to the world of the Oyo Empire. Its population may have reached as many as 15,000 inhabitants in this period (Bay 1998:117). Four royal complexes were built at Cana by successive kings over the course of the eighteenth century. Agaja is associated with a structure now in ruins at Cana-Tota and Tegbesu with a complex at Cana-Degueli, which, at 35 ha, stands as the largest complex built by a single king on the plateau. Additionally, King Kpengla built a royal complex at Cana-Kpohon, and both Kpengla and Agonglo are remembered for building successive wings of a large structure at Cana-Agouna. The extent of building at Cana attests to the degree to which Dahomey sought to integrate this rapidly urbanizing community. From a regional perspective it is clear that the core zone of royal authority on the plateau expanded dramatically just as Dahomey emerged as the dominant political force on the Bight of Benin.

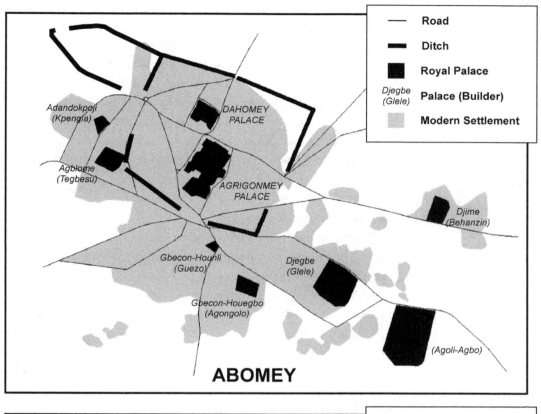
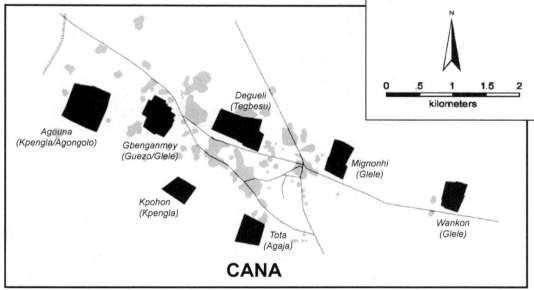

Figure 7.6
Town plans of Abomey (top) and Cana (bottom) indicating royal palace sites and their builders. The Abomey plan is compiled from maps published in Houseman et al. (1986), Antongini and Spini (1995), and Randsborg and Merkyte (2009).

In establishing hegemonic control over its territory, the kings of Dahomey in the early eighteenth century clearly expanded and intensified established ceremonial traditions. For example, in seventeenth-century Allada, "Grand Customs" were typically initiated following the death of the king to mark the accession of a new king (Law 1991, 1997). King Agaja, no doubt building upon established traditions on the plateau, is attributed with making such ceremonies an annual event (*Xwetanu*), and period accounts attest to dramatic displays of wealth and state power that took place at the Abomey palaces in this period. Historical accounts make it clear that the Abomey palaces served as the primary contexts for this ritual intensification in the eighteenth century.

The expansion of royal palace construction towards Cana, however, was part of broader attempts at expanding the state ritual sphere outwards from the capital in order to materialize royal historical claims to power and authority across the region. Cana is commonly cited as the first stop on the *Royal Road* to Abomey, a processional way that ritually linked Cana, Wawe, and Abomey during the *Xwetanu* (Alpern 1999). This processional way may have in fact originated as early as the reign of Agaja,[4] and it was clearly a significant part of royal ceremonies by the end of the century. Referring to customs performed by Agongolo to commemorate his father, for example, Dalzel wrote:

> The ancient custom, however of celebrating the memory of the deceased Dahoman Kings, by the effusion of human blood still prevailed to such a degree, that Wheenoohew [sic; Agongolo], upon his first visit to his father's tomb, took with him forty-eight men, tied, ordering, from time to time, one or two of them to be killed in the path, and saying, "He would walk in blood, all the way from Calmina [sic; Cana] to Abomey, to see his father" (Dalzel 1793: 224).

This feature ritually commemorated the historical relationship between Cana and Wawe as stops en route to Abomey in dynastic origin stories. Royal palace sites, therefore, expanded important ritual practices across a regional landscape, physically anchoring orthodox histories of dynastic origins. This reflects a broad process of ritual intensification in this period, materialized in an expanding regal-ritual landscape across the plateau.

Additionally, however, the elevated level of palace construction beyond Abomey might be read as part of a broader commitment toward establishing economic links in a chain of control from Abomey to the coast and eastwards to the Oyo sphere. Cana emerged in the eighteenth century as a primary administrative center on the plateau, and the Cana palaces doubtlessly played important roles in managing political and economic spheres. Oral traditions collected at Cana, for example, suggest that at least two of these structures (Cana-Tota and Cana-Degueli) contained areas devoted to storing human captives en route to the coast, and it is possible that an entire structure may have been devoted to this activity by the late eighteenth century (Cana-Kpohon) (Monroe 2003:238).

This pattern is in keeping with historical evidence that eighteenth-century kings expended enormous resources to build a regional infrastructure connecting political centers across the kingdom in this period. Indeed the capital itself was relocated to Great Ardra (the capital of Allada) briefly during the reign of Agaja to more effectively control coastal–inland trade. At the bureaucratic level, this shift is reflected in the early adoption of the *Yovogan*, or "Captain of the Whites," as one of the principal high ministers of Dahomey. This position was likely borrowed from Allada, since a "Captain of the Whites" is attested in Allada in the seventeenth century (Law 1997:79). The *Yovogan* was installed at Whydah by Agaja to serve as its governor and as an intermediary between Dahomey and European traders (Le Hérissé 1911:42). Dahomey also went to equally great lengths to create a regional infrastructure designed to stimulate and profit from coastal–inland trade in this period. The seeds of this process were sewn as early as the reign of Agaja. According to Le Hérissé, "After having conquered all these countries, Agaja wanted to know dimensions of his kingdom towards the south. He commanded that the distance from the palace of Dahomey to the beach of Ouidah [Whydah] be measured. It took 23,502 bamboo lengths. The bamboo which was used for this operation . . . measured from 4.5 to 5 meters" (Le Hérissé 1911:298–99, author's translation).[5]

It was not until the reign of Kpengla, however, that we have strong historical evidence for major infrastructural development in Dahomey. One of the major obstacles to the movement of people and goods in Dahomey was the biannual flooding of the *Ko* (the Lama Marsh on maps today), a low-lying swamp separating the Abomey and Allada plateaus. During periods of intense rainfall, travelers were forced to circumnavigate the Ko, which greatly inhibited travel between Abomey and the coast. In 1784, Kpengla attempted to solve this problem by initiating the construction of a major road through the Ko (Skertchly 1874:104). Writing nearly a century later, Richard Burton indicated: "Resolving to make the 'Ko' passable to his strangers, he handed over a string, ten yards long, to each caboceer, a significant hint. This passage, we are told, cost incredible labor and fatigue before the hurdle bridges over the swamps were widened and the gullies were filled up" (Burton 1864, 1:174).

This initial mobilization of labor reserves provided an essential foundation for integrating coastal and inland transport networks for a century and added additional stimulus for intraregional commerce in this period. In addition to the symbolic importance of Dahomean regional construction campaigns, therefore, the practical bureaucratic goals of the Dahomean monarchy during the eighteenth century were met by establishing centralized control over major nodes in the coastal–interior slave trade.

Importantly, however, this interest in documenting and developing the main artery of trade through the kingdom was the product of a royal desire to exploit and centrally manage the revenue-producing capacity of newly conquered territories, a notable shift in the way territorial space was viewed by the emerging state. Territory, previously conceptualized as a set of political relationships expressed along ritual and tributary lines, was increasingly perceived as quantifiable, measurable, and thereby exploitable by political elites (Scott 1999). Dahomean cities, therefore, became simultaneously integrated both economically and conceptually as part of a revenue-generating state sphere.

Despite this emerging interest in formally integrating coastal–inland trading routes, however, schemes to reach out into rural hinterlands off of the main arteries of trade are notably absent in this new system. Indeed urban–rural integration appears to have continued to depend on political strategies designed to attract followers to Abomey. Royal authority remained largely dependent on the intensification of the sorts of chiefly redistributive mechanisms so important to political order in the previous century. In the absence of new structural mechanisms that could foster urban–rural integration in this rapidly expanding polity, the florescence of the *Xwetanu* might reflect a form of ritual intensification designed to assert traditional forms of royal authority more broadly.

Historical sources suggest that this singular focus on the bureaucratic integration of coastal–interior networks resulted in some degree of regional instability. Dissent erupted on the Abomey Plateau throughout this period. Historical sources referring to the reign of Tegbesu are particular clear in this regard. Kpengla purportedly staged a rebellion against Tegbesu at Hoja, wherein he attempted to fragment the kingdom (Nondichao Bachalou, personal communication, Abomey, Bénin, 2000). Tegbesu was also forced to put down rebellion by the oft-mentioned Kingdom of Za, a minor chiefdom positioned southeast of Cana on the Abomey Plateau, during his reign (Nondichao Bachalou, personal communication, Abomey, Bénin, 2000; Le Hérissé 1911:301–2). These accounts contrast starkly with the image conjured by oral traditions that describe Dahomey, as it entered the eighteenth century, in firm control of the entire plateau, where royal authority "overflowed on its sides" (Le Hérissé 1911:295).

Overall, the eighteenth-century pattern described here suggests broad transformations in the expression of power and authority at the regional level. Ritual strategies established in the seventeenth century were intensified significantly to integrate an expanding territorial domain. New strategies were also adopted, however, to account for and stimulate economic potential along the major trade route from the interior to the coast. This period was marked by the birth of a bureaucratic landscape geared to centrally administer the movement of human captives from the interior to the coast and the subsequent flow of wealth goods back towards the capital. The eighteenth-century conquest was followed, therefore, by expanding and increasingly formalized control over coastal–inland trading networks. However, bureaucratization was essentially limited to this economic corridor and was not expressed more broadly in rural hinterlands.

The nineteenth century

The nineteenth century was also a period of dramatic change in Dahomey. The century opened with King Adandozan (1797–1818) in power, declining overseas demand for slaves, and general dissatisfaction among the elite class. In 1818, Adandozan's younger brother Gezo (1818–1858), backed by coastal merchants and various officials factions, seized the royal stool. Historically, Gezo is remembered as a great reformer who successfully ushered the kingdom through a series of major transitions (Soumonni 1980). Early in his reign,

BUILDING THE STATE
IN DAHOMEY

Gezo celebrated the collapse of the Oyo Empire, a constant thorn in Dahomey's side for nearly a century. The stability of Gezo's reign would be plagued, however, by a precipitous decline in revenue from the slave trade and an uneasy shift towards agricultural production as the primary source of royal income (Law 1995; Manning 1982; Soumonni 1995). He would expand the state bureaucracy substantially to deal with these economic transformations, creating new offices charged with managing rural production and taxing the countryside. These shifts were matched by an overall expansion in rural construction efforts in this period, reflecting broad shifts in the way the rural countryside was conceptualized by a revenue-hungry elite.

Palace construction continued in force in the core zone of royal authority in the nineteenth century. Kings Gezo and Glele (1858–1889) expanded the *Agrigonmey* palace further to the southwest (Figure 7.5), and Gezo, Glele, and Behanzin constructed private palaces on the south edge of Abomey itself along the road to Cana (Figure 7.6). Additionally, oral sources suggest that a second palace was constructed at Zassa in the nineteenth century.[6] Cana also continued to be the site of major construction campaigns in the nineteenth century, having emerged by this period as a site of major political importance (Figure 7.6). Gezo and Glele contributed to successive building phases at Cana-Gbenganmey, and Glele is remembered for building a structure referred to as *Jehoué* ("the riches of the kingdom") at Cana-Mignonhi, adjacent to Cana's precolonial marketplace. Glele also built a palace complex at Wankon, less than a kilometer along the eastern road from Cana proper towards Allahe. Sites central to royal symbolic and economic power and authority in the seventeenth and eighteenth centuries, therefore, continued to draw a great deal of royal building activity in the nineteenth.

To be sure, nineteenth-century historical accounts attest to intensifying levels of ritual activity at both Abomey and Cana. These sites continued to play central roles in the state ceremonial cycle, and nineteenth-century accounts attest to intensifying levels of royal display at both Abomey and Cana during the *Xwetanu*. Interestingly, however, these events were expanded to ritually integrate the entire region brought under control by Agaja in the previous century. King Gezo is attributed with instituting the *Gun Custom*, performed annually on the final day of the *Xwetanu* to commemorate the king's birthday (Skertchly 1874:421–22). During this ceremony, soldiers placed in small huts spaced at 100-m intervals along the road from Abomey to Whydah discharged their weapons in succession (Skertchly 1874:83). The aural experience linking coast and interior symbolically underwrote royal claims to a city-centric form of regional hegemony established in the previous century. The *Xwetanu*, which originated in the seventeenth century as redistributive ceremonies performed at Abomey, thereby evolved into a truly territory-wide event commemorating the century-long union of coast and interior. In a similar way that the *Royal Road* became an important part of the *Xwetanu* in the eighteenth century, historical events were materialized in the landscape through state ritual practices.

Archaeologically, however, this period is most notable for a major shift in the pattern of royal palace construction across the Abomey Plateau. Although Dahomean kings continued to build and modify structures at Abomey and Cana, the majority of the palace complexes constructed nineteenth-century kings were positioned largely in rural zones at a distance from urban centers (Figure 7.4). For example, a complex attributed to King Gezo stands at Tinji, to the northeast of Abomey. Oral sources claim that Gezo built this complex to commemorate the memory of his mother, a native of Tinji (Nondichao Bachalou, personal communication, Abomey, Bénin, 2008). This story is corroborated by documentary sources that indicate that Gezo traveled to Tinji in 1849 to "make custom" for his mother (Forbes 1851, 1:84). Six additional country palaces stand in ruins at Kotokpa (2), Agbanhizoun (1), Allahe (1), Tegon (1), Zassa (1) and Zagnandado (1), all but one attributed to King Glele by local traditions, a supposition confirmed by the observation of a preponderance of late-nineteenth-century imports found on the surfaces of these sites.[7] Additionally, it is possible that King Glele stationed two of his sons in palaces at Sinhoue and Oumbegame in structures inhabited and maintained by their descendants to this day. Sadly, these structures have been nearly entirely replaced by modern cement construction, and oral traditions relating to the antiquity of the sites are unclear.

Thus palace construction in the nineteenth century expanded elite control deep into Abomey and Cana's rural hinterlands. Quantitative analysis yields some insight into the underlying structure of this pattern. On the one hand, the size of palaces constructed in the nineteenth century corresponds closely with Zipf's rank-size rule for settlement size (Figure 7.7), and there is a statistically significant inverse

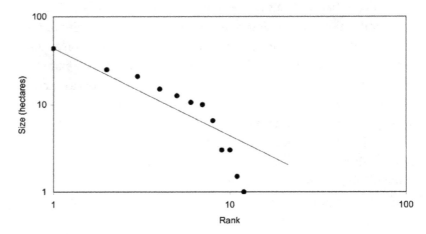

Figure 7.7
Size distribution of palace complexes conforming to the rank-size rule.

logarithmic correlation between palace size and distance from major centers on the plateau (Figure 7.8). The largest palace complexes were built at Abomey and Cana, and smaller satellite facilities were constructed in palace towns throughout their hinterlands. Additionally, the nearest-neighbor statistic, a spatial statistic commonly used to measure the degree of settlement clustering or dispersal within a region (Earle 1976), yields a value of 1.71 for the palace towns in which these structures were located, indicating a trend towards the regular spacing of such communities across the plateau in this period.[8] These patterns suggest that palace towns in the nineteenth century were ordered into a central-place hierarchy that distributed royal power evenly across the regional landscape. These data suggest the emergence of a mature administrative apparatus in this period, one that projected the power and influence of the regime down to the local level during the nineteenth century.

Broadly speaking, this pattern indicates a rising level of royal interest in establishing royal authority in the countryside around Abomey and Cana during the nineteenth century. In sharp contrast to the city-centric construction campaigns of the seventeenth and eighteenth centuries, closely tied to intensifying ritual activity and expanding trading networks, palace building in the nineteenth century created a regional bureaucratic landscape, establishing economic and political links between town and countryside in ways never before attempted. This pattern can be explained in terms of the dynamic international forces that engulfed Dahomey in this period.

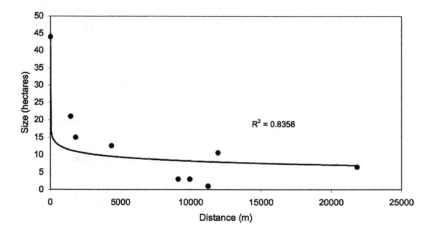

Figure 7.8
The relationship between palace complex size and distance from Abomey or Cana, revealing a statistically significant inverse correlation.

NINETEENTH-CENTURY PALACE CENTERS AS BUREAUCRATIC CENTRAL PLACES

The nineteenth century was a period of radical change across this part of West Africa, stemming from both geopolitical transformations within the region and dramatic transformation in the nature and intensity of Atlantic commerce. For example, the gradual disintegration and final collapse of Oyo between 1790 and 1823 created a political vacuum across the region, into which Dahomey and neighboring Yoruba polities happily stepped in the second and third decades of the nineteenth century. Throughout the nineteenth century, Dahomey and its southwestern Yoruba neighbors became increasingly entangled in both war and trade as they sought to fill the vacuum left in the wake of the collapse of Oyo. Additionally, royal revenue from the slave trade declined dramatically in this period and was increasingly replaced by the export of palm products. This resulted in a veritable "agricultural revolution" in West Africa generally (Hopkins 1973), and it had a profound impact on the nature of the Dahomean political economy (Law 1995). Specifically, this resulted in the overall ruralization of the Dahomean economy with two major outcomes of relevance to this study: rising interest in rural agricultural production, and the florescence of regional markets across Dahomey.

First, the shift from a slave-exporting to an agricultural economy resulted in a dramatic rise in elite interest in rural agricultural production (Le Hérissé 1911:248–49). Burton wrote that in 1864 the Toffo Plateau was "in the vulture claw of Dahome, and the officials of

BUILDING THE STATE
IN DAHOMEY

the capital have mostly houses and grounds where their palm-oil is made" (Burton 1864, 2:298). The royal family itself engaged in rural palm oil production, and Forbes wrote of one such plantation near Abomey as follows:

"Near Abomey is a royal plantation of palms, corn, &c. called Leffle-foo. It is inhabited by people from the province of Anagoo, prisoners of war, and is under the direction of a Dahoman cabooceer. The gifts of nature are all bountifully bestowed, and the soil rich and capable of producing every vegetable production" (Forbes 1851, 1:30–31).

It is conceivable then, that this palace distribution reflects state involvement in rural agricultural production. Palaces built to the southwest and east of Abomey, for example, are located in what are today considered the most agriculturally productive regions of the plateau, and both documentary and oral sources suggest that a number of royal palaces were used to centrally manage palm oil production. Skertchly notes that one palace on the road between Abomey and Cana was devoted exclusively to the production of this commodity (Skertchly 1874:154). The current king of Agbanhizoun proposed that this was the explicit function of a palace built by Gezo in this town (Da Amoussou Folly, Agbanhizoun, Bénin, July 21, 2005). Rural palace sites, therefore, could have served as central nodes in royal agricultural agendas in the countryside in this period.

However, central-place patterns more often than not result from market competition (Christaller 1966; Smith 1979), and there is clear evidence for broad shifts in the nature of regional markets in this period. Patrick Manning has argued, for example, that the decline of the slave trade and the rising internal demand for agricultural labor in this period resulted in both population increase and market growth within Dahomey (Manning 1982). Indeed, despite the fact that Dahomean elites were engaged in the large-scale production of palm oil, the particular requirements of this crop meant that commoners could easily engage in smaller-scale production also, resulting in relative economic growth across the countryside (Hopkins 1973). Patrick Manning has suggested that the net effect of rising populations and increasing purchasing power at the local level was the expansion of local markets throughout Dahomey's rural countryside (Manning 1982:22–56), and historical research has confirmed a broad distribution of large markets across the Abomey Plateau in this period (Garcia 1988:32). We might presume, therefore, that this central-place pattern was a product of the broader economic dynamics of the nineteenth century.

Dahomey, in fact, went to great lengths to profit from rural economic activities in this period, reflecting not only shifts in its economic policy but also broad shifts in the way the rural countryside was conceptualized. It is in this period that we see most clearly the countryside emerge as a commodity-producing zone in Dahomey, rather than as solely a source of tribute. This is indicated by broad adjustments to the bureaucracy as a whole, including the invention of an entire class of officials directed with managing rural activities. For example, an official named the *Tokpo* appears to have become increasingly important in the nineteenth century (Skertchly 1874:248). Oral sources suggest this individual and his agents played a major role in managing agricultural production and taxing economic activity at the local level (Le Hérissé 1911:248–49). Lieutenants of the *Tokpo*, called *Houmekponto*, were charged with dividing and parceling out land (Le Hérissé 1911:248–49) and appear to have kept track of the limits of land holdings at a local level (Le Hérissé 1911:43). They determined the areas to be devoted to palm growth or other produce throughout the kingdom and had the power to fine farmers who ignored their commands (Le Hérissé 1911:43).

According to Melville Herskovits, these controls were instituted regionally, so that entire zones within Dahomey became specialized in the production of particular crops demanded by both local and international markets (Herskovits 1938, 1:112–13). Duncan notes that "the King of Dahomey enforces cultivation over all his dominions" (Duncan 1847, 2:310) and that in the neighborhood of Whydah, caboceers enforced royal dictates demanding that every plot of uncultivated land be planted with corn or other vegetables (Duncan 1847, 1:199; Duncan 1847, 2:268–69).[9] These tactics allowed the struggling state to profit from the overall ruralization of the Dahomean economy in the nineteenth century.

The *Tokpo* was also responsible for managing tax collection throughout Dahomey in this period. The *Tokpo* managed markets that specialized in the sale of agricultural goods, and his lieutenants collected taxes on all goods for sale at such markets (Le Hérissé 1911:43). Duncan indicated that the market at Whydah was superintended by a chief constable responsible for collecting duties and maintaining the market infrastructure (Duncan 1847, 1:120–21). According to Duncan, the "chief constable, goes round the market daily, and collects the duties from each individual exposing goods for sale. A portion is exacted from every stall, whatever the goods may be" (Duncan 1847, 1:124). Officers were also sent to minor markets throughout

BUILDING THE STATE
IN DAHOMEY

214

Whydah to collect duties (Duncan 1847, 1:122). Forbes indicated that this was the case across the kingdom. Passing through Cana in 1849 on a market day, Forbes documented the presence of tax collectors on all roads leading to the market who demanded "from five to ten cowries from all who carried goods to sell" (Forbes 1851, 1:89).

In addition to taxes levied upon goods brought to market, however, a network of tax-collecting posts was created throughout the kingdom to collect duties from traveling merchants. These posts, called *denun*, were operated by minor officials "who receive cowries in number according to the value of the goods carried for sale" (Forbes 1851, 1:35–36). Potters originating near the Ko Swamp, for example, are cited as paying 10 cowries per pot transported through Allada (Skertchly 1874:85). *Denun* were established throughout the kingdom, including the Mahi territories on Dahomey's northern frontier, and they were placed at the entrance to every town in the kingdom (Burton 1864, 1:65; Skertchly 1874:8). According to Forbes,

Taxes are heavy to all parties, and farmed to collectors. The holders of the Customs have collectors stationed at all markets, who receive cowries in number according to the value of the goods carried for sale. Besides these, there are collectors on all public roads leading from one district to another, and on the lagoon on each side of Whydah; in short, every thing is taxed, and the tax goes to the king. (Forbes 1851, 1:35–36)

At one such *denun*, Duncan found "numerous traders from different parts of the country, resting their carriers until their several duties were paid and permits obtained" (Duncan 1847, 1:284). They were relatively insignificant complexes, containing only a few small structures for storing taxes and housing officials (Figure 7.9), yet they helped to engender broad transformations in the nature of regional authority in the nineteenth century.

Forbes' observation, cited above, that tax collection was "farmed out to collectors" suggests that that rural tax collectors were allowed to keep a share of what they collected as payment. Indeed tax-collection posts appear to have been a primary source of income for various state officials. The *denun* at Setta Dean, described above, was managed by the *Meu*, or Dahomey's prime minister himself (Duncan 1847, 1:290), and it appears that profits from rural production were a source of revenue for all the primary male ministers (*Bonu-gan Daho*) in Dahomey (Le Hérissé 1911:87). We can assume, therefore, that Dahomean taxation depended on the speculative activities of both urban and rural officials. This practice, commonly referred

NINETEENTH-
CENTURY PALACE
CENTERS AS
BUREAUCRATIC
CENTRAL PLACES

Figure 7.9
Dahomean tax-collection station, or *denun* (Chaudoin 1891:103).

to as "tax-farming" by economic historians, has been observed in a wide range of both ancient and modern contexts (Balsdon 1962; Bushkovitch 1978; Butcher and Dick 1993; Evers 1987; Falola 1989; Gregory 2005; Howatson 1989; Islamoglu-Inan 1994; Kiser and Kane 2001; Stroud 1998). Such systems are commonly the most cost-effective source of state revenue in emerging bureaucratic systems, and reflect the ruralization of centralized political economies.

Dahomean royal complexes can be viewed as central nodes in an increasingly bureaucratic landscape, serving as staging centers for taxes collected by rural officials from merchants at local markets and along major trade routes. Complexes located at greater distance from Abomey received taxes on traded goods and local produce collected at local *denun*, awaiting transshipment on to Abomey or the coast.

The close relationship between country palaces and rural taxation is supported by contemporary documents. Referring to a palace complex that historical accounts place in Arimey (probably a 1-ha palace complex identified at nearby Tegon), Richard Burton recounted: "Agrimen – 'In the wall' – derives its name from an old legend. When Jemeken was the chief, it was predicted to him that his wall must shake unless he daily 'ate' (i.e., exacted a tax upon goods passing the place) a 'kene' and a 'tene' (160 and 9) of cowries" (Burton 1864, 1:178). Rural palace complexes thereby allowed the nascent state to profit from rural production and exchange, and they stood as notable extensions of royal authority into the countryside in the nineteenth century.

The expansion of royal authority into the countryside allowed the state unprecedented access to and knowledge of rural social, economic, and political dynamics. This emerging landscape broadly reflected, therefore, elite reconceptualizations of rural territories from reservoirs of tribute to commodity-producing zones, a critical component of creating exploitable subjects. In this way, Dahomean rural expansion resulted in both an economically and conceptually integrated countryside, one fostering the centrally controlled flow of people and goods into and throughout its territories.

CONCLUSION

The Kingdom of Dahomey came to prominence on the Bight of Benin in a period of dramatic economic change, successfully weathering both the slave trade and an unstable shift to an agricultural export economy. Regional construction campaigns were clearly a centrally important component of royal attempts at establishing order and projecting authority across a broad territory over time. This chapter has examined how Dahomean elites remade the regional landscape over the course of this tumultuous period, drawing from a variety of strategies fostering ritual, economic, and conceptual integration at the regional level. Historical and archaeological evidence documents a broad shift from a relatively decentralized political apparatus, in which regional networks and urban–rural ties were expressed in terms of ritual and tributary relationships, toward a landscape that integrated urban centers and rural countrysides in ways never before attempted. The patterns presented here suggest a dynamic regional landscape involving changing directions of regional control, closely interconnected with contemporary shifts in the nature of Atlantic commerce. The ultimate result was an increasingly bureaucratic landscape that grounded elite agendas in the countryside and recast the nature of urban–rural interaction specifically – and the political economy as a whole more broadly. This strategy contributed substantially to Dahomey's comparative stability in the wake of the destabilizing forces of Atlantic commerce.

AKNOWLEDGEMENTS

The research presented herein was conducted in the Republic of Bénin during 2000–02 and 2005–09. I benefited greatly from the assistance and support of a number of individuals during the initial phases of this project and during ensuing years. In particular I would like to acknowledge Alexis Adandé, Joseph Adandé, Christian Assogba, Obare Bagodo, Zephiran Daavo, Da Langanfin Glélé Aïhotogbé, Kenneth Kelly, Da Nondichao Kpengla, Merrick Posnansky, and Elisée Soumonni for providing critical guidance and assistance in both shaping and implementing this research. I would also like to express my sincere gratitude to Rowan Flad, Jeffrey Fleisher, Neil Norman, Andrew Matthews, Akin Ogundiran, Jason Ur, and two anonymous reviewers for providing invaluable comments on previous drafts of this chapter.

BIBLIOGRAPHY

Adediran, B. (1994). *The Frontier States of Western Yorùbáland, Circa 1600–1889: State Formation and Political Growth in an Ethnic Frontier Zone*. IFRA, Ibadan, Nigeria.

Akinjogbin, A. (1967). *Dahomey and Its Neighbours, 1708–1818*. Cambridge University Press, Cambridge.

Alpern, S. B. (1999). Dahomey's Royal Road. *History in Africa* **26**: 11–24.

Antongini, G., and Spini, T. (1995). *Les palais royaux d'Abomey: espace, architecture, dynamique socio-anthropologique*. UNESCO.

Ashmore, W. (1989). Construction and Cosmology: Politics and Ideology in Lowland Maya Settlement Patterns. In Hanks, W. F., and Rice, D. S. (eds.), *Word and Image in Maya Culture: Explorations in Language, Writing, and Representation*. University of Utah Press, Salt Lake City, 272–86.

Balsdon, J. P. V. D. (1962). Roman History, 65–50 B.C.: Five Problems. *The Journal of Roman Studies* **52**: 134–41.

Bay, E. (1998). *Wives of the Leopard: Gender, Politics, and Culture in the Kingdom of Dahomey*. University of Virginia Press, Charlottesville.

Blier, S. P. (2005). Razing the Roof: The Imperative of Building Destruction in Danhomè (Dahomey). In Atkin, T., and Rykwert, J. (eds.), *Structure and Meaning in Human Settlements*. University of Pennsylvania, Philadelphia, 165–84.

Burton, R. F. (1864). *A Mission to Gelele, King of Dahome*. 2 vols. Tinsley Brothers, London.

Bushkovitch, P. (1978). Taxation, Tax Farming, and Merchants in Sixteenth-Century Russia. *Slavic Review* **37**: 381–98.

Butcher, J., and Dick, H., eds. (1993). *The Rise and Fall of Revenue Farming: Business Elites and the Emergence of the Modern State*. St. Martin's, New York.

Chaudoin, E. (1891). *Trois mois de captivité au Dahomey*. Hachette, Paris.

Christaller, W. (1966). *Central Places in Southern Germany*. Prentice-Hall, Englewood Cliffs, NJ.

Dalzel, A. (1793). *The History of Dahomey, an Inland Kingdom of Africa*. Printed by T. Spilsbury and Son and sold by J. Evans, London.

DeMarrais, E., Castillo, L. J., and Earle, T. K. (1996). Ideology, Materialization and Power Strategies. *Current Anthropology* **37**: 15–31.

Dietler, M. (2001). Theorizing the Feast: Rituals of Consumption, Commensal Politics, and Power in African Contexts. In Dietler, M., and Hayden, B.

(eds.), *Feasts: Archaeological and Ethnographic Perspectives on Food, Politics, and Power*. Smithsonian Institution Press, Washington, DC, 65–114.

Duncan, J. (1847). *Travels in Western Africa, in 1845 & 1846, comprising a journey from Whydah, through the kingdom of Dahomey, to Adofoodia, in the interior*. R. Bentley, London.

Earle, T. K. (1976). A Nearest-Neighbor Analysis of Two Formative Settlement Systems. In Flannery, K. (ed.), *The Early Mesoamerican Village*. Academic Press, New York, 196–223.

Ellis, A. B. (1965). *The Ewe-Speaking Peoples of the Slave Coast of West Africa: Religion, Manners, Customs, Laws, Languages, Etc.* Benin Press, Chicago.

Evers, H.-D. (1987). Trade and State Formation: Siam in the Early Bangkok Period. *Modern Asian Studies* **21**: 751–71.

Fakambi, J. (1993). *Routes des esclaves au Bénin (ex-Dahomey) dans une approche regionale*. Musée d'Histoire de Ouidah, Ouidah.

Falola, T. (1989). The Yoruba Toll System: Its Operation and Abolition. *Journal of African History* **30**: 69–88.

Forbes, F. E. (1851). *Dahomey and the Dahomans; being the journals of two missions to the King of Dahomey and residence at his capital in the years 1849 and 1850*. Frank Cass, London.

Fox, R. G. (1977). *Urban Anthropology: Cities in Their Cultural Setting*. Prentice-Hall, Englewood Cliffs, NJ.

Fritz, J. (1986). Vijayanagara: Authority and Meaning of a South Indian Imperial Capital. *American Anthropologist* **88**: 44–55.

Garcia, L. (1988). *Le royaume du Dahomé face à la pénétration coloniale*. Éditions Karthala, Paris.

Gregory, T. E. (2005). *A History of Byzantium*. Blackwell, Malden, MA.

Herskovits, M. J. (1938). *Dahomey: An Ancient West African Kingdom*. Northwestern University Press, Evanston, IL.

Herskovits, M. J., and Herskovits, F. S. (1958). *Dahomean Narrative: A Cross-Cultural Analysis*. Northwestern University Press, Evanston, IL.

Hopkins, A. G. (1973). *An Economic History of West Africa*. Columbia University Press, New York.

Howatson, M. C. (1989). *Oxford Companion to Classical Literature*. Oxford University Press, Oxford.

Islamoglu-Inan, H. (1994). *State and Peasant in the Ottoman Empire: Agrarian Power Relations and Regional Economic Development in Ottoman Anatolia during the Sixteenth Century*. Brill, Leiden.

Kelly, K. (1995). *Transformation and Continuity in Savi, a West African Trade Town: An Archaeological Investigation of Culture Change on the Coast of Bénin During the 17th and 18th Centuries*. Ph.D. dissertation, University of California at Los Angeles.

Kelly, K. (1997a). The Archaeology of African-European interaction: Investigating the Social Roles of Trade, Traders, and the Use of Space in the Seventeenth- and Eighteenth-Century Hueda Kingdom, Republic of Bénin. *World Archaeology* **28**: 351–69.

Kelly, K. (1997b). Using Historically Informed Archaeology: Seventeenth- and Eighteenth-Century Hueda-Europe Interaction on the Coast of Bénin. *Journal of Archaeological Method and Theory* **4**: 353–66.

Kelly, K. (2002). Change and Continuity in Coastal Bénin. In DeCorse, C. (ed.), *West Africa during the Atlantic Slave Trade: Archaeological Perspectives*. Leicester University Press, New York, 81–100.

Kiser, E., and Kane, J. (2001). Revolution and State Structure: The Bureaucratization of Tax Administration in Early Modern England and France. *American Journal of Sociology* **107**: 183–223.

Law, R. (1991). *The Slave Coast of West Africa, 1550–1750: The Impact of the Atlantic Slave Trade on an African Society*. Oxford University Press, Oxford.

Law, R. (1995). *From Slave Trade To "Legitimate" Commerce: The Commercial Transition in Nineteenth-Century West Africa*. Cambridge University Press, Cambridge.

Law, R. (1997). *The Kingdom of Allada*. Research School CNWS, Leiden.

Le Hérissé, R. (1911). *L'ancien royaume du Dahomey: Moeurs, religion, histoire*. Emile Larose, Paris.

Leone, M. (1984). Interpreting Ideology in Historical Archaeology: Using the Rules of Perspective in the William Paca Garden in Annapolis, Maryland. In Orser, C. (ed.), *Images of the Recent Past*. AltaMira, Berkeley, CA, 25–35.

Manning, P. (1982). *Slavery, Colonialism, and Economic Growth in Dahomey, 1640–1960*. Cambridge University Press, New York.

Monroe, J. C. (2003). *The Dynamics of State Formation: The Archaeology and Ethnohistory of Pre-Colonial Dahomey*. Ph.D. dissertation, University of California at Los Angeles.

Monroe, J. C. (2004). The Abomey Plateau Archaeological Project: Preliminary Results of the 2000, 2001, and 2002 Seasons. *Nyame Akuma* **62**: 2–10.

Monroe, J. C. (2007a). Continuity, Revolution, or Evolution on the Slave Coast of West Africa: Royal Architecture and Political Order in Precolonial Dahomey. *Journal of African History* **48**: 349–73.

Monroe, J. C. (2007b). Dahomey and the Atlantic Slave Trade: Archaeology and Political Order on the Bight of Benin. In Ogundiran, A., and Falola, T. (eds.), *The Archaeology of Atlantic Africa and The African Diaspora*. Indiana University Press, Indianapolis.

Monroe, J. C. (2010). Power by Design: Architecture and Politics in Precolonial Dahomey. *Journal of Social Archaeology* **10**: 477–507.

Nast, H. J. (1996). Islam, Gender, and Slavery in West Africa circa 1500: A Spatial Archaeology of the Kano Palace, Northern Nigeria. *Annals of the Association of American Geographers* **86**: 44–77.

Nast, H. J. (2005). *Concubines and Power: Five Hundred Years in a Northern Nigerian Palace*. University of Minnesota Press, Minneapolis.

Norman, N. (2010). Feasts in Motion: Archaeological Views of Parades, Ancestral Pageants, and Socio-Political Process in the Hueda Kingdom, 1650–1727 AD. *Journal of World Prehistory* **23**: 239–54

Norris, R. (1789). *Memoirs of the reign of Bossa Ahádee, King of Dahomy an inland country of Guiney: to which are added, the author's journey to Abomey, the capital; and a short account of the African slave trade*. Printed for W. Lowndes, London.

Ojo, G. J. A. (1966). *Yoruba Palaces*. University of London Press, London.

Pique, F., and Rainer, L. (1999). *Palace Sculptures of Abomey: History Told on Walls*. Thames & Hudson, Los Angeles.

Polanyi, K. (1966). *Dahomey and the Slave Trade: An Analysis of an Archaic Economy*. University of Washington Press, Seattle.

Schreiber, K. (1987). Conquest and Consolidation: A Comparison of the Wari and Inka Occupations of a Highland Peruvian Valley. *American Antiquity* **52**: 266–84.

Schwartz, G. M., and Falconer, S. E. (1994). *Archaeological Views from the Countryside: Village Communities in Early Complex Societies.* Smithsonian Institution Press, Washington, DC.

Scott, J. C. (1999). *Seeing Like a State: How Certain Schemes to Improve the Human Condition Have Failed.* Yale University Press, New Haven, CT.

Skertchly, J. A. (1874). *Dahomey As It Is: Being A Narrative Of Eight Months' Residence In That Country.* Chapman and Hall, London.

Smith, A. (2003). *The Political Landscape: Constellations of Authority in Early Complex Polities.* University of California Press, Los Angeles.

Smith, M. E. (1979). The Aztec Marketing System and Settlement Pattern in the Valley of Mexico: A Central Place Analysis. *American Antiquity* **44**: 110–25.

Soumonni, E. A. (1980). Dahomean Economic Policy under Ghezo, 1818–1858: A Reconsideration. *Journal of the Historical Society of Nigeria* **10**: 1–11.

Soumonni, E. A. (1995). The Compatibility of the Slave and Palm Oil Trades in Dahomey, 1818–1858. In Law, R. (ed.), *From Slave Trade To "Legitimate" Commerce: The Commercial Transition in Nineteenth-Century West Africa.* Cambridge University Press, Cambridge.

Stanish, C. (1994). The Hydraulic Hypothesis Revisited: Lake Titicaca Basin Raised Fields in Theoretical Perspective. *Latin American Antiquity* **5**: 312–32.

Stroud, R. S. (1998). *The Athenian Grain-Tax Law of 374/3 B.C.* American School of Classical Studies at Athens, Princeton, NJ.

Tilley, C. (1994). *A Phenomenology of Landscape: Places, Paths and Monuments.* Berg, Oxford.

Ur, J. (2003). CORONA Satellite Photography and Ancient Road Networks: A Northern Mesopotamian Case Study. *Antiquity* **77**: 102–15.

Wilkinson, T. J. (2003). *Archaeological Landscapes of the Near East.* University of Arizona Press, Tucson.

NOTES

1. This form of feasting fits Dietler's model of the "patron-role feast," in which asymmetrical reciprocal ties between leaders and followers are materialized through the consumption of food and drink (Dietler 2001).

2. Anthropologists have documented the use of public feasting as a political strategy in many societies around the world at a similar scale of social complexity. See Dietler (2001) for discussions on the role of such events in establishing political integration and marking status distinction in a variety of contexts.

3. Zassa is also mentioned in eighteenth-century sources as the hiding place for the royal family during an Oyo raid in the year 1738 (Ellis 1965:294; Norris 1789:14).

4. Agaja was reported to be performing the Annual Customs at Cana-Tota in 1733 (Levet, cited in Law 1991:326). Robin Law suggests the possibility that the Annual Customs began with a royal procession from Cana to Abomey as early as Agaja's reign (Law 1992:326).

5. This figure results in a distance of approximately 50 km, half the distance from Abomey to the coast, but very close to that of Allada, suggesting

Agaja was measuring from Allada, the capital of the kingdom for a period under his reign.

6. There is significant disagreement in local oral traditions about the history of construction campaigns at Zassa in the nineteenth century. Two structures have been identified on the ground at Zassa, whereas only one space devoted to palace construction is recognized by many local informants. According to residents of neighboring Hoja, an earlier structure, nearly entirely in ruins, dates to the reign of Agaja, whereas informants from Zassa itself suggest that a clearly later structure to the south was built by Glele on the remains of Agaja's palace. Additionally, contemporary informants from Abomey suggest that Gezo converted Agaja's private palace at Zassa into a barracks for female soldiers during his reign, an argument supported by Le Hérissé and likely reflecting an Abomean variation on the palace construction history at Zassa (Nondichao Bachalou, Abomey, Bénin, 2000; Le Hérissé 1911:66–67). Future oral and archaeological research will, I hope, shed light on this confusion, but suffice it to say that there are two structures at Zassa, an early palace most likely constructed by Agaja in the eighteenth century, and a later structure constructed sometime in the nineteenth by either Gezo or Glele.

7. One of two structures built at Kotokpa is attributed to King Behanzin (1889–94) by some local informants.

8. The nearest-neighbor statistic (R) is defined as $R = r_A/r_E$, where r_A is the average distance between all points and their nearest neighbors in a given region, and r_E is the expected average if those sites were distributed across the same region by completely random processes (Earle 1976). The nearest-neighbor statistic thus measures the departure from randomness of an observed pattern on the ground and is an extraordinarily useful tool for evaluating the degree of spatial structure within archaeological distribution patterns. For maximally aggregated sites, a hypothetical (and impossible) scenario in which all sites are located at the same point in space, the mean distance observed between nearest neighbors will be zero ($R = 0$). For a randomly distributed population of settlements, observed and expected mean distances will be the same ($R = 1$). For maximal spacing, however, all settlements will be distributed in the evenly spaced hexagonal pattern predicted by central-place theory, where $R = 2.15$. Thus the nearest-neighbor ratio can range from 0 to 2.15, $R = 1$ serving as a useful watershed, with values less than 1 indicating a tendency towards aggregation, and values greater than 1 suggesting a trend towards regular spacing.

9. There is some evidence that the state, in fact, overmanaged agriculture in this period. During the Customs of 1850, for example, the assembled officials agreed "that the corn grounds were insufficient in extent to meet the demands, and remarked that the country which formerly supplied this necessary article of food was Ahjar, and that now war was about to preclude the practicability of depending on that market" (Forbes 1851, 2:102). This suggests the possibility that state schemes for agricultural management did not reflect the realities of production on the ground.

8

The Formation of an Oyo Imperial Colony during the Atlantic Age

Akinwumi Ogundiran

INTRODUCTION

Of the numerous Yoruba polities – city-states and kingdoms – that emerged between about A.D. 800 and the 1700s, only one attained imperial status (Figure 8.1). This was the Old Oyo Empire (Figure 8.2). It came into prominence in the seventeenth century, but its imperial foundations were laid in the sixteenth century or even earlier (Law 1977). The Oyo Empire, from the seventeenth century through its collapse in the first quarter of the nineteenth century, fits the definition of an imperial state in the sense that it expanded beyond its core area in northwest Yorubaland, controlled regions and peoples far beyond its heartland, took over other polities, indirectly controlled other hegemonic and expansionist states, and succeeded in manipulating the political structures of those other polities in ways that made it exercise sovereignty over them (see Schreiber 1992:3; Sinopoli 1994:160 for the characteristics of an empire). Oyo can be called an Atlantic Age empire not only because it flourished in the high noon of the Atlantic period but, more importantly, because its imperial expansion was a response to the impacts of the Atlantic commercial revolutions in the seventeenth and eighteenth centuries (Law 1977:235).

Archaeological investigations have focused on the capital of the empire itself, Oyo-Ile (Agbaje-Williams 1983; Soper 1992, 1973–77; Soper and Darling 1980) and its core area in northwest Yorubaland (Agbaje-Williams 1989a, 1989b) (Figure 8.1). It seems that the occupation of the area of Oyo-Ile (capital of the Old Oyo Empire) by thriving and hierarchical agricultural communities was well in place around the ninth century A.D. (Agbaje-Williams 1983). We can only speculate

223

INTRODUCTION

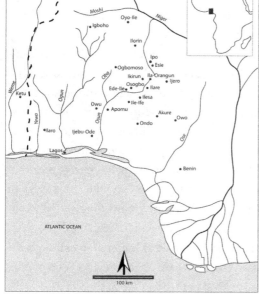

Figure 8.1
Yorubaland, showing major kingdoms before the nineteenth century.

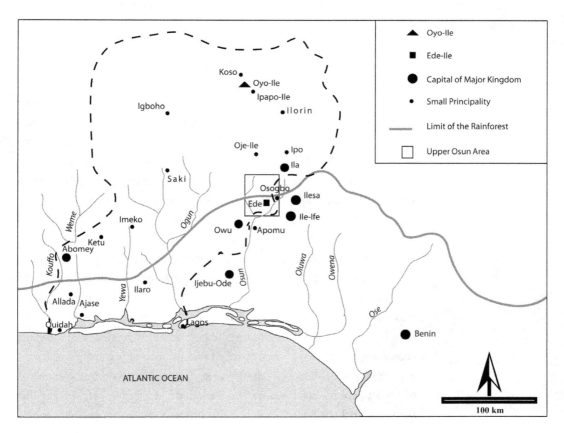

Figure 8.2
Upper Osun region.

THE FORMATION OF
AN OYO IMPERIAL
COLONY DURING
THE ATLANTIC AGE

at this point, on the basis of historical sources (e.g., Abimbola 1964; Adeyemi 1914), that Oyo-Ile was constituted into a full-fledged kingdom and a *primus inter pares* by the thirteenth century (Ogundiran 2003). The next two centuries were marked by travails for the polity due to dynastic changes, external attacks, internal conflicts, and settlement displacements (Johnson 1921). Oyo-Ile, as a viable kingdom, rebounded in the fifteenth century. And, at the close of the sixteenth century, the reinvigorated polity had developed and consolidated important institutional structures that would enable it to become, during the next two centuries, the largest political unit in West Africa south of the Niger River. Archaeological surveys have revealed that five major wall systems were built in Oyo-Ile between the sixteenth and late eighteenth centuries. At its peak in the mid-eighteenth century, the imperial capital covered an area of more than 5,000 ha, with diameters of 10 km north–south and 6 km east–west. Agbaje-Williams (1986) has estimated that between 60,000 and 140,000 people occupied the city in the eighteenth century.

Oyo's imperial expansion proceeded in five simultaneous ways: (1) conquest and formation of client states (e.g., Igbomina), (2) conquest and formation of tributary states (e.g., Dahomey), (3) the transformation of independent states into junior "gift-giving" partners (e.g., Ilesa), (4) the outright absorption of existing polities in the heartland (e.g., Ikoyi), and (5) the establishment of Oyo colonies in the frontier zones. The first four were associated with military conquest, favorable diplomatic relations, and tributary accumulation, whereas the fifth strategy – colonization – was directly linked to the settling of populations from the core of the empire in the frontiers and extraction of capital from a (proto-) market economy – commerce and tolls. Colonization is, however, the least understood of the five imperial strategies in both historical and archaeological scholarship. Yet, colonization could give us a deeper understanding of the political economic processes that drove Oyo imperialism, because these colonies were the sites of imperial innovations in economic, social, and cultural terms. Because all empires are characterized by expansion beyond their political cores to regions and frontiers of diverse ecologies, identities, and cultures, it is arguably as important to focus on such frontiers in the study of the processes involved in the making of an empire as on the imperial heartland itself. In fact, it is in the frontiers and the provinces that the process, motives, and strategies of imperial expansion and control are most observable (Schreiber 1992:265).

This study is a contribution to our understanding of colonization in empire formation based on the archaeological and historical research project in the Upper Osun area of central Yorubaland (Figure 8.2). One aspect of the research goal is to examine the nature of Oyo imperial expansion in the Upper Osun region during the sixteenth through the eighteenth centuries. I argue in this chapter that we will be better able to account for the mechanisms and processes that transformed the Oyo metropolis into an imperial power by focusing on the frontier colonial outposts of the empire rather than on the metropolis itself. The focus here is on the settlement of Ede-Ile because the convergence of the trails of oral historical sources and of archaeological investigations shows that Ede-Ile was most likely the first successful colony that Oyo-Ile established towards achieving its imperial ambitions. Hence, drawing from the existing body of literature, especially anthropology, archaeology, and historiography, I identified the Upper Osun of Yorubaland as a suitable area to investigate one strategy of Oyo imperial expansion – colonization.

The questions that I tackle here are: What was the nature of Oyo's intrusion into Upper Osun (central Yorubaland) and how did the Oyo metropolis maintain its presence in a foreign and presumably hostile territory? My answers to these questions draw from the perspective of the landscape as a socially constructed space in the negotiation of political and economic relations, usually between unequal powers (e.g., Smith 2003). The very act of colonization involves the manipulation of the interpenetrating cultural, historical, and natural elements of the landscape to achieve the political and economic goals of the colony. Indeed, any form of social complexity, especially one that involves territorial expansion and appropriation, intrinsically involves the elaborate manipulation of the landscape and its resources for the coordinated movement of people and goods and for the mobilization of power, authority, and legitimacy at a large scale. Rather than being the backdrop for the enactment of these political actions, however, the landscape is an active instrument for establishing, contesting, and reproducing political relationships (Falconer and Redman 2009:5; Knapp and Ashmore 1999:2; Smith 2003:272). I shall demonstrate that Ede-Ile was a community of colonists set up to appropriate and safeguard the southeast frontiers of the Oyo Empire.

The settlement of Ede-Ile was therefore part of the political landscape of Oyo Empire. We expect this form of political landscape to generate its own material signs consistent with the purpose and dynamics of its origins. Far more important, we expect that the character of these signs on the landscape would tell us something specific about the mechanism of colonization as a strategy of Oyo imperial project.

Empirical African case studies are generally missing in almost all of the literature on the archaeology and cross-cultural models of colonization; when they are present, they tend to be limited to North Africa (e.g., Adams 1984). Almost all of the recent writings on the archaeology of colonization have focused on South America, the Mediterranean, and Asia, often dating to much earlier periods (e.g., Alcock et al. 2001; Stein 2005a). Moreover, the study of colonization in the early modern period tends to focus on European imperial formations around the globe. This tendency is a holdback from the World Systems perspective and is one that homogenizes non-Western societies vis-à-vis Western domination. This chapter is therefore a contribution to the comparative archaeology of colonization as a strategy of expansion by state-level societies and as a mechanism for empire formation. Whereas most studies of political colonization have focused on colonial encounters between the colonizers and the local populace (Schreiber 1992; Stein 1999, 2002a; also see D'Altroy 1992), here I emphasize the cultural and political relationship between colonists and the metropolis/homeland. In the following pages, I will first examine the evidence of Oyo colonial intrusion into Upper Osun and the implantation of an Oyo settlement – Ede-Ile – in the region. The nature of the evidence – the social landscape of colonization – provides indications of the motivations and strategies of Oyo's colonization program. The empirical evidence will then be used to interrogate the archaeology of colonization in Upper Osun.

COLONIZATION AND COLONY IN EMPIRE STUDIES

Historical and anthropological interest in the role of colonies and colonization in the process of empire formation have received a boost in recent years (Stein 2005a). These studies challenge earlier conceptualizations of colonies based solely on European experience. This idea is best demonstrated in Finley's model of colonies as implanted settlements that dominate technologically backward, small-scale polities, with weak resistance capability in the face of a superior European military system, political organization, and cultural institutions (Finley 1976:177). Finley has been roundly criticized for equating colonies with domination and control of the neighboring regions and for his ethnocentric assumption that colonizers are inherently superior in technological, political, and cultural terms to the peoples of the host region (Stein 2005b:10). According to Stein (2005c), colonies generally share four universal characteristics, universal in the sense of cutting across time, political economies, space, and cultures:

1. An implanted settlement established by one society in either uninhabited territory or the territory of another society.
2. An implanted settlement established for long-term residence.
3. An implanted settlement that is both spatially and socially distinguishable from the communities of a host society.
4. A settlement with a distinct corporate identity as a community with cultural/ritual, economic, military, or political ties to its homeland.

The other two characteristics identified by Stein (2005c) are features that are not always present. They are caveats and are contestable. These are

1. that the homeland needs not politically dominate the implanted settlement; and
2. that the colonies need not necessarily control the regions in which they settled, or are allowed to settle.

Recent scholarship has made important contributions by eschewing a unitary model for conceptualizing colonies, giving us an expansive view of the different motives behind colonization and the different roles that colonies played. Some may be trading, religious, and/or economic outposts. However, the recent tendency, most exemplified in the collection of essays edited by Gil Stein (2005a), to make the case that not all colonies were and have been associated with conquest and domination or were related to political control of the host communities, makes the definition and conceptualization of colonies a chimerical project. In Stein's scheme, diasporic trading communities and cohesive migrant populations who settled away from their homelands, and maintain weak or no political linkages to the political institutions of the homeland, are also considered colonies. It is important to distinguish these or other forms of frontier migrations (e.g., Kopytoff 1987) from colonies that were integrally related to political expansion and that were tools for political economic control of the frontier and the outlying territories. These are two different processes of implantation that require different terminologies and conceptualizations.

For colonization and colonies to have analytical value in the study of imperial expansion, it is important to develop a tighter definition of colonies. First, let us put our working definitions in order. Whereas colonization refers to the process, methods, and motives by which colonies are made, colonies are implanted communities or settlements in a foreign territory. Imperialism is a set of processes and practices by which a polity (a state) expands into the territories of other polities and establishes political and economic control over the territories for the sole purpose of diverting wealth, resources, and profits to the coffers of the metropolis and its heartland through tributes, levies, taxes, and terms of trade that favor the imperial state. Therefore, imperialism has always been a political-economic project or has a political-economic dimension to it, and colonization is only one of the mechanisms by which imperialism could take place. However, colonization seems to be an instrument of expansion associated only with societies with sociopolitical complexity, such as a state (Algaze 1993). Such expansion would be for the control of a foreign territory and exploitation of its resources for the interest of the metropolis.

Given the association between colonization and state-level societies, it is then important to add that for an implanted community to qualify as a colony, its functions must be to advance both the political and economic interests of its homeland (especially the corporate interest of the metropolis), and it must enjoy the patronage of the metropolitan homeland through political protection. Whereas a colony need not politically dominate its host society, it must be able to dominate the terms of relationship with its neighbors and culturally, politically, economically assert its interests, and, by extension, advance the interest of its metropolis in the host community. Hence, to qualify as a colony, the immigrant population must not be subjected to the control of the host, as in the case of some trading Mesopotamian communities in Anatolia, which Stein (2002b, 2005c) refers to as colonies but are best described as trading diasporas (for comparative examples, see Cohen 1971; Spence 2005). Even when there is a symmetric relationship between the economic spheres of the colonists and the first-comers, the colony must serve as an arena for projecting the power, authority, and grandeur of the metropolis in a distant land, as a direct means of enabling the metropolis and its colonists to have access to a larger share of resources than would have been otherwise possible without the implantation of the settlers.

ARCHAEOLOGY OF OYO COLONIZATION AT EDE-ILE

The broad agenda of my research program in Upper Osun – archaeological survey and excavations, ethnographic and ethnohistorical studies – is driven by two related themes: the regional political economic aspects of Oyo imperial expansion in the frontier area of Upper Osun and the impacts of the Atlantic economy on this Yoruba hinterland. The archaeological investigations involved survey and excavations in two contemporaneous but now abandoned settlements, Ede-Ile and Old Osogbo (also known locally as Ohuntoto), 15 km apart (Figure 8.1). Archaeological reconnaissance was also carried out in three other abandoned settlements in the area – Ejigbo, Awo, and Ojoo – all occupied in the sixteenth through the eighteenth centuries. This chapter will focus primarily on the results of archaeological research at Ede-Ile, although mention will be made where necessary to the surrounding sites. The excavations at Ede-Ile were carried out in four loci and focused on refuse mounds, domestic house structures, crafts centers (dye-making/cloth dyeing zone, and a blacksmithing/ironworking area (Figure 8.3). A total area of 79 m² was excavated at Ede-Ile. All the excavated units show that Ede-Ile was founded on an unoccupied land. There was no prior settlement or occupation before the Oyo colonists settled in the site that later became Ede-Ile. However, the prior ownership of the land on which Ede-Ile was founded is attributed to Awo, a neighboring small polity that came under the rule of Oyo as soon as Ede-Ile was established (personal communications/interviews, Alawo of Awo, April 2004). Upper Osun was a weak political landscape in the sixteenth century, a frontier coveted by three powerful rainforest belt kingdoms: Ilesa, Ile-Ife, and Owu. Yet, this frontier was not a cultural and political tabula rasa. It was in the heartland of Yorubaland, an area that was culturally within the sphere of influence of Ile-Ife and in which Ilesa was having active political and economic interests (Ogundiran 2009a).

The historians of Oyo Empire, especially Johnson (1921) and Law (1977), suggest that Ede-Ile was founded in the sixteenth century, but radiocarbon dates securely place the foundation of Ede-Ile within the seventeenth century and show that the town was occupied throughout the eighteenth century. Historical sources indicate that the town was abandoned in the early fourth decade of the nineteenth century (Adegboyo 1972; Olagunju 1991). Most of the eight samples of charcoal and bone collagen assays submitted for radiocarbon dating were returned, expectedly, with multiple probability age ranges, due to short-term variations in the atmospheric 14C contents at certain time periods during the sixteenth through the eighteenth centuries (see McIntosh and McIntosh, 1986). These multiple probability age ranges are more pronounced for the 2-sigma (98 percent probability) calibration. When these dates are combined with oral traditions and known age of imported artifacts, such as cowries and tobacco pipes, we are certain that Ede-Ile was occupied during the seventeenth and eighteenth centuries.

Ceramics accounted for the majority of the artifacts, including bowls and jars, clay tobacco pipes, oil lamps, and spindle whorls. Other items are animal bones of both domesticated and wild species;

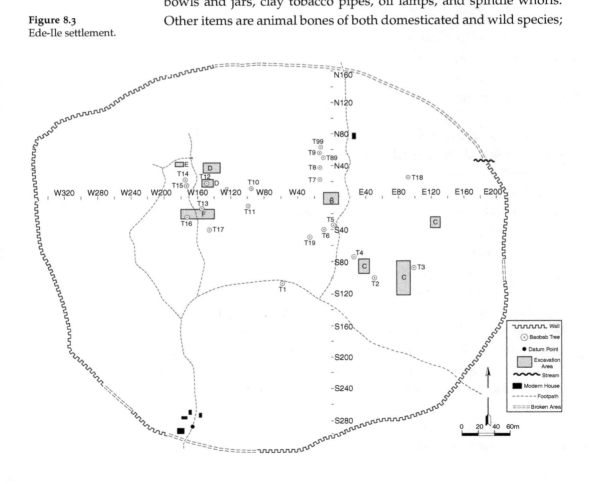

Figure 8.3
Ede-Ile settlement.

metal artifacts, including iron and brass of both utilitarian and decorative forms: knives, arrows, rings, and bangles. The presence of iron slag, tuyere, and iron furnace demonstrates that active iron smelting took place in the town. Other artifacts are wooden combs, cowries, and glass beads of blue, white, and green colors (for details, see Ogundiran 2009b). The prolific presence of horse bones demonstrate the militaristic aspects of Ede-Ile settlement and illustrates its representation in the oral historical sources as an outpost of the Oyo Empire (Johnson 1921:156). The results of the archaeological investigations suggest we can explore the dynamics of Oyo colonization in Upper Osun in three evidential domains: ceramics, landscape, and horse remains.

Ceramics as indicator of Oyo colonization at Ede-Ile

The stylistic lexicon of the ceramics at Ede-Ile, especially the forms and surface patterns (e.g., decoration), are exactly the same as those at Oyo-Ile, the imperial metropolis, and other settlements in the heartland of the empire such as Ipapo-Ile and Koso (Agbaje-Williams, 1983, 1989a, 1989b).[1] The characteristic diagnostic surface patterns of Oyo ceramic complex include brush marking, shell-edge, scallop impressions, dot punctates, and incised and rouletted geometric symbols (crosses, triangles, squares, and perpendicular motifs) (e.g., Ogundiran 2001:31). Ten distinctive bowl types of Oyo ceramic complex predominate in the Ede-Ile assemblage (Figure 8.4). These bowl forms are described below:

B4X: Serving bowls (*awo*) with nodular, slightly everted rims, flared-to-vertical body profile, and round base. The decorations forms are wide ranging but are predominantly of carved roulettes, incisions, and dot-punctates. The surface and paste fabric are mainly gray to dark gray; with burnished exterior and a gritty paste.

B6: Shallow serving bowls (*awo*) with everted rim, angular body profile, and flat base. Rouletted and incised geometric motifs, with burnished dark-gray exterior fabric and grayish fine paste, are predominant.

B7: Cooking bowl – *isaasun* – with flared, everted rim (sometimes fluted), vertical body profile, and round base. It tends to be well burnished, often with dark-gray to black exterior, and light-gray to dark-gray paste. The form is sparsely decorated. Such few decorations tend to consist of bands of incisions, and combinations of incisions and dot punctuates in geometric patterns.

B9: Cooking bowls – *isaasun* (for soup/stew) – with everted, often fluted, rims; carinated shoulders, and round body/base. This form exhibits decorations that range from rouletted to stamped and incised geometrics. The paste fabric is fine with lots of mineral temper and different shades of brown, gray, and black. The surface fabric is generally burnished and smooth.

B14: Serving bowls with outwardly slanted body and round base. Both the rim and body are continuous, but there is often a sharp discontinuity between the body and the base. This form is generally deep, and mainly has carved rouletted and incised decorations; with gray to dark-gray fabrics; and, for the most part, burnished exterior.

B16: A rare bowl form with very restricted orifice, in-turned, slanted and horizontal rim, shouldered, with round body and base. The fabric is dark gray, burnished and fine with occasional quartzite temper. The function is unknown but it was likely used for storing valuables, given its restricted orifice, 4–6 cm in diameter.

B17: Another variety of cooking bowl – *isaasun* – with everted, often fluted rims, slanted body profile, and round base (there is a sharp discontinuity between the body and the base). The predominant decoration motifs include lattices of geometric lines with dot-punctates, other carved rouletted motifs, and incisions. The fabric is generally grayish to black, burnished exterior, and fine paste with mineral inclusions.

B18: An assortment of serving bowls with both pronounced and slightly in-curving body wall profile, often with thick rounded rim, and with round base. This form tends to be deep, and there is a sharp discontinuity between the body wall and the base. It is mostly plain but has occasional incised, stamped motifs, and carved motifs. It is generally burnished with a dark-gray exterior fabric and light-gray paste.

B22: A shallow serving bowl with a rounded and slightly everted rim, as well as a vertical body profile that is continuous with a round-to-flat base. This form mostly bears bands of incisions, carved roulettes, and stamped geometric motifs.

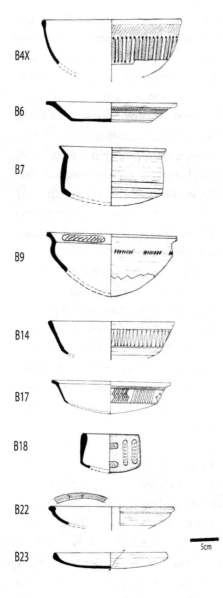

Figure 8.4
Oyo ceramic complex-diagnostic bowls.

The fabric varies between shades of gray and black, and has smooth/burnished exterior, and gritty paste.

B23: Serving bowl, mostly shallow, with vertical body wall profile and flat-to-round base, often with thin rim. This form is undecorated but has occasional occurrence of incisions and brushmarks. The fabric generally has exterior gray color and reddish brown paste.

Ongoing analysis of the formal properties of Ede-Ile assemblage indicates that more than 98 percent of the bowls, and related paraphernalia (such as lids), bear the diagnostic characteristics of the ceramic complexes in Oyo-Ile and its environs. This shows that Ede-Ile belonged, throughout its existence, to the Oyo ceramic sphere. There is substantial evidence that the initial expansion of the Oyo ceramic complex from Oyo-Ile into other parts of Yorubaland, especially in the seventeenth century, followed the directions and routes of Oyo imperial expansion and political economic influence (Ogundiran 2001). The stylistic aspects of Oyo ceramic complex at Ede-Ile, especially the bowl and lid forms and their surface decoration patterns, when compared to those at Oyo metropolis (Agbaje-Williams 1983), offer useful insights into the kinds of relationship between the two settlements, especially the political economic role that Ede-Ile played in the expansion of Oyo imperial power.

We have now learned, via neutron activation analysis (NAA),[2] that about 67 percent of the 105 vessels examined from Ede-Ile were locally produced within or in the vicinity of the settlement and about a third of the ceramics were traded in from the direction of north-west Yorubaland – Oyo-Ile and Ilorin areas. The NAA result reveals multiple sources of production, and this implies that the production and distribution of the twelve dominant bowl/lid forms possibly resulted from a decentralized production/distribution network (Ball 1993:247). That is, the production and circulation of pottery was neither centralized at the state level nor conducted at the household level. Rather, the standardization of the dominant bowl/lid forms and the decorative patterns associated with them strongly indicate that there were only a few workshops both in Ede-Ile and in the heartland of Oyo. These production sites specialized in producing the same categories of Oyo service/cooking vessels and these workshops supplied the pottery needs of Ede-Ile residents. Both the stylistic and chemical analyses of the ceramics indicate that about two-thirds of Oyo ceramic forms and design vocabularies were replicated in Ede-Ile. The only strong explanation for this is that immigrants from the Oyo-Ile metropolis and its environs founded Ede-Ile and that among these immigrants were potters. Ethnographic and ethnoarchaeological studies have demonstrated that potting was a female occupation in Oyo in particular, and Yorubaland in general (Agbaje-Williams 1983; Ajekigbe 1998; Anifowose 1984). We are then on a secure ground to speculate that women were responsible for setting up and operating the pottery workshops at Ede-Ile and that these potters were among the settlers who populated this frontier town, about 150 km from the metropolis, in the seventeenth century.

Serving/cooking bowls are an integral part of a community-based social and cultural world. They could be explicit ingredients in the formation of historical group identities and for differentiating the self and the "other" because they are linked to foodways, one of the most conservative cultural features cross-culturally. The uniformity of the stylistic properties of the utilitarian pottery at Ede-Ile indicates that its residents belonged to or adopted the same embodied practices associated with the social service of food. In subsequent sections, I will combine the uniformity of the ceramics across Ede-Ile with other lines of evidence to argue that these immigrants were colonists from Oyo-Ile and that distinctive Oyo ceramic attributes were important components for establishing their corporate identity in a frontier zone with a different ceramic stylistic vocabulary. Although the stylistic "lexicon" of the Oyo utilitarian pottery was likely part of their enculturated practices, perhaps taken for granted in the metropolis, these material aspects of everyday life would have been emblematic and meaningfully active for the immigrants in the frontier field. Their mission as colonists and vanguards of the imperial project would have made it even more necessary for the immigrants to define themselves as close as possible to the Oyo metropolis in order to accomplish their colonization project.

Baobab trees and transformation of the landscape

Ede-Ile is located in the upper reaches of the rainforest belt. However, a characteristic tree at the settlement is a savanna tree – baobab (*Adansonia digitata*). Twenty-one standing baobab trees and two recently fallen ones were found concentrated within the settlement area (Figure 8.3). Baobabs are generally indicators of habitation sites in the dry zones of Africa and are found naturally in the Sahel and savanna parts of West Africa. Their occurrence in the rain forest can only be by deliberate introduction and maintenance (Owen 1970:25). The distribution of the baobab trees coincides with the area of surface ceramic distribution – the primary index of the settlement's occupation area. The distribution of these trees thus gives us a rough estimate of the size of the settlement. The baobab trees concentrate the most in the heavily occupied part of the settlement (Loci II, III, and IV). Toward the edges of the town, the trees decrease in number and disappear at the town's outskirts.

Baobabs are known to live several hundred years, and different authors have attributed ages ranging from about 400 to over 1,000 years to baobab trees based on their girth and enormous size (Newbold 1924; Swart 1963). Following the unsatisfactory results from attempts to apply chronometric dating methods to baobab trees, several works have indicated that reliable age estimates of baobab cannot be determined from its growth rates because its girth tends to vary in response to different moisture regimes. Neither, it is claimed, is it possible to use baobab's ring-width measurement to determine its age because the absorbent nature of this fibrous wood tends to distort upon drying (Fenner 1980; Guy 1970; Robertson et al. 2006; Wickens 1982). The earlier proposition made by Rosemary Hollis (1963) about the possibility of assessing the developmental stages and relative ages of baobab trees from the color and texture of their bark, however, seems to remain valid. According to her, "The young tree has a distinctly shiny texture and pinkish-bronze tint; this color changes to bluish-mauve in middle-age and, as old age supervenes, the back becomes rough, wrinkled, and grey, like the skin of an elephant." The baobab trees at Ede-Ile are in different stages of development. Fourteen of the standing baobab trees at Ede-Ile have rough, wrinkled, and gray skin, and they also have the widest trunk circumference (ranging between 7.0 and 12.7 m). Both their rough surface texture and their sizes would indicate they are the oldest baobab trees on the site (Figure 8.5). These trees most likely dated to the period of Ede-Ile occupation, from about 400 to nearly 200 years ago.

Ethnobotanical survey in Oyo-Ile shows that the baobab is the prime tree in that savanna ecology (Sowunmi 1983). Unlike the guinea savanna environment of the Oyo metropolis, Ede is located in the upper reaches of the rainforest belt. The occurrence of this grove of baobab trees in a rainforest vegetation zone suggests that the immigrants into Ede-Ile made a successful attempt to implant a savanna landscape in a rainforest environment in order to build a town in the image of the metropolis – Oyo-Ile. Frontier immigrants from Oyo-Ile thereby successfully recreated an Oyo physical landscape in Ede. In the process, they cognitively transformed a rainforest landscape, especially the settlement area, into a savanna one.

Figure 8.5
Baobab trees.

Comparative studies have indeed shown that empires tend to change the landscape of conquered territories with different ecological systems so that they bear more resemblance to the core territory. This often involved introducing familiar plants and animals by colonists and imperial administrators into foreign territories (Crosby 1986). This was clearly the case at Ede-Ile. In contrast to Ede-Ile, however, none of the neighboring and first-comer settlements of Ojoo, Ejigbo, Awo, and Old Osogbo, contemporaneous seventeenth- and eighteenth-century settlements, yielded baobab trees. Hence, in the overall settlement geography and social identity of Upper Osun during the mid-Atlantic Age, Ede-Ile was unique with the prevalence of baobab trees. It would have served as a critical cultural and identity marker, separating the colonists/new immigrants from their first-comer neighbors.

Horse remains as an indicator of Oyo militarism

The historical narratives of the founding of Ede-Ile unambiguously state that the process of migration and settlement involved military activities sponsored by the Oyo metropolis (Johnson 1921:156; also Olunlade 1961; the Late Oba Tijani Oyedokun, personal communication, 2004). Hence, the Oyo frontier warrior – Timi – who established the colony is appellatively referred to as *Alapo ofa tiemi tiemi*: "owner of a heavy bag of arrowpoints" (personal communication, Safiriyu Atanda, a.k.a. Babanla Oba of Ede, March 2004; also see Johnson

1921:156). Likewise, the people of Ede-Ile and their contemporary descendants are referred to in Yoruba praise poetry as "children of the flaming arrows" in order to emphasize the duties of Ede-Ile as the vanguard of the empire.

Cavalry was the backbone of Oyo army and imperial expansion (Law 1975). Horses are in fact the most important weaponry that enabled Oyo to assert its control over is outlying territories. It was the quintessential instrument of imperial expansion. It is insightful, therefore, that horse remains were present in Ede-Ile. In fact, no other archaeological site in Yorubaland, including Oyo metropolis itself, has yielded as many horse remains as present in the very preliminary excavations conducted at Ede-Ile (Figure 8.6). Fifty-seven individual horse elements were collected from the excavations at Ede-Ile, mostly from a single 2 m × 2 m excavation unit in Locus B. These specimens represented a range of ages from fetal to adult, indicating that horse breeding took place at the settlement.[3]

A minimum number of ten horses are represented in the sample, but this figure will likely be revised upwards at the end of the ongoing fauna analysis. Knowing the species of the horses represented in the archaeological record will be useful for understanding the likely sources of the horses and the trading networks through which the horses were procured. Perhaps then we will be able to understand the proportions of the smaller pony breed to the larger Dongola breed and the "barbs" that originally came from the Nile Valley and the Maghrib respectively (Law 1976:115–17). Whereas the pony breed was a pre-Islamic introduction to West Africa, the Dongola breed began arriving in the subcontinent after the fourteenth century.

Again, it is of interest that the excavations conducted at the peer settlement of Osogbo, also a frontier town established by a competing hegemonic power – Ilesa – in the seventeenth century did not yield horse remains. The ponies/horses at Ede-Ile would have served to showcase imperial prestige in a horseless environment, to intimidate the neighboring peoples with these exotic animals, and to inflict swift attack-and-withdraw tactics on the "enemies." But more importantly, the horses would have served defensive purposes for the colony, an expensive endeavor that only the royalty could have afforded. The presence of horses alone indicates that the settlement of Ede-Ile was patronized and underwritten by the metropolis. That Oyo-Ile went so far as to invest heavily in the security of Ede-Ile shows the importance of this frontier town in the future of Oyo's political economy.

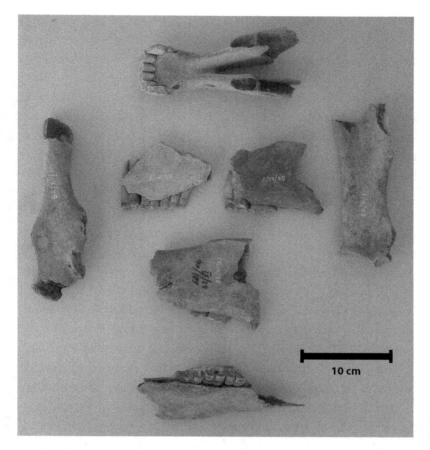

Figure 8.6
Horse remains from Ede-Ile.

COLONIZATION AS A STRATEGY OF IMPERIAL EXPANSION: EDE-ILE AS CASE STUDY

The archaeological study of Ede-Ile shows that a broad-based immigrant group, comprising men and women of diverse socioeconomic stations, were the colonists of Ede-Ile. The presence of spindle whorls in house units, the evidence of iron smelting and smithing, the extensive dye-making/cloth dyeing workshop in the settlement, and the horse remains all indicate that dyers, weavers, blacksmiths, traders, farmers, horse handlers – feeders, riders, and veterinarians, among others – settled in the colony. Likewise, the presence of cowries, glass beads, and tobacco pipes reveals that Ede-Ile was well integrated into the circuit of cowry currency, diverse market spheres, and regionwide adoption of new taste and consumption patterns in Yoruba hinterlands during the seventeenth and eighteenth centuries (Ogundiran 2002, 2007).

The picture that emerges from the combination of archaeological data and the oral historical and ethnographic sources is that sometime between the late sixteenth and early seventeenth century, the Oyo imperial agents used Ede-Ile as the base for launching Oyo's political and economic influence in Central Yoruba. By the mid-seventeenth century, Ede was an economically diversified township and the headquarters of an imperial province, protecting Oyo imperial interests in the heartland of Yorubaland and managing the commercial traffic between the Atlantic coast and the hinterland on behalf of the empire.

Colonization was an expensive investment in terms of the labor, skills, and personnel being diverted from the metropolis into the frontiers; in terms of the resources being expended by the metropolis to maintain the colonists in hostile and foreign territory; and in terms of the level of risk involved in maintaining the colony in an unpredictable and often hostile environment. The cost would be reduced if the colony was able to become self-sufficient within a short period and was able to deliver the desired resources at handsome profit margins to the metropolis. But first, the metropolis must be able to mobilize a large number of people of different skills from an integrated heartland for the colonization project to be effective as a strategy of imperial expansion (see Bauer and Covey 2002:847). Archaeological investigations in the vicinities of Oyo-Ile, the imperial metropolis, have not been directed to understanding the sociopolitical, economic, cultural, and ecological conditions that favored the ambitions of Oyo leaders of embarking upon an imperial colonization project in the sixteenth century. However, the surveys and excavations conducted by Agbaje-Williams (1989a, 1989b) in northwest Yorubaland strongly indicate that by the end of the sixteenth century, Oyo-Ile had developed into an urbanized center with satellite towns and villages, such as Koso, Ipapo-Ile, and Igboho, among others, within a radius of 30 to 40 miles of the city (personal communication, 2004). One could then argue that the only reason that the metropolis succeeded in mobilizing large numbers of people from its heartland into embarking on colonization was because the core area of the empire was unified politically, ideologically, economically, and culturally. Here, I believe, lies the explanation for the rapid success of Ede-Ile as a colony of the metropolis 150 miles from the heartland. Ede-Ile not only achieved self-sufficiency within a generation but also succeeded in becoming a small but compact town of about 850 m² (85 ha), similar to the sizes of the satellite towns in the metropolis such as Ipapo-Ile and Koso.

How the colony was populated is a subject that cannot be fully known at this stage of the research. Were the colonists only from the Oyo metropolis or did they also come from the adjoining areas of the metropolis? Or, were some of the colonists members of conquered population relocated to Ede-Ile under the leadership of Oyo soldiers? It is most likely that the colonists came from different parts of the heartland, especially in the northwest region of Yorubaland, and that the initial colonists were a mixture of soldiers, traders, adventurers, and their dependents. The success of these pioneer colonists would have encouraged others from the metropolis and the adjoining areas to settle in the colony. But one thing is clear: the cultural flavor of Oyo was maintained throughout the colony's existence as the ceramic evidence and the transformations of the landscape show. A major challenge that faces us in understanding the process of colonization in Ede-Ile, as in other studies of imperial processes (e.g., Sinopoli 1994:173), is that archaeological chronological resolution is not amenable to documenting sequences of imperial growth and settlement expansion, especially one that flourished for only about 200 years.

The traditional world systems theory's explanation that imperial frontier migrations and colonization was a strategy of population redistribution from the core to the periphery in order to relieve local population pressures in the core is not applicable to the Oyo colonization project (Santley and Alexander 1992:23). This core-periphery model is a very mechanical explanation of how the core population expanded into the periphery or how colonies were established. Historical narratives hint at a more complex picture, namely that young men and women became colonists to pursue commerce and wealth at a scale not possible in the metropolis (personal communication/interviews, Ibilola Omileye, a.k.a. Yeye Osun Osogbo, June 2003; Adeleke Oyelami, a.k.a. Chief Ajagemo, April 2004; Oba Tijani Oyedokun Agbonran II, April 2004; also see various references in Johnson 1921:169–217). The materiality of archaeological evidence broadly supports these historical accounts, especially in showing that Ede-Ile was attuned to the commercial revolutions taking place in the Atlantic basin during the seventeenth and eighteenth centuries.

There is a wide range of motives for imperial expansion, chiefly among which are security concerns, (proto-) market economics, tributary exploitation, population pressure, scarcity of and demands for prime resources (e.g., land, raw materials), and ideology. Whereas there may be a prime motive for expansion, there are often feed-back relations among these motives, and it may be difficult to pinpoint a singular explanation for the instigation of an imperial expansionist project. Hence, many scholars tend to seek explanation in the interaction of two or more of the above factors for imperial expansion (Sinopoli 1994:162). However, the strategies of imperial expansion may sometimes reveal the most important motive, especially when it is possible to combine archaeological data with other parallel evidence, such as oral traditions and documentary sources.

Ede-Ile was the product of an effort to implant the Oyo metropolis in a faraway territory. With baobab trees, the Oyo imperial agents animated the rainforest environment with the vision of a savanna landscape; with horses, they projected the source of Oyo's military strength to Upper Osun; and with ceramics, they affirmed Oyo ethnicity in a foreign land. None of these three features appear in the four contemporaneous and neighboring settlements – Awo, Osogbo, Ojo, and Ejigbo – so far surveyed in Upper Osun. None had baobab trees, based on the excavation at Osogbo, there were no horse remains, and the ceramics of each belong to the Ife ceramic sphere, not Oyo. Ede-Ile was therefore an ideological statement, but a statement intended to give Oyo-Ile access to new economic and political opportunities in the hinterland of Yorubaland. In all, the Oyo imperialists exported Oyo-Ile to a critical frontier zone of interaction.

Hence we can begin to understand what kind of colony Ede-Ile was and then begin to understand the primary goals and agenda of Oyo's imperial ambition. This first Oyo colony sustained a large-scale emigration from the Oyo metropolis and probably its suburbs; it was established on a previously unoccupied land that it appropriated from one of the local small polities in Upper Osun; it politically dominated small-scale polities within about 10-km radius of the colony-settlement; and in turn, the metropolis established, through its agent-ruler, the formal political and economic control of the Ede-Ile colony. All these features are consistent with Finley's definition of what a colony is. However, contrary to Finley's insistence that a defining characteristic of a colony is that it serves to control the local labor force on behalf of the metropolis, it is very unlikely that Ede-Ile served this function for the Oyo Empire because the very form of resource extraction that Oyo sought to achieve in Upper Osun was not conducive to the control of the local labor force.

Oyo's imperial ambition was guided by an interest in partaking in the booming commercial networks that connected the coast to the Upper Osun hinterland. In this regard, Oyo was a trading empire in origin. Unlike the contemporaneous empires of the Atlantic world, Oyo did not control the market mechanisms that characterized the Atlantic mega-empires of Portugal, Britain, Spain, and the Netherlands. Nonetheless, its rise was shaped and even conditioned by the world economic systems and the political economies that these mega-empires created. The political entrepreneurs of Oyo-Ile ventured into Upper Osun primarily for economic reasons. The goal was not to plunder, ravage, and cart away loot, to merely set up a tributary dependency, or to control the flow of specific preciosities. Its primary interest in founding the colony of Ede was to set up political control over Upper Osun in order to establish a permanent base for commercial activities and take charge of some of the trade routes in the region. In doing so, it created a market niche for its citizens and supplied them with military protection in the form of archers, horsemen, and cavalry. All these served as a means, of course, to divert profits and wealth to the metropolis. With this colonization strategy, Oyo was responding to a new economic order.

Following the establishment of Portuguese trading factories on the coast of Benin kingdom in the course of the sixteenth century, and the gradual transformation of the Bight of Benin into a slave-trading mall in the course of the seventeenth and throughout the eighteenth centuries, Upper Osun became a hotbed of economic activities, a critical link between the coast and the far hinterlands. Before the end of the sixteenth century, two commercial centers were flourishing at Apomu and Osogbo, each under different political powers: Ilesa and Ile-Ife, respectively. The Ilesa kingdom was on its way to bringing the whole of Upper Osun under its control when Oyo entered the contest, determined to have a large piece of the pie. Strategically, Ede was placed at a location between Osogbo and Apomu so that it could control part of the commercial traffic. The diverse craftworks (iron, dye, and weaving) that archaeological evidence portray, the standardization revealed in the ceramic complex, and the profusion of cowries used as currency strongly indicate the commercial components of everyday life in the colony.

Ede-Ile was most likely the first colony that Oyo established as an offensive mechanism in pursuing the economic and hegemonic aspects of Oyo imperial ambitions. It was therefore not a loose/independent frontier town of a trading diaspora but a colony that depended politically and ideologically on Oyo metropolis. No doubt, the metropolis also depended on the colony for commercial opportunities, revenue (through tributes, taxes, and profits), and as a critical means of extending metropolitan hegemonic powers, territorial control, and cultural influence in central Yorubaland. In order to have access to the economic opportunities of the Upper Osun and its strategic links to the coastal trade via the Ijebu country, the Oyo metropolis embarked upon colonization. This gave birth to Ede-Ile as the pivot for establishing and maintaining Oyo's formal political and economic control in Upper Osun.

Santley, Yarborough, and Hall (1987:87–88) have suggested that the ethnic identity of a colonial enclave should be identifiable from the archaeological records via the public rituals, architecture, burial customs, and the stylistic, iconographic, and symbolic elements of the material culture. Ede-Ile maintained significant features of the metropolis in terms of ceramics, military strategies, and the landscape plan. Ede-Ile thus expressed an Oyo identity throughout its 200-year existence. The ceramics, so far, offer the most convincing clue to the Oyo identity of this colonial enclave. Although it is likely that the colonists were not all from Oyo metropolis, one could surmise that maintaining sociocultural ties (aside from political and economic ties) to the Oyo metropolis gave the colonists in Upper Osun the tool to "assert a distinct ... identity in their interactions with the indigenous groups" (Stein 2005b:25).

The investment in modifying the landscape to mimic the metropolis by planting baobab trees, the supply of ponies/horses for transportation, defensive and offensive strategies, and the preponderance of Oyo ceramics all indicate that Ede was intended as a long-term settlement for an Oyo metropolis population and that, ideologically, the settlement was intended to maintain a distinct formal corporate identity as a community with economic, cultural, military, and political ties to Oyo metropolis. The large numbers of scarce ponies/horses (about ten horses from only a 4 m² excavation unit) and the likely high mortality rate of ponies/horses in the rainforest environment of Upper Osun would suggest further that Ede-Ile was politically dominated directly by the metropolis. This would have been the case because only the royal court had the resources to procure horses and invest them in such an environment that was endemic for ponies/horses. For practical purposes, the only reason for such investment was to protect the colony from attacks by the neighboring competing interests. Indeed, it was the access that Oyo had to ponies/horses that gave it military superiority over the other interest groups in the area.

Yet, one could argue that the role of Ede-Ile as a military and administrative outpost of Oyo was only a means to secure a market niche for Oyo citizens in Upper Osun, not for setting up a primarily tributary system. Unlike the military and administrative colonies that have been identified in other parts of the world, such as in the prehispanic Andes and Mesoamerica and in the Mediterranean and in the Near East (e.g., Stein 2005a), there were no fortified garrisons in Ede-Ile. It is the contextual interpretation of the remains of ponies/horses that gives us the clues that Ede was an implantation of Oyo cavalry in the heartland of the rainforest belt. Likewise, Oyo did not invest in building durable structures that bear the markings of Oyo material culture. In fact, Oyo immigrants did not possess a better building technology than the first-comer settlers in Upper Osun. Yet, Oyo colonists and their mentors in the metropolis understood the cognitive power of the built landscape in social engineering. Oyo transformed the physical landscape and built Ede-Ile in the conceptual image of the metropolis by planting baobab trees at the very same time that it was implanting its colonizers. The demarcation of Ede-Ile settlement landscape with baobab trees defies the dichotomy between nature and culture. Baobab trees are cultural trees par excellence, bearing significant cognitive value in the mentality of the people. This makes the trees a resourceful tool in Oyo's colonization strategies in Upper Osun.

Thus far, the baobab trees at Ede-Ile serve as one component of settlement arrangement that the colonists developed to optimally align themselves with the order and balance of the metropolis (also see Willey 1983:462, for comparative work in Central and South America), to create a visualscape that legitimizes Oyo's presence in a foreign and contested territory. This visualscape refers to a set of socially constructed features that constitute the visual panorama (intimately linked to both the private and public spheres) by which a community cognitively defines its collective/communicative sense of space. In this regard, Oyo's imperial colonists creatively exported Oyo-Ile to Upper Osun as the efficient means of bringing the empire, through resources from the provinces and provincial markets, to the capital. Thus, whereas baobab trees served as the ideological imprints of

Oyo's imperial colonization in the frontiers, ponies/horses served to project the power of the empire to the contested zone, and the ceramics served a dual purpose. First, they highlighted cultural continuity in cuisine and foodways between the colony and the metropolis, and second, they fostered a continuous economic relationship between the two. The baobab and the horse/pony remains make it possible for us to claim that the users of the Oyo wares were immigrants and settlers from the metropolis. The near absence of Oyo pottery in the surrounding communities highlights the fact that Ede-Ile was an Oyo colonial enclave.

CONCLUSION

This chapter is an inquiry into whether Ede-Ile was indeed an Oyo colony and, if so, what strategies of colonization were employed by Oyo in this outlying territory. Beyond these objectives, the investigation in the Upper Osun area of Yorubaland is giving us insights into the economic systems, imperial political economy, accommodation and resistance to imperial domination, and the political aspects of colonization, migrations, and interactions at the regional levels (for some of the comparative frameworks, see Alcock et al., 2001; Sinopoli 1994; Smith 2004; Stein 2005a; Tracy 1991; Yoffee 1995). As we secure a better understanding of the regional political economy and multisettlement contexts in which Ede-Ile flourished, and as we expand our study to other Oyo colonies, especially in western Yorubaland, it may become clearer that the strategy of imperialism that Oyo pursued in critical commercial zones was colonization. We would expect Oyo's colonization strategies to differ from place to place, and this diversity will, we hope, enrich our understanding of the unique place of colonization as probably the most sustaining feature of Oyo imperialism in the age of the Atlantic economy.

Against the background of the many definitions of colonies that suffuse the literature these days, Ede-Ile was an epitome of a frontier settlement project initiated or patronized by the metropolis. It was a colony set up purposely to further the political economic agenda of the metropolis, and, for this reason, it enjoyed the patronage of Oyo-Ile throughout its existence. We need a more diachronic approach to, and a more focused conceptualization for, the theorizing of colonization and colonies. It is indeed the case that colonies may be established for overlapping reasons, and the status of an immigrant community in the outlying territory may change from that of an apolitical trading post to a political weapon of imperial control. Likewise, a colony originally set up as a political act directly controlled by the metropolis may gain its political freedom but remain close to the metropolis in ideological and cultural terms, and it may continue to do the bidding of its metropolis in political and economic matters. Moreover, a colony that had maintained a separatist cultural sphere may eventually become open and be infiltrated by the neighboring groups to the extent that in due course it loses its enclave identity. Even then, the strategies for maintaining colonies may vary widely and across time. Moreover, although all colonies are implanted communities, they may not be set up necessarily to reproduce major cultural features of the homeland and, therefore, may be difficult to recognize in the archaeological records. In the case of Ede-Ile, we have a situation in which the colonists not only owed their identity but also their political allegiance to the imperial heartland. As a result, Ede-Ile reproduced some of the major cultural features of the homeland.

Ede-Ile was a universe of imperial presence in a frontier region away from the metropolis where the idea of political expansion was originally dreamed up and put into action. As a colony, Ede-Ile was constructed as a political landscape to conceptualize and actualize the dreams of the Oyo expansionists. Its material signs – pottery, baobab trees, and horses – disciplined the mind and the visualscape in order to create a new community and a new identity, and to evoke the authority and power of Oyo in Upper Osun. The political landscape of Oyo was not culturally homogenous, nor was it uniformly continuous. It was therefore important for Oyo to replicate versions of itself in the different spatial nodes of its conquered territory in order to effectively project its power, authority, and legitimacy. Ede-Ile was the first most successful product of that political experiment, as an imperial settlement space and a spatial expression of the Oyo imperial political authority. It is no doubt the most visible expression of the toll collection spots, the turnpikes, the guarded roads, and the protected/subdued villages and towns that collectively formed part of the cartographies of the Oyo political landscape. In other words, Ede-Ile has attracted our attention because it was the centrifugal force harnessing instruments of power and authority on behalf of the empire in its southeastern frontiers. It was therefore in Ede-Ile that both the colonists and their neighbors in the southeast frontiers experienced, perceived, and imagined the empire the most.

All three material indices of Oyo imperial presence account for the socialization of the conquered territory into an Oyo landscape, serving as the rope that tied the outlying frontiers of the empire to the metropolis. The particular signs and materialities of colonization at Ede-Ile reveal that the process and mechanism of Oyo Empire formation was constituted into the practice of everyday life in which individuals, whether as forced or voluntary colonists, participated in enacting the sensibility of a unified imperial community (Smith 2003:70). In that everyday life, the residential marker – baobab; the wares of cuisine, social, and domestic activities – Oyo pottery; and the military hardware of imperial power – horses – were united within the singularity of Oyo identity. These signs and materialities of the political landscape were embedded in the "ways of living and being" to unite the political, social, cultural, and economic elements of the Oyo Empire (Knapp and Ashmore 1999:13). It was this political landscape that gave social order to the Oyo expansionist agenda in its early stage, allowing that agenda to flourish and move forward to produce what we now know as the Oyo Empire.

ACKNOWLEDGEMENT

This chapter is a product of the *Upper Osun Archaeological and Historical Project* funded by Wenner-Gren Foundation for Anthropological Research (Grant Number 7099), with additional research funds from the Office of the Dean, College of Liberal Arts and Sciences, University of North Carolina at Charlotte. My gratitude goes to Nigeria's National Commission for Museums and Monuments for granting the permission to carry out the fieldwork, especially to the following officers of the commission: Dr. Seyi Hambolu, Mr. M. O. Adesina, and Mr. James Ameje. The support of His Royal Highness, the Late Timi of Ede, Oba Tijani Oyedokun Agbonran II; the Ojisun family; and Alagba Safiriyu Atanda, a.k.a. Babanla Oba, made the research at Ede-Ile possible. I am grateful to the faculty and staff of the Department of Archaeology and Anthropology and the Institute of African Studies at University of Ibadan, especially Dr. Babatunde Agbaje-Williams, Mr. Philip Ajekigbe, Dr. Raphael Alabi, Dr. Bayo Folorunso, and Dr. Bolanle Tubosun for their assistance in a variety of ways. The hard work of all members of the research team is highly appreciated. I have benefited from the comments provided by Dr. Babatunde Agbaje-Williams, Dr. Dele Odunbaku, Dr. Adria LaViolette,

Dr. Ann Stahl, and Dr. Norman Yoffee on the earlier drafts of the chapter, but I alone am responsible for any omission or error that may be present and for the interpretations advanced here.

BIBLIOGRAPHY

Abimbola, W. (1964). The Ruins of Oyo Division. *African Notes* **2** (1): 16–19.

Adams, W. (1984). The First Colonial Empire: Egypt in Nubia, 3200–1200 B.C. *Comparative Studies in Society and History* **26** (1): 36–71.

Adegboyo, J. (1972). *Ede: Ascendancy at the Left Wing of Old Oyo Empire in the First Half of the Nineteenth Century.* B.A. Essay in History, University of Ibadan, Nigeria.

Adeyemi, M. C. (1914). *Iwe Itan Oyo-Ile ati Oyo Isisiyi abi Ago-d'Oyo.* Ibadan.

Agbaje-Williams, B. (1983). *A Contribution to the Archaeology of Old Oyo.* Ph.D. dissertation, University of Ibadan, Nigeria.

Agbaje-Williams, B. (1986). Estimating the Population of Old Oyo. *Odu* (NS) **30**: 3–24.

Agbaje-Williams, B. (1989a). Archaeological Reconnaissance of Ipapo-Ile, Kwara State, Nigeria: An Interim Report. *West African Journal of Archaeology* **19**: 21–36.

Agbaje-Williams, B. (1989b). The Discovery of Koso: An Ancient Oyo Settlement. *Nigerian Field* **54**: 123–27.

Ajekigbe, P. (1998). Pottery Making in Ilora and its Relationship with Old Oyo Pottery Finds. In Wesler, K. W. (ed.), *Historical Archaeology in Nigeria.* Africa World Press, Trenton, NJ.

Alcock, S. E., D'Altroy, T. N., Morrison, K. D., and Sinopoli, C. M., eds. (2001). *Empires: Perspectives from Archaeology and History.* Cambridge University Press, New York.

Algaze, G. (1993). Expansionary Dynamics of Some Early Pristine States. *American Anthropologist* **95** (2): 304–33.

Anifowose, M. (1984). *An Ethnoarchaeological Study of Pottery in Ilorin.* B.A. Essay, University of Ibadan, Nigeria.

Ball, Joseph W. (1993). Pottery, Potters, Palaces, and Polities: Some Socioeconomic and Political Implications of Late Classic Maya Ceramic Industries. In J. A. Sabloff, J. A., and Henderson, J. S. (eds.), *Lowland Maya Civilization in the Eighth Century A.D.* Dumbarton Oaks Research Library and Collection, Washington, DC, 243–72.

Bauer, B. S., and Covey, A. A. (2002). Processes of State Formation in the Inca Heartland (Cuzco, Peru). *American Anthropologist* **104** (3): 846–64.

Cohen, A. (1971). Cultural Strategies in the Organization of Trading Diasporas. In Meillassoux, G. (ed.), *The Development of Indigenous Trade and Markets in West Africa.* Oxford University Press, Oxford, 266–81.

Crosby, A. W. (1986). *Ecological Imperialism: The Biological Expansion of Europe, 900–1900.* Cambridge University Press, Cambridge.

D'Altroy, T. N. (1992). *Provincial Power in the Inka Empire.* Smithsonian Institution Press, Washington, DC.

Falconer, S. E., and Redman, C. L. (2009). The Archaeology of Early States and their Landscapes. In Falconer, S. E., and Redman, C. L. (eds.), *Polities and*

Power: Archaeological Perspectives on the Landscapes of Early States. University of Arizona Press, Tucson, 1–10.

Fenner, M. (1980). Some Measurements on the Water Relations of Baobab Trees. *Biotropica1* **2**: 205–9.

Finley, M. I. (1976). Colonies – An Attempt at a Typology. *Transactions of the Royal Historical Society* **26** (5th series): 167–88.

Guy, G. L. (1970). *Adansonia digitata* and Its Rate of Growth in Relation to Rainfall in South Central Africa. *Proceedings & Transactions* 54. Rhodesia Scientific Association, Salisbury, 68–84.

Hollis, R. (1963). Reflections on Baobabs. *Nigerian Field* **28** (3): 134–38.

Johnson, S. (1921). *The History of the Yorubas.* CSS Bookshop, Lagos.

Knapp, A. B., and Ashmore, M. (1999). Archaeological Landscapes: Constructed, Conceptualized, Ideational. In Ashmore, W., and Knapp, A. B. (eds.), *Archaeologies of Landscape: Contemporary Perspectives.* Blackwell, Malden, MA, 1–30.

Kopytoff, I. (1987). The Internal African Frontier: The Making of African Political Culture. In Kopytoff, I. (ed.), *The African Frontier.* Indiana University Press, Bloomington, 3–81.

Law, R. (1975). A West African Cavalry State: The Kingdom of Oyo. *Journal of African History* **16** (1): 1–15.

Law, R. (1976). Horses, Firearms, and Political Power in Pre-colonial West Africa. *Past and Present* **72**: 112–32.

Law, R. (1977). *The Oyo Empire c. 1600–c. 1836: A West African Imperialism in the Era of the Atlantic Slave Trade.* Oxford University Press, Oxford.

McIntosh, S. K., and McIntosh, R. J. (1986). Recent Archaeological Research and Dates from West Africa. *Journal of African History* **27**: 413–42.

Newbold, D. (1924). More Notes on Tebeldis. *Sudan Notes and Records* **7** (1): 135–37.

Ogundiran, A. (2001). Ceramic Spheres and Historical Process of Regional Networks in Yoruba-Edo Region, Nigeria, A.C. 13th–19th Centuries. *Journal of Field Archaeology* **28** (1&2): 27–43.

Ogundiran, A. (2002). Of Small Things Remembered: Beads, Cowries, and Cultural Translations of the Atlantic Experience in Yorubaland. *International Journal of African Historical Studies* **35** (2–3): 427–57.

Ogundiran, A. (2003). Chronology, Material Culture, and Pathways to the Cultural History of Yoruba-Edo Region, Nigeria, 500 B.C.–A.D. 1800. In Falola, T., and Jennings, C. (eds.), *Sources and Methods in African History: Spoken, Written, Unearthed.* University of Rochester Press, Rochester, NY, 33–79.

Ogundiran, A. (2007). Living in the Shadow of the Atlantic World: Material Life, History and Culture in the Yoruba-Edo Hinterland, ca. 1600–1750. In Ogundiran, A., and Falola, T. (eds.), *Archaeology of Atlantic Africa and African Diaspora.* Indiana University Press, Bloomington, 77–99.

Ogundiran, A. (2009a). Frontier Migrations and Cultural Transformations in Yoruba Hinterland, ca. 1575–1700: The Case of Upper Osun. In Falola, T., and Usman, A. (eds.), *Movements, Border and Identities in Africa.* University of Rochester Press, Rochester, NY, 37–52.

Ogundiran, A. (2009b). Material Life and Domestic Economy in a Frontier of Oyo Empire during the Mid-Atlantic Age. *International Journal of African Historical Studies* **42** (3): 351–85.

Olagunju, O. A. (1991). A History of the Development of Kingship Institution in Ede, c. 1840–1980. *B.A. Essay in History*, University of Ibadan, Nigeria.

Olunlade, E. (1961). *Ede: A Short History. General Publications Section, Ministry of Education*, Ibadan.

Owen, J. (1970). The Medico-Social and Cultural Significance of Adansonia Digitata (Baobab) in African Communities. *African Notes* 1: 24–36.

Rice, P. (1996). Recent Ceramic Analysis: I. Function, Style, and Origins. *Journal of Archaeological Research* 4: 133–63.

Robertson, I., Loader, N. J., Froyd, C. A., Zambatis, N., Whyte, I., and Woodborne, S. (2006). The Potential of the Baobab (*Adansonia digitata* L.) as a Proxy Climate Archive. *Applied Geochemistry* 21: 1674–80.

Santley, R., and Alexander, R. (1992). The Political Economy of Core-Periphery Systems. In Schortman, E. M., and Urban, P. A. (eds.), *Resources, Power, and Interregional Interaction*. Plenum, New York, 23–49.

Santley, R., Yarborough, C., and Hall, B. (1987). Enclaves, Ethnicity, and the Archaeological Record at Matacapan. In Auger, R., Glass, M., MacEachern, S., and McCartney, P. (eds.), *Ethnicity and Culture*. University of Calgary Archaeological Association, Calgary, 85–100.

Schreiber, K. (1992). *Wari Imperialism in Middle Horizon Peru*. Anthropological Papers, Museum of Anthropology, No. 87. University of Michigan, Ann Arbor.

Sinopoli, C. M. (1994). The Archaeology of Empires. *Annual Review of Anthropology* 23: 159–80.

Smith, A. T. (2003). *The Political Landscape: Constellations of Authority in Early Complex Polities*. University of California Press, Berkeley.

Smith, M. E. (2004). The Archaeology of Ancient State Economies. *Annual Review of Anthropology* 33: 73–102.

Soper, R. (1973–77). *Archaeological Work at Old Oyo*. Unpublished Report, Department of Archaeology, University of Ibadan, Nigeria.

Soper, R. (1992). The Palace at Oyo Ile, Western Nigeria. *West African Journal of Archaeology* 22: 295–311.

Soper, R., and Darling, P. (1980). The Walls of Oyo Ile, Oyo State, Nigeria. *West African Journal of Archaeology* 10: 61–81.

Sowunmi, M. A. (1983). Appendix A. The Vegetation of Old Oyo Field Trip of 8th-10th May, 1979. In Agbaje-Williams, B., *A Contribution to the Archaeology of Old Oyo*. Ph.D. dissertation, University of Ibadan, Nigeria, 375–79.

Spence, M. W. (2005). A Zapotec Diaspora Network in Classic-Period Central Mexico. In Stein, G. J. (ed.), *The Archaeology of Colonial Encounters: Comparative Perspectives*. School of American Research Press, Santa Fe, 173–205.

Stein, G. J. (1999). *Rethinking World-Systems: Diasporas, Colonies, and Interaction in Uruk Mesopotamia*. University of Arizona Press, Tucson.

Stein, G. J. (2002a). Colonies without Colonialism: A Trade Diaspora Model of Fourth Millennium B.C. Mesopotamian Enclaves in Anatolia. In Lyons, C., and Papadopoulos, J. (eds.), *The Archaeology of Colonialism*. Getty Research Institute, Los Angeles, 27–64.

Stein, G. J. (2002b). From Passive Periphery to Active Agents: Emerging Perspectives in the Archaeology of Interregional Interaction. *American Anthropologist* 104: 903–16.

Stein, G. J. (2005a). *The Archaeology of Colonial Encounters: Comparative Perspectives*. School of American Research Press, Santa Fe.

Stein, G. J. (2005b). Introduction: The Comparative Archaeology of Colonial Encounters. In Stein, G. J. (ed.), *The Archaeology of Colonial Encounters: Comparative Perspectives*. School of American Research Press, Santa Fe, 3–32.

Stein, G. J. (2005c). The Political Economy of Mesopotamian Colonial Encounters. In Stein, G. J. (ed.), *The Archaeology of Colonial Encounters: Comparative Perspectives*. School of American Research Press, Santa Fe, 143–72.

Swart, E. R. (1963). Age of the Baobab Tree. *Nature* **198**: 708.

Tracy, J. D. ed. (1991). *The Political Economy of Merchant Empires*. Cambridge University Press, New York.

Wickens, G. E. (1982). The Baobab: Africa's Upside-Down Tree. *Kew Bulletin* **37**: 173–209.

Willey, G. (1983). Settlement Patterns and Archaeology: Some Comments. In Vogt, E., and Leventhal, R. (eds.), *Prehistoric Settlement Patterns: Essays in honor of Gordon R. Willey*. University of New Mexico, Albuquerque, 445–62.

Yoffee, N. (1995). Political Economy in Early Mesopotamian States. *Annual Review of Anthropology* **24**: 281–311.

NOTES

1. The analysis of the ceramic complex at Ede-Ile was conducted in comparison to the ceramic collections from Oyo-Ile. The later were generated by (1) the fieldwork conducted by the University of Ibadan Archaeological Field School led by Robert Soper (1973–77, unpublished); and (2) the excavations conducted by Babatunde Agbaje-Williams in 1981 and discussed in his dissertation (1983). The collections are now housed in the Department of Archaeology and Anthropology, University of Ibadan. Reference was also made, secondarily, to the ceramics from the capital's satellite towns, Ipapo-Ile, Koso, and Igboho, based on the fieldworks led by Babatunde Agbaje-Williams from 1987 to 1991 and involving the present author and other students.

2. *Report on Instrumental Neutron Activation Analysis of Pottery and Clay from Upper Osun, Yorubaland, Nigeria*. Report prepared by Leslie G. Cecil, Robert J. Speakman, and Michael D. Glascock, Archaeometry Laboratory, Missouri University Research Reactor, University of Missouri, Columbia, September 22, 2006.

3. *Preliminary Faunal Report: Ede-Ile and Osun Grove Settlement, 2004 Season*, by Clayton M. Tinsley, State University of New York, Binghamton. May 2006.

PART III

INTERNAL
FRONTIER
LANDSCAPES

9

The Rise of the Bassar Chiefdom in the Context of Africa's Internal Frontier

Philip de Barros

INTRODUCTION

This volume uses the concept of landscape production as a paradigm for understanding the nature and dynamics of political economies and cultural ideologies, including ideologies of power and resistance, with an emphasis on the use and manifestation of power in symbolic, materialistic, and integrative ways. This chapter examines the concept of Africa's internal frontier as described by Kopytoff in the context of the rise of the Bassar Chiefdom of Northern Togo in the late eighteenth century, including its interaction with corporate descent groups, regional power relationships, and the degree of political economy.

More than twenty years ago, Kopytoff (1987) elaborated on the role of the "internal frontier" in the rise of political entities in sub-Saharan Africa. This chapter examines his ideas in the context of the rise of the Bassar Chiefdom in the late eighteenth century and finds there are major parallels supporting Kopytoff's model. However, although the study of the internal frontier is by definition the study of regional processes (de Barros 2001; Stahl 2004), Kopytoff (1987) spends little time discussing the impacts of two major regional phenomena on the political processes of this frontier: (1) the immigration of specialist ironworkers associated with the rise and decline of regional ironworking centers; and, (2) the regional impact of slave raiding by centralized polities in peripheral areas associated with the internal frontier. It is suggested that Kopytoff's (1987:41) exclusion of societies with pronounced specialist occupations (such as ironworking) leaves a big hole in his model and that, indeed, iron-workers could be an important catalyst for the initial stages of polity formation, particularly in their search for apprentices and the social-ization of these apprentices into kinsmen. In addition, it is apparent that the slave trade had a major impact on Africa's internal frontier so that the frontier process was not just primarily the result of "steady little local quarrels and raids" (Kopytoff 1987:21). Finally, this chapter uses both archaeological and ethnohistorical data to document the processes of the internal frontier.

AFRICA'S INTERNAL FRONTIER

Kopytoff (1987, 1999) argues that most African political entities did not evolve out of preexisting simpler forms; rather, they grew out of immigrant settlements that split off from existing central polities – immigrants who migrated into the "internal frontiers" between fully formed regional political systems (Kopytoff 1999:88). These areas were empty or occupied by small, decentralized groups or "weak local hegemonies." These new immigrant groups brought with them preexisting social and political models from their former polity (Kopytoff 1987:14). The principle of first-comer primacy, a key to legitimate authority in African societies, led newcomers to strug-gle to "co-opt the mystical powers of the earliest settlers in relation to the land"; and, in the context of acephalous societies, "a hierar-chy can emerge through the simple process of adding new layers of immigrants under the kin groups that settled the area first" (Kopytoff 1987:51; McIntosh 1999:21).

A recently arrived immigrant group sought to attract followers and new members as kinsmen or pseudo-kinsmen using a corporate kin group model; however, as the new polity became well established and had developed a modus vivendi with earlier first-comer groups, including the ritual "owners of the land," adherents increasingly were added under a contractual model between ruler and subjects (Kopytoff 1987:40–52). An ideological duality thus develops that tells the story of the polity's creation from the differing views of ruler and subjects, offering political counternarratives often associated with sacred geographies. This process of polity creation is useful for under-standing processes of political change and continuity among and between African polities, large and small (Kopytoff 1987; McIntosh 1999; Robertshaw 1999; Schoenbrun 1999; Vansina 1990, 1999).

THE BASSAR REGION

The Bassar region of northern Togo is bisected by the Katcha River and is bordered by iron-rich hills and mountains, including the nearly pure hematite ores at Bandjeli (Figures 9.1 and 9.2). It has alternating dry and rainy seasons and an annual rainfall of 140 cm. The savanna-woodland vegetation has been heavily impacted by cultivation and deforestation. Subsistence is based on shifting agriculture focused on yams, sorghum, millet, groundnuts, but also cassava, cowpeas, okra, peppers, shea butter nuts, and nere (*Parkia biglobosa*). For centuries, Bassar exported foodstuffs and iron for cloth, charcoal, slaves, and cattle.

Around the beginning of the German colonial rule in 1890, the Bassar region was home to the Bassar and Kabu chiefdoms in eastern Bassar and the relatively autonomous western region extending from Bandjeli to Dimuri. In precolonial times, western villages were likely presided over by lineage elders. The Bandjeli Chiefdom is not discussed in colonial literature, but it probably resulted from a Bissib (Lamba) migration in the nineteenth century.

Early German observers exaggerated the extent of the Bassar Chiefdom, suggesting it once held sway over the entire Bassar region and that the late-nineteenth-century Dagomba war had weakened its power. Actually, the chiefdom was relatively small – 25 to 80 km^2 with a population of 5,000 to 10,000 (Cornevin 1957:96; de Barros 1985; Dugast 1988). It was centered on the community of Bassar and may have included Kalanga to the west. It was created between A.D. 1780 and 1810 (de Barros 1985:723–29), which coincides with the onset of intensive slave raiding by the Dagomba from the west and the Tyokossi from the north, and the growth of a major Hausa kola route through Bassar into the Volta Basin (Barbier 1982; de Barros 1985:325–29; Norris 1984). The only other documented chiefdom is Kabu, founded in the 1850s (Gnon 1967).

Since around 1800, most Bassar have lived in the four centers of Bassar, Kabu-Sara, Bandjeli, and Bitchabe. The Bassar are an amalgam of indigenous Paragourma-speaking groups and immigrants from the north (Lamba, Konkomba, Gurma, Gangan, and Tyokossi), west (Gouang or Gondja and Dagomba), and east (Tem or Kotokoli and Tchamba). Immigrants came to Bassar for its farm land, its iron industry, and as a place of refuge from regional slave-raiding activities (Cornevin 1962:24). The neighboring Kabiye often traded slaves

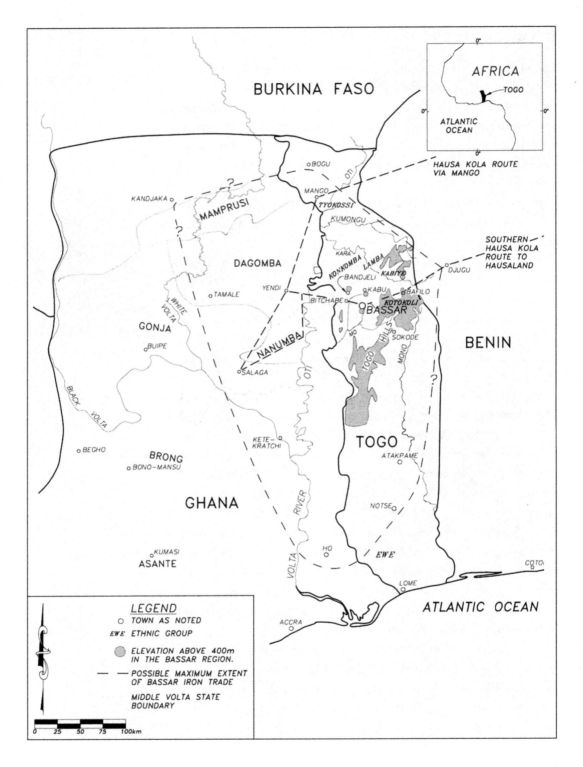

Figure 9.1
Bassar and Bassar iron trade in West Africa, showing relationship to states of the Middle Volta Basin and Hausa kola routes circa A.D. 1800.

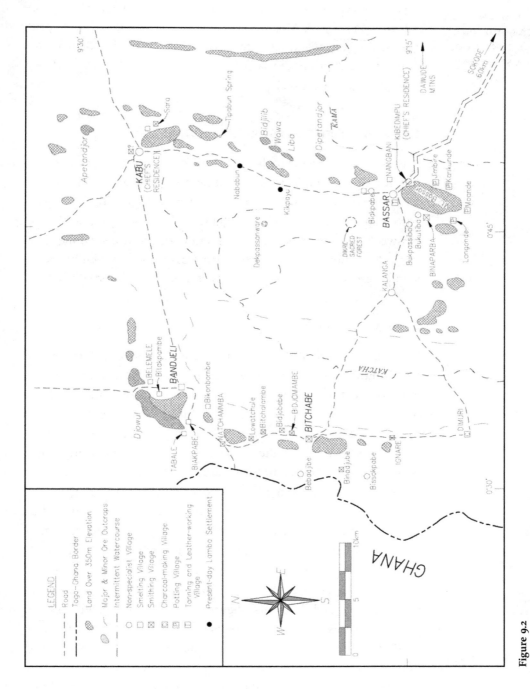

Figure 9.2
Bassar region showing iron ores, chiefdoms centered on Bassar and Kabu, and specialist villages at contact (1890s). The early Iron Age (400 B.C.–150 A.D.) ironworking site of Dekpassanware is also shown.

to the Bassar for food. Slaves were used for field labor and as wives who farmed, made charcoal, and mined iron ore. Children begotten from enslaved women were, however, free (Cornevin 1962; Klose 1903a, 1903b, 1964). Most immigrants were assimilated and speak Bassar. The largest and most important Bassar clan, the Nataka Clan, claims an origin from the sacred forest of Dikre northwest of Bassar (Dugast 1992; Figure 9.2).

THE RISE OF THE BASSAR CHIEFDOM

After a brief discussion of the nature of chiefdoms, this section examines the rise of political centralization and the Bassar Chiefdom in the light of both ethnohistorical and archaeological data contexts. Particular emphasis is placed upon the role of iron production and ironworker immigration and the impact of the transatlantic slave trade. In a subsequent section, these narratives will then be examined in terms of their degree of fit with Kopytoff's internal frontier.

Defining the nature of chiefdoms

Given the multiple and often ambiguous usages of the term "chiefdom" in the literature, it is useful to define how it is used here. The office of chief is usually hereditary; however, a new chief might be only mildly related to the former chief as a member of a chiefly lineage or clan; selected from outside the clan or may be a foreigner; or selected from alternating clans. Fried (1967) distinguished between simple and complex chiefdoms. The former was chief of a single village with satellite hamlets or farmsteads; the latter minimally had a paramount chief ruling over local village chiefs in a regional polity. Simple chiefdoms have populations in the thousands and complex chiefdoms in the tens of thousands. Johnson and Earle (2000) view chiefdoms as a continuum of variability evolving from the big man collectivity to the threshold of the state; chiefly hierarchies and heterarchies are also viewed on a continuum, with the latter typical of sub-Saharan Africa (Johnson and Earle 2000:266; McIntosh 1999). For some, the term "chiefdom" has lost much of its meaning (Yoffee 1993), essentially covering all intermediate-level societies (Stanish 2004). For Bassar, the position of chief is quasi-hereditary and its scale and degree of hierarchy most closely resemble a simple chiefdom.

Ethnohistorical context of the Bassar Chiefdom

Oral traditions speak of indigenous first-comer elements and the later in-migration of peoples from the west, north, and east into the Bassar region internal frontier. They also provide evidence of the ideological duality of the Bassar Chiefdom and the integration of first-comer elements into the ritual of chiefly installation and the agricultural cycle, both part of the modus vivendi between rulers and subjects that is an important part of the processes of the internal frontier. Finally, they provide insights into the actual authority of the chief over the everyday lives of his subjects and the place of the Bassar Chiefdom within the hierarchical-heterarchical continuum.

As for first-comer populations, oral traditions suggest there were once indigenous "Lama" populations (ancestors of the Lamba and Kabiye) in the Bassar region (de Barros 1985; Dugast 1992:138ff; Froelich and Alexandre 1960; Froelich et al. 1963). Gbikpi-Benissan (1976, 1978) suggests Lamba are present in the indigenous community of Kankunde; Dugast (1992) found no evidence of this, but admits the Lamba origins are a mystery. Although the Bissib (Lamba) clan is a relatively recent arrival, local informants agree they are the "owners" of the four iron hills north of Bassar (Dugast 1992:136; Figure 9.2). The community of Biakpabe-Bassar, of Gurma origin, also claims first-comer (but not indigenous) status and emphasizes its ritual role in the installation of the chief, which the Nataka (chiefly) clan rejects (Dugast 1992:868–70). The possibility of Biakpabe's long-term presence in the area is strengthened by the role it plays in harvest ceremonies. Cornevin (1962:22–51) and Gbikpi-Benissan (1978:4ff; see Dugast 1992) state that the major component of early "Bassar" populations came from Ghana (Gurma and Gondja), including the composite Nataka clan, which also claims first-comer status. Immigrant farmers and ironworkers also came over the centuries: Gurma from Burkina Faso to Biakpabe and Bandjeli; Dagomba smiths (Koli clan) to Bitchabe and Binaparba; Lamba ironworkers (Bissib clan) to Bandjeli, Bassar, and Sara; Kotokoli smiths to Bassar-Nangbani; Tchamba ironworkers to Bandjeli; and Gangan ironworkers fleeing the Tyokossi (Cornevin 1962; de Barros 1985; Dugast 1987; Froelich and Alexandre 1960; Martinelli 1982).

In the Bassar Chiefdom, the chief is chosen from the Nataka clan. Pioneering clan elements consisted primarily of Gondja (Guang) peoples from near Kete Kratchi in Ghana (Figure 9.1), some fleeing

THE RISE OF THE
BASSAR CHIEFDOM
IN THE CONTEXT OF
AFRICA'S INTERNAL
FRONTIER

the Dagomba (Gbikpi-Benissan 1976:81), before establishing themselves at the forest of Dikre centuries ago. Nataka elements are in Kibedimpu, Nangbani, and Bukpassiba; in Wadande, Ketangbao, and Kpaajadumpu in Bassar; and in indigenous Kankunde by incorporation (Dugast 1987, 1992; Gbikpi-Benissan 1978:8). Oral traditions offer conflicting narratives about who came first to Mount Bassar – those from the Nataka clan or elements associated with possibly indigenous "Lama." In legitimizing indigenous status for the whole clan, Chief Ouro Bassabi Atakpa told Gbikpi-Benissan (1978:7) that the first Nataka lived in holes in Bassar Mountain. The issue of origins resulted in a complicated balancing act (modus vivendi, after Kopytoff 1987:57–60) in the structure, installation, and functioning of the Bassar Chiefdom (Dugast 1988, 1992, 2004).

The Kankunde immigrants were integrated into the Nataka clan, and they begrudgingly accept that their affiliation with the Nataka gave them access to land to settle when they arrived. Although the Kankunde do not have legitimate right to the chieftaincy, they do play an essential ritual role during the installation of a new Bassar chief (Dugast 1992:759–60).

Biakpabe also claims first-comer status even over Kankunde (Dugast 1992:874–76). The author's research found that Biakpabe claims involvement in the selection and/or installation of the chief. One story stated the new chief has to choose between two stones, one representing the "earth" and the other "secular power"; if he mistakenly chooses the "earth" stone, a special ceremony must be performed in Biakpabe and a secret one in Bukpassiba where his head is shaved. A similar story was told to Dugast (August 1, 2010, personal communication) about a stone and wooden bench that he was shown. Biakpabe also brings the first yams to the chief and has the right to sow the first fonio seeds (Dugast 1992:877). Gbikpi-Benissan (1984:17–18) was told the following in Biakpabe: Biakpabe introduced yams to the area; Biakpabe is more interested in deities than the office of chief, which explains why the chief is at Kibedimpu; and, finally, Kibedimpu chooses the chief who is then elected in Nangbani. However, the chief is only installed if he can distinguish the royal stone from other stones presented to him in Biakpabe and can identify those who belong to the royal line versus those first-comers associated with the Dikre divinity. Although first-comer and chiefly installation claims by Biakpabe are rejected by the Nataka, Dugast (1992:679, 868–70) emphasizes that all Bassar clans attribute magical powers to Biakpabe, especially related to yam germination. Biakpabe also has the honor of planting the first yams. These conflicting stories of first-comer status reflect the modus vivendi that develops between indigenous first-comers and immigrant latecomers described by Kopytoff (1987).

Dugast (1988:274–79) argues the Bassar Chiefdom was a reinvention and improvement upon an earlier, less centralized, perhaps even failed "chiefdom." The primary goal was to reduce clan factionalism and to create an institution that could deal with the huge influx of foreign refugees, including ironworkers, created by intense slave raiding, by bringing in a neutral, impartial outsider who could arbitrate constant disputes that were creating anarchy within the old chiefdom. Thus, the Nataka clan was a political composite consisting of indigenous and foreign elements and associated ritual leaders, including the *utandaan*s associated with the divinity for the entire Bassar agglomeration and that associated with ancient origins of the Nataka clan at Dikre, along with other ritual leaders linked with rain, wind, and fertility. This grouping of indigenous and other ritual leaders within a single clan provided the spiritual legitimacy the chief needed to rule, but at the same time it tightly circumscribed his authority (Dugast 1988:274–75; 2004). In fact, contrary to what often occurs in the classical African chiefdom, where the growth of sacred chiefly authority is associated with a rupture between the chief and his clan, this did not occur in Bassar, a point emphasized with the chief's disappearance upon his death into the Dikre sacred forest (Dugast 1992:241).

What kind of authority did the Bassar chief have over his subjects? Economically, the Bassar chief had no influence over planting and harvesting decisions, which were made in close coordination with elders and the *utandaan*s, and he had no control over iron production and exchange (Dugast 1988; de Barros 1985, 2011). The chief could decide to go to war but, in principle, only with the consent of his council. The chief was the head of the judicial tribunal (*bosolib*), a larger assembly of elders (*unatchebe*), and the executive council (*diber*), yet decisions were generally reached through consensus. The chief's primary powers lay in his power to make judgments and in his ritual power associated with controlling malevolent forces. Using his judicial powers, the Bassar chief focused on preventing and settling internal disputes, encouraging cooperation at all levels, and mitigating social inequalities (Gbikpi-Benissan 1976:148–59). Despite

THE RISE OF THE
BASSAR CHIEFDOM
IN THE CONTEXT OF
AFRICA'S INTERNAL
FRONTIER

structural elements that sought to diminish tension, inter- and intra-clan conflicts were common (Gbikpi-Benissan 1976:123–26). The first were often between the Nataka and foreign (latecomer) clans; the latter between senior and junior clan members. Sources of conflict included women, cattle, and farm land. Gbikpi-Benissan 1976:126) describes clans as pressure groups, reflecting the chiefdom's heterarchical nature. The use of physical force to make people comply was problematic; moral persuasion and peer pressure were the best tactics, including the threat of exile. No formal police force existed to enforce decisions (Gbikpi-Benissan 1976:134–35).

In terms of ritual power, the organization of a fire dance was central to Bassar ritual activity at both the residential and Bassar agglomeration level. It involves diviners discerning the silhouette of potential evil influences in the flames, concentrating this evil in the cinders, and then disposing of them at a crossroads at the edge of town. The chief and his clan have the responsibility of organizing a fire dance for all Bassar; more importantly, if the chief has the visionary powers to foresee evil, he can order ritual action to render harmless that evil at the town's crossroads without a fire dance. No one else has such power in Bassar (Dugast 2004:210, 232–34).

In summary, the chief's authority was legitimated at several levels: practical – justice, order, and the general welfare were promoted and maintained; religious – the chiefly installation and harvest festival ceremonies provided the ritual support and legitimization he needed to rule and his unique powers associated with keeping out malevolent forces through the fire dance and associated rituals; and ideological – he was chosen from and by the legitimate Nataka clan and its composite elements. In terms of the hierarchical-heterarchical continuum, the Bassar Chiefdom was decidedly heterarchical (see also the case of Eguafo discussed by Spiers in this volume).

ARCHAEOLOGICAL CONTEXT

Archaeological studies (de Barros 1985, 1986, 1988, 2001, 2003, 2006, 2011) provide important evidence linking both iron production and the indirect effects of the transatlantic slave trade to major demographic and settlement shifts that are related to the rise of political centralization within the Bassar region. These studies also provide support regarding both the nature of indigenous (first-comer) populations and the later in-migration of ironworking (and other) latecomer populations.

Iron production and political centralization

A regional archaeological sample survey (10 km²) of the east central portion of the Bassar region between the Katcha River and the *Bidjilib* iron ore source (Figure 9.2) was conducted to look for associations between the rise of iron metallurgy and the rise of political centralization (de Barros 1985, 1988). No evidence for a settlement site hierarchy was found until the early Iron Age with the site of Dekpassanware (late first millennium B.C.), and then again with the later Iron Age settlements associated with large-scale iron production beginning in the fourteenth century and reaching peak production levels after CALIB A.D. 1550. In both cases, the site hierarchy consisted of a village-satellite hamlet complex with little or no evidence for residential segregation, the production of elite goods, monumental architecture, or other signs of more complex political centralization. In short, it is hypothesized that political centralization was no greater than that associated with generic big man systems or simple chiefdoms. The only centralized polities recognized in local oral traditions are the relatively recent Bassar and Kabu chiefdoms, both best characterized as simple chiefdoms.

During the early Iron Age, two concordant sets of radiocarbon dates from Dekpassanware date early iron production to CALIB 400–200 B.C. (de Barros 2011), where small, probable bellows-driven furnaces were used to meet primarily local iron needs. As noted earlier, oral traditions suggest the Bassar region was formerly inhabited by the Lama, peoples ancestral to the present-day Kabyie and Lamba, whose homelands today are just to the north and northeast (Figure 9.1). The excavations at Dekpassanware strongly suggest the inhabitants of this 30-ha site were ancestral to the Kabiye (de Barros 1985, 2011). This evidence includes the following: (1) the dominant ceramic ware (Bright Mica Ware) is made from clays derived from gneisses and granites, which are not present in the Bassar region but do exist in the Kabiye area; (2) the ceramic forms, including pots with flared hollow bases and carinations (along with the frequent use of grooves and incisions), are similar to modern Kabiye forms; (3) the people at Dekpassanware buried their dead in family or communal tombs as do the Kabiye (Posnansky and de Barros 1980), along with iron grave goods, whereas local Bassar informants stated this is contrary to Bassar burial practices; and, (4) Dekpassanware contains iron bloom crushing mortars (*lukomandjole*) and fragments of large stone forging hammers, practices used in northern Togo today by only the Bassar and the Kabiye (Dugast 1986). Thus, it would appear that early Bassar-region metallurgists were probably ancestors of the present-day Kabiye, and perhaps the Lamba as well, given the Bissibi clan's Lamba origin noted earlier. In short, archaeological data support the ethnographic evidence for an indigenous Lama people.

Turning to the later Iron Age, induced draft furnace technology appears in the fourteenth century (de Barros 1985, 1986) when iron and iron tools began to be produced for trade with neighboring populations, such as the Konkomba and Kotokoli. The emergence of the Dagomba, Mamprusi, and Gonja states to the west (Figure 9.1) during the fifteenth and sixteenth centuries greatly increased the demand for iron weapons, horse paraphernalia, and protective chain mail for their cavalries. These states, along with Bono-Mansu and then Asante, stimulated long-distance trade into the Middle Volta Basin by the Hausa. Bassar responded with a spectacular growth in iron production between the late sixteenth and eighteenth centuries (de Barros 1986, 2001). Major iron production centers developed north of Bandjeli and Kabu and at Tipabun (Figure 9.3). Bassar iron markets thrived (e.g., Natchammba) and Bassar blacksmiths organized trading parties to adjacent areas. Bassar iron was traded throughout Togo and eastern Ghana with the help of Tyokossi and perhaps Hausa traders (de Barros 1985, 1986; Dugast 1986, 1988). The thriving iron industry led to a marked population increase due to better living standards, the import of slaves as field laborers, and the immigration of farmer-ironworkers from regions that had either exhausted local wood supplies (Goucher 1984) or were plagued by slave raiding.

Large-scale iron production led to larger, more sedentary villages; a population shift closer to major ore deposits (de Barros 1988); specialization within the iron industry (Figure 9.3); and a rising standard of living for ironworkers, especially clan elders who often amassed wealth in the form of food, cowry shells, cattle, slave labor, and imported goods (Dagomba brass rings, Kirotashi agate beads on the Niger, and European glass and native ground beads; Klose 1964:162–63). It is not known whether the new regional settlement pattern of larger villages with satellite hamlets resulted in incipient big men or simple chiefdoms (de Barros 1988). A simple chiefdom was perhaps at Dikre before the rise of the Bassar Chiefdom (Dugast 1988), but no chief names are remembered.

Cornevin (1962) and Dugast (1992) have documented the importance of in-migration to the Bassar region during the seventeenth

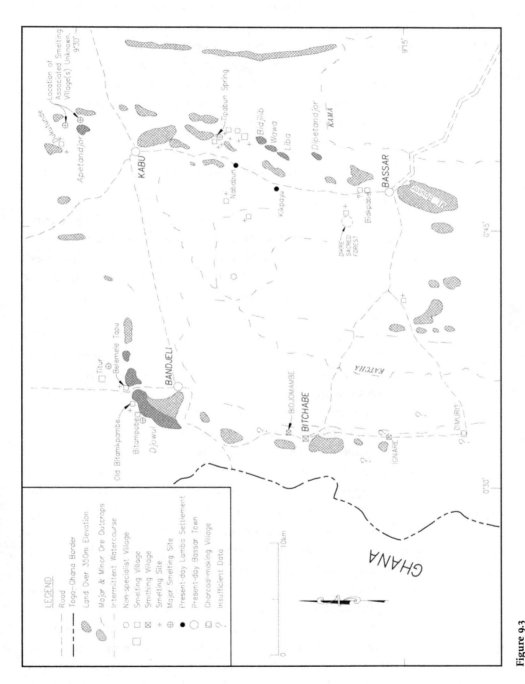

Figure 9.3
Bassar region circa A.D. 1600–1750. Major ironworking villages and sites are shown near Bandjeli, Kabu, Nababun (Tipabun), and Bassar. Insufficient data are available for the Bitchabe area.

THE RISE OF THE
BASSAR CHIEFDOM
IN THE CONTEXT OF
AFRICA'S INTERNAL
FRONTIER

through nineteenth centuries. Many of these immigrants were farmer-ironworkers attracted to the region's good farm land and its important iron industry with its excellent ores at Bandjeli. This period of in-migration corresponds well with archaeological studies described above, which show a pronounced rise in site size and regional site density and the appearance of a village-hamlet site hierarchy beginning in the late sixteenth century. In short, farmer-ironworker migration was an important force in the production of the internal frontier landscape of the region.

The impact of the slave trade on Bassar political centralization

Beginning in the late 1700s, Bassar was subjected to major slave raiding by the Dagomba from the west and the Tyokossi kingdom to the north (de Barros 2001). The Dagomba sought slaves and cattle to pay tribute to the Ashanti, and the Tyokossi sought slaves to raise food. Some of the slaves sent to the Ashanti ended up in the transatlantic slave trade, and one can argue that the displacement of the Tyokossi from the Ivory Coast to northern Togo in the late eighteenth century was an indirect result of the turmoil caused by this same trade (de Barros 2001). In 1873–76, the Dagomba laid siege to the town of Bassar. Although they never conquered Bassar, there is some evidence Bandjeli may have periodically paid tribute or gifts (Dugast 1992:62; Rattray 1932:580). The Tyokossi may have briefly collected tribute from Kabu (de Barros 2001:69–70).

Archaeological data (de Barros 1985, 1988) confirm this intensive slave raiding led to the abandonment of the Bassar peneplain between 1775 and 1825 and the regrouping of populations in mountain refuge areas like those inhabited today (Figure 9.4). Major ironworking centers moved to new locations: (1) in Bandjeli, populations and smelting sites moved from the north to the south side of Djowul Mountain; (2) the major iron-producing areas north of Kabu and to the south at Tipabun were abandoned, with some populations later regrouping at Sara with the rise of the Kabu Chiefdom in the 1850s; (3) new smelting sites developed north of Nangbani; and, (4) smithing populations north of Bitchabe moved closer to the mountains. People left Dikre and settled near Mount Bassar at Nangbani, Bukpassiba, Wadande-Bassar, and Kibedimpu. The last group at Dikre (Old Ussakar) left in the early 1800s. Oral traditions from the composite Nataka clan state their ancestors left Dikre under Bangaraku.

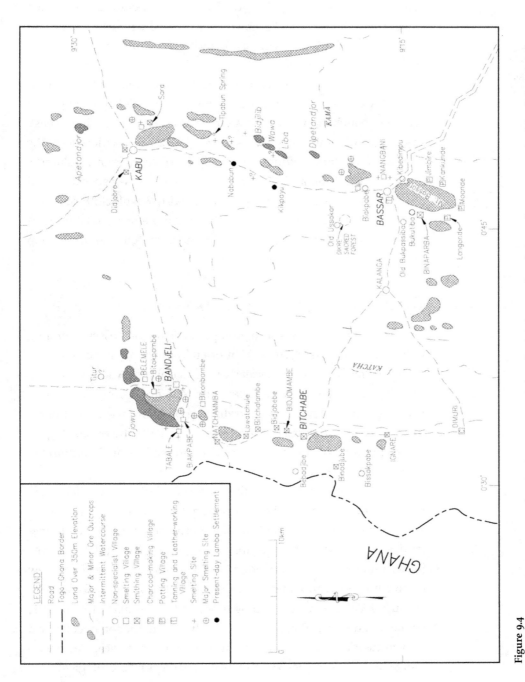

Figure 9.4
Bassar region circa A.D. 1825–50. There has been a major shift in the distribution of smelting settlements to south of Bandjeli and closer to the large mountains adjacent to Kabu and Bassar. Tipabun and Dikre have been abandoned, and two major smelting centers appear north of Bassar.

Kibedimpu became the new chiefly residence, close to Mount Bassar for protection; Nangbani, Bukpassiba, and Wadande were spaced across the landscape to alert the Bassar of impending slave raids (de Barros 1985:662–67). Bissib smelters settled between Bassar and Nangbani (Gbikpi-Benissan 1976), and some smiths from Bitchabe settled at Binaparba (Figure 9.4).

In the last decade of the nineteenth century, regional specialization in the west continued with smelting near Bandjeli, smithing from Ignare to Natchammba, and charcoal making at Dimuri; in the east, smelting and smithing villages developed in association with the Bassar and Kabu chiefdoms (Figure 9.4). Women from Kankunde, Langonde, Jimbire, and Moande near Mount Bassar specialized in potting, and Bassar women dyed imported Kotokoli cloth obtained in exchange for iron. This slave raiding and major population shift coincided with the rise of the Bassar Chiefdom and the production of its associated cultural landscape.

THE INTERNAL BASSAR FRONTIER

To a great extent, the Bassar region parallels the processes operating within Kopytoff's (1987:16–17) "internal frontier." With the exception of Dekpassanware during the early Iron Age, which was a major iron-working center and may have been the center of a simple chiefdom, it was a region of small, decentralized groups or "weak local hegemonies" with no evidence of centralized polities in the archaeological record for at least eleven centuries prior to the Bassar Chiefdom (de Barros 1985, 2006, 2011).

Another key similarity is the importance of in-migration from neighboring regions – "the production of frontiersmen" (Kopytoff 1987:16–23) – some seeking to avoid internal disputes in their homeland, others seeking better farmland, still others fleeing slave raiders. Such immigrants also included farmer-ironworkers seeking new opportunities because of depleted wood fuel (Goucher 1984) and/or because local ores were no longer accessible because of civil strife or slave raiding (de Barros 2000:185). This phenomenon of collapsed iron industries was widespread in sub-Saharan Africa. For example, Schmidt (1997:265–88) presents archaeological, ecological, and technological evidence showing how thriving "early Iron Age" communities in northwestern Tanzania collapsed because of wood fuel depletion. By the seventh century, ironworking had ceased in many areas and would not be reestablished until the thirteenth century when the land had become reforested. Similarly, it is likely that the ironworking industry of Mema in the empire of Ghana also went into serious decline as a result of regional deforestation (Haaland 1985:66; see de Barros 2000:186). A similar decline in Burkina Faso may have led to the immigration of ironworkers to the south, including the Bassar region. And, deforestation was becoming a serious problem in Bassar when the Germans arrived in 1890 – they described how the entire core region was denuded of forest and how wood charcoal was imported from the Konkomba to the north and from Dimuri to the south (de Barros 1985; Goucher 1981; Hahn 1997; Kuevi 1975). In short, immigrant ironworkers were probably a common phenomenon over the centuries (de Barros 2000:186; McIntosh 1994:177), often contributing to the migration of frontiersmen to the internal frontier landscape.

Kopytoff (1987) describes how the growth of polities in the internal frontier consists of obtaining adherents (kinsmen and pseudo-kinsmen) and how each latecomer group is added on as a layer in the political and social structure. This process is evident in the Bassar region where immigrants from different cultural areas have been assimilated into the structure of Bassar society, resulting in smelting and smithing groups or clans of diverse origins. The author found that when village elders were assembled by the chief to answer questions, they spoke of a common origin in the Bassar region; however, if these same elders were asked similar questions within their family vestibule, one suddenly discovered a diverse range of origins (Gonja, Gurma, Dagomba, and so forth).

First-comer primacy also played a major role in the structuring and legitimization of the Bassar Chiefdom. The ethnohistorical and archaeological evidence presented earlier indicates this internal frontier was "initially" characterized by first-comer Lama populations, followed perhaps by later Gurma migrations (Biakpabe), followed by later immigrants, including elements of the Nataka clan and ironworkers of diverse origins during the mid-to-late second millennium A.D. The archaeological evidence suggests these later ironworking populations brought induced draft furnace technology to the Bassar region during the early fourteenth century A.D. (perhaps from Burkina Faso; see de Barros 1986). Such populations would have had an important "edge" as latecomers: (1) as ironworkers they had an independent means of wealth production that could be used to

THE RISE OF THE BASSAR CHIEFDOM IN THE CONTEXT OF AFRICA'S INTERNAL FRONTIER

attract adherents (especially through marriage to the daughters of other groups) allowing them to build up potential embryonic polities; and, (2) they could solve their latecomer status paradox by claiming to have brought a "new order" of wealth and production (thanks to induced draft furnaces) to the internal frontier (see Kopytoff 1987:50). This appears to have led to the rise of an earlier, simple chiefdom associated with the populations living near the sacred forest of Dikre. This polity was apparently relatively small and the chief's powers relatively constricted, because no list of chief names comes down to us from that period, though Chief Ouro Atakpa told Szwark (1981:19) that fourteen other chiefs are buried at Dikre in a communal tomb. Chiefs of the new chiefdom are said to disappear into the ground at Dikre upon their death (Dugast 1992:237).

The combined ethnohistorical and archaeological evidence also suggests that the first-comer Lama populations were largely displaced to the east and north of the Bassar region, with remnants perhaps at Kankunde. Similarly, Gurma first-comers lost their preeminence with the growth of the probable latecomer and heterogeneous Nataka clan. These first-comer remnants were then ritually integrated into the politics of the Bassar Chiefdom when it arose in the late eighteenth century, which helps explain Biakpabe claims about involvement in the chiefly installation ceremonies described earlier. It is also noteworthy that Biakpabe has the honor of planting the first yams in the chief's fields and the right to sow the first fonio seeds.

Kopytoff (1987) emphasizes that the internal frontier often attracted royal or chiefly elements that fissioned off from nearby centralized polities and that as a polity grew in importance within the internal frontier, it sought to situate itself in a regional context by identifying with common values, themes, and historical precedents. Here the Bassar case only partially parallels the Kopytoff model. The Nataka clan selected a foreign (Kotokoli) element to serve as first chief, but traditions do not describe him as part of a chiefly or royal lineage (Dugast 1992:868–72). A critical difference between the Bassar Chiefdom and the neighboring Dagomba, Gondja, Tyokossi, and Kotokoli centralized polities was that the latter were all influenced by Islam, whereas the Bassar Chiefdom was not. The smaller Kabu Chiefdom (formed in the 1850s), however, was partly influenced by the organizational structure of Islamic Kotokoli chiefdoms and adopted some of its administrative terms (de Barros 1985:68). The composite nature of the Nataka and other Bassar clans also applies to Kopytoff's (1987:40–48) kin-group model for attracting adherents, where latecomers become incorporated as "pseudo-kinsmen" as the polity grew by increasing its "wealth in people." In the latter case, the "first-comers" would have included a number of layers created over time, including the Lama remnants and various immigrating groups. Indeed, Kopytoff (1987:48) suggests that internal frontier processes can result in a new ethnic identity – in this case, "the Bassar," whose identity was probably strongly influenced by the common ironworking traditions of many of its people (de Barros 2000:185–86). Finally, the chiefdom's ideological duality (Kopytoff 1987:62–69) is reflected in the conflicting versions of first-comer status between the chief and ritual first-comers described earlier. It is also reflected in the severe internal conflict created when the German and French colonial administrations attempted to violate the alternating foreign versus indigenous chief pattern that had been negotiated prior to their arrival (Dugast 1988).

It was mentioned earlier that Kopytoff's (1987) original model tends to emphasize in-migration into the internal frontier in terms of the results of "steady little local quarrels and raids." In the case of the rise of the Bassar Chiefdom, however, and probably for many other embryonic politics in the internal frontier during the many centuries of the transatlantic slave trade, a critical factor included the immigration of refugee populations and the dislocation and trauma inflicted on existing populations by constant slave raiding. In the Bassar case, it led to major relocations of its population and its iron production centers from the plain to refuge mountain areas, ultimately creating an untenable political situation where a combination of local quarrels, quarrels between local and immigrant populations, and quarrels between immigrant populations required the negotiation of a stronger chiefdom to deal with these problems (Dugast 1988; Gbikpi-Benissan 1976:123–26). Indeed, one might argue that the Bassar Chiefdom might not have come to pass without this disruption, especially considering that iron production and trade were fully under the control of corporate kin groups before and *after* the rise of this chiefdom (de Barros 2001; Dugast 1988). The rise of the Bassar Chiefdom shows that the presence of pronounced specialist production need not be excluded from the processes of the internal frontier. To the contrary, one can argue that the immigration of substantial numbers of ironworkers was an important element in the creation of a new ethnic identity and a new regional polity, using the very processes described by Kopytoff for Africa's internal frontier. In short, the production of the internal frontier landscape of the Bassar region was strongly impacted by major regional forces to which local polities had to adapt.

In conclusion, the history of the Bassar region internal frontier as deduced from both archaeological and ethnohistorical evidence provides considerable support for Kopytoff's (1987) description and explanation of its processes. This includes the nature of local polities; the production of frontiersmen; the process of acquiring adherents in polity formation; the importance of first-comer primacy and the processes of integrating first-comers and latecomers; the ideological duality of the new polity (the Bassar Chiefdom) in terms of rulers versus subjects; and the resolution of this duality in terms of the ritual integration of first-comers in the political processes of the chiefdom, particularly in the chiefly installation ceremony and the selection of alternating foreign and indigenous chiefly lineages. It differs in that there was no imported political model in the Bassar case, and no ruler-subject dichotomy developed because there was never a complete rupture between the chief and his clan. The Bassar case also illustrates the importance of internal frontier processes not emphasized by Kopytoff: (1) the importance of specialist ironworker immigration and how it fits within the political processes of the internal frontier, and, (2) the major impact of slave raiding on these same political processes.

ACKNOWLEDGEMENTS

This chapter is derived from a larger project dealing with the Bassar Chiefdom in the context of theories of political economy. The original manuscript was reviewed by Tim Earle, Nic David, Scott MacEachern, Susan McIntosh, Chip Stanish, David Killick, and J. Cameron Monroe. This subsequent version, focusing on Africa's internal frontier, was reviewed by Amanda Logan and anonymous reviewers from Cambridge University Press. It also benefited enormously from extensive discussions and commentary by Stéphan Dugast. Thanks go to all for their time so graciously spent. I also thank Merrick Posnansky for his constant encouragement and Tim Earle for inspiring me to study African political economies. Finally, thanks go to my dear friend, Joel Paulson, for his excellent maps.

BIBLIOGRAPHY

Barbier, J.-C. (1982). L'Histoire Présente, Exemple du Royaume Kotokoli du Togo. Manuscript on File, Centre d'Études d'Afrique Noire, Bordeaux.

Cornevin, R. (1957). Étude sur le Centre Urbain de Bassari (Togo). *Bulletin de l'IFAN* **19** (Série B), No. 1: 72–110.

Cornevin, R. (1962). Les Bassari du Nord Togo. *Mondes d'Outre Mer*. Berger-Levrault, Paris.

de Barros, P. (1985). *The Bassar: Large-Scale Iron Producers of the West African Savanna*. Ph.D. dissertation, University of California at Los Angeles.

de Barros, P. (1986). Bassar: A Quantified, Chronologically Controlled, Regional Approach to a Traditional Iron Production Centre in West Africa. *Africa* **56** (2): 148–74.

de Barros, P. (1988). Societal Repercussions of the Rise of Large-Scale Traditional Iron Production: A West African Example. *African Archaeological Review* **6**: 91–113.

de Barros, P. (2000). Iron Metallurgy in its Sociocultural Context. In Vogel, J. (ed.), *Ancient African Metallurgy*. AltaMira, Walnut Creek, MA, 147–98.

de Barros, P. (2001). The Effect of the Slave Trade on the Bassar Ironworking Society. In DeCorse, C. (ed.), *West Africa during the Atlantic Slave Trade: Archaeological Perspectives*. Leicester University Press, London, 59–80.

de Barros, P. (2003). Recent Early Iron Age research in Bassar, Togo. *Nyame Akuma* **59**: 76–78.

de Barros, P. (2006). Dekpassanware: Early Iron Age Site in the Bassar Region of Northern Togo. 18th Biannual Meeting of the Society for Africanist Archaeologists, Calgary.

de Barros, P. (2011). A Comparison of Early and Later Iron Age Societies in the Bassar Region of Togo. *Proceedings of the World of Iron Conference, 16–20 February 2009, London*. Archetype, London.

Dugast, S. (1986). La Pince et le Soufflet: Deux Techniques de Forge Traditionnelles au Nord-Togo. *Journal des Africanistes* **LVI** (2): 29–53.

Dugast, S. (1987). L'Agglomération de Bassar: Classement Selon le Clan fondateur; Classement par Village. Manuscript produced for ORSTOM, Lome, Togo.

Dugast, S. (1988). Déterminations Économiques *versus* Fondements Symboliques: La Chefferie de Bassar. *Cahiers d'Études Africaines* **110**, XXVIII (2): 265–80.

Dugast, S. (1992). *Rites et Organisation sociale: l'Agglomération de Bassar au Nord-Togo*. Doctoral thesis, EHESS, Paris.

Dugast, S. (2004). Une Agglomération Très Rurale: Lien Clanique et Lien Territorial dans la Ville de Bassar (Nord-Togo). *Journal des Africanistes* **74** (1–2): 203–48.

Fried, M. (1967). *The Evolution of Political Society*. Random House, New York.

Froelich, J.-C., and Alexandre, P. (1960). Histoire Traditionnelle des Kotokoli et des BiTchambi du Nord-Togo. *Bulletin de l'IFAN* **12** (Série B), Nos. 1–2.

Froelich, J.-C., Alexandre, P. and Cornevin, R. (1963). *Les Populations du Nord-Togo*. Presses Universitaires de France, Paris.

Gbikpi-Benissan, D. F. J. (1976). Pouvoirs politiques anciens et pouvoir politique moderne au Togo – la chefferie dans la nation contemporaine – essais de sociologie politique sur les chefferies en pays Bassari, Akposso et Mina. Thèse de IIIème Cycle, Université R. Descartes, Paris V.

Gbikpi-Benissan, D. F. J. (1978). Entretiens en pays Bassar I: origines, migrations, fondations de villages, conflits armés. *Études de Documents de Sciences Humaines*, Série B, No. 1. INSE, Université du Bénin, Lome.

Gbikpi-Benissan, D. F. J. (1984). Rapport d'Enquêtes du 27–03-84 dans le Village de Kibedipou sur L'Histoire Bassar. Manuscript on File, Université de Lome, Togo.

Gnon, A. (1967). *L'Aménagement de l'espace en pays Bassari – Kabou et sa région*. Master's thesis, DES Géographie, Université de Caën.

Goucher, C. (1981). Iron is iron 'til it is rust: trade and ecology in the decline of West African iron-smelting. *Journal of African History* **22**: 179–189.

Goucher, C. (1984). *The Iron Industry of Bassar, Togo: An Interdisciplinary Investigation of African Technological History*. Ph.D. dissertation, University of California at Los Angeles.

Haaland, R. (1985). Iron Production, its Socio-Cultural Context and Ecological Implications. In Haaland, R. and Shinnie, P. (eds.), *African Iron Working – Ancient and Traditional*, Norwegian University Press, Bergen, 50–72.

Hahn, Peter H. (1997). *Techniques de Métallurgie au Nord-Togo*. Presses de l'Université du Bénin, Lomé.

Johnson, A., and Earle, T. (2000). *The Evolution of Human Societies*, 2nd ed. Stanford University Press, Stanford, CA.

Klose, H. (1903a). Das Bassarivolk I. *Globus* **83** (20): 309–14.

Klose, H. (1903b). Das Bassarivolk II. *Globus* **83** (22): 341–44.

Klose, H. (1964). Klose's Journey to Northern Ghana, 1894. Translated by I. Killick. Manuscript on File, Institute of African Studies, University of Legon, Ghana. [Originally *Togo unter deutscher Flagge*, 1899, 285–44.]

Kopytoff, I. (1987). The Internal African Frontier. In Kopytoff, I. (ed.), *The African Frontier*. Indiana University Press, Bloomington, 3–84.

Kopytoff, I. (1999). Permutations in Patrimonialism and Populism: The Aghem Chiefdoms of Western Cameroon. In McIntosh, S. K. (ed.), *Beyond Chiefdoms: Pathways to Complexity in Africa*, Cambridge University Press, Cambridge, 88–96.

Kuevi, D. (1975). Le travail et le commerce du fer au Togo avant l'arrivée des Européens. *Etudes Togolaises* **11–12** (n.s.): 22–43.

Martinelli, B. (1982). Métallurgistes Bassar: Techniques et Formation Sociale. *Etudes de Documents de Sciences Humaines*, Série A, No. 5. INSE, Université du Bénin, Lome.

McIntosh, S. K. (1994). Changing Perceptions of West Africa's Past: Archaeological Research since 1988. *Journal of Archaeological Research* **2** (2): 165–98.

McIntosh, S. K. (1999). Pathways to Complexity: An African Perspective. In McIntosh, S. K. (ed.), *Beyond Chiefdoms: Pathways to Complexity in Africa*. Cambridge University Press, Cambridge, 1–30.

Norris, E. G. (1984). The Hausa Kola Trade through Togo, 1899–1912: Some Qualifications. *Paideuma* **30**: 161–84.

Posnansky, M., and de Barros, P. (1980). An Archaeological Reconnaissance of Togo, August 1979. Report prepared for H. E. The Minister of National Education and Scientific Research of the Republic of Togo, under the Sponsorship of the United States International Communications Agency. University of California at Los Angeles. Mimeographed and bound.

Rattray, R. S. (1932). *The Tribes of the Ashanti Hinterland*. Oxford University Press, Oxford.

Robertshaw, P. (1999). Seeking and Keeping Power in Bunyoro-Kitara, Uganda. In McIntosh, S. K. (ed.), *Beyond Chiefdoms: Pathways to Complexity in Africa*. Cambridge University Press, Cambridge, 124–35.

Schoenbrun, D. (1999). The (In)visible Roots of Bunyoro-Kitara and Buganda in the Lakes Region: A.D. 800–1300. In McIntosh, S. K. (ed.), *Beyond Chiefdoms: Pathways to Complexity in Africa*. Cambridge University Press, Cambridge, 136–50.

Schmidt, P. (1997). *Iron Technology in East Africa: Symbolism, Science, and Archaeology*. Indiana University Press, Bloomington.

Stahl, A. (2004). Comparative Insights into the Ancient Political Economies of West Africa. In Feinman, G., and Nicholas, L. (eds.), *Archaeological Perspectives on Political Economies*. University of Utah Press, Salt Lake City, 253–70.

Stanish, C. (2004). The Evolution of Chiefdoms: An Economic Anthropological Model. In Feinman, G., and Nicholas, L. (eds.), *Archaeological Perspectives on Political Economies*. University of Utah Press, Salt Lake City, 7–24.

Szwark, M. (1981). Proverbes et Traditions des Bassar du Nord-Togo. *Collections Instituti Anthropos* 22. Edited by J. Thiel. Haus Voker und Kulturen, St. Augustin.

Vansina, J. (1990). *Paths in the Rainforests*. University of Wisconsin Press, Madison.

Vansina, J. (1999). Pathways of Political Development in Equatorial Africa and Neo-Evolutionary Theory. In McIntosh, S. K. (ed.), *Beyond Chiefdoms: Pathways to Complexity in Africa*. Cambridge University Press, Cambridge, 166–72.

Yoffee, N. (1993). Too Many Chiefs? (or, safe tests for the '90s). In Yoffee, N., and Sherratt, A. (eds.), *Archaeological Theory: Who Sets the Agenda?* Cambridge University Press, Cambridge, 60–78.

10

Fortified Towns of the Koinadugu Plateau: Northern Sierra Leone in the Pre-Atlantic and Atlantic Worlds

Christopher R. DeCorse

INTRODUCTION

This chapter examines sociopolitical formation on the Koinadugu Plateau, northern Sierra Leone. Drawing on oral traditions, limited documentary sources, and archaeological data, this research examines the fortified towns that were the centers of historically known Limba, Yalunka, and Kuranko chiefdoms. The major impetus for the establishment of these Atlantic-period settlements was defense against slave raiding and interethnic conflict during the eighteenth and nineteenth centuries. In this respect, their appearance during the era of the Atlantic world can be seen as both an internal African frontier and the frontier of an expanding Eurocentric world economic system. Archaeological data, however, suggest the initial occupations of some of these settlements took place during the first or early second millennia A.D., thus predating the advent of the Atlantic world. Although poorly known archaeologically, these occupations may represent an earlier period of settlement hierarchy and nascent complexity. These sites and their associated polities are examined in light of the region's *longue durée*, the impacts of the transatlantic slave trade, and Kopytoff's concept of the internal African frontier.

The fortified towns of the Koinadugu Plateau, northern Sierra Leone, are the most striking aspect of the region's archaeological record. Defensive sites of this kind represent an ancient settlement form in West Africa, one that predates the advent of the Atlantic economy. However, many defensive sites were established in response to slave raiding and interethnic conflict during the period of the Atlantic trade. During the eighteenth and nineteenth centuries some of the fortified towns of the Koinadugu Plateau emerged as the center of small, fluid polities, with limited centralized authority. Political organization was centered on larger towns that extended limited control over surrounding villages. Within the Yalunka area, increasingly centralized political authority emerged during the late eighteenth century within the Solima Yalunka kingdom.

Koinadugu's past is examined in light of limited documentary sources, oral traditions, and surveys and excavations at twenty-eight town sites. Covering approximately 4,500 km², northern Sierra Leone lies within the Koinadugu Plateau, an extension of the Guinea Highlands. The topography consists of intricately dissected plains, hills, and mountains; many of these natural features were utilized in fortified settlements. The region is today part of Koinadugu District, including the modern Limba chiefdoms of Wara Wara Yagala and Wara Wara Bafodia; the Yalunka chiefdoms of Musaia Dembelia, Sinkunia Dembelia, and Solima; and the Kuranko chiefdoms of Mongo and Sengbe (Figure 10.1). Though sharing subsistence practices and some cultural features, language and a variety of cultural practices allow the groups to be distinguished ethnographically (see DeCorse 1989; Ottenberg 1988). To some extent the current political boundaries and distribution of ethnic groups reflect divisions that extend back to the eighteenth century, possibly earlier. These polities were, however, modified and transformed with the advent of colonial rule in 1896 and subsequently by an independent Sierra Leone beginning in 1961.

Koinadugu's pre-nineteenth-century past is poorly known. Early documentary sources on this portion of West Africa primarily relate to the coast. References to the interior prior to the twentieth century are confined to isolated travel accounts, and oral traditions only afford limited time depth. Archaeological data thus provide an important means of reconstructing the region's early history. The area's initial occupation long predates the Atlantic world. Archaeological research, including some of the research presented here, indicates a Late Stone Age settlement dating back to at least 2500 B.C. (Atherton 1969, 1972a, 1979, 1984). Iron appears in the eight century A.D., but a quartz and ground stone lithic tradition continues into the second millennium A.D. (Atherton 1979:32; 1984). There is limited evidence for settlement size and distribution prior to the second millennium A.D., but the region was likely settled by agricultural communities long before the period of the Atlantic trade

280

FORTIFIED TOWNS OF
THE KOINADUGU
PLATEAU

(Atherton 1969:147–50; DeCorse 2010). Scatters of Late Stone Age quartz lithics and ground stone tools, particularly celts, occur in many areas, including the level, fertile river plains later occupied by eighteenth- and nineteenth-century Yalunka fortified towns. The initial settlement of Koinadugu District may have been at least partially related to developments in the Upper Niger, including consolidation and fragmentation within the Mande kingdoms of the savanna and the exploitation of the Bure gold fields. Atherton (1980:266–70) has speculated that gold and diamonds from Sierra Leone may have reached North Africa during classical times, and George Brooks has suggested that the region was incorporated into the Mande world through trade beginning circa 1100 A.D. (Brooks 1993:69–73).

Surveying place names, Fyle (1979a:5) has suggested that the Limba were among the first inhabitants of the region, having gradually expanded out of the Wara Wara mountains beginning in the eighth century (also see Atherton 1969:139–45). They may have already occupied their current territory by the sixteenth century, a supposition based on oral traditions and limited textual sources (Fyle 1976:109–10, 1979a:4–5). The predominance of Mandinka names among Limba ruling families may suggest the arrival of Mande settlers in connection with the founding of the principal Limba towns discussed here (Fyle 1976:108; also see Finnegan 1965:15). The Kuranko and Yalunka may have been more recent arrivals, perhaps entering the region in the sixteenth and seventeenth centuries (Fyle 1976:109–10, 1979a:4–5, 1979b:6–8). They are closely related Mande peoples, who share similar language and ritual practices with other Mande groups to the north (see DeCorse 1989; Greenberg 1970:8). The Kuranko may have arrived in the area now covered by the present Mongo Kuranko Chiefdom at the end of the sixteenth century and expanded further south during the following century, the Yalunka arriving somewhat later (Demougeot 1944:12; Donald 1968:31–33; Fyle 1976:109–10; cf. Jackson 1977:2–3).

Though plausible, these oral traditions, reconstructions of population movements, and their timing are difficult to anchor chronologically. There are few references to datable historic events, and the few there are generally date to the late nineteenth century (Figure 10.2). Much of the information contained in the traditions consists of lists of previous town chiefs that are repeated when a new chief assumes his position. Accounts often narrate events only a few generations

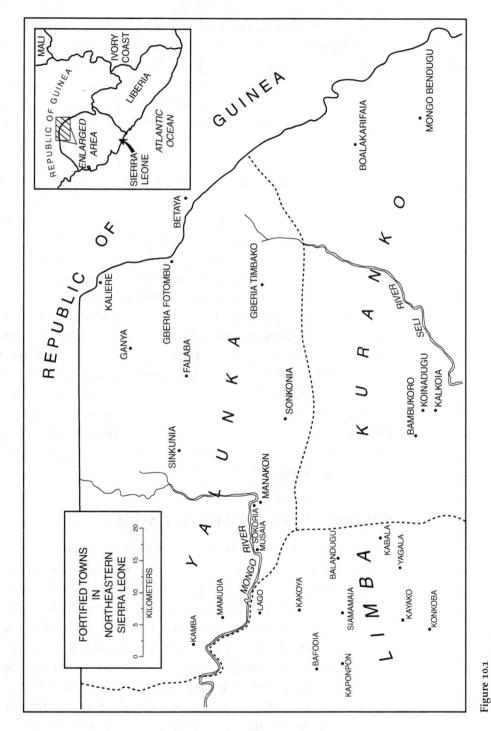

Figure 10.1
Map of northeastern Sierra Leone showing the areas currently occupied by the Limba, Yalunka, and Kuranko and the principal fortified towns.

prior to the time of telling, suggesting a time depth only extending to the late eighteenth century (see Hill 1981:3; Howard 1972:v, Jones 1983:11). The settlement founder is often described as a farmer and/or hunter, who arrived in an area that was uninhabited or who was given unoccupied land (e.g., Donald 1968:75–77; Fyle 1979a:6–7). He is said to have then been joined by his kinsman and other settlers. Traditions then recount the names of succeeding rulers. These foundation stories likely do not refer to actual events, and the list of rulers may not be accurate or complete genealogies. Rather, they represent partial, collapsed, or even created lineages that begin in the distant past with mythical or semimythical events and then present the genealogy of the current chief, thus validating present authority patterns (see Kopytoff 1987 for discussion of founder stories). As Hill notes, "Locating such validation in a single event [the founding] frees the narrator from the need to regress indefinitely into the past and permits him to begin his narration at a convenient point" (Hill 1981:3).

There is archaeological evidence for the occupation of some fortified sites of the Koinadugu Plateau in the late first millennium or early second millennium A.D., but the lack of continuity in archaeological evidence dating between the fifteenth and the eighteenth centuries makes it difficult to evaluate claims of continuous occupation prior to eighteenth century. Genealogies, and the limited historical and archaeological data, suggest that the Limba, Yalunka, and Kuranko fortified towns and political structures reported on here date to the eighteenth century or later (Donald 1968:77; Fyle 1976:108; Fyle 1979b:37–38; Howard 1972:iii–vii).

NORTHERN SIERRA LEONE IN THE ATLANTIC WORLD

Europeans arrived in coastal Sierra Leone in the fifteenth century, and there is some evidence that trade connections between the coast and the Futa Jallon, via Koinadugu, had been established by the early sixteenth century (Atherton 1979:33; Hair 1977:31; Hill 1971:7; Rodney 1970:2). Substantive evidence, however, does not appear until much later. Trade, including gold, ivory, hides, salt, firearms, and slaves, was well established by the late nineteenth century, aided by the expansion of the Sierra Leone colony (Deveneaux 1973; Fyle 1979b:93–98; Howard 1972:37–40, 150–60; Mitchell 1962). Although a variety of factors may have been involved, the development of trade undoubtedly provided additional impetus for the formation of the

Solima Yalunka kingdom in the nineteenth century (Fyle 1977a:4–6). Yet, as will be seen, archaeological evidence for trade in manufactured goods and its connection with the fortified towns of the Koinadugu Plateau is limited. Prior to the twentieth century, northeastern Sierra Leone's direct connections with British and French political spheres of influence remained very limited. The first European expedition passed through Koinadugu in 1822 and only a handful of Europeans had visited the region by the end of the nineteenth century (e.g., Blyden 1873; Garrett 1892; Laing 1825; Lipschutz 1973; Reade 1873; Trotter 1898; Zweifel and Moustier 1880).

There is, however, no question that the Sierra Leone hinterland was dramatically impacted by Africa's intersection with the Atlantic world, particularly during the period of the slave trade. The region provided fewer numbers of slaves than some areas, but it had more direct connections with North America. Rice was an important crop in Sierra Leone, and enslaved Africans from this part of Africa were seen as particularly desirable for work on the rice plantations of South Carolina. Africans from Sierra Leone subsequently provided an important part of the labor force (e.g., Carney 1996, 2001; Littlefield 1981). The major European trade post in this portion of the African coast was Bunce Island in the Sierra Leone estuary. Founded in 1670s, the island reached it apogee during the second half of the eighteenth century, during which time it became one of the most lucrative slave-trading centers on the West African coast (Fyfe 1962:7; Kup 1961:21–22, 26; also see DeCorse 2007). Despite British abolition of the slave

Figure 10.2
A Yalunka elder in Kamba holding a battle ax used in the Samori wars, dating to the 1880s and 1890s. Oral traditions of many Limba, Yalunka, and Kuranko sites are associated with slave raiding and interethnic conflicts of the eighteenth and nineteenth centuries (photograph by C. DeCorse 1980).

284

FORTIFIED TOWNS OF
THE KOINADUGU
PLATEAU

trade in 1807, it remained important in parts Sierra Leone and, in fact, expanded during the nineteenth century. In southern Sierra Leone, in the Galinhas country, the slave trade reached it apogee during this period (Jones 1983:37–38). In Koinadugu, slave raiding remained a threat throughout the nineteenth century. Raiding was primarily by Fulani polities from the north, but there was also raiding between groups within the region (e.g., Suret-Canale 1969). The Yalunka, in particular, raided both Limba and Kuranko towns for slaves and foodstuffs (e.g. Donald 1968:63–66; Jackson 1977:2; Laing 1825:235–37, 243–44, 264; 318–19, 344, 353, 381, 399–419).

The Samori invasions between 1884 and 1892 were partly directed at slave raiding (e.g. Fyle 1979b:117–24; Lipschutz 1973:62–79). Samori Touré's Islamic state expanded across the West African savannah from the Futa Jallon in Guinea eastward through Mali and Burkina Faso, to northern Ghana in the 1880s and early 1890s (e.g., Donald 1968:35–36; Koroma 1977; Lipschutz 1973; Newland 1933; Peterson 2008). Defeated polities either submitted and converted to Islam or saw their people enslaved. The British established a Frontier Police Post at Falaba in 1890s, and Samori's armies left Koinadugu in 1892. The region, along with the rest of Sierra Leone, was incorporated into the British Sierra Leone Protectorate, and district administration extended to Koinadugu in 1896 (Alie 1990:126–63; Donald 1968:37–38; Lipschutz 1973:62–79).

Apart from the Atlantic trade and Fulani slave raiding, domestic slavery remained important well into the twentieth century, an anomaly in a region that had been established as a refuge for freed slaves (Lipschutz 1973:180–97; Peterson 1969). With the extension of the British Protectorate over the Sierra Leone hinterland in the late nineteenth century, the abolition of the slave trade became an increasing concern. A series of legislative acts aimed at eliminating slavery were instituted in the Protectorate during the 1890s and early twentieth centuries. Slavery was finally abolished in 1928.

SOCIOPOLITICAL ORGANIZATION

The precolonial sociopolitical organization of northern Sierra Leone is difficult to characterize, in part because of the limited information available prior to the late nineteenth century. Modern chiefdoms are the result of administrative boundaries imposed by the colonial administration during the late nineteenth and twentieth centuries and later by the Sierra Leone government (e.g., Alie 1990:152–57; Donald 1968:128–35; Fyle 1979b:12–13; Lipschutz 1973; Mitchell 1971). Traditional rules of governance and succession were overlaid by British policies, making it difficult to extrapolate the nature of sociopolitical organization prior to the late nineteenth century. In addition, the inconsistencies of terms such as "chiefdom," "tribe," and "kingdom" that have historically been used to describe sociopolitical organization further complicate interpretation (e.g., Earle 1987; Kopytoff 1987; Mitchell 1971; McIntosh 1999). To some extent, the seven Limba, Yalunka, and Kuranko chiefdoms currently located within Koinadugu are representative of earlier spheres of influence, yet oral traditions suggest that these divisions were fluid, even during the more recent past. Prior to the twentieth century, a series of Limba, Yalunka, and Kuranko polities extended influence over varying territories, which at times stretched outside the borders of modern-day Sierra Leone. Features of centralized political authority (e.g., Cohen 1991; Southhall 1988, 1991), such as institutionalized bureaucracy, taxation, centralized redistribution of goods and labor, stratified accumulation of wealth, and military control, that have been traditionally seen as markers of state-level organization were limited.

Political authority among the Limba, Yalunka, and Kuranko was vested in individuals historically referred to as chiefs who inherited their positions patrilineally. These positions did not, however, necessarily follow strict rules of descent; a chief might have many sons and brothers, the most prominent of whom would be his successor (e.g., Fyle 1979a:9–13). Polities centered on charismatic leaders in larger towns who extended limited control over surrounding villages and, sometimes, other larger settlements. On a classificatory continuum the Limba and Kuranko polities were structurally more akin to political organizations sometimes classed as "simple chiefdoms," with a slightly greater degree of centralization emerging among the Yalunka in the nineteenth century (Fried 1967; also see de Barros this volume; Johnson and Earle 2000; Service 1975:74–80, 104–64). Simple chiefdoms (following Fried 1967) are characterized by a principal settlement surrounded by smaller villages, with a total population in the thousands. Hence they may be seen as a bridge in a sociopolitical hierarchy ranging from big men polities to states (see Johnson and Earle 2000). Yet, as Southall (1991:80) and others have cautioned, the terms "chiefdoms" and "chiefs" are ambiguous, and the latter can be equally if not better described as "big men, local ritual leaders, notables, or *primi inter pares*." In addition, specifically with regard to the Limba, Yalunka, and Kuranko, other sociopolitical structures, such as kinship groups (both maternal and paternal), affines, age grades, and secret societies (evidence for which is all poorly perceived archaeologically), provide crosscutting forms of more heterarchical social organization.

The position and influence of a chief greatly depended on the charismatic qualities of the individual. For example, among the well-described and centralized Biriwa Limba located to the south of Koinadugu, alliances were transitory and dependent on political negotiation (Fyle 1977b; 1979a:9–13). Rulers exerted only limited influence beyond their immediate hinterlands. Oral traditions and limited documentary sources suggest that, during the nineteenth century, the Mansaray clan of Bafodia dominated the settlements within the current Limba chiefdoms of Wara Wara Bafodia and Wara Wara Yagala and parts of the Kasunko Chiefdom to the south (Finnegan 1965:16; Garrett 1892:443). Yet, although oral traditions recount that certain settlements were nominally "under" (i.e., subservient to) Bafodia, individual towns nevertheless retained a great deal of autonomy (Fyle 1976:108,111). Among the Kuranko of Mongo and Sengbe chiefdoms, the Mara clan seems to have occupied a similar position until dominated by the Yalunka in the later nineteenth century (Fyle 1976:110–11; Jackson 1977:2; Laing 1825:195). When faced with an external threat, as in the case of the Samori Touré's invasions in the late nineteenth century, various Limba, Yalunka, and Kuranko towns of Koinadugu seem to have often negotiated their own fate, some electing to fight others suing for peace (e.g., Donald 1968:59–61; Lipschutz 1973:85–92).

Within the Yalunka area, precolonial sociopolitical organization was somewhat different, exhibiting a greater degree of centralized authority. During the eighteenth century the political situation may have been similar to that noted in the neighboring Limba and Kuranko areas, with spheres of influence centered on the principal towns of Kamba, Musaia, Sinkunia, and Falaba. By 1800, however, under the Samura of Falaba, these settlements had coalesced into what Fyle (1976, 1979b) refers to as the Solima Yalunka kingdom. Falaba emerged as a regional, judicial, and administrative center with the Manga, or king of Falaba, as its leader (Fyle 1979b:49–64; also see Donald 1968:9–12, 44–55). Important cases were tried at

Falaba, and all trading and redistribution was supervised by the Manga (Fyle 1979b 55, 84, 88; also see Donald 1968:46–49). The kingdom could also bring wayward towns into line with military force (Donald 1968:58–59, 122–23; Fyle 1979b:41–44). Solima came to include all of the Yalunka chiefdoms of modern-day Koinadugu and Yalunka settlements now in the Republic of Guinea to the north and Kuranko Sengbe Chiefdom to the south (Fyle 1976:111; 1979b:13; Laing 1825:346–47). Yet the power of Falaba and the Manga was not absolute. Important decisions of state could not be made without representatives of the other towns, and leaders met regularly at Falaba to decide matters of policy (Fyle 1979b:53–55; also see Laing 1825:356–67). As in the case with Limba and Kuranko towns, the Yalunka settlements of Musaia, Sinkunia, and Falaba seem to have independently undertaken negotiations with Samori Touré, the British, and the French (e.g., Donald 1968:59–61; Lipschutz 1973:85–92, 106, 125–26).

Ethnographic and historical data suggest that towns formed the basis of precolonial political organization and, indeed, form an important aspect of sociopolitical organization today. With a few exceptions, most notably the modern district capital of Kabala, most people in Koinadugu continue to live in small settlements of between thirty and a few thousand inhabitants, with Limba towns generally somewhat smaller than those of the Yalunka and Kuranko. In light of limited archaeological data, this may have been the pattern throughout most of the second millennium A.D. Traditionally, larger settlements incorporated several irregular clusters of clan groups, a feature recognizable archaeologically (Figure 10.3).

New settlements formed by fissioning (e.g., Hill 1970:36; Jackson 1977:13, 41–42; McCulloch 1950:102; Siddle 1968, 1969, 1970). A man might settle near his farm and gradually attract kinsmen to join him. New villages might also result from political dissension within the town; movement away from a town provided a means of gaining independence that was not possible within the settlement. Older, larger towns came to be surrounded by newer hamlets and villages with which they might have alliances and exert limited influence – for example, acting together in warfare and conflicts. It has been suggested that by the nineteenth century the settlement pattern throughout Sierra Leone centered on large, fortified towns, which were in turn surrounded by smaller satellite villages within an 8-km radius, sometimes occupied by slaves (e.g., Donald 1968:122–25;

FORTIFIED TOWNS OF
THE KOINADUGU
PLATEAU

288

Jones 1983:169–70; Siddle 1968, 1970:89). Settlements may have aggregated during periods of conflict, the inhabitants of smaller, unfortified settlements seeking protection in the larger towns. During times of conflict, large areas were occasionally abandoned, particularly as a consequence of Samori's practice of destroying settlements both as punishment and as a means of hindering French and British incursions. Passing through Koinadugu in the 1880s, British expeditions reported many destroyed and deserted settlements, people perhaps having sought shelter in larger fortified towns, fled even further afield, or been enslaved (e.g., Garrett 1892; Trotter 1898:34).

A key point to be made is the nature of the political economy that underlaid these Limba, Yalunka, and Kuranko settlements and their associated political structures. As Jackson (1977:9) has pointed out specifically with regard to the Kuranko, the labor demands of subsistence farming in some instances necessitated locality-based economic groupings at the community level that likely transcended other aspects of sociopolitical organization. The limited degree of centralized political authority seen in the Limba, Kuranko, and early Yalunka polities is indicative of this. Although poorly accessible on the basis of the available information, the availability, control, and management of slave labor may have played a key role in transforming the basis of agricultural production. Available data suggest that there was a significantly higher proportion of slaves within the Yalunka area (Lipschutz 1973:185). Hence, within the Solima Yalunka kingdom the ability to control agricultural production and distribution through the management of slaves more effectively than neighboring polities may have been a key factor in the kingdom's expansion. Transformations in political economies seen here during the period of the Atlantic trade resonate with observations made in other parts of West Africa (DeCorse 1991, 2001a, 2001b; DeCorse and Spiers 2009; Inikori 1982; Kelly 1997; Ogundiran and Falola 2007; Richard 2007; Smith 2008; Spiers 2007; Stahl 1999, 2001; de Barros this volume).

THE INTERNAL AFRICAN FRONTIER IN THE ERA
OF THE ATLANTIC WORLD

The available information on precolonial Koinadugu accords very well with aspects of Kopytoff's (1987; 1999) conceptualization of the internal African frontier. The relatively shallow histories of the

THE INTERNAL
AFRICAN FRONTIER
IN THE ERA OF THE
ATLANTIC WORLD

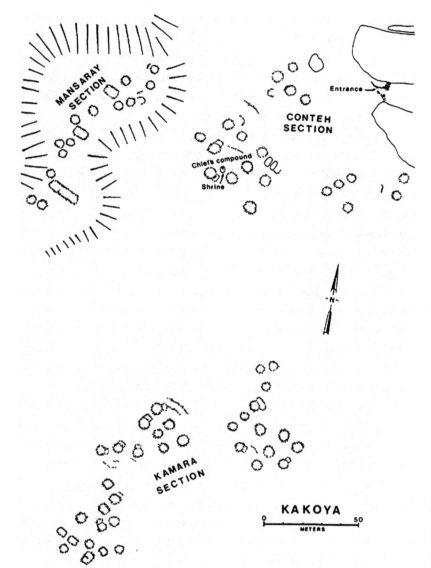

Figure 10.3
Sketch map of Limba hilltop settlement of Old Kakoya, now unoccupied, showing distribution of clan groups.

ethnographically known Limba, Yalunka, and Kuranko polities are consistent with Kopytoff's (1987:4) frontier polities that neither show nor claim much time depth. The core group (see Kopytoff 1987:7) that bounded the Koinadugu frontier and historically played the key role in identity formation in Koinadugu was the Mande, including the ancient states of Ghana and Mali. Depending on the author's reconstruction, the borders of ancient Mali appear just north of Koinadugu in what is now the Republic of Guinea (e.g., Bird 1970; Brooks 1993: d'Azevedo 1962; Dalby 1971; Dieterlen 1957; Hiskett 1984; Levtzion 1973; 1976). Located beyond the borders of these ancient savanna

290

FORTIFIED TOWNS OF
THE KOINADUGU
PLATEAU

states, northern Sierra Leone was likely an area of lower population density, located on the margins of the more established, "mature" societies to the north (see Kopytoff 1987:5). The migration of Mande settlers into the region, particularly the Yalunka and Kuranko, may have been precipitated by conflicts, population pressure, or a search for greater access to agricultural lands.

The role of the Mande as a source of technology, cultural features, and a model for political authority in much of western West Africa is a point made strongly by Brooks (1993), who argues that Mande groups, moving southward out of the inland Niger Delta, arrived in the Sierra Leone hinterland early in the second millennium A.D. Brooks (1993:44–46) particularly underscores the link between Mande secret societies and smiths that he sees as spreading Mande power associations throughout non-Mande groups, such as the West Atlantic Limba. Some of Brooks' assessments both with regard to chronology and content need evaluation in light of future data. Brooks links the initial movement of Mande populations to the south to the circa 1100–1500 A.D. dry period that led to environmental stress in the savanna. Though plausible, this period of settlement cannot yet be substantiated on the basis of the data at hand. In fact, archaeological and oral historical evidence from settlements such as Falaba, the founding of which Brooks associates with the circa 1100–1500 dry period, rather points to later occupation during the eighteenth and nineteenth centuries. Apart from the chronology, the Mande origins of some cultural practices remain unclear. A case in point is the distribution and relative importance of secret societies or power associations, which have a stronger association with non-Mande groups in southern Sierra Leone. The Poro and Sande (Bundu) societies are, for example, particularly prominent among the Limba but poorly represented among the Yalunka and Kuranko, where they appear as more recent traditions. The hunter and fisherwomen societies of the Yalunka and Kuranko (the *dunsu banna* and *yxsuxona*) are distinct from and have less authority than the Poro and Sande among the Limba. This may suggest that some of these power associations are remnants of earlier cultural practices that predate the arrival of the Mande or a distinctive, localized response to the confluence of varied cultural influences (see d'Azevedo 1962:528). The Limba, Yalunka, and Kuranko polities also do not display the ritual centralization and sacred kingship noted in some societies of the internal African frontier (Kopytoff 1987:62–68).

Arriving Mande groups, nonetheless, clearly influenced cultural practices among earlier Limba populations. Mande elements, including place names, weaving, technology (such as ironworking), and Islam, were borrowed from the incoming groups. As noted, Mande names are common in Limba king lists, possibly suggesting that the Mande newcomers overlaid models of political authority on the earlier Limba peoples. The Yalunka and Kuranko also present cultural characteristics distinct from the Mande groups to the north (see DeCorse 1989; also see Conrad and Frank 1995). These observations are consistent with the mixing of cultural traits and the fluidity of cultural identity within the internal African frontier. The fluidity of the various Limba, Yalunka, and Kuranko chiefdoms, which lacked a "clear body of customary law, and unambiguous legitimacies," was a frustration to colonial administrators and is reflected in the created chieftaincy boundaries of the colonial period (see Kopytoff 1987:5).

THE FORTIFIED TOWNS OF THE KOINADUGU PLATEAU

Traces of the Limba, Yalunka, and Kuranko polities of Koinadugu lie across the landscape. Their most prominent features are the fortified towns of the eighteenth and nineteenth centuries. Often located on hilltops and surrounded by a variety of walls, ditches, and other obstacles, they are clearly defensive works rather than symbols of sociocultural identity or political authority. Such defensive features have a wide distribution within the Mande area and among other West African groups. Fortified towns are found throughout present-day Guinea, Sierra Leone, and Liberia and are associated with the majority of ethnic groups in the region (e.g., Abraham 1975:129–31; Alldridge 1901:219, 230, 298–300; Atherton 1968, 1972b, 1983:86–90; Dapper 1668:397; DeCorse 1980, 1981, 1983, 1989; Haselberger 1964:99; Jones 1983:169–73; Kup 1975: 26; Laing 1825:220–21, 264; Malcolm 1939:48–49; Siddle 1968). Fortified, hilltop, and entrenchment sites also occur to the north throughout the Upper Guinea coast, and farther east, including portions of modern-day Ghana (e.g., Brooks 1993:238–39, 246, 250, 255–56; Chouin 2002, 2008, 2010; Chouin and DeCorse 2010; Kiyaga-Mulindwa 1982; Kup 1975:26). The fortifications employed in these defensive sites were sometimes very elaborate. For example, among the Mende of southern Sierra Leone, towns were sometimes surrounded by more than ten fences or walls, defensive ditches, and guard towers

FORTIFIED TOWNS OF
THE KOINADUGU
PLATEAU

(Alldridge 1901:230; Malcolm 1939:48–49). Among the Susu in north-western Sierra Leone (a Mande group closely related to the Yalunka), defense was provided by mud walls, some of which were over 15 ft thick (Alldridge 1901:298–300). In many cases, winding entrances through dense brush were also employed (e.g., Alldridge 1901:97, 115).

The fortified towns of the Limba, Yalunka, and Kuranko of Koinadugu possess many of these features and also distinctive characteristics (Atherton 1968, 1972b, 1983:86–90; Laing 1825:220–21, 264). The twenty-eight Limba, Yalunka, and Kuranko settlements discussed here were located using a variety of sources, including primary and secondary documentary sources, oral traditions, and archaeological survey (DeCorse 1980, 1981, 1983, 1989). Black-and-white and infrared false-color aerial photographs also proved useful in locating some settlements. Surface surveys were conducted at each site, and limited surface collections of diagnostic artifacts undertaken. The diagnostic artifacts recorded primarily consisted of datable, European trade materials, such as gunflints, beads, ceramics, and glass, and locally produced ceramics with representative examples of decorations, rim forms, or vessel shapes. Test excavations were also undertaken at the Yagala Old Town site.

The specific defensive features employed by the Limba, Yalunka, and Kuranko varied because of vegetation and topographical considerations, along with some cultural biases. The settlements of the Yalunka are primarily located on low riverine plateaus or interfluves, but defensible hilltop sites are also found. Located, for the most part, in the thinly forested, transitional savanna, the towns were protected by mud walls, which had small portals near the gates that allowed men to fire at attacking forces. Encircling ditches were sometimes dug outside of the walls. Portions of the entrenchments at Falaba and Musaia are still 20 ft across and 15 ft deep, despite the fact that a substantial amount of sedimentation and erosion has occurred. In some cases, the walls were made up of stockades of living trees, interspersed with timber or mud walls (Figures 10.4 and 10.5). The Kuranko made use of defenses similar to those used by the Yalunka. The settlements of Mongo Bendugu and Masadugu, for example, had stockades of living trees. In more densely forested areas, however, dense brush was cultivated as a living barrier. Walls or stockades provided additional defenses at entrances. The entrances themselves consisted of low doorways that could be closed with a wooden slab.

THE FORTIFIED
TOWNS OF THE
KOINADUGU
PLATEAU

Figure 10.4
Cotton trees surrounding the Yalunka town of Musaia (photograph by C. DeCorse 1980).

Located to the west of the Yalunka and Kuranko, the Limba of the Wara Wara Mountains also employed these defensive methods. Limba towns such as Kaponpon were surrounded by stockades of cotton trees. Others defenses included thickets of thorn bushes the Limba call *inthiri*. In addition to being heavily forested, this area is also more mountainous and the terrain more irregular. The Limba sometimes utilized these topographical features to their advantage. Limba settlements such as Kakoya and Yagala were located atop steep slopes that afforded them natural protection (see discussion of Yagala Old Town below). In these towns, stone was used to construct defense works and houses, giving the sites a striking appearance (Figure 10.6).

The archaeological data from these sites are consistent with the principal occupation of these settlement sites by the Limba, Yalunka, and Kuranko during the eighteenth and nineteenth centuries, with occupation in many instances continuing up to the present. Hence, they clearly date to the era of the Atlantic world, including the period of slave trade. Only limited amounts of European trade materials were noted in surface collections, and these primarily date no earlier than the eighteenth century. In fact, no trade materials clearly predating the twentieth century were found at any of the Kuranko settlements. The small amount of trade materials noted archaeologically is consistent with written accounts of the region that suggest limited trade in imported materials from the coast (e.g., Alldridge 1901:232; Blyden 1873:129; Garrett 1892:444; Laing 1825:372; Lipschutz 1973:80,

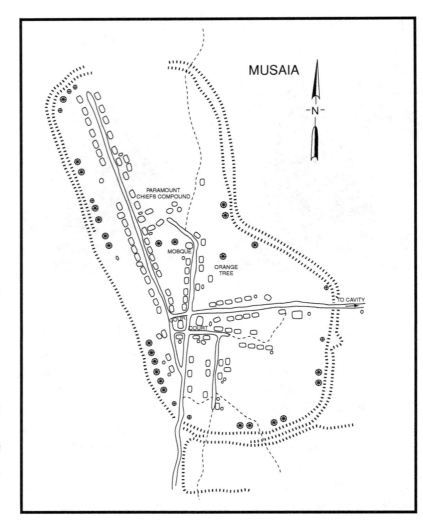

Figure 10.5
Yalunka settlement of Musaia showing the entrenchment surrounding the town and the interior ring of cotton trees. Houses are now oriented along roads built in the 1950s and 1960s. The paramount chief's house is distinct in having a very large, traditional thatched roof house and large compound. Clan groups are associated with different areas of the settlement, but these are continuous and less clearly delineated than they were traditionally.

117–18; Trotter 1898:50; Winterbottom 1803, 1:172). The major exception was in the trade in firearms, including both guns and powder; Port Loko and Freetown were major sources of guns for Samori Touré (e.g., Lagassick 1966: 100–101; Lipschutz 1973:96–97). Notably, the most common type of European artifact recovered at the town sites was gunflints. At least one is represented in every surface collection, and over one hundred were found at the Yalunka town of Musaia alone. The number of gunflints may reflect the role of these settlements as defensive sites. Local ceramics made up the largest portion of the surface material recorded. The majority of the sherds is consistent in manufacture, form, and decoration with ethnographically observed ceramics and so is consistent with the information from

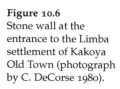

Figure 10.6
Stone wall at the entrance to the Limba settlement of Kakoya Old Town (photograph by C. DeCorse 1980).

oral traditions and imported trade materials that suggest occupations dating between the eighteenth century and the present.

Variation in settlement size provides some indications of settlement hierarchies and political centralization. The Limba settlements were substantially smaller than those of the Yalunka and Kuranko. The Limba hilltop settlements of Kakoya and Yagala had fewer than a hundred houses, a fraction of the hundreds reported at some of the Kuranko and Yalunka sites. Large Yalunka towns may have had populations of thousands. Laing (1825:288, 352), for example, states that Falaba had 400 houses and a population of between 6,000 and 10,000 inhabitants in 1822. Laing's estimate may have been somewhat high, but there is no question that there was a gradation in settlement size. The striking appearance of the larger Yalunka settlements was captured by Reade in 1873:

On arriving at the top of a small hill the people stood still, and pointing with their hands, pronounced the word *Falaba*! I saw beneath me beautiful plain covered with sheep and goats and red cattle, and a black avenue of trees marking the course of a river. In the midst of this plain was a large grove, as it seemed, of gigantic silk-cotton trees; and on looking more carefully I perceived now and then a brown roof between the foliage. At the same time I heard the distant booming of a drum... We entered and were led a roundabout way, that we might be impressed with the size of the town. (Reade 1873:408–9)

In 1872, Blyden reported that Falaba was surrounded by a natural stockade of over 500 huge trees. One of the seven gates of the town was said to have been cut through the trunk of one of the larger trees (Blyden 1873:128). Notably, Laing's (1825:227, 352–54) account, written fifty years earlier, suggests that the trees sprouting from the stockade were already well established. The descriptions of Falaba and its larger size are consistent with the historical data that suggest a greater degree of centralization and political authority within the Solima Yalunka kingdom.

The principal fortified towns of the Limba, Yalunka, and Kuranko are relatively evenly distributed across the landscape, mostly located less than ten miles from each other, their distribution being somewhat denser within the Limba area. This may reflect the smaller size of the Limba settlements and the topography of the Wara Wara Mountains. It should be noted here, however, that the survey presented is not entirely comprehensive, and some settlements have likely been omitted, particularly in the southern Kuranko and western Limba areas. Based on current evidence it is also impossible to evaluate the number of villages and hamlets that surrounded these principal towns in the past. Smaller settlements are referred to in traveler accounts, but their size and population are left unmentioned (e.g., Laing 1825:215–20). There is some evidence for separate slave villages. For example, Laing (1825:221–22) notes the town of Konkodoogore "a slave-town belonging to Falaba" that was "very spacious" and contained 3,000 to 4,000 inhabitants. The walled Yalunka settlement of Sokoria, just over a mile from Manakon, encloses an area significantly less than the larger Yalunka settlement, perhaps representing a secondary, dependent settlement.

Within the larger towns, different sections were associated with individual clan groups, usually three or four within a settlement. Notably smaller villages still seem to, at least in some cases, present similar divisions. This suggests some degree of cohesion in organization within settlement clusters; smaller villages or hamlets appear not to represent the fissioning of larger settlements along clan divisions. These clan groupings are visible archaeologically in some settlements (Figure 10.3) (DeCorse 1989; Donald 1968: 67–71; Finnegan 1965:59; Jackson 1977:41–43). This pattern is still common today, although divisions are often contiguous and so less clearly recognizable archaeologically. In the past five decades, settlements with discrete clan divisions have been increasingly replaced by more linear arrangements along motor roads (e.g., Jackson 1977:41–43; Siddle 1968, 1969). Further disruption has resulted from the civil war.

A PRE-ATLANTIC INTERNAL AFRICAN FRONTIER?

Although historical data, oral traditions, and the archaeological record clearly associate fortified towns with occupations by the Limba, Yalunka, and Kuranko during the eighteenth and nineteenth centuries, there is archaeological evidence for the occupation of some sites during the first and early second millennium A.D., predating the advent of the Atlantic trade. These early occupations are noted in hilltop sites that were likely chosen for defense and are characterized by distinct ceramic industries. One of these sites is Kawoya, a settlement located on a steep-sided hill just east of the modern Limba town of Bafodia. Oral histories indicate that this was the place where the "first people" of Bafodia settled. The site consequently predates the establishment of the valley town, which dates to the middle of the eighteenth century. Ceramics from Kawoya are very distinct from sherds noted at other, historically known Limba fortified towns, but they are comparable to late Iron Age ceramics from nearby Kamabai Rock Shelter, dated to first and early second millennia A.D. (Atherton 1969:59–60; 125–28). Thermoluminescence dates were obtained on three of the distinctive Kawoya ceramics recovered from surface contexts. These yielded dates of A.D. 1209 +/− 104; A.D. 1536 +/− 190; and A.D. 1560 +/− 98 (University of Washington UW976, UW977, and UW978). These dates suggest an occupation dating prior to the sixteenth century. The age and distinctive characteristics of the Kawoya collection may indicate an older, pre-Atlantic component distinct from the later eighteenth-century Limba occupation of the area.

Yagala Old Town

Further support for a pre-sixteenth-century occupation of some fortified settlements is evidenced by excavations at the Wara Wara Rock Shelter in Yagala Old Town. Because of its clearly defensive location, this settlement was considered to be ideal for archaeological investigation of the initial establishment of a fortified settlement. Excavations at the site suggest two distinct periods of occupation: an initial occupation late in the first millennium or early second millennium A.D., followed by a later eighteenth- to nineteenth-century occupation clearly associated with the Limba.

Yagala and the other Limba fortified towns in Koinadugu are mentioned in early documentary accounts of the region. The earliest

Figure 10.7
Stone house ruins at the Yagala Old Town site (photograph by C. DeCorse 1980).

and most detailed account is provided by Zweifel and Moustier, who visited the Yagala in 1879. Their published account provides a brief description of the town, but it affords no insight into the settlement's history and organization. Because the settlement was occupied until 1952, some of the older people in the present town remembered life in the Old Town, the succession of chiefs, and the settlement's history. The information and the chronologies provided by these narratives are comparable to those collected at other Limba, Yalunka, and Kuranko settlements. They include an account of the settlement's founding, recount the names of past chiefs, offer few highlights of past events, and suggest a time depth extending back to the eighteenth century. Now the center of the Wara Wara Yagala chieftaincy, Finnegan (1965:16) notes, the town of Yagala was at times under Bafodia and at others under Bumban far to the south. Some oral traditions further suggest that during some periods the town of Yagala was independent.

Yagala Old Town is one of the most striking Limba fortified towns (Figure 10.7). Located just 3 miles south of the district capital of Kabala, the town is positioned on top of an almost inaccessible crag of plutonic grano-diorite, a site clearly chosen for defense. The site extends across a hilltop 800 ft above the modern settlement of Yagala (Figure 10.8). The northern and southwestern approaches to the Old Town are protected by sheer rock faces, and the western, southern, and eastern sides are steep slopes of bedrock or loose soil. A steep slope also protects the northeast approach, but ascent is possible.

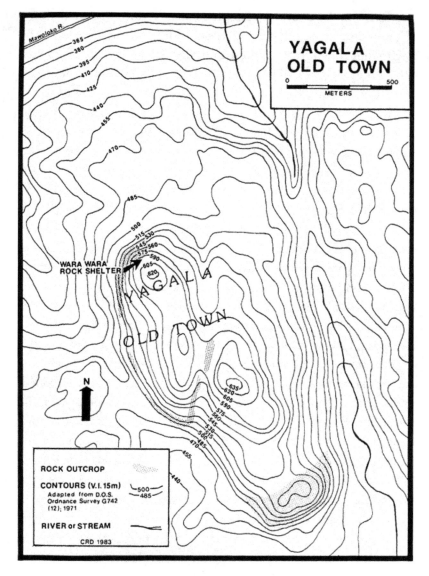

Figure 10.8
Map of the hilltop settlement of Yagala. The steep slopes of the hill provided natural protection.

Oral histories indicate that in the past the more accessible approaches to the settlement were protected by thickets of *inthiri* planted by the Limba. These thickets have been largely cleared by the extension of farmland and the harvesting of grass on the site. One oral tradition indicates that other areas considered vulnerable to attack were also protected by stone walls, including a narrow stone entrance that one man could guard. These defensive walls could not be delineated archaeologically, and they may have been built of mud. In any case, the natural topography afforded the settlement's principal means of defense. Water was gathered from two streams at the base of the

300

FORTIFIED TOWNS OF
THE KOINADUGU
PLATEAU

hill and from the pools of water that collect in the exposed bedrock of the hilltop during the rainy season. Many of the houses in the town were constructed of mud mortared stone, giving the town's ruins the appearance of what one researcher described a "miniature Zimbabwe" (Atherton 1972b:12).

Archaeological data provide evidence for an earlier occupation of the site, predating the historically documented Limba settlement. Excavations within the Old Town were undertaken in Wara Wara Rock Shelter. Seven 1 m × 1 m units were excavated by natural stratigraphic levels, subdivided into artificial levels of 10 or 20 cm, with a maximum depth of 2.5 m. The assemblage recovered included almost 1,600 sherds of local ceramics, imported trade materials (ceramics, beads, and glass), lithics, metal, tuyere fragments, a spindle whorl, faunal remains, and worked bone. Trade materials, including imported ceramics, English gunflints, glass beads, and fragments bottle glass, were confined to the upper levels of the excavations. They provide a *terminus post quem* of circa 1780 for the historic period levels. The locally produced ceramics associated with the eighteenth- to nineteenth-century levels were relatively homogenous and similar to ceramics noted ethnographically and in surface collections at other Limba sites. Two trends are notable in the uppermost levels: the percentage of decorated sherds decreases, but the cord rouletting increases through time. These trends in the upper levels may correspond to a decline in local ceramic production during the twentieth century. Overall, the imported materials and the ceramic assemblage in the upper levels are consistent with eighteenth- to nineteenth-century Limba settlement.

The lower levels of the excavation were distinct both stratigraphically and in terms of the assemblage recovered. The artifacts included local ceramics, iron and iron slag, and a small quartz lithic component. The ceramics recovered from the lower levels were few in number and mostly nondiagnostic. However, those found nevertheless suggest distinct forms and decorative inventory. The paste and temper in the sherds recovered are consistent with that found in the upper levels. Rather than continuity in the industry, however, this likely reflects exploitation of similar clay sources and similarity in firing techniques. Two of the intact rims recovered are unrepresented in the upper levels of the excavation or in ethnographically noted forms. One of the vessels represented (consisting of eight co-joinable pieces) is more finely made than other ceramics in the assemblage and has an elaborate carved roulette decoration. The decoration and vessel forms are distinct from any of the ceramics found in the upper part of the excavation and, indeed, from ceramics found at any of the other sites surveyed. The vessel bears some similarity to beaker-ware from assemblages in southern Sierra Leone, tentatively dated to between 1000 and 1400 A.D. (Hill 1971:5, 1972:8; also see Cole-King 1976; Ozanne 1966; Ozanne 1968). It is, however, somewhat distinct from the published examples. The age and distribution of the beaker-ware is, in any case, still poorly defined.

In addition to ceramics, the lower levels of the excavations also included evidence of iron production and a lithic component consisting of three quartz flakes and a small core with random striking platforms. Evidence for iron production included slag and tuyere fragments and iron. Though limited, these materials are consistent with the age and characteristics of the Late Stone Age in the area. Based on material from nearby excavations at Kamabia and Yagala Rock Shelters, Atherton (1979:32) reported that following the appearance of iron in the eighth century A.D., the lithic industry continued into the second millennium A.D.

Charcoal samples for radiocarbon dating and sherds for thermoluminescence assessment were taken from the lower levels of the excavations, discrete from the levels containing historic material. The charcoal fragment yielded a calibrated age of A.D. 1154 +/− 101 (840 +/− 120 BP; UCLA-2382). The two thermoluminescence dates on the ceramics yielded a date of A.D. 774 +/− 107 (UW975) from a sherd recovered stratigraphically above the charcoal sample and a date of A.D. 610 + 20% (1340 +/− 20%BP; Alpha-553) on a sherd at the bottom of the excavation stratigraphically below the radiocarbon date and the other thermoluminescence date. These dates indicate a settlement occupation with an iron industry in the late first millennium or early second millennium A.D.

CONCLUSION

Archaeological and historical evidence reveals changes in the sociopolitical landscape of Sierra Leone during the first and second millennia A.D. Lying on the margins of the savanna kingdoms of ancient Ghana and Mali, and later the Fulani polities of the Futa Jallon, northern Sierra Leone in many respects epitomizes the physical and cultural interstices of the internal African frontier. The political organization of the ethnographically and historically known Limba, Yalunka, and Kuranko polities had a kinship mode of production, with political economies based on the labor needs of a subsistence economy. Chiefs, who largely functioned as secular leaders, utilized personal ties and charismatic authority to extend their political influence. Centralization was limited with regard to the control of wealth (whether in land, agricultural surplus, people, or prestige goods) and with regard to ritual authority. The power of rulers remained transitory and counterbalanced by heterarchical means of social control. Although political leaders, kin groups, and class associations were important, cooperative groupings at the household and community level provided the basis of social organization. The location of settlements near farmlands may have been a major concern in the initial establishment of settlements. During times of conflict, however, these concerns were overshadowed by the needs of defense, particularly during the slave-raiding and interethnic conflicts of the Atlantic period. Larger, fortified towns with more centralized political authority afforded protection. Hence the eighteenth- and nineteenth-century fortified towns of Koinadugu may at once be seen as representative of both local and global frontiers. On the one hand they are local, situated on the margins of the Mande and later Fulani states to the north. Yet, on the other hand, they are global in their connections – the catalyst of their formation being the slave trade.

The overarching point to be made with regard to the internal African frontier is its nonlinear nature and the probability of multiple periods of frontier expansion. Although the genesis of the historically and ethnographically known Limba, Yalunka, and Kuranko fortified towns was driven by an expanding Eurocentric Atlantic economy, previously existing and locally evolving political, social, and cultural traditions also played important roles in structuring the nature and unfolding of these transformations. The expanding frontier was not unidirectional – expansion followed by an evolutionary progression in complexity to chiefdom or state. Rather, regions may have been frontiers multiple times, witnessing renewed periods of migration, consolidation, and ethnic re-formation. Polities such as those of the Limba, Yalunka, and Kuranko either continued to grow in size and complexity, emerging as new chiefdoms or states (as appears to have been the case of the Solima Yalunka kingdom), or experienced renewed processes of fissioning, collapse, and migrations to new areas. Hilltop and fortified sites such as Yagala and Kawoya dating to the first millennium A.D. may represent an earlier period of frontier expansion, perhaps associated with the advent of iron technology. Rather than in a unidirectional trend toward complexity in sociopolitical organization, it was characterized by ebbs and flows; the oscillation from centralization to decentralization, from fragmentation to consolidation. This model of political formation has relevance to other parts of Africa and beyond.

ACKNOWLEDGEMENTS

I thank J. Cameron Monroe, Akin Ogundiran, and the anonymous reviewers at Cambridge University Press for their many useful comments on initial drafts of this chapter.

BIBLIOGRAPHY

Abraham, A. (1975). *The Pattern of Warfare and Settlement among the Mende of Southern Sierra Leone in the Second Half of the Nineteenth Century*. Institute of African Studies, Fourah Bay College Occasional Paper No. 1. Freetown, Sierra Leone.

Alie, J. A. D. (1990). *A New History of Sierra Leone*. Macmillan, Oxford.

Alldridge, T. J. (1901). *The Sherbro and Its Hinterland*. Macmillan, New York.

Atherton, J. H. (1968). Válečné Jeskyně Kmene Limba. *Nový Orient* October: 237–38.

Atherton, J. H. (1969). *The Later Stone Age of Sierra Leone*. Ph.D. dissertation, University of Oregon.

Atherton, J. H. (1972a). Excavations at Kamabai and Yagala Rock Shelters, Sierra Leone. *West African Journal of Archaeology* 2: 39–74.

Atherton, J. H. (1972b). Protohistoric Habitation Sites in Northeastern Sierra Leone. *Bull. Soc. Roy. Anthrop. Prehist.* **83**: 5–17.

Atherton, J. H. (1979). Early Economies of Sierra Leone and Liberia: Archaeological and Historical Reflections. In Dorjohn, V. R., and Issac, B. L. (eds.), *Essays on the Economic Anthropology of Sierra Leone and Liberia*. Institute for Liberian Studies, Philadelphia, 27–43.

Atherton, J. H. (1980). Speculations on Functions of Some Pre-historic Archaeological Materials from Sierra Leone. In Swartz, B. K., and Dumett, R. E. (eds.), *West African Culture Dynamics: Archaeological and Historical Perspectives*. Mouton, The Hague, 259–75.

Atherton, J. H. (1983). Ethnoarchaeology in Africa. *African Archaeological Review* **1**: 75–104.

Atherton, J. H. (1984). La Préhistoire de la Sierra Leone. *L'Anthropologie* **8** (2): 245–61.

Bird, C. S. (1970). The Development of Mandekan (Manding): A Study of the Role of Extra-Linguistic Factors in Linguistic Change. In Dalby, D. (ed.), *Language and History in Africa*. Africana, New York, 146–59.

Blyden, E. W. (1873). Report on the Expedition to Falaba, January to March 1872. *Proceedings of the Royal Geographical Society* **17** (2): 117–33.

Brooks, G. E. (1993). *Landlords and Strangers: Ecology, Society, and Trade in Western Africa, 1000–1630*. Westview, Bolder, CO.

Carney, J. (1996). Landscapes of Technology Transfer: Rice Cultivation and African Continuities. *Technology and Culture* **37** (1): 5–35.

Carney, J. (2001). *Black Rice: The African Origins of Rice Cultivation in the Americas*. Harvard University Press, Cambridge, MA.

Chouin, G. L. (2002). Sacred Groves as Historical and Archaeological Markers in Southern Ghana. *Ghana Studies* **5**: 177–96.

Chouin, G. L. (2008). Archaeological Perspectives on Sacred Groves in Ghana. In Sheridan, M. J., and Nyamweru, C. (eds.), *African Sacred Groves: Ecological Dynamics and Social Change*. James Currey, Oxford, 178–94.

Chouin, G. L. (2010). *Forests of Power and Memory; An Archaeology of Sacred Groves in the Eguafo Polity (c. 500–1900 AD)*. Ph.D. dissertation, Syracuse University.

Chouin, G. L., and DeCorse, C. R. (2010). Prelude to the Atlantic Trade: New Perspectives on Southern Ghana's Pre-Atlantic History (800–1500). *Journal of African History* **51** (1): 123–45.

Cohen, R. (1991). Paradise Regained: Myth and Reality in the Political Economy of the Early State. In Claessen, H. J. M., and van de Velde, P. (eds.), *Early State Economics*. Political and Legal Anthropology Series, Volume **8**. Transaction, New Brunswick, 109–29.

Cole-King, P. A. (1976). *Sierra Leone: Development of the New National Museum and Preservation of Antiquities*. UNESCO, Paris.

Conrad, D. C., and Frank, B. E. (1995). Nyamakalaya Contradiction and Ambiguity in Mande Society. In Conrad, D. C., and Frank, B. E. (eds.), *Status and Identity in West Africa: Nyamakalaw of Mande*. Indiana University Press, Bloomington, 1–23.

d'Azevedo, W. (1962). Some Historical Problems in the Delineation of a Central West Atlantic Region. *Annals, New York Academy of Sciences* **96** (2): 512–38.

Dalby, D. (1971). Distribution and Nomenclature of the Manding People and Their Language. In Hodge, C. (ed.), *Papers on the Manding*. Indiana University Press, Bloomington, 1–13.

Dapper, O. (1668). *Naukeurige beschrijvinge der afrikaensche gewesten*. Amsterdam.

DeCorse, C. R. (1980). An Archaeological Survey of Protohistoric Defensive Sites in Sierra Leone. *Nyame Akuma* **17**: 48–53.

DeCorse, C. R. (1981). Additional Notes on Archaeological Fieldwork in Northeastern Sierra Leone. *Nyame Akuma* **19**: 14–17.

DeCorse, C. R. (1983). Fortified Towns of the Koinadugu Plateau: Ethnoarchaeological Research in Northeastern Sierra Leone. M.A. Paper in Archaeology, University of California at Los Angeles.

DeCorse, C. R. (1989). Material Aspects of Limba, Yalunka and Kuranko Ethnicity: Archaeological Research in Northeastern Sierra Leone. In Shennan, S. (ed.), *Archaeological Approaches to Cultural Identity*. Unwin Hyman, London, 125–40.

DeCorse, C. R. (1991). West African Archaeology and the Atlantic Slave Trade. *Slavery and Abolition* **12** (2): 92–96.

DeCorse, C. R., ed. (2001a). *West Africa during the Atlantic Slave Trade: Archaeological Perspectives*. Leicester University Press, New York.

DeCorse, C. R. (2001b). *An Archaeology of Elmina: Africans and Europeans on the Gold Coast, 1400–1900*. Smithsonian Institution Press, Washington, DC.

DeCorse, C. R. (2007). Bunce Island: A Cultural Resource Management Plan. Unpublished report. Sierra Leone Monuments and Relics Commission, Freetown, Sierra Leone.

DeCorse, C. R. (2010). Culture History, Agricultural Origins, and the Atlantic World in the Sierra Leone Hinterland, 3000 BC–1800 AD. 13th Pan-African Archaeological Association for Prehistory and Related Studies, Dakar, Senegal, November 1–7, 2010.

DeCorse, C. R., and Spiers, S. (2009). A Tale of Two Polities: Sociopolitical Change and Transformation on the Gold Coast in the Atlantic World. *Australian Journal of Historical Archaeology* **27**: 29–42.

Demougeot, A. (1944). *Notes sur l'organisation politique et administrative du Labé avant l'occupation Française*. Larose, Paris.

Deveneaux, G. K. (1973). *The Political and Social Impact of the Colony in Northern Sierra Leone, 1821–1896*. Ph.D. dissertation, Boston University.

Dieterlen, G. (1957). The Mande Creation Myth. *Journal of the International African Institute* **28** (2): 124–38.

Donald, L. H. (1968). *Changes in Yalunka Social Organization: A Study of Adaptation to a Changing Cultural Environment*. Ph.D. dissertation, University of Oregon.

Earle, T. (1987). Chiefdoms in Archaeological and Ethnohistorical Perspective. *Annual Reviews in Anthropology* **16**: 279–308.

Finnegan, R. H. (1965). *Survey of the Limba People of Northern Sierra Leone*. Her Majesty's Stationery Office, London.

Fried, M. (1967). *The Evolution of Political Society*. Random House, New York.

Fyle, C. (1962). *A History of Sierra Leone*. Oxford University Press, London.

Fyle, C. M. (1976). The Kabala Complex: Koranko-Limba Relationship in the Nineteenth and Twentieth Centuries. In Abraham, A. (ed.), *Topics in Sierra Leone History: A Counter-Colonial Interpretation*. Leone Publishers, Freetown, 106–19.

Fyle, C. M. (1977a). Commerce and Entrepreneurship: The Sierra Leone Hinterland in the Nineteenth Century. Institute of African Studies, Fourah Bay College Occasional Paper No. 2.

Fyle, C. M. (1977b). Collaboration, Co-Operation and Resistance: The Case of Almany Suluku of Biriwa Limba and the British. *Journal of the Historical Society of Sierra Leone* **1** (1): 3–15.

Fyle, C. M. (1979a). *Almamy Suluku of Sierra Leone, c. 1820–1906: The Dynamics of Political Leadership in Pre-Colonial Sierra Leone*. Evans Brothers, Ibadan.

Fyle, C. M. (1979b). *The Solima Yalunka Kingdom*. Nyakon, Freetown.

Garrett, G. H. (1892). Sierra Leone and the Interior, to the Upper Waters of the Niger. *Proceedings of the Royal Geographical Society* **14** (7): 433–55.

Greenberg, J. H. (1970). *The Languages of Africa*. University of Indiana, Bloomington.

Hair, P. E. H. (1977). Sources on Early Sierra Leone: (12) The Livro of the "Santiago" 1526. *Africana Research Bulletin* **8** (1): 28–49.

Haselberger, H. (1964). *Bautraditionen der Westafrikanischen Negerkulturen*. Herder, Austria.

Hill, M. (1970). *Ceramic Seriation of Archaeological Sites in Sierra Leone, West Africa*. Ph.D. dissertation, Southern Illinois University.

Hill, M. (1971). Towards a Cultural Sequence for Southern Sierra Leone. *Africana Research Bulletin* **1** (2): 3–12.

Hill, M. (1972). Speculations on Linguistic and Cultural History of Sierra Leone. International Conference on Manding Studies, School of Oriental and African Studies, University of London, June 30–July 3, 1972.

Hill, M. (1981). The Hunter/Founder in Mende Histories. Unpublished Monogragh.

Hiskett, M. (1984). *The Development of Islam in West Africa*. Longman, New York.

Howard, A. M. (1972). *Big Men, Traders, and Chiefs: Power, Commerce, and Spatial Change in the Sierra Leone-Guinea Plain, 1865–1895*. Ph.D. dissertation, University of Wisconsin.

Inikori, J. E., ed. (1982). *Forced Migration: The Impact of the Export Slave Trade on African Societies*. Africana, New York.

Jackson, M. (1977). *The Kuranko: Dimensions of Social Reality in a West African Society*. Hurst, London.

Johnson, A., and Earle, T. (2000). *The Evolution of Human Societies*, 2nd ed. Stanford University Press, Stanford, CA.

Jones, A. (1983). From Slaves to Palm Kernels: A History of the Galinhas Country (West Africa), 1730–1890. *Studien zur Kulturkunde* **68**. Franz Steiner, Wiesbaden.

Kelly, K. G. (1997). The Archaeology of African-European Interaction: Investigating the Social Roles of Trade, Traders, and the Use of Space in the Seventeenth- and Eighteenth-Century Hueda Kingdom, Republic of Bénin. *World Archaeology* **28** (3): 351–69.

Kiyaga-Mulindwa, D. (1982). Social and Demographic Changes in the Birim Valley, Southern Ghana, c. 1450 to c. 1800. *Journal of African History* **23**: 63–82.

Kopytoff, I. (1987). *The African Frontier*. Indiana University Press, Bloomington.

Kopytoff, I. (1999). Permutations in Patrimomialism and Populism: The Aghem Chiefdoms of Western Cameroon. In MacIntosh, S. K. (ed.), *Beyond Chiefdoms: Pathways to Complexity in Africa*, Cambridge University Press, Cambridge, pp. 88–96.

Koroma, A. K. (1977). Samori Toure and the Colony and Hinterland of Sierra Leone: Diplomatic and Military Contacts, 1880–1892. *Journal of the Historical Society of Sierra Leone* **1** (2): 2–17.

Kup, A. P. (1961). *A History of Sierra Leone, 1400–1787*. Cambridge University Press, New York.

Kup, A. P. (1975). *Sierra Leone: A Concise History*. St. Martin's, New York.

Lagassick, M. (1966). Firearms, Horses, and the Samorian Army Organization 1870–1898. *Journal of African History* **8** (1): 95–115.

Laing, A. G. (1825). *Travels in the Timanee, Kooranko and Soolima Countries*, vols. 1 and 2. J. Murray, London.

Levtzion, N. (1973). *Ancient Ghana and Mali*. Africana, New York.

Levtzion, N. (1976). The Early States of the Western Sudan to 1500. In Ajayi, J. F. A., and Crowder, M. (eds.), *History of West Africa*, vol. 1. Columbia University Press, New York, 114–51.

Lipschutz, M. R. (1973). *Northeast Sierra Leone after 1884: Responses to the Samorian Invasions and British Colonialism*. Ph.D. dissertation, University of California at Los Angeles.

Littlefield, D. C. (1981). *Rice and Slaves: Ethnicity and the Slave Trade in Colonial South Carolina*. Louisiana State University Press, Baton Rouge.

Malcolm, J. M. (1939). Mende Warfare. *Sierra Leone Studies* **21**: 47–52.

McCulloch, M. (1950). *Peoples of the Sierra Leone Protectorate*. International African Institute, London.

McIntosh, S. K. (ed.) (1999). *Beyond Chiefdoms: Pathways to Complexity in Africa*. Cambridge University Press, Cambridge.

Mitchell, P. K. (1962). Trade Routes of the Early Sierra Leone Protectorate. *Sierra Leone Studies* (n.s.) **16**: 204–17.

Mitchell, P. K. (1971). Peoples, Localities and Territories: "Tribe" and Chiefdom in Sierra Leone. *Sierra Leone Geographical Journal* **15**: 55–77.

Newland, C. H. (1933). The Sofa Invasion of Sierra Leone. *Sierra Leone Studies* **19**: 162–71.

Ogundiran, A. O., and Falola, T., eds. (2007). *Archaeology of Atlantic Africa and the African Diaspora*. Indiana University Press, Bloomington.

Ottenberg, S. (1988). Religion and Ethnicity in the Arts of a Limba Chiefdom. *Africa* **58** (4): 437–65.

Ozanne, P. (1966). A Preliminary Archaeological Survey of Sierra Leone. *West African Archaeological Newsletter* **5**: 31–36.

Ozanne, P. (1968). Sierra Leone Problems. *West African Archaeological Newsletter* **9**: 14–17.

Peterson, B. J. (2008). History, Memory and the Legacy of Samori in Southern Mali, c. 1880–1898. *Journal of African History* **49** (2): 261–79.

Peterson, J. (1969). *Province of Freedom: A History of Sierra Leone, 1787–1870*. Northwestern University Press, Evanston, IL.

Reade, W. (1873). *The African Sketch-Book*, vols. 1 and 2. Smith, Elder and Co., London.

Richard, F. (2007). *From Cossan to Colony: Exploring Archaeological Landscape Formations and Socio-Political Complexity in the Siin (Senegal), A.D. 500–1900*. Ph.D. dissertation, Syracuse University.

Rodney, W. (1970). *A History of the Upper Guinea Coast*. Monthly Review Press, New York.

Service, E. R. (1975). *Origins of the State and Civilization*. W. W. Norton, New York.

Siddle, D. J. (1968). War-Towns in Sierra Leone: A Study in Social Change. *Africa* **38** (1): 47–56.

Siddle, D. J. (1969). The Evolution of Rural Settlement Forms in Sierra Leone circa 1400 to 1968. *Sierra Leone Geographical Journal* **13**: 33–34.

Siddle, D. J. (1970). Location Theory and the Subsistence Economy: The Spacing of Rural Settlements in Sierra Leone. *Journal of Tropical Geography* **31**: 79–90.

Smith, J. N. L. (2008). *Archaeological Survey of Settlement Patterns in the Banda Region, West-Central Ghana: Exploring External Influences and Internal Responses in the West African Frontier*. Ph. D. dissertation, Syracuse University.

Southhall, A. W. (1988). The Segmentary State in Africa and Asia. *Comparative Studies in Society and History* **30**: 52–82.

Southhall, A. W. (1991). The Segmentary State: From the Imaginary to the Material Means of Production. In Claessen, J. M., and van de Velde, P. (eds.), *Early State Economics*. Political and Legal Anthropology Series, Volume 8. Transaction, New Brunswick, 75–96.

Spiers, S. (2007). *The Eguafo Kingdom: Investigating Complexity in Southern Ghana*. Ph.D. dissertation, Syracuse University.

Stahl, A. B. (1999). The Archaeology of Global Encounters Viewed from Banda, Ghana. *African Archaeological Review* **16**: 5–81.

Stahl, A. B. (2001). *Making History in Banda: Anthropological Visions of Africa's Past*. Cambridge University Press, New York.

Suret-Canale, J. (1969). Les origins ethniques des anciens captives au Fouta-Djalon. *Notes Africaines* **123**: 91–92.

Trotter, J. K. (1898). *The Niger Sources*. Methuen, London.

Winterbottom, T. (1803). *An Account of the Native Africans in the Neighborhood of Sierra Leone*. C. Whittingham, London.

Zweifel, J., and Moustier, M. (1880). *Voyage aux sources du Niger*. Barlatier-Feissat, Marseille.

11

Rethinking the Mandara Political Landscape: Cultural Developments, Climate, and an Entry into History in the Second Millennium A.D.

Scott MacEachern

INTRODUCTION

In Western historiography, the middle of the second millennium A.D. has usually been considered a period of transition in coastal West Africa, the time of the first encounter between Europeans and the different peoples of the region, when this part of Africa entered fully into history and an engagement with the outside world (Stahl 2001:19–25). It is no coincidence that there is also an important transition in West Africanist archaeology during this period as well, marked by a decreasing intensity of research on later communities: history progressively replaces archaeology as the privileged mode for investigating human experience through the last 500 years. In addition, the focus of archaeological research undertaken shifted through this period, from the analysis of indigenous cultural processes before about A.D. 1500 to a concern with the archaeology of culture contact, sites implicated in the slave trade, and European colonization – to a certain degree, that is, with the archaeology of Europeans in West Africa – afterward (MacEachern 2005).

The situation in more northerly areas of the subcontinent is somewhat different, in part because of the greater time depth of written sources for the regions to the south of the Sahara (Levtzion and Hopkins 1981; Lewicki 1974) and in part because of the greater distance between this area and the disruptions associated with European contact along the coast. These circumstances have combined to render the historiographical transition in that region less abrupt and have in turn had distinct effects upon historical (and archaeological) perceptions of the Sahelian and Sudanic zones of West Africa. Both external and internal written sources have tended to view the region through the lenses of Islam and state-level societies, and this has resulted in some privileging of the study of political systems and external contacts in regional analyses at the expense of smaller-scale societies (often assumed explicitly or implicitly to be "people without history") and local cultural sequences (Anignikin 2001; MacEachern 1993; Tymowski 2005). In the southern Lake Chad Basin, the political continuity of the Kanuri state through almost a millennium has also been the focus of archaeological research (Gronenborn 2001a, 2001b), and – unusually for West and Central Africa – significant data have been accumulated on recent archaeological sites in some areas (e.g., the "Âge du Fer Final" of Marliac 1991). These influences have somewhat lessened the contrast between "prehistoric" and "historic" research stances, as these are seen along the coast.

Nevertheless, research priorities and historical understandings change, and the last twenty-five years of archaeological investigations in West Africa have seen significant progress in our understandings of sociopolitical change in the region through the mid- to late second millennium A.D. This understanding has been reached particularly through fieldwork and writings critical of received assumptions about idealized dichotomies (between "prehistory" and "history," "precolonial" and "colonial," for example) and through research that has specifically focused on examination of African communities and their creative adaptation to the encounter with Europeans (DeCorse 2001; Kelly 1997, 2001; McIntosh 1999; Stahl 1993, 2001, 2005). To the extent that this dichotomization was never so clear-cut in the Sahelian and Sudanic zones of West Africa, less attention has probably been paid to its critique. The demonstration through the last thirty years that complex societies in West Africa were not originally gifts from the Mediterranean world (McIntosh 1995; McIntosh and McIntosh 1980; but see also Lange 2004) has been salutary, but at the same time there remains to the south of the Sahara a tendency to leave more recent centuries to historical analysis, to concentrate archaeological efforts upon earlier periods and processes, and to privilege centralized and usually Islamic states as the motivating factor in social and political developments.

In this chapter, I will examine a subset of archaeological data from the southern Lake Chad Basin in light of these issues. The area under consideration is the northern Mandara Mountains of

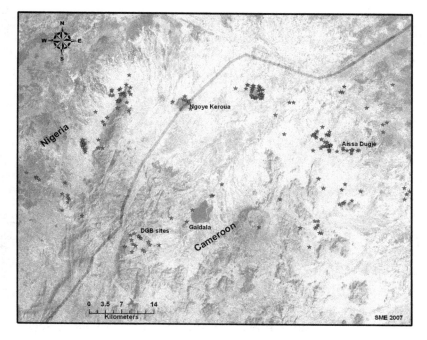

Figure 11.1
Sites in and around the northern Mandara Mountains in Cameroon and Nigeria, with sites mentioned in the text noted.

Cameroon and Nigeria and the immediately neighboring plains to the north, between the mountains and Lake Chad, an area where I have worked since the mid-1980s (Figure 11.1). Today, the northern Mandara Mountains are one of the most intensively managed cultural landscapes in Africa, a situation that involves terrace agriculture, ecosystem management, and population densities of up to 250 people/km² in a dry Sudanic environment. The diverse communities that live in the Mandara Mountains, with their different cultural and political forms, traditionally existed at the interstices of more powerful plains-based states, most notably Kanem-Bornu and the Sokoto Caliphate and, more locally, the Wandala state. The region historically fits well within a typological category of *internal frontier polities*, as described by the editors of this book (Monroe and Ogundiran, this volume). It might, in fact, be argued that it continues to play the same role today (Roitman 2004).

Some years ago, I argued that the Mandara cultural landscape was largely the product of the activities of predatory slave-raiding states on the plains north of the Mandara massif in the mid-second millennium A.D. (MacEachern 2001). However, the accumulation of archaeological data in this region, especially through the past five to ten years, necessitates reexamination of assumptions – among them my own – about the origins of the Mandara landscapes, and of the polities that it now contains, and about environmental and cultural processes during the mid-second millennium A.D. The appearance of political and social hierarchies in this region seems to have been a rather more complicated process than seemed to be evident one or two decades ago.

AN "IRRUPTION OF STATES": THE SOUTHERN LAKE CHAD BASIN IN THE SECOND MILLENNIUM A.D.

When archaeologists have written about the culture history of the area, including the northern Mandara Mountains and the plains between the mountains and Lake Chad, they have often identified the middle of the second millennium A.D. as a period of significant transformation in regional political and social relationships (Connah 1976, 1981; David and MacEachern 1988; Holl 1996; MacEachern 1993, 2001, 2003 [1991]; Marliac 1991). This period is often seen to be one of rupture, a time in which preexisting social and political systems (as seen through their archaeological manifestations) were broken down and reformulated according to new models. There is thus a sense that things changed during this period, in a variety of different ways, and that it will thus be more difficult for researchers to apprehend the forms and structures of societies existing before this rupture than those that existed afterward – because the reformulated social and political relationships existing afterward were more or less directly ancestral to those encountered by Europeans in their first visits to the region from the early nineteenth century onward. The contours of earlier communities are, however, somewhat more mysterious.

The reasons for this recognition of a rupture in local social/political systems are complex but involve essentially two factors. The first is the historically attested activity of state-level political units – especially Bornu, but also Wandala, Baghirmi, and eventually a number of other polities – in the area at this period, and the effects of these states upon the smaller-scale communities already existing in the region (Figure 11.2) (Barkindo 1985; Forkl 1983; Lange 1977; Mohammadou 1982; Reyna 1990). These effects were especially manifested in Kanuri attempts to enforce vassalage on local political leaders around the northern Mandara Mountains, most dramatically perhaps by Mai Idris Alauma of Bornu during the late sixteenth century (Lange 1987, 1989), and the expansion of slave raiding into the

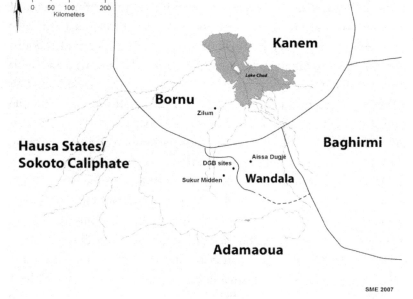

Figure 11.2
The Mandara sites in regional context. Precolonial state boundaries are extremely approximate.

region at generally the same period (MacEachern 2001; Morrissey 1984). These influences also led to the adoption of elements of especially Kanuri political terminology and relationships by nascent polities in the region over the next centuries (David 2006; Mohammadou 1982; Sterner 2003; Vaughan 1970) and probably to a significant increase in the level of political centralization and hierarchy in those groups, as they became progressively incorporated into regional and even continental networks of political and economic interchange (Gronenborn 2001a; MacEachern 2001, 2002a). Such formulations also fit comfortably into the evolutionary schemas that have dominated West African historiography throughout the twentieth century (MacEachern 2005). From this point of view, state formation in the Mandara area is seen as ultimately a "gift of outsiders" – a poisoned gift, perhaps, borne to the area by slave raids, but introduced from beyond the region nevertheless.

Archaeologists and historians have posited that these events led to widespread rearrangements of social and political systems in the region, through the movement of people from plains communities into the Mandara massif, heretofore more or less unoccupied, and to the shores and islands of Lake Chad and the Logone-Chari river system (Baroin 2005; de Garine 1964; Lange 1989; MacEachern 2002b, 2003 [1991]). A major factor behind these historical models was the lack of evidence for prehistoric occupation of the Mandara Mountains coupled with the linguistic diversity of modern montagnard populations (Barreteau and Dieu 2000; David and MacEachern 1988; MacEachern 2003 [1991]). This paradox – with substantial modern populations and languages diversifying through time, in an area with little archaeological evidence for occupation – might be explained by a relatively recent movement of numerous small groups of people into peripheral areas of the massif already occupied at low population densities, with the newcomers being assimilated into preexisting communities (MacEachern 2003 [1991]).

These immigrant populations would have come from long-established habitation sites in the plains around the Mandara Mountains, and those archaeologically known plains sites are the second element in this belief that the middle of the second millennium A.D. constituted a period of political transformation in the southern Lake Chad Basin. At some point during the second millennium A.D. there appears to have been a significant degree of abandonment of these habitation sites north of the Mandara Mountains, sites that had in many cases been occupied for centuries (Bourges et al. 1999; Connah 1981; David and MacEachern 1988; Gronenborn 1998; Lebeuf 1969; Lebeuf et al. 1980; MacEachern in press; Marliac et al. 2000). For the most part, this abandonment occurred on the mound sites that are characteristically associated with occupation by the semilegendary "Sao" and "Maya" populations of the region. At least twenty-five of these sites exist within about 30 km from the edge of the massif, and hundreds are known in the Nigerian, Cameroonian, and Chadian sections of the southern Lake Chad Basin. There are major challenges involved in dating the end of occupation of these sites, however, because most of them have not been adequately dated and because erosion effects often tend to remove the upper (and thus most recent) levels of such mound sites (Connah 1981; see also Rosen 1986). It should also be noted that a variety of settlements south of Lake Chad were not in fact abandoned during this period, although their internal characteristics and external sociopolitical relationships were probably significantly modified (Bourges 1996; Holl 1988; Jones 2001; MacEachern 2002a).

In isolation, both of these claims in their general form – that external states began playing progressively more of a role in the area around the Mandara Mountains during the second millennium A.D. and that a number of ancient settlement sites were abandoned during that period – are almost certainly correct. However, in earlier writing on this region, I at least have tended to link these two observations in ways that may not be useful (MacEachern 2001, 2002a; MacEachern et al. 2001). Such a linkage assumes that the very limited chronological data that can be extracted from the historical sources can be used to supplement the even more limited chronological data available from the archaeological sites and thus that the sites were abandoned in about the middle of the second millennium A.D., at the same time that the earliest historical sources on the area become available. The appearance of states is thus taken not merely to be coeval with the abandonment of Iron Age sites but to largely explain that abandonment – along with a resulting movement of refugee populations from these communities into the Mandara massif. Although it is quite likely that the two processes are related, we should keep in mind that the evidence for a chronological relationship between state formation and state activities, on the one hand, and site abandonment, on the other hand, is not at all conclusive. In addition, such assumptions risk overemphasizing the discontinuity between archaeological manifestations from the first and early second millennia A.D. and the succeeding communities of the precolonial period.

To some degree, the knowns and unknowns of southern Lake Chad Basin prehistory supported these assumptions through the 1980s and 1990s. As noted, there was no significant evidence for occupation of the northern Mandara Mountains themselves, a striking contrast to the abundant archaeological evidence for agricultural communities on the plains around the massif – especially given the complexity and density of human occupation through much of the region today (Boulet et al. 1984). This, along with the oral historical evidence (MacEachern 2003 [1991]), suggested that occupation of the mountains was associated with site abandonment on the plains, that there had been a population transfer between the two regions. Similarly, there seemed to be only quite ambiguous evidence for state formation, political centralization, or intercommunity conflict on the plains around the Mandara Mountains before the Kanuri state of Kanem and its successor in Bornu took an interest in the region, perhaps by the fourteenth century A.D. A number of sites dating before this time seem to have been walled (Connah 1981; Lebeuf 1969; MacEachern 2002a), but the period of construction of such walls is usually unclear, and in some cases (as at Manaouatchi-Gréa [PMW 602]) their defensive potential is quite doubtful. Other sites seem not to have been walled at all and are frequently located in areas where defensive possibilities were rather limited. Again, this could be interpreted as indicating a very significant change in the region in the middle of the second millennium A.D.

COMPLICATING THE PICTURE: WALLS AND HORSES

Over approximately the last ten years, however, the archaeological picture of cultural sequences in and around the Mandara Mountains has become significantly more complicated, in ways that tend to vitiate models of an evolutionary trajectory toward political central-ization and of an historical rupture in the region in the middle of the second millennium A.D. This complication has involved a number of different elements. In the first place, it now appears that some ele-ments of prehistoric culture, frequently taken to be temporally associ-ated with historically known states and the conflicts they engender, actually possess significantly greater time depth in this area. This is strikingly true in the cases of community walls. The discovery of a probable ditch-and-(possible)-wall system at the site of Zilum, about 60 km southwest of Lake Chad and dating to the middle of the first millennium B.C. (Magnavita 2004; Magnavita et al. 2004, 2006; Magnavita and Schleifer 2004), forces some degree of rethink-ing about the chronology of these architectural features in the region, because the Zilum wall is at least 1,000 years older than other claimed wall systems south of Lake Chad. If, as the excavators claim, this site included a defensive wall and was thus a fortified commu-nity – and in fact a large (12–13 ha) nucleated site, at the apex of a small site hierarchy – then one must also rethink assumptions about scales of political organization and the potentials for inter-community conflict south of Lake Chad at this very early period. These data imply a considerably earlier appearance of large-scale nucleated communities and sociopolitical complexity in the south-ern Lake Chad Basin than was hitherto thought to be the case; they also imply that such developments were substantially indige-nous, existing well before the synthesis of local practice and intro-duced Islamic culture begun by the rulers of Kanem in the tenth century A.D.

The technological associations of Zilum – it dates to the time when iron was first being produced in this region, but there is as yet no trace of iron or iron production technologies on the site – and the degree of cultural continuity between Zilum and sites of the first millennium A.D. in the region are not well understood. It is notable, however, that the populations of the southern Lake Chad Basin encountered by the Kanuri as they began to move into this region were designated as Sao or *sawé*, inhabitants of walled towns, indicating that those architectural features were already well known south of the lake (Gronenborn 1998) – although they were not as common close to the Mandara massif as to the north. Such questions may render inadequate any simple model of evolutionary increases in sociopolitical complexity in this region originating in Kanem in the late first millennium A.D., the default origin in many historical reconstructions.

In a similar fashion, the discovery of pony remains dated to the mid- to late first millennium A.D. and afterward at the Aissa Dugjé site, to the northeast of the Mandara Mountains (MacEachern et al. 2001; Diana Crader, Portland, personal communication 2007) invalidated a number of previous historical reconstructions. These were chiefly mine (MacEachern 2003 [1991]) – but see also Mohammadou (1982) – and located the first appearance of these animals on the peripheries of the Mandara massif as an element in the irruption of predatory states into the region in the mid-second millennium A.D. Horses served as potent markers of social hierarchy throughout the Sudanic zone through most of the last 1,000 years and were also significant elements in regional economic and military power, making possible the cavalry forces used in fighting and slave raiding (Holl 1994; Law 1980; Seignobos 1987). The discovery of ponies in this area at this period is perhaps not as surprising as the discovery of walls at Zilum 1,000 years beforehand, because horses/ponies also appear in other areas of West Africa at the same time (MacDonald and MacDonald 2000; Togola 1996:106), but it again implies a long indigenous tradition of use of these animals around the Mandara Mountains, well before the historically attested processes of state formation began.

In later periods, there was some degree of contrasting use of ponies by non-Muslim communities in this region, where they tended to be associated with less formalized and structured sociopolitical hierarchies than was the case for the larger horses used in Islamic states (such as that of the Wandala). As with the Zilum walls, we cannot easily discern the roles that horses played in regional social, political, or economic systems during the first millennium A.D.

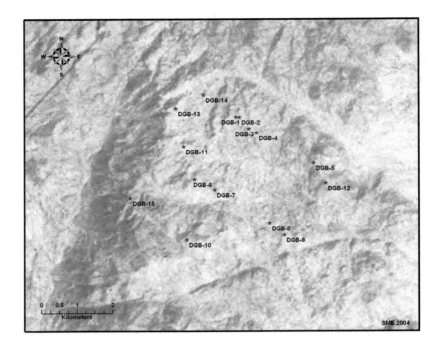

Figure 11.3
The DGB sites.

(when the Muslim/non-Muslim and [presumably] state/nonstate distinctions would not be significant), although their contexts of discovery at Aissa Dugjé indicates that they were probably valuable possessions. The absence of horse remains at contemporary sites in the region may also imply some status differentiation between inhabitants of Aissa Dugjé and neighboring sites.

COMPLICATING THE PICTURE: THE DGB SITES

Perhaps the most important complicating factor in recent views of regional prehistory has been the identification, excavation, and (limited) dating of a set of substantial sites in the northwestern Mandara Mountains, the DGB sites (David 2008; David and Sterner 2006; MacEachern et al. 2010). "DGB" stands for *diy-gid-biy*, which can be translated from the Mafa language of the region as "place of chiefly residence," with the contraction used to avoid assumptions about site functions (David 2008). The sixteen DGB sites (Figures 11.1 and 11.3) are complexes of platforms and terraces of varying size (Figure 11.4). Other architectural features include integrated staircases, passageways, internal chambers, and silos/courtyards. They are characterized by very distinctive and carefully made dry-stone walling, different than that used by modern populations in the region

(Figure 11.5). The ceramics found on the DGB sites is also different from that of modern Mafa inhabitants of the area, although belonging to the same general montagnard ceramic tradition. At this point, no data on habitation sites associated with the DGB phenomenon exist. It has proven difficult to locate prehistoric sites in a context of very intensive modern use of mountain landscapes – the DGB sites are an exception in large part because of their size and distinctive architecture. We assume from DGB site locations that the builders of the sites were montagnard terrace farmers, as are their modern successors in the area, but have no specific data on their economies. Gathering data on ancient Mandara economies, and especially on the creation of the complex terracing systems characteristic of the mountains, is a priority for further research on the DGB sites.

The DGB sites appear to have been built up in a sequence of construction stages, although the total time span involved in their construction is difficult to establish. The DGB-1 and DGB-2 sites are only about 100 m apart and probably should be considered as a single site; they form a very striking architectural complex, roughly comparable in size, for example, to the Khami site in Zimbabwe (Figure 11.6). Radiocarbon dates from DGB-2 and DGB-8 indicate that those two DGB sites were in use in the late fifteenth century A.D., and DGB-1 was occupied between the fourteenth and seventeenth centuries A.D. (David 2008; MacEachern et al. 2010). More dates will be needed to evaluate the timing of the DGB phenomenon more generally. Evidence for early occupation of the mountains is the existence

Figure 11.4
View of DGB-1, from below.

Figure 11.5
Dry-stone walls at DGB-1.

of grinding hollows in boulders in various parts of the massif (David 1998), in contexts that imply significant changes in ground level – and thus the passage of significant amounts of time – since those grinding hollows were created (Figure 11.7). However, these hollows cannot be dated, and their numbers imply much lower population densities than exist in the region today. They may well then date from an earlier, and far less intensive, occupation of some regions of the mountains than the occupation associated with the DGB sites.

There is limited evidence for extensive habitation on the DGB sites themselves, although domestic debris and especially ceramics are found in the vicinity of a number of these sites (including the DGB-1/DGB-2 complex) and settlement probably existed nearby. They appear to have had no defensive function: no protective walls are found atop their open platforms and terraces, they are frequently overlooked by neighboring physical features, and they have no

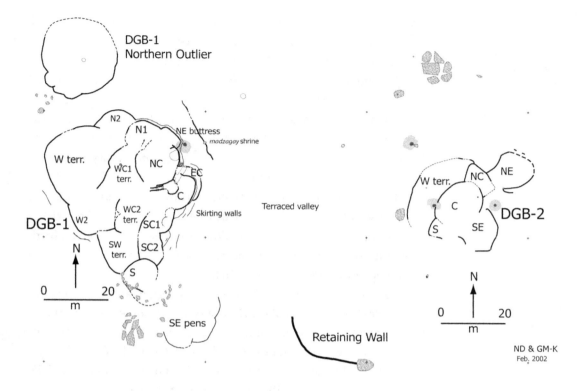

protected access to water. The DGB sites are provisionally identified by the researchers who originally studied them as combining functions of surveillance and rituals relating to rain, possibly in a context of environmental stress associated with a severe, century-long drought in the middle of the second millennium A.D. – that is, the period of occupation of these sites – indicated primarily by very

Figure 11.6
Ground plan of the DGB-1 and DGB-2 sites.

Figure 11.7
Grinding hollows near DGB-15.

low water levels in Lake Chad (David 2008; David and Sterner 2006; see also Brunk and Gronenborn 2004). According to this hypothesis, the sites themselves served to a significant extent as stages for community ritual performances, with those performances coordinated by individuals with ritual functions at least somewhat analogous to those of modern "masters of the rain" in Mafa, the *bi yam*. This status has variable ritual and political implications in different parts of the Mandara Mountains, derived from a recognized ability to control rainfall in a semiarid environment.

This model places the DGB sites firmly within the context of modern social and ideological institutions and practices that exist in Mandara populations, and so it allows for a very rich and sophisticated interpretation. At the same time, some additional issues need to be kept in mind. There are, first, some problems in using Lake Chad levels as a proxy for climates in this region, and thus in positing that the construction of the DGB sites was in some way a response to an extremely severe drought. The catchment area of the lake lies primarily farther to the south, in the headwaters of the Chari-Logone river system, leading to situations in which one can find higher lake levels correlated to aridity in the areas immediately surrounding Lake Chad and vice versa (Brunk and Gronenborn 2004:114).[1] There is, however, also written and oral historical evidence, both direct and circumstantial, for an arid episode in the southern Lake Chad Basin during the fifteenth century A.D. (Brunk and Gronenborn 2004; Maley 2000), although the magnitude of that arid episode, compared to other periodic droughts in the region through a progressively desiccating second millennium A.D., remains unclear.

One would also expect that such sites, if functioning in the context of an environmental crisis, would be seen to retain their ritual efficacy once that crisis passed, especially given crises in later centuries and the substantial climatic variability in the area even in noncrisis conditions. This explanation thus leaves open the question of when the DGB-1/DGB-2 complex, at least, ceased to be used. In addition, it seems likely that the spectacular DGB-1/DGB-2 site complex (Figures 11.4–11.6) also has some regional political significance, even if such significance accreted through use and was not the original aim of the initial phases of construction. The size and complexity of DGB-1/DGB-2 would have provided a potent stage for the presentation of ritual power, and one wonders why, if the other, smaller, less complicated DGB sites could serve the same ritual function, so much extra effort was invested in the construction and progressive modification of that particular site complex. Further research will be required to further elucidate the functions of these sites.

It is important to note that the DGB sites are specifically a montagnard phenomenon: there is no evidence for habitation sites in the plains immediately below the massif whose inhabitants could be responsible for their construction (personal observation, 2007–08), and their layout and the striking skill in dry-stone architecture demonstrated by their builders would in any case have been more or less irrelevant on the plains. The DGB sites very strongly indicate that there was already a substantial population in at least one part of the Mandara Mountain at the time when we first find evidence for significant Kanuri activity on the plains immediately to the north. Moreover, their distinctiveness implies that their builders had already occupied and explored the architectural potential of that mountain landscape for some extended period of time. We have not merely evidence for occupation in the massif significantly before the middle of the second millennium A.D. but also evidence for communal mobilization of resources, and ritual/political activity, on a scale at least equal to anything going on in the plains around the Mandara Mountains at the same time.

The position of the DGB sites in the northern Mandara political landscape is particularly interesting. By the "Mandara political landscape," I mean the constellation of small ethnopolitical territories that cover the mountains, politically competitive but culturally fairly similar and intimately associated with particular physical areas of the massif. On the one hand, the sites are today embedded in a specifically montagnard cultural world and can at least conceptually be compared to a number of ethnographically known montagnard polities in different parts of the Mandara massif, including Sukur (David 1996; Smith and David 1995; Sterner 2003) to the southwest and the Mofu "princedoms" to the southeast (Vincent 1991). In both of these cases, montagnard political leaders – often with relatively limited coercive power – are nevertheless associated with substantial dry-stone architectural systems, albeit not of the DGB type. The similarities are obvious, and, indeed, ethnographic data from these political units (along with data from the Mafa communities now occupying the DGB distribution area) are primary sources of comparative analogy for interpretation of the DGB sites (David 2008; David and Sterner 2006). At the same time, the DGB sites are positioned only

30–40 km south of the Pulke–Keroua area, known historically as the area of origin of the Wandala state, which would later, and after borrowing many of the Sudanic trappings of Islamic state functioning, dominate the plains around the northern peripheries of the mountains (Forkl 1986; MacEachern 1993; Mohammadou 1982; Morrissey 1984). The DGB sites are, in fact, about the same distances from Pulke and Keroua as they are from Sukur and the Mofu area.

There are connections in material culture (especially with the so-called funnel-mouth pots) and oral traditions between the DGB sites and the present montagnard inhabitants of the Gwoza Hills, just to the south of Pulke – and through that region to Wandala itself (Muller-Kosack 2004). However, the timing of such connections remains unclear; it is quite possible that it postdates the period when the DGB sites were occupied. The first historical references to Wandala – in Italy – date to the early fifteenth century A.D. (Gasparrini Leporace 1956; MacEachern 2003 [1991]), and thus to exactly the period of known use of the DGB sites. One would minimally expect that Wandala leaders and the makers of the DGB sites[2] would have been aware of one another, and it is entirely likely that some interaction between these two regions would have taken place, because in more recent times linkages with Gudur have been at least conceptually important for a number of communities in the northern Mandara massif (Jouaux 1991; Seignobos 1988; Sterner 2003).

The nature of such potential interactions between the DGB sites and the Keroua–Pulke area is at present unknown. On the one hand, the differentiation between mountains and plains lifeways at that time would presumably not have been as marked as it is today, after five centuries of slave raiding and cultural and political divergence – although this of course depends to some degree upon an unknown, the length of occupation of the mountains at that time. Even today, substantial parallels between the two regions exist (MacEachern 2002a). On the other hand, the very different architectural characteristics of the DGB sites and the habitation mound sites found on the plains to the north of the massif seem to imply correspondingly different cultural backgrounds at the time. It is worth noting that habitation mound sites, the most distinctive prehistoric site type between the Mandara Mountains and Lake Chad, do not appear to be found in the Koza Plain just to the east of the DGB sites, even in locations – as around the edges of the Galdala inselberg – that are favored for such sites just 25–30 km to the north (Figure 11.1) (personal observation, 2007; MacEachern in press). Given that such mound sites appear in the area in the early first millennium A.D., this absence cannot be due to the Koza Plain's relative inaccessibility to Kanuri attack from the north a millennium later. Further archaeological research is required to elucidate the relationships between these different regions through the first and early second millennia A.D.

ENVIRONMENTAL AND POLITICAL CONTEXTS

As David (2008) noted in his argument that the DGB sites combine functions of surveillance and rituals relating to rain, the available radiocarbon dates from DGB-2 and DGB-8 closely match the timing for very low lake levels in the Lake Chad Basin and other evidence for drought in the region during the middle of the fifteenth century (see also Brunk and Gronenborn 2004). It is likely that this period of drought contributed to political changes more generally in this region, most obviously by providing impetus to the final shift of the center of gravity of the Kanuri state from Kanem, northeast and east of Lake Chad, toward Bornu, in the better-watered lands southwest of the lake. This shift was almost certainly associated in turn with Kanuri territorial expansion, warfare, and increases in slave raiding south of Lake Chad, which ultimately affected most of the societies in that region (MacEachern 2003 [1991]). Perhaps as important as gross measures of drought conditions would be the year-to-year variability in rainfall that farmers must deal with, but data on that variability are not at present available for the region. It is unlikely that such variability was qualitatively different over the long term from the case today (Nicholson 2000; Street-Perrott et al. 2000). On a larger scale, we need to think of the mid-fifteenth century drought as just one in a series of such episodes to afflict this area through the last 1,000 years, after relatively wetter conditions during the mid- to late first millennium A.D. It was almost certainly this progressive desiccation through time that played a role in generating greater Kanuri interest in the region from the *fourteenth* century onward and possibly for a hundred years before that (Brunk and Gronenborn 2004; Gronenborn 2001a; Lange 1984; Seidenstecker-Brikay 2004). The establishment of a new Kanuri capital southwest of the lake at Birni Ngazargamo in the late fifteenth century was the culmination of this process, not its beginning.

Such a perspective again moves the focus away from a decisive set of events occurring at mid-millennium and toward consideration of an extended set of social and political interactions happening over centuries in the southern Lake Chad Basin. In such a case, the effects of changing climates need to be considered not merely as an isolated impetus for Kanuri expansionism or DGB construction in the fifteenth century but as providing a context for changes on longer timescales. It is likely that the availability of high-yield sorghum during the relatively moist centuries of the first millennium A.D. (Langlois 1995:503, 608; Magnavita 2002), alongside the dry-tolerant *Pennisetum* millet already known in the region (Klee and Zach 1999), contributed to the establishment of sedentary agricultural communities, now known archaeologically through their habitation mound remains. Availability of both sorghum and millet would provide alternatives during drought periods, and at this point no data indicate gross changes in settlement patterning, or interruptions in site habitation, on the plains south of Lake Chad in the early second millennium A.D. – although historical data do provide evidence for such disruptions in Kanem to the northeast (Brunk and Gronenborn 2004:114–17; MacEachern in press). It would appear that the agricultural system in use south of the lake was sufficiently resilient to cope with these increased drought frequencies on a regional scale. This does not, of course, rule out the likelihood of more localized disruptions and indeed catastrophes that might afflict particular communities, nor does it rule out increased levels of population movement and intercommunity conflict, of the sort that accompanied later drought episodes, during this period.

The near-total absence of archaeological data from the Mandara Mountains beyond the DGB sites makes reconstructions of cultural sequences in this region nearly impossible. However, some considerations of local environmental effects, and their potential cultural consequences, may be permissible. Modern environments in this area are very heavily affected by human activities, to the extent that many parts of the massif may be described as anthropically derived farm- and parkland, but areas like the Gokoro Forest Reserve, derived from farmland and now heavily overgrown, do not offer reliable indications of ancient vegetation regimes (Boutrais 1984:93–99; World Wildlife Fund 2004). However, the presence in areas of low population density, and in relict stands throughout the northern massif, of associations of Sudanic tree species, including *Isoberlinia doka*, *Daniellia oliveri*, and *Anogeissuss leiocarpus*, indicates that the vegetation of the massif before human occupation was probably a Sudanic or even Sudanic-Guinean forest (Boutrais 1984:26–28). This would have been quite possible in the context of increased rainfall levels in the first millennium A.D. Modeling of late Holocene environments in the African Sahelian zone indicates that two stable equilibria for vegetation patterns exist: (1) the present case, with sparse vegetation in the Sahel; and (2) an alternate case, with different rainfall–ecosystem interactions, where wooded grasslands and shrublands are found at up to 600 km north of their present limits (Street-Perrott et al. 2000:299). If this latter equilibrium existed in the first millennium A.D., as seems likely, we would expect a corresponding northward expansion of Guinean and Sudanic woodland as well.

A forest environment on the Mandara Mountains would have been a significant deterrent to settlement in this region. On the other hand, a progressive trend toward desiccation in the early second millennium A.D. might well have increased the attractiveness of a montagnard way of life to people living on the plains close to the massif, given that such a trend would have increased pressure (both environmental and, potentially, political) on plains communities, while at the same time contributing to the diminution of forest cover in the mountains – which would in addition have received more rainfall than the neighboring plains, as they do today. This would not provide an all-encompassing explanation for occupation of the Mandara Mountains, especially given that archaeological and ethnohistorical data indicate that much of the massif remained largely empty until a few centuries ago (MacEachern 2003 [1991]). However, it may help to provide a context for interpretation of the DGB sites and the populations that built them, and especially for thinking about those unknown centuries in the mountains before those sites were constructed.

A COMPLEX ENTRY INTO HISTORY

This brief and somewhat idiosyncratic survey of the complications of Mandara prehistory, and of the origins of the intensively managed and complex northern Mandara landscape that we see today, perhaps serves best as a guide to what we do not know – about the origins of the DGB sites, about the role of horses in the first millennium A.D., about settlement walls in the region and their antecedents, and so on. At the same time, the fact that such complications exist is an indication of just how much our knowledge of prehistory around the Mandara Mountains has increased over the last twenty-five years: there is, after all, nothing less complicated than a (nearly) blank slate.

Perhaps one element of (near-) blank-slate thinking is an assumption that what we do know, and especially what is well known and universally agreed upon, must provide an explanation for what we do not know – or, at least, must play a dominant role in such an explanation. An emphasis on the role of the Kanuri state as a *deus ex machina* in bringing political centralization and sociopolitical hierarchy to the lands around the Mandara Mountains through a clockwork mechanism of impacts on local populations, while at the same time disrupting settlement patterns in the region (MacEachern 1993, 2003 [1991]), may be an example of such thinking. These elements may well be part of the overall trajectory of Mandara culture history – which we are probably many decades from understanding in any detailed way – but they are unlikely to be the whole story.

The available data indicate that the settlement history of the Mandara region, and the appearance of political centralization and eventually states in that region, was a significantly complicated process. In this process, the movement of the Kanuri state's center of gravity from Kanem to Bornu, starting in or before the fourteenth century A.D. and probably at least in part a response to deteriorating environments east of Lake Chad, almost certainly played an important role. This should not, however, lead us to ignore the accumulating data for cultural change and innovation indigenous to the southern Lake Chad Basin itself. Data from sites such as Zilum and Aissa Dugjé indicate that some of the elements historically incorporated into regional definitions of sociopolitical complexity were already in place many centuries before Kanuri contact, although the roles that horses and walled communities played in wider sociopolitical systems during that period remain obscure. Perhaps equally significant, the absence of similar remains from other, contemporary sites indicates that these elements were not equally available to everyone.

The beginning of the second millennium A.D. saw significant changes in the landscapes of the Lake Chad Basin more widely defined, with a turn toward significantly drier environments and an increased frequency of droughts through time. Both palaeoenvironmental and historical data indicate that these processes first affected areas to the east and west of Lake Chad itself, as might be expected given the sensitivity of the Sahelian zone to changes in rainfall. However, we can expect that secondary effects, likely including a diminution of forest cover in the Mandara Mountains, would have followed soon after. These changes may well be implicated in an expansion of human settlement into the Mandara Mountains, especially in circumstances where increased levels of conflict on the plains (both indigenous and, eventually, involving Kanuri and other outsiders) made such a move more attractive.

We know relatively little about how such settlement would have taken place, and especially about the history of terrace farming in the Mandara massif, which made possible the intensely managed human landscape that exists there today. The DGB sites prove that the distinction between mountain-dweller and plains-dweller cultural worlds was developing in at least the northwestern massif in the early second millennium A.D. This obviously raises questions about the circumstances of mountain settlement but also about how societies in these areas progressively differentiated themselves from their neighbors in the plains nearby. The cultural and political characteristics of the Mandara landscape are to a significant degree the results of interactions and accommodations with neighboring plains-based states, notably including that of the Wandala; it is after all within that relationship that the region can be thought of as an internal frontier landscape (see Chapter 1). Some understanding of the cultural characteristics of "proto-Wandala" communities – that is, of sites around the northwest extension of the Mandara Mountains and dating to the first half of the second millennium A.D. – would thus be very helpful for our understanding of relationships between mountains and plains during this critical period, especially because the Wandala would go on to become unambiguously identified with the wider cultural milieu of the Islamic Sudanic zone of West and Central Africa. To this point, we have no archaeological remains certainly associated with early Wandala occupations, partly because of the political difficulties of excavations on sites at Keroua, very close to the frontier between Cameroon and Nigeria.[3]

As noted at the beginning of this chapter, there has been a tendency to assume on both historical and archaeological grounds that a cultural break occurred in the southern Lake Chad Basin in the middle of the second millennium A.D., one associated with the intrusion of state-level societies into the region and the corresponding disruption of preexisting local communities. The available data do not, however, strongly support this conclusion, for two reasons. In the first place, a number of significant cultural features associated with sociopolitical hierarchy and political centralization actually have deep indigenous roots in the region, raising the likelihood that local states were the result of a synthesis of local and foreign elements. Second, it is quite likely that the cultural and environmental processes associated with the putative disruptions at mid-millennium actually took place over many centuries, probably from the beginning of the second millennium A.D. onward. At this point, the challenge for archaeologists working in this region is to gather data relevant to these issues so that we can better understand the complex genesis of Mandara landscapes and societies.

ACKNOWLEDGEMENTS

I want to thank Genevieve LeMoine for her valuable comments on different drafts of this chapter. I have not followed all of these suggestions, but they were very much appreciated. The research behind this chapter has been supported through a Kenan Research Fellowship from Bowdoin College and through grants from the National Science Foundation (Research Grant 0743058), the Social Sciences and Humanities Research Council of Canada (Research Grants 410-83-0819, 410-85-1040, 410-88-0361, 410-92-1860, and 410-95-0379), and the National Geographic Society.

BIBLIOGRAPHY

Alkali, M. N. (1983). The Political System and Administrative Structure of Borno under the Seifuwa Mais. In Usman, B., and Alkali, M. N. (eds.), *Studies in the History of Pre-colonial Borno*. Northern Nigeria Publishing Company, Zaria, 101–26.

Anignikin, S. (2001). Histoire des Populations Mahi. À propos de la Controverse sur l'ethnonyme et le Toponyme "Mahi." *Cahiers d'Études Africaines* 41 (162): 243–66.

Barkindo, B. M. (1985). The Mandara Astride the Nigeria-Cameroon Boundary. In Asiwaju, A. I. (ed.), *Partitioned Africans: Ethnic Relations across Africa's International Boundaries 1884–1984*. Hurst, London, 129–42.

Baroin, C. (2005). What Do We Know about the Buduma? A Brief Survey. In Baroin, C., Seidensticker-Brikay, G., and Tijani, K. (eds.), *Man and the Lake*. Centre for Trans-Saharan Studies, Maiduguri, 199–217.

Barreteau, D., and Dieu, M. (2000). Linguistique. In Seignobos, C., and Iyebi-Mandjek, O. (eds.), *Atlas de la Province Extrême-Nord, Cameroun*. Éditions de l'IRD/MINREST, Paris, 64–70.

Boulet, J., Beauvilain, A., and Gubry, P. (1984). Les Groupes Humains. In Boutrais, J. (ed.), *Le Nord du Cameroun: des Hommes, une Région*. Collections Mémoires. Éditions de l'ORSTOM, Paris, 103–57.

Bourges, C. (1996). *Ceramic Ethnoarchaeology and Historical Process: The Case of Gréa, North Cameroun*. M.A. thesis, University of Calgary.

Bourges, C., MacEachern, S., and Reeves, M. (1999). Excavations at Aissa Hardé, 1995 and 1996. *Nyame Akuma* **51**: 6–13.

Boutrais, J. (1984). Les unités naturelles. In Boutrais, J. (ed.), *Le Nord du Cameroun: des Hommes, une Région.* Collections Mémoires. Éditions de l'ORSTOM, Paris, 23–62.

Brunk, K., and Gronenborn, D. (2004). Floods, Droughts, and Migrations: The Effects of Late Holocene Lake Level Fluctuations and Climate Fluctuations on the Settlement and Political History in the Chad Basin. In Krings, M., and Platte, E. (eds.), *Living with the Lake: Perspectives on History, Culture and Economy of Lake Chad.* Rüdiger Köppe, Cologne, 101–32.

Connah, G. (1976). The Daima Sequence and the Prehistoric Chronology of the Lake Chad Region of Nigeria. *Journal of African History* **17** (3): 321–52.

Connah, G. (1981). *Three Thousand Years in Africa: Man and his Environment in the Lake Chad Region of Nigeria.* Cambridge University Press, Cambridge.

David, N. (1996). A New Political Form? The Classless Industrial Society of Sukur (Nigeria). In Pwiti, G., and Soper, R. (eds.), *Aspects of African Archaeology: Proceedings of the Tenth Pan-African Congress.* University of Zimbabwe Press, Harare, 593–600.

David, N. (1998). The Ethnoarchaeology and Field Archaeology of Grinding at Sukur, Adamawa State, Nigeria. *African Archaeological Review* **15** (1): 13–63.

David, N. (2006). The Origins of Sukur Titles. http://www.sukur.info/Soc/TitleOrig.htm.

David, N. (2008). *Performance and Agency: The DGB Sites of Northern Cameroon.* British Archaeological Reports International Series, 1830. Oxford.

David, N., and MacEachern, S. (1988). The Mandara Archaeological Project: Preliminary Results of the 1984 Season. In Barreteau, D., and Tourneux, H. (eds.), *Le Milieu et les Hommes: Recherches Comparitives et Historiques dans le Bassin du Lac Tchad.* Collection Colloques et Séminaires. Éditions de l'ORSTOM, Paris, 51–80.

David, N., and Sterner, J. (2006). DGB Sites of Northern Cameroon: Performance and Landscape. Paper presented at the biennial conference of the Society of Africanist Archaeologists, Calgary, June 2006.

de Colombel, V. (1985). La Naissance d'Aguedzavernda: Un Pouvoir Enfanté et Transmis par les Femmes. In Barbier, J.-C. (ed.), *Femmes du Cameroun: Mères Pacifiques, Femmes Rebelles.* Karthala-ORSTOM, Paris, 219–31.

DeCorse, C. (2001). *An Archaeology of Elmina: Africans and Europeans on the Gold Coast, 1400–1900.* Smithsonian Institution Press, Washington, DC.

de Garine, I. (1964). *Le Massa du Cameroun.* PUF, Paris.

Forkl, H. (1983). *Die Beziehungen der zentralsudanischen Reiche Bornu, Mandara und Bagirmi sowie der Kotoko-Staaten zu ihren südlichen Nachbarn unter besonderer Berücksichtigung des Sao-Problems.* Münchner Ethnologische Abhandlungen 3. Minerva, Munich.

Forkl, H. (1986). Sozial- und Religiongeschichte der Wandalá in Nordkamerun. Paper presented at Conference on Comparative Studies in the Development of Complex Societies. Southampton.

Gasparrini Leporace, T. (1956). *Il mappamondo di Fra Mauro. (With Reproductions of the Fra Mauro Map of 1459).* Instituto Poligrafico dello Stato, Rome.

Gronenborn, D. (1998). Archaeological and Ethnohistorical Investigations along the Southern Fringes of Lake Chad, 1993–1996. *African Archaeological Review* **15** (4): 225–59.

Gronenborn, D. (2001a). Kanem-Borno – A Brief Summary of the History and Archaeology of an Empire in the Central Bilad-el-Sudan. In DeCorse, C. R. (ed.), *West Africa during the Atlantic Slave Trade: Archaeological Perspectives.* Leicester University Press, London, 101–30.

Gronenborn, D. (2001b). Princedoms along the Lakeshore: Historical–Archaeological Investigations on the Development of Complex Societies in the Southern Lake Chad Basin. *Berichte des Sonderforschungsbereichs* **268** (14): 55–69.

Holl, A. (1988). *Houlouf I: Archéologie des Sociétés Protohistoriques du Nord-Cameroun.* BAR International Series 456. Oxford.

Holl, A. (1994). The Cemetery of Houlouf in Northern Cameroon (AD 1500–1600): Fragments of a Past Social System. *African Archaeological Review* **12**: 133–70.

Holl, A. (1996). Genesis of Central Chadic Polities. In Pwiti, G., and Soper, R. (eds.), *Aspects of African Archaeology. Papers from the 10th Congress of the Pan-African Association for Prehistory and Related Studies.* University of Harare Press, Zimbabwe, 581–82.

Jones, K. (2001). *The Archaeology of Doulo, Cameroon.* M.A. thesis, University of Calgary.

Jouaux, C. (1991). La chefferie de Gudur et sa politique expansionniste. In Boutrais, J. (ed.), *Du Politique a l'Économique: Études Historiques dans le Bassin du Lac Tchad.* Éditions de l'ORSTOM, Paris, 193–224.

Kelly, K. (1997). The Archaeology of African-European Interaction: Investigating the Social Roles of Trade, Traders and the Use of Space in the Seventeenth and Eighteenth Century Huéda Kingdom, Republic of Bénin. *World Archaeology* **28** (3): 77–95.

Kelly, K. (2001). Change and Continuity in Coastal Bénin. In DeCorse, C. (ed.), *West Africa during the Atlantic Slave Trade: Archaeological Perspectives.* Leicester University Press, London, 80–100.

Klee, M., and Zach, B. (1999). The Exploitation of Wild and Domesticated Food Plants at Settlement Mounds in North-east Nigeria (1800 cal BC to today). In van der Veen, M. (ed.), *The Exploitation of Plant Resources in Ancient Africa.* Kluwer Academic/Plenum, New York, 81–88.

Lange, D. (1977). *Le Diwan des Sultans du (Kanem)-Bornu: Chronologie et Histoire d'un Royaume Africain de la Fin du 10e Siècle Jusqu'à 1808.* Franz Steiner, Stuttgart.

Lange, D. (1984). The Kingdoms and Peoples of Chad. In Niane, D. T. (ed.), *General History of Africa, IV: Africa from the Twelfth to the Sixteenth Century.* UNESCO and Heinemann, Paris, 238–65.

Lange, D. (1987). *A Sudanic Chronicle: The Borno Expeditions of Idris Alauma (1564–1576).* Franz Steiner, Weisbaden.

Lange, D. (1989). Préliminaires Pour une Histoire des Sao. *Journal of African History* **30** (2): 189–210.

Lange, D. (2004). *Ancient Kingdoms of West Africa: Africa-Centred and Canaanite-Israelite Perspectives.* J. H. Röll, Dettelbach.

Langlois, O. (1995). *Histoire du Peuplement Post-néolithique Ndu Diamaré.* Ph.D. dissertation, Université de Paris I, Pantheon Sorbonne.

Langlois, O. (2004). Distributions Anciennes et Actuelle des Décors Imprimés au Diamaré (Nord-Cameroun) et à ses Marges. *Préhistoire Anthropologie Méditerranéennes* **13**: 109–126.

Law, R. (1980). *The Horse in West African History*. Oxford University Press, London.

Lebeuf, A. M. D., Lebeuf, J.-P., Treinen-Claustre, F., and Courtin, J. (1980). *Le Gisement Sao de Mdaga (Tchad): Fouilles, 1960–1968*. Société d'Ethnographie, Paris.

Lebeuf, J.-P. (1969). *Carte Archéologique des Abords du Lac Tchad (Cameroun, Nigeria, Tchad)*. Éditions du CNRS, Paris.

Levtzion, N., and Hopkins, J. H. (1981). *Corpus of Early Arabic Sources for West African History*. Cambridge University Press, Cambridge.

Lewicki, T. (1974). *Arabic External Sources for the History of Africa to the South of the Sahara*. Translated by M. Abrahamowicz. Prace Komisji Orientalistycznej. Polska Akademia Nauk, Warsaw.

MacDonald, K., and MacDonald, R. H. (2000). The Origins and Development of Domesticated Animals in Arid West Africa. In Blench, R., and MacDonald, K. (eds.), *The Origins and Development of African Livestock: Archaeology, Genetics, Linguistics and Ethnography*. UCL Press, London, 127–62.

MacEachern, S. (1993). Selling the Iron for Their Shackles: Wandala-Montagnard Interactions in Northern Cameroon. *Journal of African History* **34** (2): 247–70.

MacEachern, S. (2001). State Formation and Enslavement in the Southern Lake Chad Basin. In DeCorse, C. (ed.), *West Africa during the Atlantic Slave Trade: Archaeological Perspectives*. Leicester University Press, London, 130–51.

MacEachern, S. (2002a). Beyond the Belly of the House: Space and Power in the Mandara Mountains. *Journal of Social Archaeology* **2** (2): 179–219.

MacEachern, S. (2002b). Residuals and Resistance: Languages and History in the Mandara Mountains. In Joseph, B., Destefano, J., Jacobs, N., and Lehiste, I. (eds.), *When Languages Collide: Perspectives on Language Conflict, Language Competition and Language Coexistence*. Ohio State University Press, Columbus, 21–44.

MacEachern, S. (2003) [1991]. *Du Kunde: Processes of Montagnard Ethnogenesis in the Northern Mandara Mountains of Cameroon*. Mandaras, London. http://www.mandaras.info/electronicisbnpublication/maceachern_dukunde_phd.pdf.

MacEachern, S. (2005). Two Thousand Years of West African History. In Stahl, A. (ed.), *African Archaeology: A Critical Introduction*. Blackwell, London, 441–66.

MacEachern, S. (in press). Mandara Prehistory. In David, N. (ed.), *Iron in the Mandara Mountains: Technology, Economy and Society*. Red Sea Press, Trenton NJ.

MacEachern, S., Bourges, C., and Reeves, M. (2001). Early Horse Remains from Northern Cameroon. *Antiquity* **75** (287): 62–67.

MacEachern, S., Datouang Djoussou, J. M., and Janson-Lapierre, R. E. (2010). Excavations at DGB-1, Northern Cameroon, 2008. *Nyame Akuma* **73**: 37–45.

Magnavita, C. (2002). Recent Archaeological Finds of Domesticated *Sorghum bicolor* in the Lake Chad region. *Nyame Akuma* **57**: 14–20.

Magnavita, C. (2004). Zilum: Towards the Emergence of Sociopolitical Complexity in the Lake Chad Region (1800 BC–1600 AD). In Krings, M., and Platte, E. (eds.), *Living with the Lake: Perspectives on History, Culture and Economy of Lake Chad*. Rüdiger Köppe, Cologne, 73–100.

Magnavita, C., Breunig, P., Ameje, J., and Posselt, M. (2006). Zilum: A Mid-First Millennium BC Fortified Settlement near Lake Chad. *Journal of African Archaeology* 4 (1): 153–69.

Magnavita, C., Kahlheber, S., and Eichhorn, B. (2004). The Rise of Organisational Complexity in Mid-First Millennium BC Chad Basin. *Antiquity* 78 (301). http://antiquity.ac.uk/ProjGall/magnavita/index.html.

Magnavita, C., and Schleifer, N. (2004). A Look into the Earth: Evaluating the Use of Magnetic Survey in African Archaeology. *Journal of African Archaeology* 2 (1): 49–64.

Maley, J. (1981). *Études Palynologiques dans le Bassin du Tchad et Paléoclimatologie de l'Afrique Nord-tropicale de 30,000 Ans à l'Epoque Actuelle.* Éditions de l'ORSTOM, Paris.

Maley, J. (2000). Les variations des niveaux du lac Tchad au cours du dernier millénaire: rôle des conditions climatiques régionales et des apports fluviatiles. Réactions des populations régionales. Comparaison avec le lac Naivasha en Afrique orientale. *Bulletin Méga-Tchad* 2000 (1/2):21–26. http://lah.soas.ac.uk/projects/megachad/bulletin-fr.html.

Marliac, A. (1991). *De la Préhistoire à l'Histoire au Cameroun Septentrionale.* Éditions de l'ORSTOM, Paris.

Marliac, A., Langlois, O., and Delneuf, M. (2000). Archéologie de la Région Mandara-Diamaré. In Seignobos, C., and Iyebi-Mandjek, O. (eds.), *Atlas de la Province Extrême-Nord, Cameroun.* Éditions de l'IRD, Paris, 71–76.

McIntosh, S. K. (1995). *Excavations at Jenné-Jeno, Hambarketolo and Kaniana (Inland Niger Delta, Mali), the 1981 Season.* University of California Publications in Anthropology 20. University of California Press, Berkeley.

McIntosh, S. K. (1999). *Beyond Chiefdoms: Pathways to Complexity in Africa.* Cambridge University Press, Cambridge.

McIntosh, S. K., and McIntosh, R. J. (1980). Excavation and Survey at Djenné-Djeno, Mali: Preliminary Results of the 1977 Field Season. *Proceedings of the Panafrican Congress of Prehistory and Quaternary Studies* 8: 369–72.

Mohammadou, E. (1982). *Le Royaume du Wandala ou Mandara au XIXe Siècle.* Institute for the Study of Languages and Cultures of Asia and Africa, Tokyo.

Morrissey, S. R. (1984). *Clients and Slaves in the Development of the Mandara elite: Northern Cameroon in the Nineteenth Century.* Ph.D. dissertation, Boston University.

Muller-Kosack, G. (2004). DGB Sites and the "Godaliy": Funnel Pots and Ceremonial Walling. Mandaras, London. http://www.mandaras.info/DGB-Godaliy_Research/index.htm.

Nicholson, S. (2000). The Nature of Rainfall Variability over Africa on Time Scales of Decades to Millennia. *Global and Planetary Change* 26: 137–58.

Reyna, S. P. (1990). *Wars without End: The Political Economy of a Precolonial African State.* University Press of New England, Hanover, NH.

Roitman, J. (2004). Productivity in the Margins: The Reconstitution of State Power in the Chad Basin. In Das, V., and Poole, D. (eds.), *Anthropology in the Margins of the State.* School of American Research Press, Santa Fe, 191–224.

Rosen, A. (1986). *Cities of Clay: The Geoarcheology of Tells.* University of Chicago Press, Chicago.

Seidenstecker-Brikay, G. (2004). Lake Chad: Arabic and European Imagination and Reality. In Krings, M., and Platte, E. (eds.), *Living with the Lake: Perspectives on History, Culture and Economy of Lake Chad*. Rüdiger Köppe, Cologne, 133–47.

Seignobos, C. (1987). *Le Poney du Logone et les Derniers Peuples Cavaliers*. Institut d'Élevage et de Médecine Veterinaire des Pays Tropicaux, Paris.

Seignobos, C. (1988). Le rayonnement de la chefferie théocratique de Gudur (Nord-Cameroun). 4th Colloque Mega-Tchad, Paris.

Smith, A., and David, N. (1995). The Production of Space and the House of Xidi Sukur. *Current Anthropology* **36** (3): 441–71.

Stahl, A. (1993). Concepts of Time and Approaches to Analogical Reasoning in Historical Perspective. *American Antiquity* **58** (2): 235–60.

Stahl, A. (2001). *Making History in Banda: Anthropological Visions of Africa's Past*. Cambridge University Press, Cambridge.

Stahl, A. (2005). Introduction: Changing Perspectives on Africa's Pasts. In Stahl, A. (ed.), *African Archaeology: A Critical Introduction*. Blackwell, London, 1–23.

Sterner, J. (2003). *The Ways of the Mandara Mountains*. Rüdiger Köppe, Cologne.

Street-Perrott, F. A., Holmes, J. A., Waller, M. P., Allen, M. J., Barber, N. G. H., Fothergill, P. A., Harkness, D. D., Ivanovich, M., Kroon, D., and Perrot, R. A. (2000). Drought and Dust Deposition in the West African Sahel: A 5500-year Record from Kajemarum Oasis, Northeastern Nigeria. *The Holocene* **10** (3): 293–302.

Togola, T. (1996). Iron Age Occupation in the Méma Region, Mali. *African Archaeological Review* **13** (2): 91–110.

Tymowski, M. (2005). Le territoire et les frontières du Songhaï à la fin du XVe et au XVIe siècle. Le problème du centre et des territoires périphériques d'un grand État de l'Afrique occidentale. In *Des frontières en Afrique du XIIe au XXe siècle*. UNESCO, Paris, 213–38.

Vaughan, J. H. (1970). Caste Systems in the Western Sudan. In Tuden, A., and Plotnicov, L. (eds.), *Social Stratification in Africa*. Free Press, New York, 59–92.

Vincent, J.-F. (1991). *Princes Montagnards: Les Mofu-Diamare et le Pouvoir Politique (Cameroun du Nord)*. Éditions Harmattan, Paris.

World Wildlife Fund. (2004). Terrestrial Ecosystems of the World: Afrotropics. http://www.worldwildlife.org/wildworld/profiles/terrestrial_at.html.

NOTES

1. Thus, for example, palaeolimnological data indicate an extremely severe drought period in northeastern Nigeria just over 1,000 years ago, with droughts succeeding periodically thereafter, at a time when lake levels in Lake Chad were still quite high (Maley, 1981; Street-Perrott et al. 2000).

2. It should be noted that when archaeologists, historians, and anthropologists speak of "leaders" and "elites" in and around the Mandara Mountains, they are in virtually all cases implicitly assuming such individuals to be males. This is in large part a function of the available data; there is

almost no consideration of female political roles in the ethnographic or historical literature of the Mandara region, except in some cases in the realm of myth (de Colombel 1985) and in semimythical Wandala historical accounts (Mohammadou 1982), which also have parallels in Hausa oral histories. However, ibn Fartuwa's contemporary account of the activities of the *gumsu* (principal wife) of the "ruler of Margi," in supporting her husband when he was being pursued by Mai Idris Alauma of Bornu (Alkali 1983; Lange 1987), implies the active participation of women in significant political functions in the region at that period. This question certainly deserves further consideration.

3. It also needs to be noted that the prior discussion implicitly privileges cultural relationships with plains populations to the north of the Mandara Mountains over relationships with other communities living farther to the south. In part, this is because a detailed comparison between archaeological research results to the north of the massif and those from sites to the southeast (Langlois 1995, in press) has not yet been undertaken; this must be a priority in future work. Almost no archaeological research has been undertaken to the south and southwest of the Mandara Mountains.

PART IV

CONCLUSION

12

The Local and the Global: Historiographical Reflections on West Africa in the Atlantic Age

Ray A. Kea

There is no History apart from Universal History which must be written as it really is.

(Leopold von Ranke)

INTRODUCTION

To begin, I would like to cite a statement made several decades ago by historian Marshall Hodgson. It serves as a point of reference and a point of departure for my reflections: "It was also necessary that there exist large areas of relatively dense, urban-dominated populations, tied together in a great interregional commercial network, to form the world market which had gradually come into being in the eastern hemisphere, and in which European fortunes could be made and European imaginations exercised" (Hodgson 1993:47). Hodgson introduces the idea of vast urban and commercial landscapes beyond Europe and contends that Europe's interactions with these landscapes were necessary social conditions for European mercantile profits and the emergence of an *imaginaire sociale* about exotic "Others" (Barker et al. 1985; Braudel 1982, 1984; Campbell 2006; Gallouët et al 2009; Mudimbe 1988; Said 1978; Wells and Stewart 2004). Investigations into the histories of the non-European world, including West Africa, are encouraging scholars to make fundamental reevaluations of conventional conceptions and interpretations of remote and recent pasts.

In an academic climate of historical revisionism, Hodgson's words still resonate because world regions beyond Europe are now, more often than not, subjects rather than objects in world history narratives and comparative world history studies. Evidence for this is abundant and can only be suggested here. Janet Abu-Lughod, for example, refers to the "complexly reticulated system of world production and trade" in pre-fifteenth-century Eurasia thereby decentering Europe as a focal point of investigation (Abu-Lughod 1989a, 1989b, 1990; also Chakrabarty 2000; Frank 1998). A wide range of other works has also challenged master narratives about the "miracle" of Europe's historical ascendancy and its role in the making of modernity. These works typify revisionist historiographies and new methodological approaches that set forth, in various strategic ways, conceptual and methodological shifts from Eurocentric master narratives and Europe as the domain of history, economics, political science, philosophy, and sociology to theoretical paradigms grounded, for example, in comparative and global perspectives. They ask reflexive questions and introduce new sources, methodologies, subjects of inquiry, and themes (Abu-Lughod 1989a; Bailyn and Denault 2009; Barendse 2002; Bin Wong 1997; Buck-Morss 2009; Burke and Prochaska 2008; Campbell 2006; Diawara 1990; Falola and Childs 2009; Frank 1998; Fuchs and Stuchtey 2002; Gills and Frank 1993a, 1993b; Greene and Morgan 2009; Guha 2002; Howard and Shain 2005; Jayasuriya and Pankhurst 2003; Mbembe 2001; Pomeranz 2000; Prestholdt 2008; Ross 1994; Zegeye and Vambe 2006). Constructing a revisionist West African past involves, in effect, the appropriation of decolonized modes of representing the subjects and objects of historical knowledge. The chapters in this volume indicate that the work of archaeologists is crucial to the development of any revisionist approach to the study of West African history (cf. Haour 2007; Holl 2006; Stahl 2009).

I find current archaeological research, masterfully exemplified in the preceding chapters, stimulating and groundbreaking in the varied ways it represents and explains the diverse historical forms of cultural, material, political, and social life in West Africa. It also provides West African historiographical practices with new premises and an expanded table of contents, thus allowing for a more complex understanding of the processes of West African history. The chapters describe in engaging detail different landscape sites, which extend across various historical moments (temporalities) and geographical scales (spatialities), from Senegambia to the Chadian basin. Through case studies they demonstrate that archaeological fieldwork effectively delineates the multiple empirical contours of West Africa's time and space in past centuries. Richard's account of the Siin kingdom presents a political landscape that differs considerably from the landscape of an imperial Oyo as described in Ogundiran's chapter. The Mandara political landscape, as analyzed by MacEachern, is vastly different from the landscapes of Hueda (Norman) and Bassar (de Barros). This kind of research is indispensable to historians' understanding of West African history, especially with regard to the complexity of cultural processes, the concrete specifics of material culture, and the production of identity, place, and locality. Monroe's analysis of the development of the Kingdom of Dahomey will oblige historians to rethink the processes at work in that kingdom's history and MacDonald and Camara's chapter on the Segu kingdom adds a new and detailed dimension to the development of its historical landscape. DeCorse highlights material and other features of the eighteenth- and nineteenth-century urban landscape of the Koinadugu Plateau, features that have hitherto escaped the eye of historians' investigations. Thiaw's study of Gajaaga and Bundu is an eye-opener because it illuminates details that escape the framework of standard historical interpretations of the Upper Senegal basin. Spiers' study of the Eguafo polity on the Gold Coast describes in careful detail the political and social transformations that occurred there in the context of an expanding Atlantic commerce. In short, archaeological research offers fascinating particulars that the historians' methods and interpretive procedures are unable to capture. I am not suggesting that historians hand over research on West African history to archaeologists who, of course, establish their disciplinary *praxis* through the production of their own objects of study, their own empirical and conceptual problems, and their own methodological procedures. I would suggest that if historians wish to produce illuminating and challenging narratives about West Africa in the Atlantic Era, they must engage, as integral to their investigations and paradigms, the kind of archaeological research and imaginative interpretations that are offered in this volume.

"Power and landscape" serves as a thematic point of departure and as a conceptual tool. Based on the volume's archaeological case studies, the editors propose three "broadly inclusive landscapes," namely "fragmented landscapes," "state-generated landscapes," and "internal frontier landscapes." Do these spatial categories define the historical specificity of West African social and political development? If they do, how is this achieved? What histories do the landscapes carry? What continuities, ruptures, and discontinuities do they engender? Linked to landscapes are practices, institutions, ideologies, and discourses that developed within particular worldviews. We may be assured that political, cultural, material, and social relations developed within the contexts of landscape-based histories. By grounding political landscapes in different historical and sociopolitical configurations, the editors seek to establish a dynamic relationship between the conceptually general and the historically concrete. For the discussion that follows, the editors' differentiation of landscapes is a useful starting point. They direct critical attention to the specificity of West African historical development. My historiographical reflections are intended to address as well as to complement archaeological conceptual and empirical understandings of West Africa's disparate landscape formation.

What is a "landscape" from a historian's perspective? A ready response is that the category "landscape" specifies history's geographical or spatial dimension. African historians have long recognized that there are sound reasons for a spatial approach to historical construction and interpretation (Howard 1999, 2000; Howard and Shain 2005). An implicit presupposition, as I see it, is that in the West African world region, a landscape is foundational and therefore general; and that place (locality) is contingent and therefore particular (for a discussion of "world region," see Frank and Gills 1993; Gills and Frank 1993a, 1993b; Hall 1996). For the purpose of my discussion, West Africa may be viewed as organized around the spatiality of landscape, place, and networks. "Power" may be deemed a constitutive and appropriative relationship with regard to language groups and linguistic relations, social organization, cultural systems, commercial networks and relationships, and political organization and political relations. Relations of power articulate particular cultural, economic, and social spaces, being discernable in a definable and designed life-world (*Lebenswelt*), which designates the self-evident or the given of social existence. Power is exercised within and across spatialities. A "landscape of power" is archaeologically revealed as a layered formation of differentiated strata ("stratigraphies") and as a historical "record" of events, actions, connections, and climatological and ecological processes. Above all, a landscape is a site of agency. From a conceptual and methodological standpoint, each stratum, as an archaeological or historical datum, implies a dense complexity of the products of history – knowledge(s), conventions, practices, technologies, institutional agencies, and representational systems or structures of meaning and thought (Allman and Parker 2005; Dawson 2009; Holl 2002). The landscape was the infrastructure of quotidian life.

World systems analysts identify four kinds of networks that define societal interaction and, I would add, landscape formation. They include (1) bulk goods networks; (2) prestige or luxury goods networks; (3) military-political networks; and (4) cultural-informational networks. The interacting networks constitute different levels and patterns of spatial integration, management, and organization. They expand and contract over time and, in the words of two historical sociologists, were "fundamentally social structures that include different cultural groups and polities within them" (Chase-Dunn and Hall 1997a:88, 90; 1997b:2; also see Braudel 1984). Across West Africa's landscapes was a dense and extensive field of network-based "social structures," each with its own geographical scale and its substantive content of managerial problems, techniques, and developments. Within them households, lineages, cultural groups, and polities accumulated wealth, public offices, rights, information, and power. Historically, the long-distance movements of goods and people throughout West Africa occurred to such a degree that interactive networks of flows became integral and indispensable to the maintenance of daily life and political rule, and to the shaping and reshaping of landscapes (Howard and Shain 2005; Sharpe 1986; Skinner 1964). Interacting networks were foundational in the shaping of the West African world region.

A HISTORIOGRAPHICAL EXCURSUS

The late Eric Wolf wrote that social patterns always occur in the multiform or the plural and are constructed in the course of historical interchanges, internal and external, over time (Wolf 1988). I would like to expand on the notion of historical interchanges and processes with reference to their subjective and objective components:

Humans make their world; they make their world in conditions they inherit and that are not all within their control; theoretically understanding this "making" involves redefining social structure and cultural institutions as not simply given but constituted, and hence containing the possibility of being changed. Culture is best appreciated as defining the realm of human choices in (potentially) definable contexts, choices of individuals as potentially self-aware agents.

(Mohanty 1989)

"Making a world," or, more to the point, making landscapes of power with their manifold social patterns, involves, from a materialist point of view, a considerable organization of social labor that, as the case studies show, is dense in its passages, habitations, and ateliers. Furthermore, making a landscape includes as a necessary circumstance culturally embedded, self-aware, and motivated social agents and structures and institutionalized agencies. I conceptualize the heterogeneous social patterns of a landscape in terms of its material, ideational (symbolic), and political life, its practices, and its historical interchanges. This way of understanding means presenting the details of a (spatialized) political economy (e.g., networks of interaction), the *mentalités* (e.g., beliefs, thought, ideas, values, ideology, religion, and language), and the subjective experiences and phenomenology of a social group or community (cf. Holl 2002; MacEachern 1994). The archaeological record identifies sequentially the materiality of a given community's world; however, in order to identify particular social actors in a community's history, archaeologists are obliged to resort to supplementary sources, such as oral and written documentation. The methodological question that arises concerns the conceptual articulation of archaeological evidence and historical evidence.

There is another matter of historiographical concern, namely chronology. The temporal scale of West African landscape formation and development is neither homogeneous nor necessarily continuous. Fernand Braudel's works demonstrate the complexity of chronological reckoning. His smallest temporal scale focuses on particular events or episodes and individual actors. He calls it the scale, or history, of events (*l'histoire événementielle*) or individual time. However, as Michel Foucault reminds us, there are actually a whole order of levels of different types of events differing in amplitude, chronological breadth, and capacity to produce effects (Foucault 1980:78–108). In other words, an event is a differentiated phenomenon. Braudel makes the argument that individual events can obscure their own context if they are subject to an inordinate focus. Thus, he recognizes a wider time dimension, one that contextualizes events. His second scale is "social" time or conjunctural history (*l'histoire conjoncture*). It represents the time of short- and medium-term change and encompasses a multitude of events. It highlights large-scale cultural, demographic, social, and economic changes over a period of decades or generations. Economies expand and contract, populations grow and shrink, and centers of wealth and power rise and fall and shift from one landscape to another. Seen through the wider lens of the conjuncture, individual events look very different. Braudel identifies a still larger temporal context. The third scale is "geographical" time or history of the long duration (*longue durée*), and it is measured according to centuries rather than decades or generations and encapsulates histories of events and conjunctures without conflating them. It refers to the scale of "material life" and those "structures of everyday life" that change very slowly and set limits to human action and interaction: diets and foodways, lifeways and productive methods, methods of transportation and communication, and patterns of demographic growth and decline (Braudel 1972a, 1972b, 1979, 1982, 1984). Social agents did not live their every day in homogeneous and linear time. DeCorse's account of the fortified towns on the Koinadugu Plateau discloses the effects of military and other events on urban settlement placement and displacement over conjunctural time. Monroe's description of the Dahomey kingdom evokes the impact of local events and regional and Atlantic conjunctural shifts on the kingdom's changing political, material, and social landscape configurations in the eighteenth and nineteenth centuries. In a similar vein, Spiers' account of post-fifteenth-century changes within Eguafo's settlement patterns and across its political landscape represent effects at specific local points or nodes where regional and Atlantic (global) phenomena were felt and acted upon. MacEachern's report on the Mandara political landscape and DGB sites is framed by *longue durée* and conjunctural perspectives, and he posits the interplay of historical events, social actions and processes, and climate change.

The case studies bring attention to two issues that are of historiographical interest to my own research agenda. One issue pertains to the actual construction of West Africa's history and the identification of the agents, agencies, and processes that populated and made that history. Appropriate frames of reference include constructs such as "human condition," "fate, fortune, and the distribution of well-being," "ways of being in the world," or the "order of things." Referential frames may be placed in event, conjunctural, or *longue durée* chronologies and may entail different historiographical approaches. For example, one may inquire about "ways of being in the world" or the "order of things" across the landscapes of Eguafo, Siin, Bassar, Oyo, Hueda, Dahomey, and inland Senegal. E. P. Thompson is famously known for having addressed certain features of historical life when he importuned historians to recall the "quality of life, the sufferings and satisfactions of those who lived and died in unredeemed time" by investigating in detail such issues as life expectancy, standards of living, technology, the distribution of income, debt levels, land and labor, and markets and commercialization (Thompson 1983). What, for example, does archaeological research in Eguafo, Siin, Gajaaga, Segu, Bassar, Hueda, Dahomey, and Oyo tell us about everyday life and the quality of life in these places for different segments of the population? I would argue quite a bit in the sense that the evidence and interpretive strategies of archaeological research point in the direction of larger historical issues and are not simply bound to the evidence of an excavated site or a surveyed expanse of sites. Braudel makes a clear distinction between the *longue durée* of material life, which is "made up of people and things," and the fast pace of economic life, which "begins at the fateful threshold of 'exchange value,'" and consists of markets, workshops, and long-distance commerce (Braudel 1979). MacEachern's study of Mandara and DeCorse's description of towns in northern Sierra Leone reveal aspects of West Africa's *longue durée*. Braudel's and Thompson's perspectives carry historical study into the realm of *Alltagsgeschichte* ("history of quotidian life") and *Alltagsleben* ("everyday life"). A focus on the quotidian does not imply a retreat into the particular but is a different way of allowing the big questions of process and structure to be posed. In my view, archaeological research has the potential to contribute significantly to a study of the everyday particular over the *longue durée*, thereby providing evidence that would enable historical studies to investigate what historical sociologist Charles Tilly calls "large processes," "big structures," and "whole populations" (Tilly 1984). The collective practices, social relations, and structured routines of everyday life organized spatial contexts or landscapes in which people produced and consumed and reproduced their languages, cultures, traditions, texts, classification systems, and organized social interests. The chapters on the Hueda and Dahomey kingdoms reveal some of these elements as integral to their historical landscapes. The same can be said about the chapter on Eguafo.

One of the historian's quests is to ascertain, through analyses of events, actions, and conjunctures, how people experienced the reality of their own activities. From the purview of archaeology, it is possible to engage analyses of stratified material culture sequences across the landscapes of Eguafo, Siin, Oyo, Gajaage, Bundu, Segu, and Bassar. But to engage the *mentalités* (subjectivities, attitudes, ideas, beliefs, etc.) of social actors, historians have to turn to other evidence, such as the vast corpus of centuries-old Arabic and Ajami writings from Timbuktu and elsewhere (Jeppie and Diagne 2008; Hunwick 1995, 2003; Kea 2003, 2010). The historian's charge is to make effective use of both sources of information in order to construct the details of everyday life with reference to events, conjunctures, and a long duration.

The second issue I wish to consider bears on the relationship between the historiography of West Africa and world history historiography. This is a topic that has been addressed in recent years by several Africanist historians and scholars who seek to decenter standard world history narratives that, because of their Eurocentric orientation, minimize and marginalize Africa's historical presence at a world-historical level (Ahluwalia 2005; Chrétien 2006; Keita 2001, 2002; Mbembe 2001; Smythe 2004). To counter the Eurocentric, I emphasize that West Africa, as a world region, was one of Marshall Hodgson's "large areas of relatively dense, urban-dominated populations, tied together in a great interregional commercial network." My point needs a brief elaboration.

Because of its gold production, West Africa was for centuries a center of the world economy. Economic historian Ian Blanchard's multivolume study aims to illustrate the history of mining, metallurgy, and the minting of gold and silver from the decline of the Roman Empire until 1575. This is a study over the *longue durée*. Blanchard asserts that there was a westward shift ("an industrial diaspora") of silver and gold production from Central Asia to Europe and Africa (with West Africa as the principal gold producer). He recognizes four main cycles of gold-silver production: a transitional period (930–1125); the first long cycle (1125–1225) of African-European supremacy in gold-silver production; the second long cycle (1225–1450); and the third long cycle (1450–1540/1575). During the third long cycle there occurred the transfer of supremacy in bullion production from Europe and Africa to the Americas. The flows of gold and silver between the two continents created in the Mediterranean basin in the twelfth century "a single Afro-European [bullion] market, which was characterized by the long term, stable distribution of gold and silver, as well as by falling prices which increased consumption, fuelling a new international economy which lasted for a further three centuries" (Blanchard 2001, 2005; De Rosa 2002; also Ross 1994). I contend that the global cycles of gold and silver production described by Blanchard were part of West Africa's *longue durée*.

There is every indication, as several studies have shown, that the central and western half of the pre-sixteenth-century world economy was based on African gold and that by means of this economy, one writer relates, "Africa continued as before to be fully integrated into the mainstream of world history and participated in its highest developments" into the early modern period (Ross 1994). Another study concludes that the continent's gold-bearing regions were so productive that by the fourteenth century Africa was supplying as much as two-thirds of the world's gold (west of the Straits of Malacca) (Banaji 2007; Blanchard 2001, 2005; Braudel 1972a, 1972b; also Haour 2007; Keita 2001; Lunde 2004; Messier 1974; Phillips 1998, chap. 8; Vilar 1984). Gold was exchanged in part for European copper for which West Africa was a huge market – to the extent that the demand for copper "may have contributed its share to the pressure to open up a sea route to West Africa" in the fifteenth century (Willett and Sayre 2006). The globalization of West African gold production and the, later, globalization of African labor were phenomena of world-historical dimensions. To fully appreciate these phenomena it is necessary for archaeological and historical scholarship to have a detailed knowledge of the landscapes of the West African local.

As a gold producer, West Africa participated fully at the center of the world economy, and any appraisal of "medieval" economic geography or of West African historical life has to take this role into account. The point cannot be overstated. A gold-producing West Africa was fundamental to the maintenance of the Mediterranean's commercial-monetary system (Blanchard 2001, 2005; Braudel 1972a, 1972b; Kea 2004; Ross 1994). Given the global significance of West African gold production, there is no valid reason why the historical development of places such as Gajaaga and the Middle Niger (Marka towns) and Chad basins (Kanem; Mandara) should not be accorded a proper rank in the economic geography of what is conventionally called the "medieval" world. These places were not marginal. My interpretation of archaeological data from West Africa necessarily considers West Africa's centrality in the operations of markets and capital in the Mediterranean and Islamic worlds (Kea 2004; Ross

1994). In what ways are this centrality and its structural legacy registered in the archaeological record of, say, Bassar, the Koinadugu Plateau, Oyo, Mandara, Gajaaga, and possibly Eguafo?

In the post-fifteenth-century period, landscapes of power should also be historically assessed in the same light, because the multicentric West African world region participated fully and centrally in the slave circuits that populated the plantations and mines in the Americas. This too was an activity of world-historical dimensions. It has been noted, for example, that the French slave trade transported more than a million Africans across the Atlantic to the islands of the Caribbean and that it enabled France to establish Saint Domingue as the single richest colony in the world. It was the "bank" that paid for France's eighteenth-century wars (Blackburn 1997; Miller 2008; Villiers 1993). It seems to me that the phenomenon of Saint Domingue cannot be separated from the structures and strategies of West Africa's interacting networks and political landscapes. The varied landscapes of Eguafo, Siin, Bundu, Gajaaga, Segu, Oyo, Hueda, and Dahomey, for example, were connected in one way or another to global slave circuits, and any historical assessment of landscape-based processes, events, relationships, and institutions must take the global dimension into consideration. The landscapes may be properly understood as local spaces of innovation, organization, differentiation, and specialization within a world regional order that was integrated into and, at the same time, constitutive of a post-fifteenth-century Atlantic world economy. In Atlantic Studies, at present, there is a fundamental contradiction between the very real absence of West African agency in the master narratives of the Atlantic world's mercantilism and its very real presence in the commercial, brokerage, and other transactions that took place on various landscapes of power in West Africa (cf. Bailyn 2005; Greene and Morgan 2009). The studies in this volume reveal that the terrain of the West African local was the site of a complex interplay of factors whose effects were in many instances translocal. A recent study of African knowledge systems spells out the relationship between the local and the global. The authors write, "African knowledge systems are the cultural expressions of the local that is not only in and of the global, but that it is the African globality from which Africa as subject can authorize views of itself, whether or not these views are taken seriously outside the continent" (Zegeye and Vambe 2006: 330–31; also Kea 2010).

If Africa's local knowledge systems are in and of the global and there is an African globality with Africa as its subject, then arguably West Africa's landscapes of power are in and of the global and are subjects of a historical African globality (Keita 2002; Ross 1994; also Lewis 1990, chap. 7). Thus, the events, actions, processes, organizations, and relationships that archaeological fieldwork has documented apropos of the landscapes of Eguafo, Oyo, Hueda, Dahomey, Bassar, Segu, the towns of the Koinadugu Plateau, Mandara, and Siin may not be regarded as local phenomena and nothing more, although it is the case that the local is "unique" and geographically specific and, historically speaking, is not necessarily and always counterpoised to the global (cf. Zegeye and Vambe 2006). Landscapes are to be perceived as constitutive and interactive components of a West African world region, and at different times and under varying conditions, they assumed global or world economy dimensions. From the sixteenth century onward, particular landscapes had differing relations to the globalization of African labor, a process that involved distinct forms of expropriation and mobilization at local levels, for example, in Oyo, Dahomey, Gajaaga, Segu, and Hueda. In these instances the local may be interpreted with reference to global relations and processes.

A perspective that embraces the idea of a West African globality dispenses with a Eurocentric notion of a one-sided incorporation of West Africa into an expanding, post-fifteenth-century European capitalism. Incorporation or integration is to be discerned as an encounter of two interacting historical processes, one European based and the other West African based. The encounter of the two implicates one facet of a dynamic world economy. The so-called Voyages of Discovery are to be read with reference to the global role West African gold played in the history of the Mediterranean basin as a whole, including the entire "Middle East," in the centuries prior to the sixteenth (Banaji 2007; Braudel 1979, 1982, 1984; also Campbell 2006). Historian Satoshi Ikeda elaborates on the matter of historical incorporation with reference to Asian history. His observation is relevant to the West African historical situation:

The recognition of the continuity of the Asian historical process before the formation of the European capitalist world-system to the present day and possibly beyond the period after the capitalist world-system not only challenges the European perspective but also provides an opportunity to expand the world-system perspective into a truly global perspective. Such a perspective will positively include the historical processes of the extra-European regions as crucial aspects of the transformation of the world-system, and it will consciously integrate various region-historical experiences for the formation of the richer and less region-biased concepts and categories for the understanding of modern history. (Ikeda 1996: 50–51)

Posited within the framework of world systems studies, Ikeda's analysis stipulates that the historical processes of extra-European regions have to be included in any study of an expanding capitalist world system. In this context, the processes that constituted West Africa as a world region have to be identified in any discussion of "incorporation." How do we speak of the incorporation of the Upper Senegal basin, representing multiple centers of organization, and the Hueda kingdom, representing a single organization, when these places were the subjects of their own historical processes, and their landscapes represent spaces of conscious historical interactions between social agents and their environment? In a revisionist historiography, the integration of the historical experiences of inland Senegal and Hueda into an expanding capitalist world economy means adding the "voices" of Senegalese and Huedan social agents in order to reframe master narratives about the development of the world economy in the Atlantic basin. Archaeology provides the data a revisionist historiography requires.

THEORIZING LANDSCAPES

The process of social/human space formation was a collective effort that involved the creation of historically specific (sub-) spaces at different temporal scales. The following passage provides a useful conceptual frame:

Spaces are created by social practices. Thus they are not universal, they are always historically specific. Spaces become socially important when they are constituted by myriad social practices. In this way they define a material spatiality of life. All spatialities are products of social agents: activities by people operating as the makers of space. There are makers of spaces of places who create worlds of "local" identities, and there are makers of spaces of flows who create worlds of connections. Through these social practices a spatiality is formed in which spaces of places and spaces of flows mutually exist but one which may be dominant.

(Taylor 2004:32)

Some of this may appear self-evident. Spaces of places and flows were endowed with different significations, depending on the motives and activities that produced them, so that the same spaces carried multiple meanings. Was this the case in Eguafo, Siin, Oyo, Segu, Hueda, Bassar, and Mandara? These landscapes may be identified with social-cultural agents, institutional agencies, and diverse social practices and events and long durations. Landscape configurations change over time as new agents, agencies, and practices emerge and older ones disappear or are drastically modified. Dahomey's defeat of the Hueda kingdom is an example of a radical reterritorialization of a conquered political landscape. Egaufo may serve as another example. There, between the seventeenth and nineteenth centuries, a political landscape, or at least sections of it, was transformed into a sacred landscape. The specificity of making or creating a "place" means giving a particular segment of space layered social-cultural meanings, whose creation occurs at the level of events and/or conjunctures (i.e., cyclical movements). Meanings and conjunctures may be identified archaeologically as stratified cultural sequences. Is this the case with the towns of northern Sierra Leone? A further point is that the making of spaces of flows or networks implies different kinds and scales of spatial interaction. The landscapes of Eguafo and the Siin Kingdom represent perhaps comparable geographical scales of activity and organization, but the Mandara political landscape represents a larger scale of societal interaction. In the *longue durée* of West African history, political, social, and cultural facts do not present themselves in discrete units in which biophysical space (e.g., ecological zones), production space (e.g., farmland), communication space (e.g., a route), political space (e.g., a battlefield), settlement space (e.g., a village), transactional space (e.g., a market), symbolic space (e.g., a cemetery), and cognitive space (e.g., mental mapping) seamlessly coincide. Thus, different kinds of spatially based activities crosscut one another in manifold intersects creating nodes of interaction and points of institution building that marked West Africa's regional dynamic in conjunctural and long durational time. The chapters on Eguafo, Oyo, Hueda, Dahomey, Segu, and Mandara conclusively demonstrate that the historical reality of intersecting and crosscutting conditions and activities complicates our understanding of West Africa's interactions with an expanding European capitalism.

In Gajaaga and Bundu, one can discern spatial-based activities where *tata* represented nodes of wealth accumulation, commercial and political interaction, and points of institution building, and adjacent European forts served as sites of commercial exchange and labor mobilization. Bassar, characterized by nonstate forms of power (before the nineteenth century), a resource extraction sector (iron ore mining), and an artisanal sector (based on smithery), developed the institution of chieftaincy in the nineteenth century as a centralized form of state power. In the eighteenth century in the Segu kingdom, the *Sifinso* settlement system – an institutional and cultural innovation – was linked to the kingdom's slave economy and the coercive power of the kingship. The hegemonic logic in operation in the political economies of the Hueda and Dahomey kingdoms generated the formation of palace-centered projects and complexes in the seventeenth and eighteenth centuries as nodes of interaction and sites of institution building and resource mobilization. Another case in point is the urban landscape of the Koinadugu Plateau. According to DeCorse, Koinadugu's fortified towns existed on the periphery of large-scale savanna-based societies to the north before the fifteenth century, and in the eighteenth and nineteenth centuries, they were on the periphery of Atlantic commodity circuits, because archaeological evidence indicates that European merchandise did not reach the area in large quantities before the twentieth century. He suggests that the imposition of destabilizing events in the form of raids and intense warfare resulted in the destruction and desertion of towns, the involuntary migration of people forced from their homes, and the founding of large, elaborately fortified towns of mixed populations. On the one hand, the towns were forcibly incorporated into interacting military-political networks, and on the other they were part of complex and thriving bulk and prestige-goods networks of interaction that extended deep into the interior (Howard 1976, 1999, 2000; Meillassoux 1971). In this historical situation, the towns may be described as nodes attached to different and conflicting interaction networks. In eighteenth-century Eguafo, Spiers observes that two contradictory and simultaneous developments at the height of the Atlantic slave trade were in evidence. On the one hand, there was the visible accumulation of wealth and an abundance of imported trade goods in the polity, but on the other hand there was marked political instability in the kingdom. What was the structural imbalance? It seems to me that this question has to be addressed at a regional level. Expanding Atlantic and regional commerce, I would argue, required political and spatial "fixes" of increasing scale and scope to accommodate the material expansion of trading capital; hence the eighteenth-century emergence and territorial expansion of the coastal Fante Federation and the inland Asante kingdom. Wars would have played a crucial role in destabilizing and diminishing local political capital in places like Eguafo, but at the same they created the conditions for the expansion of local and regional merchant capital.

There is another structural dimension that defines the historicity of landscapes of power. Spaces of flows, spaces of places, and spatially based activities were tied to cycles and regimes of surplus (or wealth) extraction and accumulation. A regime of accumulation may be defined as a "field" within which wealth is deployed and relations of power operate. Together, surplus extraction and accumulation constituted the internal dynamic or systemic logic of the West African world region. Andre Gunder Frank and Barry K. Gills underline the historical significance of accumulation from a world system perspective:

> Accumulation implies infrastructural investment and technological development. Infrastructural investment takes many forms in many sectors, such as agriculture, transportation, communication, the military, industrial and manufacturing infrastructure, and bureaucratic administration. There is investment even in ideological (symbolic) infrastructure, both of the cult of the state and religion.... The ultimate rationale of such investment would in all cases be to preserve, enhance, and expand the basis of accumulation itself.
>
> (Frank and Gills 1993b)

Both authors recognize "cyclical rhythms" and "secular trends" within what they call a 5,000-year-old world system. Their focus is on the accumulation of surplus and on capital accumulation as a driving force in the expansion and dynamic of the world system (Gills and Frank 1993b). This is a *longue durée* perspective. The power centers of the West Africa region functioned as sites or nodes of accumulation that, across the histories of events and conjunctures, operated at different levels of organization and effectiveness.

Associated with elite accumulation strategies and structures are regimes of surplus extraction. A surplus extractive system may be characterized as "an ensemble of inter-societal networks in which the interactions [e.g., trade and warfare] are important for the reproduction of the internal structures of the composite units and importantly affect changes which occur in these local structures" (Gills and Frank 1993b). Interacting networks were also crucial to processes of wealth extraction and accumulation. Segu's sociopolitical organization represented one kind of accumulation and surplus extraction formation, and in this respect it differed from the sociopolitical organizations found in Eguafo, Siin, Gajaaga, Bundu, Hueda, Dahomey, Bassar, and Oyo.

There are other ways of theorizing a landscape. Two categories, initially formulated in world systems analyses, are "global commodity chain" (or "global value chain") and "socio-natural regime" (or "eco-historical regime"). As conceptual tools, they may be used to examine relations between the local sociopolitical organizations, with their modes and strategies of extraction and accumulation, and the wider world. In addition, both categories define particular kinds of spaces of flows (networks) and spaces of places (localities; nodes). They relate not only to the production, circulation, distribution, exchange, and consumption of commodities, but they also relate to various practices and institutional and organizational formations. Both are integral to any study of the history of commodification and commodity values in West Africa (cf. Ehret 2002, chap. 5 and 7).

Simply defined, a commodity chain is a particular kind of interacting network or a complex of networks that result in a finished product or commodity (bulk goods or luxuries). It designates the varied ways in which productions are linked to one another. In a more elaborate definition, it may be described as a "network of labor and production processes whose end result is a finished commodity," which is situationally specific, socially constructed, and locally integrated (Gereffi and Korzeniewicz 1994; Quark 2008). The chain is embedded in labor and production processes and relations that form a mode of production of the material conditions of life. It has three systemic features: an input-output structure (i.e., a sequence of value-adding economic activities); territoriality (i.e., spatial dispersion or concentration); and a governance structure (i.e., authority and power relationships) (Quark 2008). Commodity chains were not static constructs because commodities were subject to valorizing processes. Hence a chain embodied other constitutive features, such as speech fields (discursive communities), speech networks (multilingualism), and multiple significations. Gold and slave commodity chains were global in their extent. The Upper Senegal basin (Gajaaga and Bundu) contained gold-producing sites and input-output structures in the form of occupational specialization and markets, territoriality, and governance or political structures that determined resource allocation. Social agents, in the face of events, acted in relation to chains either hegemonically or counterhegemonically.

A socio-natural regime refers to the construction of social, geographical, and ecological relations that are negotiated within one or more commodity chains by ruling elites or leading social groups (Quark 2008). The following description identifies its characteristics:

> The construction of rules, norms, and decision-making practices that create and recreate a particular configuration of matter, space, and society, in a commodity chain (and in relation to other commodity chains). That is, a socio-natural regime is generated through social struggle to manipulate social actors, matter, and space and thus create the specific ecological, geographical, and social relationships within a commodity chain.... The construction of a socio-natural regime determines which people and places can participate in the commodity chain, the terms under which they can participate, and thus the social, geographical, and ecological along the commodity chain. Social, geographical, and ecological relationships are not mutually exclusive, however, but rather are mutually constructed.
>
> (Quark 2008; also Balée 2006)

A socio-natural regime existed in and shaped a geophysical space or ecological environment in the sense that there was an environmental dimension to various economic and political ventures. In organizational terms, it may be associated with places of production and places of consumption for different kinds of commodity chain networks. Its creation entailed cultural, military, and political struggles of competing social actors or factions who sought to make a regime that would serve their interests, interests that are expressed in mixed ideological, cultural, symbolic, or religious forms (Quark 2008). At any given historical moment, the problems facing and solutions available to political, military, or commercial leaders may differ, as they attempted to construct a socio-natural regime to serve their interests, that is, to fashion cultural, social, geographical, and ecological relationships to overcome key constraints to their relations of appropriation (Quark 2008).

The monumental and massive structures to be found on the landscapes of Hueda and Mandara and the fortresses (*tata*) and walled towns that dotted different West African landscapes – Oyo, the Koinadugu Plateau, Gajaaga, Bundu, Mandara, and Dahomey – raise questions about the construction and destruction of public spaces, or what has been called "social commons," and struggles over the appropriation of the commons in the Atlantic Age. A social common (e.g., land, water, forests) is defined as an area of social existence that emerged as commons through active social struggles in the past and were subsequently formalized through institutional norms and practices as communal possession (De Angelis 2007, chap. 17). Historians have not examined this issue in any depth. Is this topic relevant to archaeological research agendas? What is the connection between social commons, their appropriation and reappropriation, and commodity chains, socio-natural regimes, and West African globality?

Ogundiran's account of Oyo's imperial expansion reveals the formation of a socioeconomic regime that was tied to different commodity chains and to other kinds of interacting networks. Oyo represents a particularly powerful geopolitical "sector" or political landscape in the Atlantic basin. Ogundiran describes it as an Atlantic Age empire, an indication of its dominance with respect to a network of global commodity chains related to the commerce in slaves. Establishing a new regime of surplus accumulation, Oyo-Ile's leaders were able to reorganize and reregulate commodity chains through a concentration of military-political power in a time of mercantile expansion. Imperial expansion enacted different strategies of rule, and these strategies of rule represent the creation of a socio-natural regime. There was an integrated ensemble of districts, polities, and cities held together by an imperial tribute-trade system centered on Oyo-Ile that regulated relations among various political jurisdictions. Excavations at Ede-Ile, apparently the early "colonial enclave" of an expansionist Oyo core area, provide data concerning the dynamic of Oyo's colonization project or, in world system's language, the formation of an expansive socio-natural regime. Ede-Ile's creation in the seventeenth century was a political and administrative act and marked a commercial and political frontier of the Oyo imperial system. With the founding of Ede-Ile, ecological space was changed, as baobab trees, a dry-zone flora in a rainforest environment, were deliberately introduced and maintained. Horse breeding took place at the site, and this phenomenon may be linked to a commodity chain for horses that were probably imported from the Nile Valley and North Africa. Occupational specialization and social differentiation were evident, and the presence of cowries, glass beads, and tobacco pipes indicate that Ede-Ile was integrated into long-distant commodity circuits and diverse market spheres, and accompanying these developments was the region-wide adoption of new taste and consumption patterns in the imperial hinterland. Did imperial expansion mean the appropriation or destruction of communal possessions by state authorities and the creation of new commons in the form of "colonial enclaves" like Ede-Ile?

The eighteenth-century Segu kingdom is another example of a socio-natural regime. It was at the crossroads of an expanding Atlantic trading system and a dense and thriving Saharan and regional trade (Abitbol 1979:178–218; Batran 1974; Hunwick 2003). The creation of a socio-natural regime may be associated with particular strategies and policies: wealth accumulation through dispossession, the breaking of established "stateless" gerontocracies, the converting of various forms of property into exclusive royal holdings, and the founding of *Sifinso*. The heartland of eighteenth-century Segu was a state-generated landscape, which represented the militarization of Middle Niger commodity chains. These were culturally and socially assimilated into the normative functioning of the state's socio-natural regime. The Segu ruler seems to have appropriated communal property (of gerontocracies) for royal purposes. Did the *Sifinso* constructions represent an appropriated social commons and the transfer of wealth and property to a slave collective (*ton jon*)?

Archaeological fieldwork reveals that local elites in inland Senegal (Gajaaga and Bundu kingdoms) responded to an expanding Atlantic economy by erecting strongholds or *tata*, which reflected the wealth and prestige of ruling elites and would seem to signal the militarization of commodity chains. The *tata* functioned as an institutionalized centerpiece of the Upper Senegal basin's socio-natural regime. In contrast, there were short-term occupation sites known as *plages*, which were the dominant form of settlement in the basin. The volatile and violent politics of the wealth-accumulating *tata* contributed to the instability and transitory nature of lowland or *plage* settlements of slaves and peasants whose agency, as makers of places, was reflected in population mobility, migration, and frequent settlement abandonment. The Atlantic commercial frontier extended into the area through an alliance of French merchant capital and local elite sociopolitical strategies and structures. Armed and fortified commodity chain networks characterized the growth and expansion of Atlantic commerce. We can differentiate between the space of the everyday – a *locus* where *subactuelle* pottery was produced – from the space of intense commercial activity and surplus accumulation, principally the *tata*.

The division between the everydayness of *plage* settlement and the commercial and accumulating capacities of *tata* sites was the source of an alienation grounded in the impermanence of places created by political subordinates and the permanence of commodity flows maintained by dominant elites and the expropriation (?) of the *plages'* social commons. In the eighteenth and nineteenth centuries, social agents (Muslim *mujahidun*) transformed particular landscapes in Upper Guinea into new sites of governance and surplus accumulation. Successful jihadist movements (e.g., the Futa Jallon jihad and Umar Tal's jihad) and the Juula revolution that brought Samory Turay to power gave rise to new socio-natural regimes (see, e.g., Person 1968, 1975). Were the struggles in the Upper Senegal basin organized around the appropriation and reappropriation of social commons and the creation of new social commons? Did the population mobility of peasants and slaves reflect the expropriation of social commons by the owners of fortresses? What social commons did jihadists create?

A different example comes from the seventeenth- and early-eighteenth-century Hueda kingdom, as described in Norman's informative chapter. As a commercially oriented polity, the Hueda kingdom was a vital component in the Atlantic economy. Between 1680 and 1727, more than a million enslaved men, women, and children passed through the world port of Hueda en route to the Americas, where they would live in perpetual intimacy with regulated physical violence. The resources and wealth of Savi, the political capital of then Hueda kingdom, were tied to the plantation economy of the Caribbean and the Americas. The kingdom was a court society dominated by a court culture, based at Savi. An essential technology of the royal court/palace regime and its role in the export of slaves was the circulation of violence through legitimated practitioners – factors, interpreters, boatmen, merchants, company's slaves, and mercenaries and guardians of the dominion. The royal palace was both the localization and institutionalized logic of the polity's production of judicial, religious, commercial, and spatial dominion. There was a court politics of deterritorialization as the palace, as a commanding institution, absorbed the wealth of Atlantic commodity trade, and the countryside remained a marginal space outside of the circuits of Atlantic capital but dependent on it. The production of the palace-based regime of power was realized through situated apparatuses and institutions (the military, the temple, the market, the trading factory), which in turn circulated power socially through various embodiments (symbolic orderings, rituals and ceremonies, and military technologies). The kingdom's capital and provincial centers were distinguished by monumental architectural structures built by rural labor. Are they evidence of the private (political) appropriation of the commons by political elites? Were communal lands and forests transferred to elites who built massive (private) structures on the appropriated commons?

The disintegration of Hueda kingdom, following its military defeat by Dahomean military forces, signaled a radical deterritorialization of one socio-natural regime and the immediate emplacement of another. In the seventeenth century, the Dahomean royal court/palace appears to have functioned like a military camp: it was expansionist oriented. In the eighteenth century, it had become a multifunctional institution, administering trade, mining, agriculture, crafts, and warfare. It was the central organizer of a new socionatural regime in Lower Guinea following the conquest of the Hueda kingdom. The Dahomean political landscape reveals a complex process of royal centralization, which was implemented through the palace and the palace system. The multifunctional palace regime constituted a complex, ritualized production of Dahomey state institutionality, coherence, and intelligibility across a wide territorial expanse. Eighteenth- and nineteenth-century palace construction projects engendered the densification of administration and political management. These projects were underpinned by the monetization of the Dahomey economy through the imposition of a cowrie shell currency by royal fiat, which established its standard of value and fixed the prices of special commodities (Gregory 1996).

After the eighteenth century, the dynamic of Dahomey's landscape seems to have been tied to a strategy that sought to politically unify social processes of production, distribution, and circulation across the rural–urban division of labor. In the nineteenth century, an "agricultural revolution" led to the "overall ruralization of the Dahomean economy." The building of palace complexes marked the establishment of a "central-place hierarchy of palace centers" across the landscape, and this hierarchy became the foundation of a re-formed socio-natural regime. Monroe argues that the expansion of royal authority into the countryside contributed to the ruling elite's reconceptualization of rural districts from sites of tribute payment (appropriation of use-vales) to commodity-producing sites (appropriation of exchange-values). In this context, one may ask whether the higher echelons of the Dahomey political order, in alliance with local merchant capital, were engaged in the appropriation of new areas of rural and urban life and social existence in the service of its accumulation priorities. Is there a centuries-long process of royal appropriation of rural commons and the transfer of communal possessions to the ruling classes?

The coastal Siin kingdom is said "to have oscillated between a variety of political arrangements throughout its history, from loosely integrated village communities to centralized polity." François Richard proposes an alternative history. What does archaeology tells us about Siin in the era of Atlantic slaving? Richard identifies two levels of authority – centralized monarchial rule at a regional level and dispersed authority at the local or village level. In the kingdom's heartland, there is no evidence of population decline, militarization of settlements, settlement abandonment, or settlement hierarchy. There is evidence of spatial dispersion of settlements. Siin was at the consumption or consumer end of a global commodity chain. How was its socio-natural regime organized? There was a market dominated by consumption of goods valued by the aristocracy and a market dominated by consumption of goods valued by peasants. Aristocratic families created a culture of conspicuous or luxury consumption. They played enterprising, defining, and controlling roles in the international market. Upper-class culture seems to have emerged as a domain in which economic and political contradictions were ritualistically expressed and symbolically resolved through lavish feasting. What does the *longue durée* of Siin history reveal with regard to struggles over the extraction and consumption of surpluses and the creation and destruction of social commons?

Historically, the Greater Voltaic Plateau where Bassar was located was a *locus* of complicated deployments – economic, cultural, demographic, political, and religious – across different landscape formations. A dense web of prestige and bulk-goods networks and cultural-information networks crisscrossed the region. From the fifteenth century it was dominated by several centralized (Islamic) polities – Dagomba, Mamprusi, Gonja, and Tyokossi (Chokossi) – and from the eighteenth by Asante (Wilks 1986, 1989; Wilks, Levtzion, and Haight 1986). The rise of the Bassar Chiefdom in the midst of "small, decentralized groups" represents another kind of landscape dynamic. A politically defined "internal frontier" becomes the site of a centralized polity in the nineteenth century. For centuries Bassar was a center of economic specialization based on a highly centralized agglomeration of iron production. De Barros examines the rise of the Bassar Chiefdom in the context of an internal frontier space, a space he describes as a political space. I would like to extend his meaning of "frontier" by recognizing Bassar as a frontier in economic specialization (concentration), that is, an economic space. For the purposes of this discussion the historical development of specialization can be understood in two senses. In one sense, there was political specialization in the form of hierarchically and centrally organized state systems and an area of political specialization characterized by noncentralized organizations. In a second sense, there was economic specialization in the form of geographically specialized centers of production, such as food production or iron production, where scale economies existed. That is to say, there existed concentrations of productive activities at particular locations. There were other areas where scale economies did not exist. The boundaries between areas of political specialization (centralization), on the one hand, and economic specialization (concentration), on the other, formed a frontier that shifted across time and space according to intensity and duration of centrifugal and centripetal forces.

The structuring and the legitimization of the Bassar Chiefdom were realized through social ideologies of property, for example, technical knowledge (a cultural capital) and right, for example, first- or latecomer status (a social capital). De Barros' account would seem to indicate that at its highest levels the chiefdom constituted and generated a highly flexible and varied "library" of methods, terms, categories, and techniques that, at a critical time, mediated relationships among a diverse population, instituted ceremonial, ritual, and prescriptive exchanges and relationships, and provided continuity through time, space, and societal depth. Was a socio-natural regime being created in this period in order to accommodate the intensification of plateau traffic along global commodity chains, or were other processes at work? What was the fate of social commons in Bassar after the founding of a chieftaincy?

WORLD-HISTORICAL CONNECTIONS

I would like to return to the issue of local–global relations by considering the connections West Africa's political landscapes maintained with the Atlantic and Mediterranean systems (Mitchell 2004; Ross 1994). As a point of departure, I cite two accounts, one by historian Paul Lovejoy and the other by anthropologist Claude Meillassoux. I begin with Lovejoy:

> For the fortunate few in Africa, as well as for the European slave merchants and slave owners in the Americas, the [Atlantic] slave route led to military success, political power, and commercial gain that enabled a level of prosperity and influence strongly affecting the organization of society and the development of culture in Africa. The towns and cities of western Africa had their palaces and courts, public gardens, prayer grounds, market places and commercial districts, as well as mosques, shrines, and, even in a few places, churches. At the centers of commercial and political power the elite was often literate, at least by the sixteenth century in Muslim towns and by the eighteenth century at the ports along the Guinea coast and in the courts of the major states in the immediate interior. Towns and cities were closely linked to the Muslim centers of North Africa and the Middle East, to the European-dominated Atlantic rim, or to both. The existence of these connections, whether to the Islamic or the transatlantic world, was long denied or misrepresented in European and North American scholarship, but a close examination of the historical record, as biographical accounts make clear, suggests otherwise. Moreover, the emphasis on memory and on the oral preservation of traditions has, to some extent, obscured the importance of literacy in connecting western Africa to the wider world. The oral tradition continued to function in the context of local religious, political, and social structures, but much of western Africa was not isolated from the Islamic and Atlantic worlds. The literate culture connected the Muslim elite to the Islamic heartland and to a "westernized" elite along the Guinea coast to the European-dominated Atlantic. Despite the scourge of slavery, the cultural history of western Africa reveals a level of education and a complexity of social interaction that demonstrates that many places in Africa were in the mainstream of world history.
>
> (Lovejoy 1997)

In terms of world systems analysis, Lovejoy specifies the cultural, ecological, economic, and social by-products of West Africa's socio-natural regimes that were globally connected via "slave routes." In particular, it is of interest that new social commons were created. West Africa's cultural history brings to light the successes of the "fortunate few," and, as he sees it, these successes ought to place West Africa "in the mainstream of world history."

Meillassoux also describes the effects of "slave route" connections, but he makes a particular point to judge the massive social cost of the successes of the "fortunate few":

The Mediterranean slave trade, followed by the Atlantic trade, spurred the formation of pillaging bands, predatory states, and market towns. These structures for waging war and commerce established to supply slaves and to export them to distant lands, contributed to the propagation of slavery on African soil and engendered huge disparities in wealth. While the slave trade devastated the peasant populations, who saw their children . . . abducted by brigands or armed troops and sold to dealers in human chattel, it brought great wealth to rapacious kings, *caboceiros*, and merchants in the market towns, as well as to aristocrats, mercenaries, and sycophants of the royal courts. Through a perversion of memory, the sumptuous trappings of the predatory kings and their go-betweens left behind a dazzling image of the slave trade as a prestigious undertaking, while the peasants who fell victim to it remained mired in wretched poverty and anonymity.

(Meillassoux 1997; also Diagne 1992)

Meillassoux views the Mediterranean and Atlantic connection as a source of instability, impoverishment, displacement, and dispossession across West Africa's political landscapes. The scenario that he presents is one in which social commons – rural communal possessions – were systematically destroyed. Does archaeological evidence document the same structural polarity that Lovejoy's and Meillassoux's descriptions separately identify – "prosperity and influence" on one side and "wretched poverty and anonymity" on the other? Both descriptions are emblematic of the complexities and contradictions of historical experience and the relationships and structural arrangements that shape it. Does Meillassoux's account apply to events in the Upper Senegal basin, in Bassar, in Eguafo, and on the Koinadugu Plateau? Do events and developments in the history of the Hueda kingdom support Lovejoy's and Meillassoux's descriptions? At one point in its history Hueda enjoyed stability, prosperity, and peace, demonstrating that it was "in the main stream of world history," but, at another time, its political landscape lay in ruins and devastation following the invasion of Dahomean armies. Do the Siin kingdom and the towns of the Koinadugu Plateau represent counterexamples to the scenarios presented by Lovejoy and Meillassoux?

Lovejoy and Meillassoux establish the interconnectedness of West African landscapes and the Atlantic and Mediterranean systems. The nature of the relationship is spelled out by Ikeda: "The regionalization of the processes of the capitalist world-system goes hand-in-hand with the globalization of non-European regional processes in the global capitalist world-system" (Ikeda 1996:64). In other words, relations of interdependence globalized West Africa's regional processes, on the one hand, and regionalized the processes of an expanding European-based capitalist world system, on the other. The processes and institutions at work in these relations of interdependence transformed people and nature into "raw materials" for the production of commodities. Arguably, the case studies in this volume provide a framework and hard evidence (for historians) for questioning the economic systems, projects, processes, and social agents that transformed the earth and humans into sellable objects. Atlantic mercantilism was part of large-scale political developments, not just in Europe but also in West Africa.

Drawing on a comment made by Braudel, historian Maghan Keita remarks that "Europe could not have developed the New World without Africa and Africans," and without the Americas there would be no modern capitalism. One argument maintains that the eighteenth-century Atlantic slave trade was more vital to European capital accumulation than slave-based commodity production in the Americas. Keita lays emphasis on West Africa's central position in the Atlantic world system (Keita 2002; Braudel 1984). In his multivolume study of the shaping of the Americas, historical geographer D. W. Meinig makes a salient point when he comments that between the sixteenth and nineteenth centuries there was a greater transfer of labor out of Africa than out of Europe (Meinig 1986). The organizing of massive labor transfers in various West African landscapes takes on a global and far-reaching historical dimension. In their studies of "plantation America," Sidney Mintz and James Blaut argue that industrialization began on commodity-producing American plantations and in South American silver mines, and that enslaved African labor – the *pieza*, a *locus* of surplus value ("abstract labor") and a "natural" social necessity – was indispensable in the capitalist world system's valorization process (Richardson 1991; Wynter 1992). No other system, Blaut relates, was as significant as the plantation system for the rise of capitalism before the nineteenth century. Sugar production and the slave trade, that is, the globalization of enslaved African labor as a force of production and globalization of the regional processes that generated captive bodies, created a global economy in the course of the seventeenth and eighteenth centuries (Blaut 1993; Braudel 1984; Mintz 1986; also Baucom 2005; Blackburn 1997; Higman 2000; Linebaugh and Rediker 2000:45–46; Santiago-Valles 2005; Tomich 2004). Under these historical circumstances it is no wonder that historian William Martin could state that world system analysis, like the capitalist world economy, has "deep African roots" (Martin 2006:381). These "roots" are embedded in the dynamic of West Africa's political landscapes.

The globality of West Africa's post-fifteenth-century polities has another, often overlooked, aspect. In the introduction to their study of metals and monies in the early modern world, two economic historians pose an interesting question. "How did African gold tie in at the global level?" They explain: "The Spanish crown needed European financiers to transfer gold to soldiers in Flanders, who always demanded at least part of their pay in gold. American silver was therefore exchanged for African gold in Italy, whereupon American silver headed off to China and African gold was forwarded to the Low Countries. African gold and slaves were both exchanged for American silver" (Flynn and Giráldez 1997:xxvii, xxviii). From this account, we are to understand that in the seventeenth century West African gold "subsidized" Spain's military occupation of the Low Countries and this gold, together with slaves, was exchanged for American silver. In other words, the global circulation and exchange of African gold were essential to Spain's military dominance in Flanders and the Netherlands. The Netherlands represents a *terminus* of consumption within a global gold commodity chain that stretched from the places where gold was produced, namely the Upper Niger and Upper Senegal basins, to sites of exchange and distribution (Marka towns) in the Middle Niger basin, across the Sahara to maritime Europe. Did the eighteenth-century Segu kingdom attempt to create a socio-natural regime, with the *Sifinso* as a centering institution, in order to dominate the sites of gold production and distribution?

There is another commercial context that throws light on the global exchange of West African gold. In the concluding chapter of his magisterial study of the seventeenth-century Indian Ocean world, Dutch historian R. J. Barendse relates that seventeenth-century trade between Europe and Asia was dominated by American silver and African gold (Barendse 2002:491). He expounds further that there were periods, for example, in the early sixteenth century and in the 1670s, when West African gold financed European commercial operations in India and other parts of Asia. What are the material representations of this commercial relationship in the archaeological record? What can excavated sites tell us about the global exchange of West African gold if the sites are viewed with reference to a Mediterranean and Indian Ocean dimension?

Barendse brings attention to another matter of substance. Even in the great "boom" period of the Atlantic slave trade, he notes, the trans-Saharan trade too was "booming" and was not in decline, contrary to a widespread viewpoint. Indeed, one study contends that from the fourteenth to the sixteenth century "the traffic of the Saharan caravans was certainly on a larger scale and more lucrative than the maritime traffic of the Mediterranean" (Chambers 2008). The commerce of the West African interior was much more oriented towards North Africa and the Nile Valley (Egypt and Nubia) than towards the Atlantic coast. Barendse continues:

Although I personally think the trans-Saharan slave trade remained about the same in volume, it is possible that the slave trade along the Saharan routes . . . declined by the late sixteenth century but this was more than compensated by an increase in trade with other commodities – salt, copper, iron, textiles, weapons, etc. . . . the slave trade made some groups very poor, but others very rich so that you should expect increasing demand for both bulk and prestige-commodities from North Africa in West Africa (after all, this is a period of Islamization in West Africa entailing a market for prestige commodities from the Islamic heartland in West Africa). The Sahara trade and the trans-Atlantic trade were thus not competing circuits – they were to a large extent complementary.

(Barendse, n.d.; also Meillassoux 1971)

The complementary nature of the Saharan and Atlantic commercial systems introduces a historical dimension that has to be taken into account in archaeological and historical studies of West Africa. The West Africa world region incorporated Saharan economic and commercial life (Goodwin 2006, pt. 3; Lydon 2005; McDougall 1991; also Abulafia 2006).

The *longue durée* of Saharan–Chadian commercial relations is evident in MacEachern's discussion of the Mandara political landscape. His presentation may be examined with reference to a statement by a historian of the Mediterranean island of Malta: "There seems to be little doubt that Malta was an important link in an economic and cultural chain that stretched from King Duname's [Dunama Dibalami, 1210–48] thirteenth century empire of Kanem to Lake Chad northwards to the Mediterranean Sea and on into Italy, and probably Malta" (Goodwin 2002:28).

The time frame corresponds to the first long cycle of gold and silver production in the Mediterranean system and a "commercial revolution" in the Mediterranean bullion market (Lopez and Raymond 2001). It also corresponds to a period when the Chad basin was a major focus of economic and politico-cultural activity and a key crossroad of global transformation, as manifested in Chadian (Kanem's) territorial expansion into the Central Sahara and its imperial dominance of a vast system of interacting networks and episodes of intense economic, political, and cultural development on the Chad basin (cf. Haour 2007; Holl 2002). The fact that Chadian basin polities and towns are named in fifteenth- and sixteenth-century Italian sources (Fra Mauro and d'Anania) and that they may have been symbolically represented in post-twelfth-century Hohenstaufen religious iconography (within the Holy Roman Empire) would suggest the global role of Chadian landscapes in the Mediterranean basin (Kaplan 1987; Lange 1972; cf. references to Chadian lands, specifically Bornu, in Martorell's and de Galba's (1983) fifteenth-century Catalonian novel *Tirant Lo Blanc*). Do the immense and architecturally distinct DGB sites denote new public spaces (property), that is, social commons, and the rural appropriation of new wealth coming out of a Chadian-based imperial system? Were wealth and property generated in bulk goods and other networks the basis for creating new social commons?

CONCLUSION

As the case studies have shown, West Africanist archaeologists have developed different procedures and methodologies in order to interpret the West African past. Their research has established the radical and empirical specificity of the West African local. The editors' conceptual and synthesizing introductory chapter provides a major reassessment of the dynamics that drove West African history in the Atlantic Age. Yet, at the same time, as my reflections have tried to suggest, West African landscapes/polities, as singular sites of agency and autonomy, need to be recognized as having shared histories and interconnections with other parts of the world. Archaeology can contribute greatly to a historical understanding of the centrality of West Africa in world history. It can serve as a point of reference for revisionist thinking among West African historians and, at the same time, have an impact on the perspectives of world history historiography, Atlantic world studies, African diaspora studies, Black Atlantic studies, Mediterranean studies, and world systems studies.

BIBLIOGRAPHY

Abitbol, M. (1979). *Tombouctou et les Arma*. Maisonneuve and Larose, Paris.

Abulafia, D. (2006). Mediterraneans. In Harris, W. V. (ed.), *Rethinking the Mediterranean*. Oxford University Press, Oxford, 64–93.

Abu-Lughod, J. (1990). Restructuring the Premodern World System. *Review* **13** (2): 273–86.

Abu-Lughod, J. (1989a). *Before European Hegemony: The World System A.D. 1250–1350*. Oxford University Press, New York.

Abu-Lughod, J. (1989b). On the Remaking of History: How to Reinvent the Past. In Kruger, B., and Mariana, P. (eds.), *Remaking History*. Bay, Seattle, 110–29.

Ahluwalia, P. (2005). Out of Africa: Post-Structuralism's Colonial Roots. *Postcolonial Studies* **8** (2): 137–54.

Allman, J., and Parker, J. (2005). *Tongnaab: The History of a West African God*. Indiana University Press, Bloomington.

Bailyn, B., and Denault, P. L., eds. (2009). *Soundings in Atlantic History: Latent Structures and Intellectual Currents, 1500–1830*. Harvard University Press, Cambridge, MA.

Balée, W. (2006). The Research Program of Historical Ecology. *Annual Review of Anthropology* **35**: 75–98.

Banaji, J. (2007). Islam, the Mediterranean, and the Rise of Capitalism. *Historical Materialism* **15** (1): 47–74.

Barendse, R. J. (2002). *The Arabian Seas: The Indian Ocean World of the Seventeenth Century*. M. E. Sharpe, Armonk, NY.

Barendse, J. R. (n.d.). Integration of Asia in the World-System. Unpublished paper. World Systems Network.

Barker, F., Hulme, P., Iverson, M., and Loxley, D., eds. (1985). *Europe and Its Others*, 2 vols. University of Essex, Colchester.

Batran, A.-A. (1974). The Qadiriyya-Mukhtariyya Brotherhood in West Africa: The Concept of Tasawwuf in the Writings of Sidi al-Mukhtar al-Kunti (1729–1811). *Transafrican Journal of History* **4** (1–2): 41–70.

Baucom, I. (2005). *Specters of the Atlantic: Finance Capital, Slavery, and the Philosophy of History*. Duke University Press, Durham, NC.

Bin Wong, R. (1997). *China Transformed: Historical Change and the Limits of European Experience*. Cornell University Press, Ithaca, NY.

Blackburn, R. (1997). *The Making of New World Slavery: From the Baroque to the Modern, 1492–1800*. Verso, London.

Blanchard, I. (2001). *Mining, Metallurgy and Minting in the Middle Ages, vol. 2: Afro-European Supremacy, 1125–1225*. Franz Steiner, Stuttgart.

Blanchard, I. (2005). *Mining, Metallurgy and Minting in the Middle Ages, vol. 3: Continuing Afro-European Supremacy, 1250–1450*. Franz Steiner, Stuttgart.

Blaut, J. M. (1993). *The Colonizer's Model of the World: Geographical Diffusionism and Eurocentric History*. Guilford, New York.

Braudel, F. (1972a). *The Mediterranean and the Mediterranean World in the Age of Philip II*, vol. 1. Translated from the French by Sian Reynolds. Harper & Row, New York.

Braudel, F. (1972b). *The Mediterranean and the Mediterranean World in the Age of Philip II*, vol. 2. Translated from the French by Sian Reynolds. Harper & Row, New York.

Braudel, F. (1979). *Civilization and Capitalism, 15th–18th Centuries*, vol. 1. Translated from the French by Sian Reynolds. William Collins, Glasgow.

Braudel, F. (1982). *Civilization and Capitalism, 15th–18th Centuries*, vol 2. Translated from the French by Sian Reynolds. William Collins, Glasgow.

Braudel, F. (1984). *Civilization and Capitalism, 15th–18th Centuries*, vol. 3. Translated from the French by Sian Reynolds. William Collins, Glasgow.

Buck-Morss, S. (2009). *Hegel, Haiti, and Universal History*. University of Pittsburgh Press, Pittsburgh.

Burke, E., III, and Prochaska, D., eds. (2008). *Genealogies of Orientalism: History, Theory, Politics*. University of Nebraska Press, Lincoln.

Campbell, K. (2006). *Literature and Culture in the Black Atlantic: From Pre- to Postcolonial*. Palgrave Macmillan, New York.

Chakrabarty, D. (2000). *Provincializing Europe: Postcolonial Thought and Historical Difference*. Princeton University Press, Princeton, NJ.

Chambers, I. (2008). *Mediterranean Crossings: The Politics of an Interrupted Modernity*. Duke University Press, Durham, NC.

Chase-Dunn, C., and Hall, T. D. (1997a). *Rise and Demise: Comparing World Systems*. Westview, Boulder, CO.

Chase-Dunn, C., and Hall, T. D. (1997b). Ecological Degradation and the Evolution of World-Systems. *Journal of World-Systems Research* **3** (3): 403–33. http://jwsr.ucr.edu/archive/vol3/v3n3a3.php.

Chrétien, J.-P. (2003). Pourquoi l'Afrique, pourquoi l'histoire? *Afrique & Histoire* **6**, http://www.editions-verdier.fr/v3/oeuvre-afriquehistoire-1.html.

Dawson, A. C., eds. (2009). *Shrines in Africa: History, Politics and Society*. University of Calgary Press, Calgary.

De Angelis, M. (2007). *The Beginning of History: Value Struggles and Global Capital*. Pluto, London.

De Rosa, L. (2002). Review Article. I. Blanchard, Minting, Metallurgy, and Mining in the Middle Ages, vol.1. *The Journal of European Economic History* **31** (1): 197–201.

Diagne, P. (1992). African Political, Economic, and Social Structures during this Period. In Ogot, B. A. (ed.), *UNESCO General History of Africa V. Africa from the Sixteenth to the Eighteenth Century*. University of California Press, Berkeley, 23–45.

Diawara, M. (1990). Reading Africa through Foucault: V. Y. Mudimbe's Reaffirmation of the Subject. *October* **55**: 80–92.

Falola, T., and Childs, M. D., eds. (2009). *The Changing Worlds of Atlantic Africa: Essays in Honor of Robin Law*. Carolina Academic Press, Durham, NC.

Flynn, D. O., and A. Giráldez (1997). Introduction. In Flynn, D. O., and Giráldez, A. (eds.), *Metals and Monies in an Emerging Global Economy*. Variorum, Aldershot, xv–xl.

Foucault, M. (1980). *Power/Knowledge: Selected Interviews and Other Writings 1972–1977*. Edited by Colin Gordon. Translated by Colin Gordon et al. Pantheon, New York.

Frank, A. G. (1998). *ReOrient: Global Economy in the Asian Age*. University of California Press, Berkeley.

Frank, A. G., and B. K. Gills (1993). The 5,000 Year World System: An Interdisciplinary Introduction. In Frank, A. G., and Gills, B. K. (eds.), *The World System: Five Hundred Years or Five Thousand?* Routledge, London, 3–58.

Gills, B. K. and Frank, A. G. (1993). The Cumulation of Accumulation. In Frank, A. G., and Gills, B. K. (eds.), *The World System: Five Hundred Years or Five Thousand?* Routledge, London, 81–114.

Fuchs, E., and Stuchtey, B., eds. (2002). *Across Cultural Borders: Historiography in Global Perspective*. Rowman & Littlefield, Lanham, MD.

Gallouët, C., Diop, D., Bocquillon, M., and Lahouati, G., eds., (2009). *L'Afrique du Siècle des Lumières: Savoirs et Représentations*. Voltaire Foundation, Oxford.

Gereffi, G., and Korzeniewicz, M., eds. (1994). *Commodity Chains and Global Capitalism*. Greenwood, Westport, CT.

Gills, B. K. and Frank, A. G. (1993a). The Cumulation of Accumulation. In Frank, A. G., and Gills, B. K. (eds.), *The World System: Five Hundred Years or Five Thousand?* Routledge, London, 81–114.

Gills, B. K., and Frank, A. G. (1993b). World System Cycles, Crises, and Hegemonic Shifts, 1700 BC to 1700 AD. In Frank, A. G., and Gills, B. K. (eds.), *World System: Five Hundred Years or Five Thousand?* Routledge, London, 143–199.

Goodwin, S. (2006). *Africa's Legacies of Urbanization: Unfolding Saga of a Continent*. Lexington, Lanham, MD.

Goodwin, S. (2002). *Malta, Mediterranean Bridge*. Bergin & Garvey, London.

Greene, J. P., and Morgan, P. D., eds. (2009). *Atlantic History: A Critical Appraisal*. Oxford University Press, Oxford.

Gregory, C. A. (1996). Cowries and Conquest: Towards a Subalternate Quality Theory of Money. *Comparative Study of Society and History* **38** (2): 195–217.

Guha, R. (2002). *History at the Limit of World-History*. Columbia University Press, New York.

Hall, T. D. (1996). World-Systems and Evolution. *Journal of World-Systems Research* **2** (4): 1–42. http://jwsr.ucr.edu/archive/vol2/v2_n4.php.

Haour, A. (2007). *Rulers, Warriors, Traders, Clerics: The Central Sahel and the North Sea, 800–1500*. Oxford University Press, Oxford.

Higman, B. W. (2000). The Sugar Revolution. *Economic History Review* **53** (2): 213–36.

Hodgson, M. (1993). *Rethinking World History: Essays on Europe, Islam, and World History*. Edited, with an introduction and conclusion, by Edmund Burke III. Cambridge University Press, Cambridge.

Holl, A. F. C. (2002). *The Land of Houlouf: Genesis of a Chadic Polity 1900 BC–AD 1800*. The Museum of Anthropology, Ann Arbor.

Holl, A. F. C. (2006). *West African Early Towns: Archaeology of Households in Urban Landscapes*. Museum of Archaeology, Ann Arbor, MI.

Howard, A. M. (1976). The Relevance of Spatial Analysis for African Economic History: The Sierra Leone-Guinea System. *Journal of African History* **17** (3): 365–88.

Howard, A. M. (1999). Mande and Fulbe Interaction and Identity in Northwestern Sierra Leone, Late Eighteenth Through Early Twentieth Centuries. *Mande Studies* **1**: 13–39.

Howard, A. M. (2000). Mande Identity Formation in the Economic and Political Context of North-West Sierra Leone 1750–1900. *Paideuma. Mitteilungen zur Kulturkunde* **46**: 13–35.

Howard, A. M., and Shain, R, M., eds. (2005). *The Spatial Factor in African History: The Relationship of the Social, Material, and Perceptual*. African Social Science Series. Brill, Leiden.

Hunwick, J. O. (1995). *Arabic Literature of Africa, vol. 2: The Writings of Central Sudanic Africa*. Brill, Leiden.

Hunwick, J. O. (2003). *Arabic Literature of Africa, vol. 4: The Writings of Western Sudanic Africa*. Brill, Leiden.

Ikeda, S (1996). The History of the Capitalist World-System vs. the History of East-Southeast Asia. *Fernand Braudel Center Review* **19** (1): 49–77.

Jayasuriya S. S., and Pankhurst, R., eds. (2003). *The African Diaspora in the Indian Ocean*. African World Press, Trenton, NJ.

Jeppie, S., and Diagne, S. B., eds. (2008). *The Meanings of Timbuktu*. HSRC, Cape Town.

Johnson, M. (1970a). The Cowrie Currencies of West Africa, Part I. *Journal of African History* **11** (1): 17–49.

Johnson, M. (1970b). The Cowrie Currencies of West Africa, Part II. *Journal of African History* **11** (3): 331–53.

Kaplan, P. H. D. (1987). Black Africans in Hohenstauffen Iconography. *Gesta* **26** (1): 29–36.

Kea, R. A. (2003). Science, Technology, and Learning: Eighteenth Century Moliyili (Dagomba) and the Timbuktu Intellectual Tradition. In Lauer, H. (ed.), *History and Philosophy of Science for African Undergraduates*. Hope, Ibadan, 238–70.

Kea, R. A. (2004). Expansions and Contractions: World-Historical Change and the Western Sudan World-System (1200/1000 B.C.–1200/1250 A.D.). *Journal of World-Systems Research* **10** (3): 723–816.

Kea, R. A. (2010). Intellectual Life and Scholarship in the Islamic Western Sudan during the Seventeenth and Eighteenth Centuries: A Political and Social View. In Lauer, H., and Anyidoho, K. (eds.), *Reclaiming the Human Sciences and Humanities through African Perspectives*, 2 vols. Sub-Saharan Publishers, Accra, vol. 1: 730–750.

Keita, M. (2002). Africa and the Construction of a Grand Narrative in World History. In Fuchs, E., and Stuchtey, B. (eds.), *Across Cultural Borders: Historiography in Global Perspective*. Rowman &Littlefield, Lanham, MD, 285–308.

Keita, M. (2001). Conceptualizing/Re-conceptualizing Africa: The Construction of African Historical Identity. *Journal of African and Asian Studies* **36**: 331–37.

Lange, D. (1972). L'Intérieur de l'Afrique Occidentale d'après Giovanni Lorenzo Anania (XVIe Siècle). *Cahiers d'Histoire Mondiale* **14**: 299–351.

Lewis, B. (1990). *Race and Slavery in the Middle East: An Introductory Inquiry*. Oxford University Press, New York.

Linebaugh, P., and Rediker, M. (2000). *The Many-Headed Hydra: Sailors, Slaves, Commoners, and the Hidden History of the Revolutionary Atlantic*. Beacon, Boston.

Lopez, R. S., and Raymond, I. W. (2001). *Medieval Trade in the Mediterranean World: Illustrated Documents Translated with Introductions and Notes*. Columbia University Press, New York.

Lovejoy, P. E. (1997). Daily Life in Western Africa during the Era of the "Slave Route." *Diogenes* **45** (1): 1–19. http://dio.sagepub.com/content/45/179/1.full.pdf+html.

Lunde, P. (2004). Monsoons, Mude, and Gold. *Saudi Aramco World* **56**: 4–11.

Lydon, G. (2005). Writing Trans-Saharan History: Methods, Sources, and Interpretations across the African Divide. *Journal of North African Studies* **10** (3–4): 293–324.

MacEachern, S. (1994). "Symbolic Reservoirs" and Inter-Group Relations: West African Examples. *African Archaeological Review* **12**: 205–24.

Martin, W. G. (2006). Africa and World-System Analysis. A Post-Nationalist History? In Philips, J. E. (ed.), *Writing African History*. University of Rochester Press, Rochester, NY.

Martorell, J., and de Galba, M. J. (1983). *Tirant Lo Blanc*. Translated by David H. Rosenthal. Schocken, New York.

Mbembe, A. (2001). Ways of Seeing: Beyond the New Nativism. *Introduction. African Studies Review* **44**: 1–14.

McDougall, E. A. (1991). The Quest for "Tarra": Toponymy and Geography in Exploring History. *History in Africa* **18**: 271–89.

Meillassoux, C. (1997). The Slave Trade and Development. *Diogenes* **45** (1): 23–29. http://dio.sagepub.com/content/45/179/23.full.pdf+html.

Meillassoux, C., ed. (1971). *The Development of Indigenous Trade and Markets in West Africa*. Studies presented at the Tenth International African Seminar at Fourah Bay College, Freetown, December 1969. Oxford University Press, London.

Meinig, D. W. (1986). *The Shaping of America: A Geographical Perspective on 500 Years of History, vol. 1: Atlantic America, 1492–1800*. Yale University Press, New Haven, CT.

Messier, R. A. (1974). The Almoravids, West African Gold, and the Gold Currency of the Mediterranean Basin. *Journal of the Economic and Social History of the Orient* **17** (1): 31–41.

Miller, C. L. (2008). *The French Atlantic Triangle: Literature and Culture of the Slave Trade*. Duke University Press, Durham, NC.

Mintz, S. W. (1986). *Sweetness and Power: The Place of Sugar in Modern History*. Penguin, New York.

Mitchell P. (2004). *African Connections: Archaeological Perspectives on Africa and the Wider World*. AltaMira, Walnut Creek, CA.

Mohanty, S. P. (1989). Us and Them: On the Philosophical Bases of Political Criticism. *Yale Journal of Criticism* **2** (2): 1–31.

Mudimbe, V. Y. (1988). *The Invention of Africa: Gnosis, Philosophy, and the Order of Knowledge*. Indiana University Press, Bloomington.

Person, Y. (1968). *Samori, une Révolution Dyula; la Renaissance de l'Empire Mandingue*, vols. 1 and 2. Institut Fundamentale l'Afrique Noire, Dakar.

Person, Y. (1975). *Samori, une Révolution Dyula; la Renaissance de l'Empire Mandingue*, vol. 3. Institut Fundamentale l'Afrique Noire, Dakar.

Phillips, J. R. S. (1998). *The Medieval Expansion of Europe*. 2nd ed. Clarendon, Oxford.

Pomeranz, K. (2000). *The Great Divergence: Europe, China and the Making of the Modern World Economy*. Princeton University Press, Princeton, NJ.

Prestholdt, J. (2008). *Domesticating the World: African Consumerism and the Genealogies of Globalization*. University of California Press at Los Angeles.

Quark, A. A. (2008). Toward a New Theory of Change. Socio-Natural Regimes and the Historical Development of the Textiles Commodity Chain. *Review* **31** (1): 1–37.

Richardson, D. (1991). Prices of Slaves in West and West-Central Africa: Toward an Annual Series, 1698–1807. *Bulletin of Economic Research* **43** (1): 21–56.

Ross, E. S. (1994). Africa in Islam: What the Afrocentric Perspective Can Contribute to the Study of Islam. *International Journal of Islamic and Arabic Studies* **11** (1): 1–36.

Said, E. W. (1978). *Orientalism*. Pantheon, New York.

Santiago-Valles, K. (2005). World-Historical Ties among "Spontaneous" Slave Rebellions in the Atlantic. *Review* **28** (1): 51–83.

Sharpe, B. (1986). Ethnography and a Regional System: Mental Maps and the Myth of States and Tribes in North-Central Nigeria. *Critique of Anthropology* **6** (3): 33–65.

Skinner, E. P. (1964). West African Economic Systems. In Herskovits, M. J., and Harwitz, M. (eds.), *Economic Transition in Africa*. Routledge and Kegan Paul, London.

Smythe, K. R. (2004). Africa in the World: Lessons from Africa for World History. *Teaching History: A Journal of Methods*, vol. **29**: 23–35.

Stahl, A. B. (2009). The Archaeology of African History. *International Journal of African Historical Studies* **42** (2): 241–44.

Taylor, P. J. (2004). Material Spatialites of Cities and States. *ProtoSociology: An International Journal of Interdisciplinary Research* **20**: 30–45.

Tilly, C. (1984). *Big Structures, Large Processes, Huge Comparisons*. Russell Sage Foundation, New York.

Tomich, D. W. (2004). *Through the Prism of Slavery: Labor, Capital, and World Economy*. Rowman & Littlefield, Lanham, MD.

Thompson, E. P. (1983). Visions of History/by MARHO. In Abelove, H. (ed.), *The Radical History Organization*. Manchester University Press, Manchester, 51.

Vilar, P. (1984). *A History of Gold and Money, 1420–1920*. Translated by Judith White. Verso, London.

Villiers, P. (1993). The Slave and Colonial Trade in France Just before the Revolution. In Solow, B. L. (ed.), *Slavery and the Rise of the Atlantic System*. Cambridge University Press, Cambridge.

Wells, B. R., and Stewart, P., eds. (2004). *Interpreting Colonialism: Studies on Voltaire and the Eighteenth Century*, no. 9. Voltaire Foundation, Oxford.

Wilkinson, D. (1987). Central Civilization. *Comparative Civilizations Review* **17**: 31–59.

Wilks, I. (1989). *Asante in the Nineteenth Century: The Structure and Evolution of a Political Order*. Cambridge University Press, Cambridge.

Wilks, I. (1986). The Mossi and the Akan States. In Ajayi, J. F. A., and Crowder, M. (eds.), *History of West Africa*, vol. 1. Longman Group Limited, Harlow, 465–502.

Wilks, I., Levtzion, N., and Haight, B. M. (1986). *Chronicle from Gonja: A Tradition of West African Muslim Historiography*. Cambridge University Press, Cambridge.

Willett, F., and E. V. Sayre (2006). Lead Isotopes in West African Copper Alloys. *Journal of African Archaeology* **4** (1): 55–90.

Wolf, E. (1988). Inventing Society. *American Anthropologist* **15** (1): 752–61.

Wynter, S. (1992). Beyond the Categories of the Master Conception: The Counterdoctrine of the Jamesian Poiesis. In Henry, P., and Buhle, P. (eds.), *C.L.R. James' Caribbean*. Duke University Press, Durham, NC, 63–91.

Zegeye, A., and Vambe, M. (2006). *African Indigenous Knowledge Systems. Review* **29** (4): 329–58.

Index

Abomey, 152, 192, 194, 196, 200–202, 204–206, 208–210, 220
Abomey Plateau, 151, 166, 191, 195, 197, 198, 200, 202, 207, 209, 212
Abomey Plateau Archaeological Project, 197
Abrem, 121, 130, 134
Abu-Lughod, Janet, 340
Accra, 123, 133
acculturation, 51
Adom, 121
Afro-Europeans, 50, 63, 69
Agaja, 149, 220, 221
Agbaje-Williams, Babatunde, 224, 240
Agbangala, 149
agricultural surplus, 57, 119, 132, 200, 302
agriculture, 59, 127, 169
  and settlement patterns, 50
  and slavery, 170, 171, 180. *See also* Segou
  as infrastructure, 354
  in Bassar region, 257
  in Bundu, 57
  in Dahomey Kingdom, 208, 211–213, 221, 360
  in Gajaaga, 57
  in Hueda Kingdom, 150
  in Lake Chad Basin, 326
  in Oyo Ile, 222
  in Senegambia, 71
  in Sierra Leone, 288
Ahanta, 121
Aissa Dugjé, 317, 318, 328
Aja, 191
Aja-Fon region, 19
Aja-Yoruba region, 191, 192

Akani, 19, 122–124
Alauma, Idris, 312
alcohol, 101, 102, 115, 148, 155
alcoholism, 84, 102
Allada, 26, 147, 191, 195, 198, 204, 205, 221
Almamy Dynasty, 54
Al-Yakūbī, 170
Al-Zuhri, 170
Amadji, 61
Americas, 1, 347, 349, 359, 363, 365
Anatolia, 228
Anderson, David, 142
Andes Mountains, 245
Apomu, 243
Arabic, 49
architecture
  and ethnic identity, 244
  cement, 66
  defensive. *See also* Bundu, Gajaaga, *tata*
  dry-stone, 29, 318, 323
  fired red brick, 66
  in Bassar region, 265
  in Bundu, 61, 66
  in Dahomey Kingdom, 195
  in Gajaaga, 60, 61, 66
  in Hueda Kingdom, 360
  in Sierra Leone, 291–296, 299, 300
  military, 66
  mud, 22, 61, 65, 66, 292, 300
  sand, 66
  stone, 22, 50, 65, 66, 293, 299
Arhin, Kwame, 131
Arimey, 215
Arondo, 59, 68

378

INDEX

Asante, 130, 266, 268, 354
Asia, 226, 347, 350, 366
assimilation, 51, 314
Assin, 123
Astley, Thomas, 142, 150
Atakpa, Chief Ouro Bassabi, 262, 272
Atherton, John, 280, 301
Atkins, John, 159
Atlantic Basin, 1, 7, 241, 351, 357
Atlas of African Prehistory, xvi
Atofosie, 129, 130, 133
Aujas, Louis, 84
Awo, 229, 237, 242
Axim, 123
Aysan, 149

Bacili Sempera Dynasty, 53, 54
Bafodia, 286, 297, 298
Baghirmi, 312
Bakel, 54, 55, 68
Bamana, 174, 175, 177
Bambuxu, 55
Banankoro, 182–184
Banda, 9
Bandjeli, 257, 261, 266, 268, 270
Bando Road, 130
Bangaraku, 268
Bani River, 180
baobab trees, 235–237, 242, 244–248
Barendse, R.J., 366–367
Bassar Mountain, 262
Bassar region, 18, 27–28, 255–274, 341,
        347, 353, 355, 361–362
    burial practices in, 265
    conflict in, 264, 273
    effects of iron production on, 264,
        265–268
    effects of slave trade on, 257, 264,
        268–270
    exports, 257
    fire dances in, 264
    firstcomers, 263
    immigration to, 257–260, 261, 266, 268,
        270, 271, 273
    imports, 266, 271
    iron industry, 28, 255, 257, 263,
        362
    role of chief in, 28, 263–264
    selection of chiefs in, 274
    slavery in, 28, 257, 266
    women in, 270
Bazin, Jean, 172, 176, 177
beads
    carnelian, 57

Czech, 101
European, 65
glass, 63, 231, 239, 300, 357
gold, 128
in Bassar region, 266
in Eguafo, 115, 130
in Hueda Kingdom, 149, 158
in Senegal, 57
in Siin Kingdom, 100, 101
stone, 128
Venetian, 101
Behanzin, 221
Bénin, 9, 17, 22, 25, 191
Benin City, 19
Benin Kingdom, 243
Bérenger-Féraud, Laurent, 84
*Beyond Chiefdoms: Pathways to Complexity
    in Africa*, 171
Biakpabe, 261, 262–263, 272
Bight of Benin, 9, 24, 27, 147, 243. *See also*
    Dahomey
Binaparba, 261, 270
Biriwa Limba Chiefdom, 286
Birni Ngazargamo, 325
Bissib, 261, 266, 270
Bitchabe, 257, 261, 268, 270
Blanchard, Ian, 347, 348
Blaut, James, 365
Blyden, Edward, 295
Bono-Mansu, 266
Bornu, 312, 315, 325, 328
Bosman, Willem, 150
bowls, xvii, 148, 230, 231–234, 235
brass, 231
Braudel, Fernand, 344–346, 365
bread, 148
Brenu Akyinim, 125, 129
British
    abolition of slave trade, 55, 124, 283
    in Eguafo, 120, 122, 124
    in Gold Coast, 124
    in Senegambia, 52, 55, 57
    in Sierra Leone, 283, 284, 285, 287, 288
    trade, 49, 55, 120, 124
British Sierra Leone Protectorate, 284
Brooks, George, 280, 290
Bukpassiba, 262, 268, 270
Buleban, 61
bulk goods, 343, 353, 355, 368
Bumban, 298
Bunce Island, 283
Bundu, 50, 54, 57, 59, 61, 62, 67, 70, 290,
        341, 347, 352, 355, 356
    agriculture in, 57

and the French, 55, 56
architecture in, 61, 66
conflict in, 57
conquest of Gajaaga, 54
elites in, 67, 70, 358, 359
growth of, 62, 64, 65, 70
migration from, 58
military, 62
origins of, 54
rule by Almamy, 54, 55
slavery in, 57, 349, 358
trade in, 57, 67, 70
burial practices, 130, 133, 134, 244, 265
Burkina Faso, 261, 271, 284
Burton, Richard, 206–215
Bussen, 175, 176

Cadamosto, Alvise, 98
Camara, Seydou, 25–26, 341
Cameroon, xiv, 27, 29, 311, 314, 329
Cana, 195, 202, 204, 205, 208–210, 214,
	220
capitalism, 1, 8, 31, 350, 351, 352, 364,
	365, 366
Caribbean Sea, 349
cassava, 257
cattle, 85, 180, 257, 264, 266, 268, 295
	enclosures, 66
cavalry, 238, 243, 317. *See also* horses
cemeteries, 65, 116, 129, 131, 133
census, 68
Central Region Project, 116, 125
ceramics, xvii, 244, 265, 297
	earthenware, 102, 154
	European, 100–102, 292
	in Bassar region, 265
	in Ede-Ile, 230–235, 242, 244, 246
	in Eguafo, 115, 125, 128–130
	in Hueda Kingdom, 152, 153, 155, 158
	in Mandara, 319
	in Oyo-Ile, 234
	in Senegal, 57, 65
	in Sierra Leone, 292, 294, 297, 300–301,
		319, 320
	in Siin Kingdom, 90, 101, 102
	stoneware, 102
Chad, 314
Champion, Timothy, 8
charcoal, 56, 257, 260
Chari-Logone River, 322
chiefdoms
	simple, 285
chiefdoms, defintion of, 260
China, 366

Chouin, Gérard, 125
clay, 101, 156, 230, 265, 300
client states, 224
climate change, 63, 326, 345
cloth, 57, 99, 115, 148, 257. *See also* textiles
	Kotokoli, 270
Coconut Grove, 126, 129
Cohen, David, 86
colonies, definition of, 226–229, 242
colonization, 31, 58, 225, 226, 228. *See also*
		Oyo Empire
	according to world-systems theory,
		241
	and the Americas, 1
	costs of, 240
	definition of, 228
	French, 56
commercial revolutions, 2, 6, 9, 11, 22,
	26, 222
commodity chains, 355–358, 361, 362,
	366
Compagnie de Galam, 55
conquest, 5, 227
	as a form of imperial expansion, 224
	of Allada, 192
	of Dahomey Kingdom, 192, 200
	of Gajaaga, 54
	of Hueda Kingdom, 25, 159, 160, 352,
		360
consumption, 6, 9, 31, 101, 119, 348, 357,
	361
copper, 57, 115, 130, 348
Coquery-Vidrovitch, Catherine, 119
Cornevin, Robert, 261, 266
cotton, 57, 176, 293
Coulibaly Dynasty, 174, 178, 180, 183
Coulibaly, Malamine, 180
Coulibaly, Tiema, 178, 180
Coulibaly, Zoumana, 175
cowpeas, 257
cowry, 177, 230, 231, 239, 243, 266, 357,
	360
Cross, William, 123, 124

Dagomba, 257, 261, 262, 266, 268, 271,
	272, 361
Dagomba War, 257
Dahomey, 191–216, 224, 341, 345, 346
Dahomey Kingdom, xvi, 25, 26, 147, 350,
	355, 356, 360–361
	agriculture in, 208, 211–213, 221, 360
	conquest by French, 192
	countryside, 192, 194, 196, 199, 201,
		208, 210, 212, 213, 215, 216, 360

Dahomey Kingdom (*cont.*)

elites in, 26, 194, 199, 200, 208, 209, 211, 212, 216, 360

expansion of, 149, 159, 160, 192, 201, 216, 352

exports, 211

feasting in, 199, 200

human sacrifice in, 195

in the eighteenth century, 201–207

in the nineteenth century, 216

in the seventeeth century, 198–201

kings, 192, 194, 196, 198, 204, 206, 209, 213

Adandozan, 207

Agaja, 196, 201, 202, 204, 205, 208

Agonglo, 202, 204

Akaba, 200

Behanzin, 208

Cana, 202

Dakodonu, 202

Gezo, 207–209, 212

Glele, 208, 209

Kpengla, 202, 205, 207

Tegbesu, 195, 202, 207

Wegbaja, 200

palace construction in, 26, 195, 197, 198, 200, 202, 204, 208–210, 221

palaces in, 194–216, 353, 360

Agrigonmey, 200, 202, 208

Dahomey Kingdom, 200

political organization of, 192

rituals in, 198, 200, 202, 204, 206–210

royal wives, 196

ruralization of, 211, 213, 215, 360

slave trade in, 202, 211, 216

slavery in, 205, 349

soldiers in, 197

taxation in, 196, 208, 213–215

Tokpo, 213

trade in, 201, 205, 210, 211

tribute in, 198, 199, 200

urbanization of, 202

violence in, 195, 211

women in, 157

Xwetanu, 195, 196, 204, 206, 208, 209

Yovogan, 205

Dakodonu, 195

Dalzel, Archibald, 204

Dan, 195

Dara, 61

David, Nicholas, 325

Davies, Oliver, xiii

de Barros, Philip, 18, 27–28, 341, 362

de la Fosse, Eustache, 120

de Marees, Pieter, 122, 133

de Pina, Rui, 120

Debu, 61

DeCorse, Christopher, xi, xiii, xiv, 9, 13, 28, 29, 121, 145, 341, 345, 346, 353

deforestation, 56, 69, 257, 271

Dekpassanware, 265, 270

Dembélé, Macoma, 183

DGB sites, 29, 325, 326, 329, 345, 368

Dhar Tichitt, 18

Dia, 175, 186

Diakhao, 89, 93, 98, 102

diamonds, 280

Diara Dynasty, 177

Diara, Monzon, 180, 183

diaspora, 161, 186, 228, 347

Dikre, 262, 263, 266, 268, 272

Dikre, forest of, 260, 262, 263, 272

Dimuri, 257, 270, 271

Diop, Momar-Coumba, 86

Diouf, Mamadou, 86, 87

Diouf, Niokhobaye, 114

disease, 55

Djita, 61

Djowul Mountain, 268

Dompow, 116, 125, 128, 130, 131, 133

draft furnaces, 271, 272

Drame, Mamadu Lamiin, 56, 66, 68

drought, 321, 322, 325, 326, 328, 335

Dugast, Stephan, 261–263, 266

Duncan, John, 213, 214

Dutch, 49, 120, 121, 122, 134, 149

Dyunfung, 61

Ede-Ile, 27, 225, 226, 229, 243, 252, 357, 358

ceramics, 231–235, 242, 244, 247

early colonists of, 239, 241

excavations, 229

origins of, 230

Edina, 130

Efutu, 120, 121, 135

Eguafo, 22, 23–24, 115–135, 341, 346, 347, 352, 353, 355

borders of, 121, 135

cemeteries in, 116, 129, 131, 133

decline of, 130

farming in, 126, 127, 132

gold in, 123, 130, 132, 134, 135

imports, 353

in present day, 116

in the sixteenth century, 125, 126–128, 135

in the seventeenth and eighteenth centuries, 125, 128–130, 135

in the nineteenth century, 125, 130–131
king of, 123, 124
merchants in, 122
politics in, 116, 120, 121, 125, 126, 128, 131, 135
population of, 124, 126, 131
ports in, 120, 121
sacred groves in, 116–118, 128, 131, 133, 134
settlement patterns in, 115, 116, 119, 345
slave trade in, 128, 132, 135
slavery in, 132, 134, 349
taxation in, 124, 132, 135
trade in, 115, 132
war in, 124, 128, 354
Egypt, 367
Ejigbo, 229, 237, 242
elites, 2, 11, 16, 49, 50, 147, 171, 192–194, 354, 356, 363
and political centralization, 192
consumption of prestige goods, 119
in Aja-Yoruba region, 191
in Bambuxu, 55
in Bundu, 67, 70, 358, 359
in Dahomey Kingdom, 26, 194, 199, 200, 208, 211, 212, 216, 360
in Gajaaga, 53, 70, 358, 359
in Hueda Kingdom, 360
in Mandara, 335
in Segou, 25
in Siin Kingdom, 361
in Upper Senegal Basin, 56, 66, 69, 70, 358
Muslim, 363
Elmina, 9, 116, 120, 121, 122, 125, 132, 134, 135
escarpments, 22, 50, 59, 61, 68, 70
Europe, 1, 340, 347, 365, 366
European
ceramics, 102, 156
forts, 22, 49, 50, 69, 352
influence on coast of West Africa, 309
trade, 7, 20, 24, 28, 283, 292, 293
trading posts, 84
Europeans, 4, 7
in Senegambia, 49–71
in Sierra Leone, 282, 283
Eyim, 130, 131

Faidherbe, General, 61
Falaba, 284, 286, 287, 290, 292, 295–296
Falemme River, 22, 50, 52, 53, 56, 58, 59, 61, 62, 64–68, 70
famine, 95

Fante, 9, 124, 354
Farabana, 55
Fatick, 89
Fena, 61
feudalism, 1
Finley, Moses, 242
Finnegan, Ruth, 298
firstcomer primacy, 256, 271, 274
flooding, 53, 60, 63, 68
floodplains, 50, 59, 63
Fon Dynasty, 198, 199
Fongbe, 195
Forbes, Frederick, 212, 214
forests, 19, 68, 292, 357
forowa, 130, 134
Fort Saint Joseph de Galam, 53, 55, 65
Fort Saint Pierre de Kaynura, 53, 65
Fort Senudebu, 59, 62, 65–67
fortified towns, 60. *See also* Bundu, Gajaaga, *tata*
in Sierra Leone, 278–303, 345, 353
motivations for creation of, 278
Foucault, Michel, 344
France, 49, 55, 56, 96
Frank, Andre Gunder, 354
freedom villages. *See villages de liberté*
Freetown, 294
French, 67
colonialism in Bassar region, 273
conquest of Dahomey, 192
forts, 55, 120
in Senegambia, 22
in Sierra Leone, 283, 287
in Upper Senegal Basin, 358
machine guns, 67
opinion of the Serer, 85
slave trade, 349
trading posts, 100, 120
Fulani, 28, 284, 301, 302
Fulbe, 54, 56, 58, 68, 71
Futa Jallon, 282, 284, 301, 359
Fuuta Toro, 52, 54, 61
Fyle, C. Magbaily, 286
Fyle, Magbaily, 280

Gajaaga, 50, 54, 57–59, 62, 81, 341, 347, 348, 350, 352, 355, 356
agriculture in, 57
and Islam, 54, 65
architecture in, 60, 61, 66
as decentralized polity, 67
decomposition of, 70
elites in, 358, 359
migration from, 58, 62
relations with Bundu, 54, 64

382

INDEX

Gajaaga (*cont.*)
  rulers of, 53, 54, 64
  slavery in, 57, 349, 358
  trade in, 57
Galam. *See* Gajaaga
galamsey, 117, 120, 128, 130
Galdala, 324
Gambia River, 52, 55, 81
Gangan, 257, 261
Gao, 49
Gbe, 195
Gbikpi-Benissan, Datè, 261, 262, 264
Geismar, Louis, 85
gent, 62
Germans, 257, 271, 273
Ghana, xiii, xvii, 9, 17, 18, 19, 115, 116,
    125, 129, 170, 186, 261, 266, 271,
    284, 289, 291, 301. *See also* Eguafo
Gills, Barry K., 354
glass, xvii, 57, 65, 99, 100–102, 158, 231,
    239, 266, 292, 300
globalization, 51, 350
Godelier, Maurice, 118
Gokoro Forest Reserve, 326
gold, 123, 130, 347–348, 350
  mining of, 19, 117, 123, 347
  trade, 24, 49, 115, 120, 123, 126, 132,
    134, 135, 280, 282, 355, 366
Gold Coast, 7, 23, 119, 121, 124, 125, 133,
    341. *See also* Eguafo
gold trade, 128
Gondja, 257, 261, 272
Gonja, 266, 271, 361
Goodwin, Stephan, 367
Gouang, 257
grain, 57, 156
Great Britain, 14, 55, 243
groundnuts, 180, 257
Guang, 261
Gudur, 324
Guedevi, 195, 202
Guinea, 284, 287, 291
Guinea Highlands, 279
gunflints, 294, 300
Gunjuru, 49
gunpowder, 7, 57, 99, 294
guns, 7, 55, 57, 67, 115, 131, 178, 179, 282,
    294
Gurma, 257, 261, 271, 272
Guyer, Jane, 103
Gwoza Hills, 324

Hall, Barbara, 244
Hausa, 257, 266

Hemmersam, Michael, 123
Herskovits, Melville, 213
heterarchical political system, 88, 118,
    170
  Bassar Chiefdom, 264
  in Bassar Chiefdom, 28, 264
  in Eguafo, 24
  in Middle Niger, 170
  in Sierra Leone, 29
heterarchical social organization, 18, 21,
    22, 171
  on Koinadugu Plateau, 286, 302
hierarchical political system, 88
  in Hueda Kingdom, 143
  in Middle Niger, 170
hierarchical social organization, 171
Hill, Matthew, 282
Hodgson, Marshall, 339, 347
Hoja, 221
Hollis, Rosemary, 236
Hopkins, J.F.P., 170
horses, 28, 238, 242, 244, 357
  breeding of, 357
  Dongola breed, 238
  in Ede-Ile, 244–248
  in Mandara, 317–318, 328
  pony breed, 238
  use in slave raids, 317
Hueda Kingdom, xvi, 9, 22, 24–25, 26,
    142–161, 191, 198, 341, 346, 350,
    351, 355, 359–360
  agriculture in, 150
  architecture in, 149, 158, 160, 356, 360
  borders of, 150
  celebration of deities, 148, 149
    Dangbe, 148, 149
  ceramics in, 152, 153, 155, 158
  competition with Allada, 147
  conquest by Dahomey, 149, 159, 160,
    352, 364
  countryside in, 24, 359
  destruction by fire, 159, 160
  ditches, 158
  economy of, 147–148
  elites in, 142, 143, 147, 157, 158, 160,
    360
  imports, 158
  kings of, 24, 143, 147–149, 157, 158,
    160
  markets, 147–148
  palace complexes, 143, 145, 146, 148,
    149, 155, 158, 160, 353, 359
  political organization of, 144, 156, 160
  population of, 148, 150

rural settlements, 143, 145–147, 155,
 156, 158–161
slavery in, 349, 359
taxation in, 147
trade in, 147
violence in, 143
Huffon, 149, 158, 159, 160

Ife, 19
Igboho, 240
Igbomina, 224
Ignare, 270
Ijebu, 244
Ikeda, Satoshi, 350, 351, 364
Ikoyi, 224
Ile-Ife, 191, 229, 243
Ilesa, 224, 229, 238, 243
Ilorin, 234
immigration. *See also* migration
 of ironworkers, 255
 of refugees, 273
 to Africa's internal frontier, 256
 to Bassar region, 261, 266, 268, 270,
  271, 273
 to Gajaaga, 54
imperialism
 definition of, 228
 motives for, 241–242
 Oyo Empire, 246
imports, 7, 9, 10, 24, 57, 62, 63, 65, 83, 99,
 123, 156, 157, 158, 230, 266, 271
India, 366
Indian Ocean, 1
indigo, 57
Industrial Revolution, 55
Inglis, Fred, 15
Inka Empire, 236
Intuah, Kofi, 130
Ipapo-Ile, 240
iron, 115, 153, 231, 257, 279, 301, 316
 mining of, 353
 production of, 18, 28, 231, 263, 264,
  265–268, 270, 271, 301, 362
 trade, 266
Iron Age, xiii, 59, 63, 90, 125, 128, 265,
 266, 270, 297
ironworkers, 255, 256
Islam, 50, 114, 174, 272, 291, 310, 316,
 348, 367
 in Gajaaga, 54
 in Marka towns, 175
 in Senegal, 87
 militant, 52, 55, 68
 spread of, 69, 81, 169, 170, 284, 367

teaching of, 176
Islamic states, 284, 310, 317, 324, 361, 363
Islamo-Wolof model, 87. *See also* Wolof
Italy, 324, 367
ivory, 282
Ivory Coast, 268

Jackson, Michael, 288
Jafunu, 54
Jagy, 64
Jakhanke, 68
Jemeken, 215
Jenné-Jeno, 18, 26, 49, 175, 186
jihad, 359
 of al Hadj Umar Tal, 56
 of Mamadu Lamiin Drame, 68
Jimbe, 64
Jimbire, 270
Joal, 98
Johnson, Samuel, 229
Jolof, 54
Jomboxo, 54
juula, 70

Kabala, 287
Kabiye, 257, 261, 265, 266
Kabu Chiefdom, 257, 265, 268, 270, 272
Kabu-Sara, 257
Kajoor, 95
Kakoya, 293
Kalanga, 257
Kamabai Rock Shelter, 297, 301
Kamara, Moussa, 182
Kamba, 286
Kanem Empire, 315–317, 325, 326, 328,
 348, 367
Kanem-Bornu Empire, 311
Kankunde, 261, 262, 270, 272
Kanuri, 29, 310, 312, 313, 315, 317, 323,
 325, 326, 328, 329
Kaponpon, 293
Kasunko Chiefdom, 286
Katcha River, 257, 265
Kawkaw, 170
Kawoya, 297, 303
Kaynura, 65
Kea, Ray, 30
Keita, Maghan, 365
Kelly, Kenneth, 9, 149, 150, 152, 155, 158
Keroua, 324, 329
Ketangbao, 262
Kete Kratchi, 261
Ketu, 191
Kibedimpu, 262, 268, 270

INDEX

384

kinship groups, 286
Ko swamp, 205, 206
Koinadugu, 27
Koinadugu District, 279, 280
Koinadugu Plateau, 28–29, 278–303, 341,
    345, 353, 356
  early history of, 279–282
  fortified towns of, 291–296
  slave raids, 353
  sociopolitical organization of, 303
  war on, 353
kola nuts, 257
Komenda, 120–124, 129, 130, 132,
    134
Komenda Wars, 121
Konkomba, 257, 266, 271
Kopytoff, Igor, 27, 28, 64, 169, 255
  internal frontier, 27, 28, 64. *See also*
    Bassar Chiefdom, Bassar region,
    Koinadugu Plateau, Mandara
Koso, 240
Kotokoli, 257, 261, 266, 272
Kotokpa, 221
Koza Plain, 324, 325
Kpaajadumpu, 262
kuduo, 130
Kuranko, 280, 282, 284, 285–296,
    302
Kuranko Chiefdom, 278, 279, 285–287
Kusan, 61

labor, 7, 19, 55–58, 147, 171, 348, 350, 353,
    365
Laing, Alexander, 295, 296
Lake Chad, 311–313, 322, 328, 335,
    367
Lake Chad Basin, 17, 329–330, 348, 368.
    See also Mandara
  agriculture in, 326
  drought in, 321, 322, 325, 326
  in prehistory, 315, 324
  rituals in, 325
  slave raids in, 325
Lake Toho, 152, 153
Lama, 261, 262, 265, 266, 271–273
Lamba, 257, 261, 265, 266
Lambe, Bulfinche, 196
landscape, definition of, 14–17,
    342–343
Lane, Paul, 146
Langonde, 270
laptots, 56
Law, Robin, 220, 229
Le Brasseur, 100

Le Herissé, August, 205
levees, 22, 50, 59, 61, 64, 65, 68, 70
Levztion, Nehemia, 170
Liberia, 17, 291
Limba, 280, 282, 284, 286–290, 291–292,
    293, 295, 296, 297–301, 302
Limba Chiefdom, 278, 279, 285, 286
linen, 57, 148
Logone-Chari River, 313
Lovejoy, Paul, 169, 363, 364
luxury goods, 8, 198, 343, 355

MacDonald, Kevin, 26, 171, 341
MacEachern, Scott, 29, 341, 345, 346
Mafa, 323
Maghrib, 238
maize, 148
Maka Jiba, 61
Mali, 18, 25, 171, 185, 186, 188, 284, 289,
    301
Malinke, 54
Malta, 367
Mamprusi, 266, 361
Mandara, 329–330, 341, 345, 346, 348,
    352, 356. *See also* Lake Chad
    Basin
  agricultural communities of, 315
  architecture of, 356
  DGB sites in, 318–325, 326, 329, 345
  effects of slave raids on, 311–313
  elites in, 335
  environment of, 326–327
  horses in, 317–318
  in modern times, 311, 314, 326
  in prehistoric times, 314, 318
  migration to, 313, 314, 329
  women in, 336
Mandara Highlands, 27, 29
Mandara Mountains, 310, 312, 323, 328,
    329
Mande, 172, 174, 176, 280, 290–291,
    302
Mandinka, 83, 280
Manning, Patrick, 212
Mansa, Ton, 183
maraboutism, 176
Marabouts, 176
Marka towns, 25, 169, 174–177, 186, 348,
    366. *See also* Segou
Markadougouba, 175, 176
Martin, William, 365
Masadugu, 292
Mauny, Raymond, xiii
Mauritania, 18

Maxanna, 55
Mbissel, 89
McIntosh, Roderick, 18, 144, 170
McIntosh, Susan, 18, 144
Medine, 55
Mediterranean region, 226, 245, 347, 348, 350
Meillassoux, Claude, 170, 171, 172, 174, 363–364
Meinig, Donald, 365
Mende, 291
Mengoro, Namba, 180
mercantile class, 1
mercantilism, 349, 365
merchants, 122, 364
  European, 192, 363
  in Dahomey Kingdom, 207, 214, 215
  in Eguafo, 120, 122, 133
  in Hueda Kingdom, 359
  in Segou, 176
  of the Gold Coast, 119, 124
Mesoamerica, 245
Mesopotamia, 228
metal, 57, 65
Middle East, 350, 363
Middle Niger, 170, 186–188, 348, 358, 366
Middle Passage, 28, 161
Miers, Suzanne, 140
migration, 27, 64, 68, 71, 227, 241, 358.
    See also immigration
  as response to slave trade, 64
  from Koinadugu Plateau, 353
  Mandinka, 83
  of kings, 191
  seasonal, 58
  Siin Kingdom, 84, 101
  to Ede-Ile, 237
  to Mandara Mountains, 313, 314, 329
  to Sierra Leone, 290
militarism, 2, 7, 67, 170, 171, 174, 192, 195, 231
militarization, 358
military, 57, 345
  architecture, 66
  Bundu, 54, 62
  French, 55
  garrisons, 25, 177, 178, 180
millet, 57, 100, 148, 180, 257, 326
mining, 260
  in Bassar Chiefdom, 28, 260
  in Dahomey Kingdom, 360

  in Eguafo, 123
  of gold, 19, 117, 123, 347
  of iron, 260, 353
Mintz, Sidney, 365
Moande, 270
mobility, 63–65, 68, 70, 358
Mofu, 323, 324
Mongo Bendugu, 292
Mongo Chiefdom, 279, 286
Monroe, J. Cameron, 26, 115, 151, 341, 345, 360
Moors, 52
mortality rates, 55
Moses Finley, 226–227
Mount Bassar, 262, 268, 270
Moustier, M., 298
Musaia, 286, 287, 292, 294
Musaia Dembelia Chiefdom, 279
Muslims, 4, 54, 65, 69, 87, 170, 174

Nangbani, 261, 262, 268, 270
Napoleonic Wars, 55
Nataka clan, 260–264, 268, 271–273
Natchammba, 270
Ndiaye, Moustapha, 182
Ndiongolor, 98
Near East, 245
nere, 257
nested landscapes, 118
Netherlands, 243, 366
New World, 31, 147
Ngoin, 182, 183
Niger River, 49, 177, 266
Nigeria, xiii, 17, 19, 25, 27, 29, 191, 248, 311, 314, 329, 335
Nile Valley, 238, 357
Njay Dynasty, 54
nonstate societies, 5
Norman, Neil, 24–25, 341, 359
North Africa, xvii, 226, 280, 357, 363, 367
North America, 1, 13, 283, 363
Nsawkaw, xvii
Nubia, 367
Nyamina, 172

Ogundiran, Akinwumi, 9, 26–27, 115, 341, 357
Ohuntoto. *See* Old Osogbo
Ojo, 229, 237, 242
okra, 257
Old Osogbo, 229, 237
Old Oyo, 19. *See* Oyo-Ile, Oyo Empire
Osogbo, 238, 242, 243

385

INDEX

Oumbegame, 209
outposts, 52
    British, 55, 124
    Dutch, 49
    European, 49, 50, 57, 64, 65–67, 70
    French, 55, 56
Owu, 229
Oyo Empire, xvi, 25, 27, 191, 202, 205,
        208, 211, 220, 222–248, 341, 347,
        350, 355–358
    colonization, 224, 245, 246. See also
        Ede-Ile
    imperialism, 229, 246
    methods of expansion, 224, 238
    slave trade in, 357
    slavery in, 349
Oyo-Ile, 27, 222–224, 231, 234, 235, 238,
        240–243, 245, 246, 252, 357

palaces, 25, 26, 360. See Dahomey
        Kingdom, Hueda Kingdom
palm oil, 26, 148, 212
paper, 99
Paragourma, 257
Park, Mungo, 61, 66
Patterns of African Statehood project, 171
peanuts, 58, 85
peasants, 69, 70, 84, 85, 86, 100, 358, 359,
        361, 364
Pecc Waagaan, 99, 100
Pélissier, Paul, 85
pepper, 148
peppers, 257
Pereira, Pacheco, 120
Petite Côte, 90
Peulh, 180
Phillips, Thomas, 151, 157
plages, 22, 59, 65, 68, 69, 70, 358, 359
plunder, 70
population density, 58, 71, 171
population shifts, 5, 12, 23, 28, 58, 64, 68,
        82, 120, 124, 212, 345, 358, 359
Poro, 290
Port Loko, 294
porters, 56
Portugal, 49, 52, 115, 120, 125, 128,
        243
pottery, 57, 58
    subactuelle, 63, 358
Pra River, 135
prestige goods, 7, 8, 57, 99, 100, 119, 302,
        343, 353, 361, 367
production, 6, 9, 10, 31, 101, 118, 119,
        124, 345

Pulaar, 64, 68
Pulke, 324

railroads, 50, 68, 71
rainforest belt, 235, 236, 242, 245
Rathbone, Richard, 142
Reade, William, 295
refugees, 187
Reid, Andrew, 146, 171
retinues, 53, 56, 57, 66, 69
rice, 148, 283
Richard, François, 23, 341, 361
rituals
    and ethnic identity, 244
    in Lake Chad Basin, 321, 322, 325
    on Gold Coast, 133
Roberts, Richard, 171
Royal African Company, 122
ruralization, 145, 360

Saada, Boubacar, 62
Sahelian zone, xvii, 18, 235, 310, 327,
        328
Saint Domingue, 349
Saint Louis, 53, 55
salt, 148, 282
Samori, 28
Sande, 290. See also Bundu
Sanogo, Abin, 175, 176
Sansanding, 172, 176
Santley, Robert, 244
Sara, 261, 268
savanna ecology, 235, 236, 242
Savi, 9, 24, 142–144, 146, 147–161, 359
Schmidt, Peter, 270
Searing, James, 100
secret societies, 29, 286, 290
Segou, 25–26, 169, 171–188, 341, 347, 350,
        358, 366
    agricultural villages in, 25, 26
    Cikebugu, 176–178, 180, 185,
        186
        Banankozo, 177, 178
        Dugasso, 180, 182
        Kenyé, 178, 180
    Dendugu, 177, 185
    elites in, 25
    Fadugu, 177
    Fama, 182
    Gwa, 177, 178, 180, 182, 186
    Horondugu, 176
    kings
        Diara, Monzon, 180, 183
        Mansa, Ton, 183

kings in, 177, 353, 358
Marka towns, 25, 169, 174–177, 185, 348
military in, 178, 180, 182
population of, 185
royal courts in, 177
schools in, 182
Sifinso, 184, 353, 358
slave raids in, 174, 177
slavery in, 171, 172, 174, 176, 178, 349, 353
slaves in, 169
  as soldiers, 169
  in agriculture, 169, 177, 180, 185
  jon, 174
  ton jon, 174, 176, 180, 182, 358
sociopolitical organization of, 355
spatial organization of, 172
Toeda, 172, 174, 176–178, 186
Ton Masala, 183
trade in, 358
war in, 174, 178, 179, 183
youth in, 182–184
Segoukoro, 183
Senegal, 19, 23, 56, 62, 80–104, 113, 351, 358–359. *See also* Siin Kingdom
Petite Côte, 98
Senegal River, 49, 50, 52, 53, 56, 58, 67
Senegalese Riflemen. *See tirailleurs senegalais*
Senegambia, 7, 17, 22–23, 49–71. *See also* Bundu, Eguafo, Gajaaga, and Siin Kingdom
British in, 52, 57
French in, 52–57
Sengbe Chiefdom, 279, 286
Seno, 64
Senudebu, 53, 55, 61, 62, 65, 68
Serer, 84, 114
servants, 56
Service, Elmen, 4
Shama, 120
shea butter nuts, 257
Sierra Leone, 17, 27, 28–29, 278–303, 346, 352
agriculture in, 288
architecture in, 299, 300
British in, 284, 285, 287, 288
ceramics in, 300–301
domestic slavery in, 284
Europeans in, 282, 283
fortified towns in, 291–296, 297, 301, 302, 345, 353. *See also* Kuranko, Limba, and Yalunka

French in, 287
imports, 28
slave raids in, 284
slavery in, 288
sociopolitical organization of, 284–288
trade in, 280, 284, 292
Sierra Leone Estuary, 283
Sifinso, 366
Siin Kingdom, 22, 23, 80–104, 341, 347, 352, 355, 361
agriculture in, 97
aristocratic residences in, 99, 100
aristocrats in, 100
consumption patterns in, 99–101
elites in, 84, 100, 101, 361
imports, 83, 99, 100
influence of Wolof on, 87
migration in, 101
mobility in, 97
monarchy in, 98, 99
peasants in, 84–86, 100
political organization of, 82, 85, 88, 98, 99
population density of, 90
population shifts in, 82, 90, 93, 94
settlement shifts in, 90
slavery in, 99, 100, 349
social organization of, 85, 98–101
spatial dispersal, 96
trade in, 90, 99
violence in, 95–97, 100
Siin River, 90
Siliman, 55
Silla, 49
silver, 57, 347–348, 365, 366
Sinhoue, 209
Sinkunia, 286, 287
Sinkunia Dembelia Chiefdom, 279
Skertchly, J. Alfred, 212
slave mode of production, 170, 171, 174, 187
slave raids, 2, 10, 12, 23, 170, 187
and creation of fortified towns, 278
and immigration to Bassar region, 266, 270
and migration, 273
effects on Bassar region, 263
effects on Mandara, 311–313
in Bassar region, 255
in Lake Chad Basin, 325
in Sierra Leone, 284
Koinadugu Plateau, 353
use of horses for, 317

387

INDEX

slave trade, xiv, 1, 2, 8, 10, 12, 23, 28, 58, 63, 65, 115, 120, 125, 192, 349, 353, 367
   abolition of, 7, 55, 58, 68, 124
   and mobility, 63, 64, 96
   effects on Bassar region, 264
   effects on peasants, 364
   French, 349
   impact on Africa's internal frontier, 256
   in Dahomey Kingdom, 202, 206, 207, 216
   in Eguafo, 128, 132, 135
   in Oyo Empire, 357
   in Sierra Leone, 28, 283
   in Siin Kingdom, 93
   on Bight of Benin, 243
slavery, 7, 31, 57, 58, 169, 187, 363
   commodity chains of, 355
   domestic, 70, 124, 284
   illegal, 124
   in Bassar region, 28, 266
   in Bundu, 57
   in Eguafo, 132, 134
   in Gajaaga, 57
   in Segou, 172, 174
   in Sierra Leone, 288
   indigenous, 56, 169, 170
slaves, 7, 19, 26, 49, 56, 57, 69, 70
   and gold mining, 123
   and industrialization, 365
   as artisans, 66
   in agriculture, 170, 171, 187. *See also* Segou
   in Bundu, 358
   in Eguafo, 24
   in Gajaaga, 358
   in Hueda Kingdom, 359
   in Segou, 25
   use in transport of goods, 123
   youth, 182
Snelgrave, William, 150, 158
social commons, 356–357, 358, 359, 361–364, 368
socio-natural regimes, 355–361, 363, 366
Sokoria, 296
Sokoto Caliphate, 169, 311
soldiers, 56
Solima Chiefdom, 279
Solima Yalunka Kingdom, 279, 283, 286–288, 296, 302
Somsom-Tata, 61
Songhai, 169
Soninke, 53, 55, 56, 58, 64, 68, 71, 174, 186

sorghum, 257, 326
South America, 1, 226, 365
Southall, Aidan, 285
Spain, 243, 366
Spiers, Sam, 24, 341, 345, 353
Stahl, Ann, 9, 145
Stein, Gil, 227, 228
stone, 56, 59, 61, 65, 66, 128, 153, 262, 265, 280, 293, 299, 323
Stone Age, xiii, 23, 59, 153, 154, 279, 280, 301
subactuelle, 58, 63, 358
subsistence economy, 119, 302
subsistence farming, 126, 132, 288
Sudan, 170, 171
   western, 55, 56, 57
Sudanic zone, xvii, 310
sugar, 365
Sukur, 323, 324
Susu, 292
Sy, Malik, 54
Szwark, Marian, 272

Tal, al Hadj Umar, 56, 62, 66, 68, 359
Tanzania, 270
tata, 22, 59–62, 68–70, 352, 356, 358, 359
Tata Almamy, 59, 62, 67
taxation, 120, 122, 124, 132, 134, 285
   in Dahomey Kingdom, 196, 208, 213
   in Eguafo, 124, 132, 135
   in Hueda Kingdom, 147
   in Oyo Empire, 244
   on Gold Coast, 121
taxes, 54, 68, 70, 119, 122, 123, 215, 228
tax-farming, 215
Taylor, Peter, 351
Tchamba, 257, 261
Tegbesu, 195
Tem, 257
terrace farming, 311, 318, 319, 329
textiles, 99. *See also* cloth
Thiaw, Ibrahima, 22–23, 341
Thioupane, 99
Thompson, Edward, 345, 346
Thornton, John, 7
Tilly, Charles, 346
Timbuktu, 49, 347
Timi, 237
Tinji, 209
Tipabun, 266, 268
tirailleurs senegalais, 56
Tiyabu, 62

tobacco, 57, 157
tobacco pipes, 63, 100, 101, 130, 156–158, 166, 230, 239, 357
Toffo Plateau, 211
Togo, 17, 18, 27–28, 191, 257, 265, 266, 268. *See also* Bassar Chiefdom
tolls, 122
    Oyo Empire, 224
Toto, 183
Touré, Samori, 284, 286–288, 294
Tourè, Samori, 359
trade, xvii, 2, 6, 11, 12, 20, 31, 49, 50, 52, 55, 67, 70, 146, 354
    British, 55
    competition between Gold Coast polities, 121
    entrepots, 22
    European, 9, 63
    French, 55
    global, 9, 10
    in Bundu, 57, 62
    in Dahomey, 198, 202
    in Eguafo, 23, 24, 115, 188
    in Gajaaga, 57, 70
    in Mandara Highlands, 29
    in prestige goods, 119
    in Segou, 358
    in Senegambia, 49, 50, 57
    in Sierra Leone, 280, 282–284, 292, 293
    in Siin Kingdom, 99
    international, 8, 154
    local, xvii
    long distance, xvii, 1, 8, 119, 343
    of horses, 238
    of kola nuts, 257
    routes, 5, 26, 52
    trans-Saharan, 23, 49
    with Europe, 7
trade entrepots, 5, 142
trade routes, 115, 119, 124, 132
trading diasporas, 228
trading factories, 243
trading posts, 84, 100, 247, 283
transportation, 244, 345
Trarza, 52
tributary states, 224. *See also* Dahomey
tribute, 244
tributes, 228
Trouillot, Michel-Rolph, 87
Tubabunkani. *See* Fort Saint Joseph de Galam
tunka, 54
Tyokossi, 257, 261, 266, 268, 272, 361

Uganda, 171
Ulsheimer, Andreas, 122
Upper Niger Basin, 280, 366
Upper Osun region, 27, 225, 226, 229, 231, 237, 242–247. *See also* Ede-Ile
Upper Senegal Basin, 22, 23, 56, 69–71, 341, 351, 355, 358–359, 366
urbanism, 12, 144, 145, 161
utandaans, 263

Vansina, Jan, 2
villages de liberté, 68
Volta Basin, 257
von Ranke, Leopold, 339

Wadande, 262, 270
Wadande-Bassar, 268
Wagadu, 186
Wandala, 311, 312, 317, 324, 329
war, 119, 170, 187, 188, 192, 354
    between Dahomey and Hueda Kingdom, 160
    French/Umarian, 68
    in Bundu, 57
    in Eguafo, 124, 128, 354
    in Komenda, 121
    in Segou, 169, 174, 178, 179
    in Senegambia, 54
    on Koinadugu Plateau, 353
Wara Wara Bafodia Chiefdom, 279, 286
Wara Wara Mountains, 280, 293, 296
Wara Wara Rock Shelter, 297, 300
Wara Wara Yagala Chiefdom, 279, 286, 298
Wassa, 121
water, xv, 63
Wawe, 195, 202, 204
Wegbaja, 195, 199, 200
Whydah, 192, 205, 213, 214
Wolf, Eric, 8, 343
Wolof, 81, 87, 113
women, 100, 148, 155–157, 182, 196, 234, 270
wood, 56
wool, 148
world systems theory, 226, 241
Wuli, 54

Xaaso, 54
Xaasonke, 55

Yabiw, 121
Yagala, 293, 295, 303

Old Town, 292, 297–301
Rock Shelter, 301–303
Yalunka, 280, 282, 284, 285–296, 302
Yalunka Chiefdom, 278, 279, 285–287. *See also* Solima Yalunka Kingdom
yams, 257, 262, 263, 272
Yarborough, Clare, 244
yellow amber, 57
Yoruba, 9, 191, 211
Yoruba-Edo, 19

Yorubaland, 19, 27, 222, 225, 229, 234, 238–242, 244, 246
youth, 182

Za Kingdom, 207
Zassa, 220, 221
Zawīla, 170
Zilum, 316–317, 328
Zipf, George
  rank-size rule, 209
Zweifel, J., 298

CPSIA information can be obtained
at www.ICGtesting.com
Printed in the USA
LVHW052256290721
693950LV00008B/394